INTRANSIGENCE

Ivy Graham

Intransigence – refusing to compromise or agree despite the odds. Stubborn, inflexible, unyielding.

ISBN: 0995842000
ISBN 13: 9780995842007

DEDICATIONS

Melanie Persaud, my daughter, pioneer and confidante, who was always on hand to inspire and help me with computer glitches, editing and publication.

Austin Persaud, my grandson, who motivated me, through his own storytelling, to put my thoughts into words.

My many relatives and friends who always encouraged me on.

ACKNOWLEDGEMENTS

Wikipedia – History of Guyana, and fact checking.
E.H. Gombrich – "A Little History of the World"
Frank Birbalsingh – "Indenture and Exile"

AUTHOR'S NOTES

History is part of Tabitha's journey as she searches for her roots.

How and why changes happen sometimes provide answers to questions which provoke thoughts and ideas. The early chapters of this novel deal with how world change impacted life in Guyana.

History offers insight into the many phases of "Whys" and "Wherefores" of our world today, and can provide perspicacity into our own personal journeys.

The world rotates, it never stands still. Inevitably, because human beings think beyond the tried and true, life changes. We connect the dots and we make progress.

This book is a memoir. I have tried to recreate events, locations and conversations to the best of my memory. In order to maintain anonymity, I have changed the names of individuals, character identities and details such as physical property, occupations and places of residence.

PREFACE

Life has many facets, some good, others bad, but none predictable. We turn and stretch our hands to catch the ball travelling in our direction and just when we think we've got it, the wind intercepts and it floats away out of reach, in another direction. We continue to stretch with everything our bodies permit, still hoping to grasp it, certain we'll get it. Our hopes are dashed, our hearts sink as it disappears just out of our reach. We're left with hands outstretched and disappointment in our hearts.

Each aspect of life is as distinct as it is similar. Everything looks simple but nothing flows in the direction we expect it to. We cope with what we're given. The tough survive and grow strong; the weak endure, too strong to die even as it is too tough to live. We respond to circumstances in different ways because our expectations are seldom conjoined with what life offers us.

People who were once free to do as they pleased in their homeland were caught, bound in chains, and transported with fear in their hearts, to strange lands where they were sold into slavery. Others were lured with bright thoughts of "new beginnings", never realizing that they were agreeing to accept a new form of slavery for the period of their indenture.

Money and power seduced Europeans to travel the road of enslavement of their fellow humans, and to treat those they'd enslaved as if they were less than human and certainly no better than animals. Those enslaved or indentured couldn't understand the language their masters spoke. Lack of understanding led to the belief of low intelligence.

They were simple people from different worlds caught in a web from which there was no escape, and transported to unknown domains where greed and cruelty ruled.

British Guiana was one of the scheduled destinations for human cargoes. As they endured the cramped quarters in the bowels of sailing vessels built for cargo, now used for conveying Slaves and Coolie labourers, they endured seasickness, hunger, and thirst, and many died. Women were raped and violated; hope was lost. These human cargoes became disoriented souls deprived of their humanity and placed in a class that permitted ill treatment so harsh that their willpower to fight back and free themselves took a back seat. They hated and feared their masters, and hoped freedom would one day be theirs.

It is now the year 2016 and I must travel back in time to truly understand how chance and circumstance change lives and predictions. Had movements of people from the country of their birth not taken place, perhaps I would not have been born, and certainly never outside India.

This gives rise to a question with no acceptable answer. Are our roles in life chronicled for us? Are we born with an innate map, which directs our destiny or fulfills a purpose? Does destiny play a part in our evolution? Why was my childhood destroyed by rape and sexual molestation? To whom are we accountable when we die? Can a Supreme Being give me the closure I desire? Will the transgressors receive punishment for what they've done? Can I write on my epitaph 'Destiny fulfilled or destiny deferred?'

PROLOGUE

A SCENE FROM THE PAST

The white house with its blue windows stood proud and tall amidst the urban sprawl of small cottages in the village of Vreed-en-Hoop. Two Flamboyant trees, ablaze with red blossoms decorated the front yard. The breezes from the Atlantic Ocean and the Demerara River rush through the open windows and jalousies, cooling the spaces within.

The 'kiskadees' whistled "Quesqu'il dit" as they attempted to shoo the other birds who tried to usurp their domain. These are the only sounds disturbing the peace and tranquility.

Inside a bedroom lay a young child trying to scream for help as she's being subdued by her attacker. He covers her mouth with his hand and lies atop of her. Suddenly her struggling ceases. She lies inert, immobile.

There is movement when her attacker, having at last satisfied his lust, gathers his belongings and flees. Her body bears evidence of his semen spilled over her blood.

CHAPTER ONE

TABITHA'S STORY. I'm now 86 years old and by all accounts I've led an interesting life. My friends have always told me that my journey through life is inspiring and its time to tell the story.

I was born in British Guiana and I grew up in the shadow of British rule. My Dad always impressed on us that if we were to make progress in the white man's country, we needed to learn his ways, obey his rules, and be like him in every aspect of our lives. We needed to forget our ancestry and religion and become part of the British way of life and the British Empire. This was repeated to me so often that it became part of my psyche. I'd been indoctrinated into British customs and British history. My thoughts were those of a young British woman. I was truly white inside my being, but my brown colouring set me apart. I was neither fish nor fowl.

We never learned to speak Hindi in school or at home. It was regarded as a foreign language and of little use to us in this new land, the country of our birth. We were told that India was a foreign country, not our motherland. We were British citizens and it was incumbent on us to learn everything there was to know about England and English history. Our future lay in observing the rules and regulations set by Britain and to remember that by and large we were far better off in this British colony than had we remained in India.

I was one of seven children: three girls and four boys. My parents' expectations were that the boys, Henry Aaron, Cyril Phillip, James Sebastian, and Aubrey Fitzgerald would travel to England to pursue their education at British universities and become lawyers, doctors, dentists or engineers. My sisters Irene Agatha, Edith Margaret and I, were supposed to marry well. My name is Tabitha Dolores.

I never understood the rigidity of the rules regarding education and 'proper' behaviour for women. I was told that proper behaviour was governed by cardinal rules we had to live by. Disobeying these rules could lead to ostracism and relegation to a lower level in society. Climbing out of that slough was very near impossible and could cause ruin for life.

I was very mindful about not contravening these rules. Shakespeare's *"Who steals my purse steals trash, … But he who filches from me my good name, Robs me of that which not enriches him, and makes me poor indeed"* was my mantra and has influenced me throughout my life. Untruths, half-truths, lies, and deception have all ruined many young and promising lives. Society and customs still dictate rules and behavioral conduct today. Straying from the confines of these boundaries, I believed, could only lead to ruin.

My father valued education and looked upon it as an important attribute to success in life. He regarded it as a mantle, which distinguished and defined an individual. While it was the law that all children had to attend primary school up to a certain age, few could afford to advance their education any further. Those who were lucky enough to pursue their education attained a special level, which distinguished them from 'ordinary.'

Life was not the same for girls as it was for boys. When I questioned the wisdom of my spending so much time in school when all girls were expected to do was to get married, bear children, and obey their husbands despite being more educated than the men they'd married, I was frowned upon with a forbidding stare and told to do as I was instructed.

Dad was an entrepreneur; I could almost say a visionary. He was the head of the Rajnarain family and a well-respected member of the community. A kind, considerate and loving father, he could be stern and forbidding if we disobeyed him. We basked in the sunshine of his smile and were always eager to gain his approval.

He sometimes told us a little of his own childhood and this was always fascinating. I often wondered where he acquired his vision and assimilated the acuity and foresight to venture forth into a world quite unknown to him. Looking back at him now, I can say he was truly one of the greats. He looked around at what his world offered him, was determined to succeed, and he pushed on regardless of difficulties. He once told me "you have to gird your loins and keep your nose to the grindstone, never look back, just keep going forward and learning from your mistakes." His dream of success was not limited to himself, but expanded to include the lives of his children and his siblings. Hard work, perseverance, determination, the pursuit of his dreams, and honesty were his credo. He worked from dawn to dusk until the day he died, in his eightieth year.

He was one of the six children born to his parents. His father, Ramesh, had come from India as an indentured labourer or 'bound coolie,' in the eighteen hundred's. 'Bound Coolie' was always used in a derogatory way and intended to convey that you were little better than a monkey, and illiterate, devious, and lacking in mental acuity. If the term was used by Negroes, this meant you were in a caste or category even lower than slavery. When I

3

looked at myself in the mirror, I always questioned *'Why does co-lour define me? Why am I considered to be less of a person than my 'white' school friends, when I am always ahead of them in learning?'*

But I get ahead of myself.

CHAPTER TWO

HISTORICAL CHANGES. (14TH AND 15TH CENTURIES). In order to give you a true picture of the changes history played in my story, we must go back further in time to the very beginning when European powers were vying for supremacy in a land far, far away. At that time, the New World hovered on the brink, waiting to be discovered. Potential wealth was in the grasp of those who dared to venture across the oceans on their way to discovery of new lands where untold fortunes could be made.

Myths and legends prevailed. Rumours were that Vikings had travelled across the oceans eons before, but was this fact or hearsay? The seafarers of the day chose safety over uncertainty and there were few explorers who dared to venture forth across the seas to discover a world which was unknown, or even existed. Traders journeyed eastward overland because this was the well-traversed route to the luxuries of China and India. The known was safer than the unknown and consequently the West retained its anonymity.

A new invention changed the world. The Chinese discovered that a piece of magnetized iron hanging freely always turned to the north, and the compass was born. This knowledge had remained a closely guarded secret for centuries by Chinese traders who used the device to travel westwards across mountains and deserts, towards Europe.

No secret remains hidden forever. Arabs traded their goods in return for the secret device, and then bartered it to Europeans. However, despite the riches and untold wealth that might await them in foreign lands, the device was still so mystifying a phenomenon, navigators hesitated to trust their fate to an unproven instrument; this was something beyond their comprehension.

The West remained a mystery until happenstance rewarded the vision and determination of Christopher Columbus who trusted the 'compass,' as this new device was named. He found a benefactor in Queen Isabella of Spain. In the belief that the world was round, not flat, he sailed westwards to find the East Indies, and in fact, came upon islands in the West. His discovery of this new world opened Pandora's Box, and the destiny of nations and peoples, including my own birth and destiny, changed.

Ancient civilizations, Aztecs, Mayans, and Incas, were destroyed and their peoples enslaved and forced into a religion and a way of life they couldn't understand. Landscapes changed to accommodate new settlers and the ideas that accompanied them. The inhabitants of these lands awakened to the realization that their fate rested with monarchs who lived far away, across the oceans.

Christianity itself was undergoing its own battles with Rome. Reformation of the Church began when Martin Luther, a monk of the Augustinian order, challenged an edict by the Church that atonement for sins could be bought and sold. He argued that according to the Bible, mercy could only be granted through true and full repentance. He was summoned to appear before the German Parliament by Charles V the new emperor of Germany, Holland, and Spain, to answer charges.

Martin Luther knew that dire consequences would follow his appearance at court. The summons meant he'd been condemned even before his trial. Relying on his tremendous following, he decided to take the bull by the horns. Before he could be excommunicated by parliamentary decree he announced that he and his followers had left the Church. Other sects in Germany and Holland, also in disagreement with Rome, followed suit.

Reformation gained full force when Henry VIII of England, unable to get papal agreement to a divorce from his wife, Catherine of Aragon, broke away from Rome and declared himself Head of the Anglican Church. Spain and England became bitter enemies in the succeeding years.

When Philip II inherited Spain from his father Charles V, he was determined to wrest the power of the Anglican Church from the English monarchy, then under the rule of Henry's daughter, Elizabeth I, and restore it to the papacy. The Spanish Armada, a tremendous fleet of ships, men, and weapons of warfare crossed the English Channel, determined to vanquish the English. Although they were not as well-manned and not as well-equipped, the English out-maneuvered the great Armada, and Spain suffered ignominious defeat. Spain's position as the supreme power was never regained.

English victory didn't end there. Spanish holdings on land and sea became fair game for English privateers. New English settlements were established along the coasts of North America. Christians who wanted to worship God in their own way settled there. The British Empire had begun its slow grind toward world domination. English gradually supplanted Latin as the language of choice. The world order had begun to change.

But, you ask, how does British Guiana and your own life, fit into all of this? History is important. We glean understanding from events which took place long before our time. My Dad was always wont to quote Longfellow's Psalm of Life: *"Lives of great men all remind us, we can make our lives sublime and departing leave behind us, footprints on the sands of time."*

British Guiana had a notable start in history. In the late 1500's, motivated by a lust for gold and the power it brought, Sir Walter Raleigh, a favourite at the Court of Elizabeth I, set sail for South America in search of El Dorado, the city where it was rumoured the streets were paved with gold, and buildings adorned with ornaments made from gold, silver, and precious stones. This city, which supposedly lay within the land named "Guiana" was so grand, it sparkled in the sunlight and shimmered in the moonlight. Sir Walter's voyage was unsuccessful, but he published such an exaggerated account of his journey that it earned him fame at court.

Meantime, in pursuit of his love, Sir Walter earned the disfavour of Elizabeth I. Sad to say, despite being a favourite at court, he'd forgotten the rules surrounding the Queen's favour, and courted one of her ladies-in-waiting without first gaining her permission. The consequence of this was imprisonment in the Tower of London. Elizabeth later forgave him and granted permission for him to get married, but both he and his wife, former lady-in-waiting to the Queen, were banished from court.

After Elizabeth's death, Sir Walter was accused of taking part in a plot to dethrone her successor James I, and he was again imprisoned in the Tower of London. Anxious to redeem himself and to avoid death he gave an exaggerated account of his knowledge of the whereabouts of El Dorado. The riches sparked the greed of James I, and Raleigh was freed to set off and find the city.

While exploring the Orinoco basin, he captured an Arawak Indian sailing northwards in a canoe. Through the use of sign language, the Indian indicated that he was a native of the lands where they were heading, and further could guide them there.

He led them eastwards towards the mouth of a smaller river. The area was desolate and forbidding and unlike the Islands of the West Indies, there were no lagoons or beaches for ships to land safely, and no sign of the glitter and shimmer of El Dorado.

The Arawak was threatened with execution. He calmed their disappointment and allayed their fears by explaining that El Dorado lay far within the safety of forests, which seemed to stretch endlessly on, and again promised to lead them there. To their chagrin, the Indian disappeared during the night, taking the secret of El Dorado with him. However, Sir Walter believed they could find their way inland and he remained confident that the expedition would yield access to a fortune so huge, it would diminish everything the Spaniards had amassed.

The forests proved impenetrable and forbidding, and the they were forced to abandon their search. To ease their disappointment, the sailors attacked and sacked a Spanish settlement on the mouth of the Orinoco River. This was a violation of the peace treaty signed by Spain and England. Sir Walter's fate was sealed. On his return to England he was beheaded to appease the wrath of James I.

In our history classes in school centuries later, we asked ourselves, 'Had the Indian deliberately led them up the garden path in order to spare his life?' This was a question which evoked much controversy. As children, hot on the discovery of the truth, some of us felt that El Dorado still awaited discovery; others that Raleigh was so consumed by greed, he couldn't differentiate between truth and fantasy.

Today I believe that the Indian's story that he knew the location of El Dorado was simply a clever ruse to avoid death. He knew the foreigners were greedy for gold and he played up to their expectations to escape certain death.

Be that as it may, at the time of its discovery, Guiana was inhabited by the Carib and Arawak Indians. The Arawaks were simple people cultivating the land for food, hunting, and fishing. They were displaced by the Caribs whose warlike nature quickly led to their capture and consequent dominance over the territory.

The Amerindians, as indigenous inhabitants were called, were displaced by the foreigners who came to work the lands, but their legacy, the name "Guiana," which translates into "Land of many water," remains part of their heritage.

I really loved this land where I was born. I gloried in its natural beauty, its mountains, its rivers and waterfalls, its gold, bauxite and diamonds, its culture, peoples of different colours and cultures living and working together in unison. This was indeed my El Dorado, my paradise on Earth. Sir Walter Raleigh had searched for a city, rich with gold and diamonds. We lived in a land filled with beauty, rainforests, lofty mountains and waterfalls, a country which offered us fulfillment and happiness.

Unfortunately, the world turns, circumstances change, unforeseen events occur, and lives become discombobulated. Is it possible for a diverse group of people who were born in different lands, had different skin tones and worshipped different gods to live together in harmony for ever and ever, when they'd arrived in discord?

CHAPTER THREE

LEGACY OF SLAVERY (1600 to 1800). The Dutch were the first European inhabitants of this barren country. It was the early 1700's and initially their primary purpose was to establish trading posts. Land acquisition and ownership followed; this was the usual pattern of dominant European powers at that time. The indigenous people lived in the hinterland and had no interest in settling on the coast.

Rivers and creeks provided natural roadways and this resulted in many settlements along the main river banks. Spanish marauders tried to oust the Dutch from time to time, but their attacks were easily dispersed.

Dutch ownership was established, and trade blossomed into agriculture. The tropical climate was ideal for sugar and tobacco, highly valued crops in England and Europe at the time.

Prosperity followed as the traders became prime producers. Expansion was critical to achieve market demands. Recruitment of a labour force became a necessity. Climate was an essential factor as well as a knowledge of farming.

The indigenous population, the Caribs and Arawaks, the most likely recruits, couldn't be induced to work the land. Money was foreign to their culture, and meant little to them. They preferred freedom to do as they pleased. They feared the foreigners. Deadly diseases, which they knew nothing about and which they could neither cure nor control, followed Dutch occupation of the land. Many had died. The remainder preferred to live in the forests and they stealthily escaped back into their natural habitat, which offered sanctuary and security. This was unfamiliar terrain to the foreigners as they were unable to track and capture them and force them into a life of servitude.

African slaves had solved the labour problem in North America. Much like the wild animals who roamed the plains, unsuspecting inhabitants were captured, transported across the oceans, and sold to the highest bidder. The captured had no means of redress. Brutal punishment was meted out to those who disobeyed. British citizens who didn't condone the practice, had raised objections, but their criticisms went unheeded and unrecognized.

Appreciating the value of bondage to plantation owners, enslavement became the recognized machinery for labour in the Guianas and throughout the West Indian islands; it offered the ideal solution to labour problems. Enslavement of Africans was of little or no consequence. Skin colour made them different. Combined with the simplicity of their lives, they were considered less intelligent than white people. In addition, Africans were big and strong.

Without slavery, success in the sugar industry could never have materialized. Working conditions were harsh and arduous. Slaves worked harder than animals; they feared the lash of the whip across their backs. Food and rest were ignored. Even when death resulted from this cruel treatment, it caused little concern. Slaves were cheap and plentiful.

In time, this total disregard of human compassion gave rise to rebellions. The slaves, who vastly outnumbered their masters, took control of the plantations on which they worked. The rebellion was widespread. Slaves threatened control of the colony. Owners were forced to enlist help from neighbouring colonists, who fearing the worst for themselves if their own slaves followed suit, quickly joined forces to quell the rebellion. The slaves were defeated and control restored to plantation owners.

The slaves had been as ruthless to their former masters, now under their own control, as their masters had been to them. Retribution was at hand after order was restored.

Cuffy, the leader of the rebellion was captured. He was flogged almost to death, then buried alive with his head exposed. Dismemberment was meted out to others. Escape was impossible.

Many of the white population who'd fled in fear from the country during the rebellion, didn't return. This caused a serious decline in the numbers of white people vis-a-vis black people. To remedy this situation, British plantation owners from a neighbouring Island, who were facing ruin because of poor crops, joined the plantation owners in Guiana.

In a very short time, attracted by greed and profit, English land owners outnumbered the Dutch and much to the dismay of the original Dutch owners, the English virtually took charge of the internal government in Guiana.

Plantations flourished, the economy grew, but the cost of government cut into profits. Dutch planters objected to the increased taxes levied by the English. Each sector appealed to their motherland for help.

Help came unexpectedly. Napoleon was defeated by Wellington at the Battle of Waterloo. One of the treaties signed at the end of the war (the Treaty of Utrecht) divided Guiana into three territories: British Guiana, Dutch Guiana, and French Guiana.

British Guiana became a British Colony subject to the rules and regulations imposed by the British Parliament.

In order to keep control of British Guiana, plantation owners maintained a powerful lobby in the British Parliament. Laws were enacted to make sure the interests of plantation owners were paramount. The owners saw themselves as the local aristocracy and mimicked the life and customs of the aristocracy in England. They maintained their standard of living and their own importance by making sure that any laws enacted didn't disrupt this.

In response to the groundswell of public opinion against this inhumane practice, slavery was abolished by Queen Victoria in 1833. Slaves rejoiced; freedom had come at last. Many had been born in captivity. The conditions under which they'd lived and worked were anathema to their very being; they neither loved nor respected their masters. Emancipation day arrived and they all departed without a backward glance.

Plantation owners stood by and watched in disbelief as house slaves who'd so lovingly tended their master's children up to the day before, brushed these children aside and ignored their tears and pleas as they walked away. The owners were oblivious to the fact that their cruelty had created hatred and animosity in the very people to whom they'd entrusted care of their children. They never expected their workforce, who were now no longer owned property, would simply walk away.

The masters had forgotten that cruelty, and harsh working conditions bred hatred. They'd believed that abolition meant only that slaves would remain on the sugar plantations and perform their jobs for a small salary, and that life would continue as it had for over a hundred years. Hopes were dashed when the freed slaves refused to return in spite of the inducement of payment for labour.

Workers from Portugal and China were recruited to fill the void, but the harsh climate and still harsher working conditions drove them far away from the sugar plantations. No inducement could lure them back into plantation servitude.

The industry was again in crisis; it faced extinction. Plantations were left abandoned as owners deserted them. Other plantations stood idle without the human machinery to till fields, harvest cane, and turn the juice into sugar.

The once powerful sugar magnates faced ruin. If nothing was done to help them get cheap labor, as pliable as slave labour, the sugar wealth would disappear.

Plantation owners besieged the British Parliament to find workers who could undertake the onerous task of planting and reaping the sugar canes, which flourished best in tropical countries where the heat of the sun was punishing.

Slavery was the mainstay of wealth and importance. A labour force, as pliable as slaves, was needed. Without the ability to enforce the harsh working conditions required for success, sugar plantations would perish.

Slavery left its legacy. Violence gives you strength, power, and control. This was the inheritance bequeathed to inhabitants of the land in which I was born.

History plays an important part of all our lives. It determines conditions of life and living. We can forget it for a time, but when it is used as a divisive power, it heralds unforeseen consequences. Hatred can live on for generations.

CHAPTER FOUR

B IRTH OF THE BOUND COOLIE (18th CENTURY). Years before the abolition of slavery, the British East India Company began trading with India. Spices, jewels, carpets, silks, to name a few commodities, were greatly prized items in England and Europe. As was the custom with the expansion of Colonial empires, trade blossomed into territorial acquisitions, when disputes and enmity between the governing Maharajas and Nawabs opened an opportunity for the British to establish a foothold in India. They turned disputes between the local potentates into their advantage, wrested power and became rulers of India.

In 1758, the last standing Maharajah, Suraja Dowlah, Nawab of Bengal, tired of the imposition of British rule on his country, waged his final battle in an effort to regain control of his land. He laid siege to an English fort and took many residents prisoners. They were confined and jam-packed into a small dungeon where heat and congestion caused the death of many. British historians recorded this in historical documents as 'the Black Hole of Calcutta.' A battle was fought to avenge the deaths, gain control of the territory, and defeat any attempts by the Maharajas to resume control of their country.

Britain won the battle and Suraja Dowlah was defeated. The last defiance to British rule fell and Britain became virtual rulers of India.

The Maharajas and Moguls who were supreme were now powerless. Former rulers of their once glorious empires, they were now subject to the laws of a foreign country. A British Viceroy was appointed. Calcutta became the capital of India and British colonial law became recognized as the law of the land.

Even though Britain introduced its own form of Government, India's caste system was still very much the rule. Brahmins, wealthy landowners, wielded power. Untouchables, people of the lowest caste, had no rights. Even water holes were forbidden. They had to find and locate their own. In reality, they had no rights over these either; water holes could easily be claimed by the higher castes and thus again become forbidden territory. British rule meant nothing to them. They were neither worse off, and certainly no better off.

Rural life in India continued as it had for generations. Villages sprung up hither and thither. Provided people could eke out an existence, they endured and survived. When times became tough and they could no longer make a living from the land, they picked up their few chattels and moved on.

Slavery was unknown to them. While they were prey to the greed of the landowners, they were all free. Happenings in India and indeed in the rest of the world didn't touch their lives. They neither knew nor cared that Indian soldiers who had joined Suraja Dowlah and rebelled against the British had fled to neighboring Mauritius, because they feared the long arm of British justice. A happy coincidence at this time was that plantation owners in Mauritius were recruiting labourers from India to farm their plantations.

This created a precedent for Indian indentureship to British Guiana and the West Indies. Based on the success of the Mauritius

plan, John Gladstone, a powerful lobbyist for the plantation owners in British Guiana and the British West Indies, approached
Parliament to sanction the use of labour from India for sugar
plantations in dire need since the abolition of slavery.

He argued that the climate in the countries recruiting labourers was similar, Indians were natural farmers, and therefore
ideal for work on sugar plantations. To ensure that they were
treated fairly, legislation would be enacted to provide rules and
regulations for fair treatment. At the end of their indenture,
those who wanted to return to India would be transported back
to the land of their birth, free of charge.

Unfortunately, indenture became another term for slavery.
There was no real difference between their harsh and insensi-
tive treatment, and that of the slave labour they'd replaced.
Indentured labourers had few rights; they worked long days; they
were whipped if their work wasn't satisfactory and there was no
recourse to a higher authority.

They lived in crowded conditions with very little sanitation. They weren't allowed to marry without permission from
their plantation owner; they couldn't engage in commerce; they
couldn't travel to other plantations. They were punished by whip-
pings and reputedly treated even harsher than their predecessors, the Negro slaves. Women were often raped by the white
overseers and, of course, had no legal recourse. The Coolies
feared the white overseer.

There was no one to control abuse or look into the welfare
of the unfortunates who had signed on as indentured labourers.
When the mortality rate became so high that it could no longer
be condoned, ignored, forgotten, or pushed aside, the British
Parliament couldn't withstand the outcry in England which followed, and indentureship was halted.

Humanitarians prevailed upon the British Government to re-
examine working conditions, and to impose stricter laws, and

sanctions to ensure fairer treatment for the indentured unfortunates. Under these new regulations, owners were supposed to alter their treatment of indentured Coolies. In reality this was just a panacea, as more often than not, with no one to ensure that changes were made, laws were ignored and workers still received unjust treatment.

Time passed slowly but life in British Guiana began to take on a new pattern. Christian missionaries were encouraged to establish churches and make new converts. They started schools to provide education for all. The former slaves turned to the new religion and sent their children to school. English became the language of choice, and they were able to fill vacancies in the police force, civil service, postal services, and teachers, all of which were becoming necessary.

Order became the role of the freed slaves. They were used to police the indentured Coolies and to quell rebellions or resistance when these happened on sugar plantations. Much like slavery, Coolies had few rights. When they tried to escape the harsh reality of their lives, they were caught, brought back, and punished by the freed slaves, now reclassified as Negroes, in much the same way as they themselves had been treated when they were slaves.

The Coolies feared the Negroes. The Negroes despised the Coolies. The British encouraged this, playing one against the other, and this became the pattern of life. It was easier to control the population if they were always at war or had a disagreement with each other. There was always an uneasy truce, each race fighting quietly to excel and emerge the winner. Inter-marriage between the races was frowned upon by the Coolies.

The Negroes established themselves as the elite in Government positions. The Coolies who didn't return to India were given plots of land. While half of them farmed the land and became self-sufficient, the other half remained the main workforce in the sugar industry.

As the years rolled on, labour unions were organized. When working conditions became unbearable, strikes were called. Force was used to quell the strikes. When this resulted in death, Commissions of Enquiry were set up by Parliament to resolve the issues.

My great grandparents came to British Guiana during this period and inherited the distrust between the races, as each race fought to become the dominant force.

CHAPTER FIVE

QUESTIONS WITH NO ANSWERS (1930's). I've digressed again. You may well shake your heads and ask, *"How or why is history relevant?"* We're all aware that race and religion were important elements of life, just as it is today. Our past determines this. Add poverty, wealth and power to the equation. Is it possible to meld all these differences into a cohesive whole?

I grew up with the prevailing status quo. The population of British Guiana at this time was now composed of six peoples and we all held different places in society. Whites were the rulers; they had settled the land and retained ownership of the plantations. British Guiana belonged to the British Crown and we lived under its aegis.

No one questioned the 'whys' and 'wherefores' aloud. There was a system as we saw it, and if we wanted to be somebody, or to own something, we needed to work hard to achieve our ambitions while recognizing and obeying laws, rules, and regulations which we could not understand and which we believed were unreasonable. We formed friendships with one another regardless of race, but it was accepted that we mixed with our own 'kind' and that was, of course, our own race. Sometimes things didn't work out according to plan, but we learned to live with the fallout.

As a child, I was always in the thick of things, always wanting to know. My siblings sometimes referred to me as "Meddlesome Mattie" (adopted from a story book tale in one of our Royal Reading books). After particularly heated discussions at school about racial superiority, I asked my Dad to explain what this was all about. Who and what determined superiority? I was totally confused.

He explained this was a difficult subject. As far back as he could remember, White Europeans had fought for 'superiority' because it meant acquisition of wealth and power. The British Parliament held power and influence in British Guiana because the country belonged to them. They created rules and regulations and appointed a governor to ensure that rules and regulations were followed. We were citizens and we had to obey these rules or punishment in various forms would follow.

He had come to terms with the existing situation and worked within it, and we would have to do the same.

I asked, "But Dad, what if I want to be the boss like you and someone says I can't because I'm not white", I hesitated, stared at him and shook my head, "Do I just give up?"

Dad smiled as he looked at me. We were all proud of him. We hung on his every word and hoped we would grow up to be just like him.

We were sitting around the dining table after dinner. The electric lights, which we were lucky to have, glimmered off his newly-balding head. From early photographs, I knew my Dad had a full head of hair. As he answered me, he ran his hand through what was left and offered a smile. He always smiled when he told us things we didn't want to hear. "What can one man do? We vote, nothing changes. Talk to your great grandfather, Nana, when he comes next week. Maybe if you understand our story you won't need to ask these questions anymore. We live in the White man's country. We must obey his rules and make the best of our circumstances."

"But, Dad," I persisted, "Why should they rule just because they're 'White?' Am I stupid because I am Brown?"

He wagged his finger at me and his face was stern. "That's the way it is, child. You'd better get used to it. We live under the rule of white people; they make rules so that this will never change."

My father never knew that the world could indeed change and was, in fact, undergoing a metamorphosis; that countries once taken over by force could obtain independence and self-rule.

Yet again, I've digressed and am getting ahead of myself.

My great grandfather, Nana, came to visit the following week. Even in his late eighties, he was a dapper man, fair of face, and an official in the local Pilgrim Holiness church; he always took pride in his appearance. To our childish minds, he was a man of authority, someone we had to respect. To be the first to take his straw boater hat and cane meant being rewarded with a coin, a six cents value. His manner of dress and his spoken words bespoke the aura of an educated gentleman. When Nana settled into his favourite chair, I asked him to tell my two brothers and me about Dad's father.

Nana laughed the way someone does when they know something you want to hear. He hemmed and hawed, looked at each of us in turn, then told us to get closer to him and listen carefully.

"Your grandfather Ramesh was a cheeky devil! I didn't want him to marry my daughter. At the time, I was a high ranking Muslim, and Ramesh was simply a low-caste Hindu Coolie. He kept on trying to influence me. One day, after I'd asked him about his life in India, he told me how this had changed and pitched him headlong on his journey from India to British Guiana. There were tears in his eyes as he recounted the events. I knew then that he was the right choice for my daughter even though he was Hindu and I'm Muslim." He shook his head as he remembered the past and a tear settled in his eyes.

"Listen carefully now. You may learn something from him. I'll tell you his story in his own words translated from Hindi into English, just as he told it to me. While you listen, think about your life here and compare it with the life he left when he decided it was time to leave his family home."

CHAPTER SIX

R AMESH FLEES HUNGER (The 1800's). "You won't know
what your grandfather Ramesh looked like. Think of your
Dad, only someone thinner and taller. When he told me his story, his voice was full of sadness." Now I will begin and no inter-
ruptions, please.

"*This is a day I can never forget. There was stillness in the countryside. Even the wind had forgotten that it needed to do its job to cool
the heat of the sun. My heart was heavy as I lay in the shade of the rock
wondering if death was preferable to life. Everything lay silent and un-
moving, perhaps waiting on me to disturb the atmosphere. I pulled a twig
from the ground, and stuffed it into my mouth. My throat was parched
and dry. I thought chewing would help the dryness, but the twig itself
was so dry, it became dust in my mouth and made me even thirstier. I felt
weak and weary, fed up with life, and with no sense of purpose.*"

"*The rice which my family had saved from the last crop was almost
gone. Gone also were more than half the villagers. One by one they'd disappeared in search of 'hope.' Their rice had all been eaten, and their only
choice was hunger and starvation, or depart the village in search of food.
That day the tailors I'd worked for told me they couldn't afford to pay me
any longer. That was the end for me. Despair settled in my heart as dark*

thoughts filled my being. I asked myself, 'Should I remain and starve and pray for the monsoons to come? Should I leave my family and join the bands of people who take to the road and simply disappear? Should I just lie here and wait for death?' I had two options: live or die.

"Farming was my life for as long as I can remember, but chance threw me a life-line. One-day last year I stopped at the tailor's house to gossip. While we were talking, he received a summons from the Brahmin in the big house; his presence was required immediately. He grumbled as he dropped the shirt he was making on to my lap, in his haste to get going. I picked up the garment and continued sewing. I'd watched the tailor often enough; I'd always felt stitching was a simple task. This was an opportunity I couldn't miss. I knew he would scold me when he returned but I also knew this was a gift I had to embrace. Happiness filled me when I saw that it was impossible to distinguish any difference between my stitches and the tailor's. No one could tell where the tailor left off and I started.

"The tailor boxed my ears when he returned. He was clearly annoyed, but his annoyance vanished when he saw the precision of my own stitches. He offered me work in his shop. My fortunes changed that day. Sewing was better than farming. But all of that was over now. Our village was suffering. There was little to eat, and no one was ordering new clothes. Desolation filled my soul. I asked myself, 'Why, why, why?'

"Something deep inside me whispered an answer. 'You cannot give up. Lying idle under the shade of this rock is not a choice. You must try to survive or die trying.'

As he told the story, Nana himself choked up with tears, but we were enthralled and eager. Together, it seemed, we all chanted, "What happened next, Nana?" He wiped his eyes, and coughed. "Let me catch my breath. The past is sad and telling this story takes me back to a time I'd rather forget, but I know you're anxious, so I'll continue." He drew me closer to him took my hands in his and caressed them as he smiled with me.

"These are Ramesh's own words, you know, and I'm an old man trying to remember exactly what he told me. I don't want to mislead you."

"The past year was a happy one. Laughter and joy filled my heart. My future had changed. I'd escaped the greed of the landowners, the people who controlled us. They wanted everything. We worked hard. They did nothing. But somehow I'd been saved. The Gods gave me a gift and showed me how to use it. A young girl in the next village had smiled at me and I had 'hopes.' Now this, too, has been taken from me. The Gods have forsaken me. I wanted to shout to the heavens and see if the Gods would wake up, take pity on me, and send me an answer. But I knew this was useless. We make many sacrifices to them, to appease them, but they take it all and give us nothing. In my heart I knew that nothing changes. No one could help. No one would show mercy. If I wanted to make my life better, it was up to me. I had to find my own salvation.

"I gazed up at that cloudless sky, seeking an answer. Then I felt a fly buzzing around my ear. I moved my hand to swat it. Suddenly I thought, "Nothing moves around here, but I can move. Yes, I can move. I can join the band of people on the road, and we can search for food. I don't want to starve to death, and that will surely happen if I remain here. I must and will go. But I cannot just disappear without saying goodbye to Ma and Bhap (father). I felt energy in my body. My decision brought me new life and hope. Challenges facing me would disappear. There had to be a way out and I had to find it, but if I didn't search for it, it would escape me and disappear.

"Calcutta had always been a topic of discussion around the nightly village fire. The last great battle before the British took over was told over and over again. Our soldiers were betrayed by our own people who worked for the British against our country. Those defeated in battle were forced to flee because they feared prosecution by the British.

"There was a rumour that under the new regime, we would all get work and money, and life would be better for us. Even though these

rumours had propelled some of the villagers to go in search of the proverbial fortunes to be made in the city, no one had returned home. Speculation was that they'd become so wealthy, they preferred not to return because they didn't want to share their wealth. The poor helped one another, but the rich were only interested in becoming richer, and using the less fortunate to help them in their appetite for riches and power. The practice was to preserve wealth and watch it grow, by hoarding it and keeping it to themselves.

"I stopped quickly as thoughts soared in my mind. 'You may never see this place again, once you leave, you'll never return.' I looked around me carefully with eyes and heart, trying to seal in my memory the picture of the only place I'd ever known. My steps grew slower as I neared the hovel I called home. Ma was sitting before the fire cooking the last meagre supper I'd ever taste, prepared by hands of the first person who had ever shown me love. My father and my two younger brothers were sitting close by on the mud floor. They looked up as I entered. Ma said, 'Ramesh, you're late. What's wrong?' My voice broke as I replied, 'Bad news, I'm afraid I must leave you. The tailors cannot give me work any longer.'

'Son, things will get better. The Gods will rescue us. They know how we suffer. We've prayed and offered sacrifices. Help will come soon.' Ramesh turned to his father and sobbed. 'Bhap, the time has come when I must leave you. I'm the oldest, and I cannot offer even one rupee. I'm ashamed and I cannot allow you and Ma and my brothers to starve because I have to share your food. The situation here gets worse every day. So many of our friends have died or gone to other villages! My time has come to leave also.'

"A torrent of tears, grief, and anger followed my outburst. I was sorely tempted but I knew I couldn't remain with my family. I cried out, 'My heart breaks, but my mind is made. I'll leave in the morning and try to get to Calcutta. I'll find work, and I'll never forget you. Dry your tears and let's spend this evening together. Help me with my plans. I'll remember everything I've learned, and I'll be the person you taught me to be, and hoped I'd become.'

"We ate the sparse dinner Ma had prepared, then sat talking. I saw Ma creep out shortly after. She returned with a small parcel, and later I saw she was preparing to make roti. I sensed that she'd told the villagers I was leaving, and they'd given her some of their little remaining flour to prepare food to sustain me on my travels. I knew that everyone would all be awake to see me leave the next day, and I hoped I'd still have the strength and courage to depart on a journey somewhere, hopefully to a place where my future would be brighter.

"I awoke the next day with a heavy heart. My family were all up awaiting me. Ma handed me a parcel wrapped in cotton and tied the traditional way with ends together. She told me it would keep me for a few days. Ma and Bhap blessed me and kissed my feet, my brothers hugged me, and then I went through the door. The villagers were waiting. Everyone whispered something and touched me as I passed. I barely heard what they said. My feet felt like chunks of lead, my heart whispered, 'Turn back, turn back,' but I managed to place one foot in front of the other, and suddenly found myself all alone on the dirt track which led to the main road.

"My brain whispered, 'Sit down and rest for awhile,' but something beyond me countered, 'If you do that, you'll never leave the village. You'll lose face and be branded a coward.' I plodded on, and suddenly I was on the main road. I took in a deep breath and murmured to myself, 'I'm in control of my destiny and I will succeed. I owe it to my parents and to all those people who denied themselves flour to provide roti for my journey.' I searched around for something that would help me and miraculously found a stick someone had abandoned at the roadside. This was a god omen. I held the stick aloft and with the strength of determination and bravado, I strode down the road with hope in my heart. "I travelled all day without seeing another person. The stillness was strange and unsettling.

"Towards nightfall, I came upon a group of eight travelers. They hailed out to me and asked where I was going. All eyes fell on my cotton bundle, which they eyed greedily. 'What have you got there? Come join us. We're on our way to Calcutta and we've heard that the road is full of thieves and robbers. You'll be safe in our group.' They quickly surrounded me.

"'Why did I just not run away when I saw them?' I asked myself. 'They'll take my food, beat me, and leave me by the wayside. I won't go down quietly. They outnumber me, but there must be a way. If I can create a diversion, perhaps I can escape. I can't give them all my food, but I must give them some.' My decision made, I indicated that I was agreeable to joining the band. 'It's nice to meet up with you,' I greeted them. 'I haven't seen anyone since I left home. I'll share my bundle with you. You'll tell me your news. You all look hungry. We can all eat my food and we'll get more food later down the road.' As they eagerly watched me, I quickly untied the knots holding my bundle together, then took out half the number of roti. I raised my hand and flung them as far as I could. In their anxiety to gather the food, they scattered, each scrambling to get some of what I'd pitched away.

"As they left me, I quickly secured the ends of the bundle together and raced off. I knew that what I'd flung in their direction wouldn't be enough for the band of eight, and their next move would be to catch up with me, rob me, beat me, and even perhaps kill me. But I'd had a good head start, and they were soon left behind. 'Night falls quickly,' I told myself, 'and this will force them to abandon the chase,' but I know I have to be up at the break of day and be even more vigilant when I meet up with other travelers on the road.

"I breathed deeply and pondered my good luck at having escaped. I felt that the Gods were showing me a path, and if I read the signs correctly I'd survive and life would be better. It seemed that my country was full of people who were as desperate as I was. Hunger and desperation must have turned them into thieves and robbers.

"This was my first encounter with people on the road and I'd been lucky. To get ahead I had to be the aggressor, professing a knowledge I didn't have. Even though I travelled alone, I had to show I knew what I was about.

"After a fitful night, I made an early start the next day. There was no time to dawdle. The sooner I reached my destination, the better off I'd be. After a few hours, I met a couple pushing a cart. I called out to them and walked quickly past. The couple looked at each other. I felt they were sizing me up, and had come to the conclusion that I seemed to be an upright young man, and their chances on the road would be improved if they could join me.

"'Bhia,' (brother) they chanted. 'Where are you going? You seem to be in a hurry?'

I replied, without stopping. 'I must get to Calcutta quickly. Be careful, there are thieves and cut-throats behind.'

"And that is how I met Bipal, and this wife, Champa. 'Let's join you,' they begged. 'We'll share what we have to eat, and you must share also. Together, we stand a better chance against the thieves and cut-throats you say are behind us.'

"I stopped. 'You remind me of people in my village. You seem honest. But we must be careful and we must hurry, if we are to arrive safely. With the three of us pushing your cart, we'll make better time. Bipal and I can take the handles of the cart, and Champa can push from the middle. We must be quick. We don't want to be caught.'

"And thus began the strange journey to Calcutta. We avoided would-be thieves and robbers. We gathered anything we could eat, and only ate once a day at nightfall. It seemed no time thereafter, when we saw the big buildings of the city spread out before us; we rejoiced, knelt down and thanked the Gods that had brought us safely there. We'd arrived; we'd found our way to Calcutta. We could earn a living, establish ourselves, and even return home to help our families. People called out to us, but we didn't stop. We couldn't tell the difference between the good people and the nefarious. We knew that if we showed that we needed information or direction, or even stopped to chat, we'd be easy prey for those who would take what little we had. We needed to appear to know our whereabouts. People we met on the street weren't the ones to give us helpful information or assist us in any way. They were out to use us for their own gain.

"*Champa and Bipal told me that Calcutta had become the central port for shipping Coolie labourers to foreign destinations. Indians, facing poverty and hunger, were easy recruits. They were either promised jobs and wages and a return passage after five years, or even tricked into signing on when the sales pitch didn't work on them. Tales of a good life and a triumphant return to the land of their birth seemed a better alternative than starvation. It was an open secret that the recruiters earned money, and used every trick to get the manpower they sold. However, I felt I should stay in Calcutta for a while and learn whether there were opportunities for me here.*

"*We quickly settled down to life in this vast city. We found space in one of the many ghettos that had sprung up on the outskirts. Champa remained in the 'lean-to' to guard our belongings and Bipal and I went in search of work. We had nothing much between us, but if we lost even that, life would be much worse.*

"*Calcutta was a disappointment. We were all barely surviving, and hope was quickly disappearing. When I returned to the 'lean-to' late one afternoon I found strangers in the space where Bipal, Champa, and I had set up residence. I questioned the new people who seemed to have settled there, but all they would say was that they had bought the space for a few rupees.*

'*That night I felt helpless and alone. I missed Bipal and Champa. I found some space in an area at the side of a building where beggars had congregated, stretched out my aching body and tried to focus on my future. Later that night, the police came. I was arrested and taken to the police station. Next day, I appeared before the magistrate. He told me I was a vagrant and I would be sentenced the following day and sent away to prison. Court adjourned and I was put in a prison cell with others. There I learned that if I agreed to indenture as a bound Coolie I wouldn't go to prison. I'd receive payment for work I performed, and after five years, I'd be allowed to return to India. At that time, I didn't know where I was going to be taken, and I didn't really care. I felt miserable, alone, and unhappy.*

"*Back in court the next day, the Magistrate asked me if I'd anything to say. I told him that I'd heard of the indenture scheme and asked if instead of going to prison, I could sign on for the indentureship. At that time, I had no idea that my arrest and imprisonment were a 'set-up', designed to recruit labourers for work on plantations in lands far, far away. I felt I had no choice, because English law was involved.*

"*I was led away and placed in a room, which was locked on the outside. There were others there and the news they shared gave rise to a foreboding that doom awaited me. They told me of a large ship which would cross the oceans to new lands where I'd labour in the fields.*

"*I was fearful at the thought of traveling on water. I had never seen a ship. It had been described to me as a large building that floated. I questioned my decision. Would it have been better to serve time than agree to this 'indenture'? I turned to run away, but a stiff arm pushed me back in line. After I'd put my thumbprint on the indenture certificate, I was taken to a compound where other recruits were waiting. I was given a meal, which I quickly devoured. My courage returned as my hunger eased, and my determination to survive gave me hope. I would find work for which I would be paid, and I would save my money and return home to India.*"

We were listening intently to Nana's story, absorbed in the tale of our grandfather who had come from this strange country. I'd never met him, but had heard tales of this "man from India" who had lived in our household before I was born. We were anxious to hear the rest of Nana's fascinating story, but it was time for lunch, and my mother said that Nana needed a break from our pestering.

Our chatter during lunch was all about India. This was the first time we were making the connection with our mother country and the questions we asked, more often than not, had no answers.

We quickly dragged Nana away after we'd finished eating. He pleaded that he was an old man and needed a rest, but as he looked at our eager faces, bright with anticipation, he couldn't resist our entreaties.

CHAPTER SEVEN

T HE JOURNEY ACROSS THE OCEANS. Nana continues the saga of Ramesh. *"I was taken to a compound close to the docks where we'd board the ship. Wild guesses about everything caused us to become even more worried and afraid. None of us knew exactly where we were going and how long it would take, or even what would happen to us at the end. We'd heard that waves in the ocean would toss the ship about, and this would cause us to be sick. Pain in our stomach and bowels might happen when we ate and this would lead to vomiting, 'emptying our bowels through our mouths'. This could continue for days, and we could lose our lives. There was no cure and no medicine to help us. We huddled together and tried to find answers to all the questions which troubled us.*

We made friendships and gave promises.

Suddenly, one morning, we saw a strange vessel coming toward us in the water. We wondered if this was our ship, and who or what made it float and follow directions. We later found out that wind pushed the sails and, by by adjusting these sails, sailors could control the direction and speed to take us across the oceans to the land where we would work. We became more afraid and wished we could back out of the deal, but we knew this wasn't possible. We were diligent in our prayers to the various gods in whom we'd put our trust. Those of Muslim faith could only murmur 'inshallah.'

We stared with open mouths at the passengers who left the vessel; in turn, they looked at us as if we were strange animals with little human intelligence, and only fit for work as common labourers. Some women held their skirts close to their bodies to avoid our touch. I learned later that these were English recruits for the Government who'd taken control of India. They were as puzzled about us, as we were about them.

It took many days to load the ship with spices, silks, carpets, and other merchandise destined for sale in England after at the end of our voyage to the West Indies. We all had different stories to tell about how we'd arrived at this low point in our lives, and filled the time sharing them.

There was a rumour that we would lose our position in the caste system. Because of our new association with lower castes everyone would be classified 'lower caste'. Benefits derived from being born in a higher caste would automatically disappear. The Brahmins and other higher caste members were deeply troubled, but we were all filled with fear. We were stepping into the unknown when we climbed aboard the ship. We'd lost any control we had over our lives. We wondered how many of us would survive and how many would be the lucky ones to return to India.

"When the day we all dreaded arrived, we were given a bundle with a change of clothing and a blanket and herded aboard the vessel. Sailors instructed us to climb down a ladder into a dark space called the 'hold.' We could barely see our way down. I was afraid of the darkness. I wanted to turn back, but the only way out was barred by the steady stream of people coming down. Those who were the first down rushed about to choose what they thought was a good spot, and the last comers took whatever was left. It was a tight squeeze.

Huddled in the darkness, people wept, holding on to their new friends all wondering why we'd agreed to indentureship when we knew nothing about it.

The opening above was shut with a thud. The ship made ready with her sails. Footfalls and shouts from above added to our anxiety and fear.

The start of the voyage to our unknown destination brought nothing to reduce our fears, and many uncertainties. We were given food before we left. We didn't know when we would eat again.

Sleep conquered us all. Curled up beside strangers, with no desire to do anything that would provoke a quarrel, I withdrew into my thoughts. 'What can I do to make this better? How can I find out where we were going? How many days and nights would it take to get us to our destination?'

Next morning, we were given our rations for the day. One of our fellow passengers who some had observed getting special treatment the day before, stood up and addressed us in Hindi. 'My name is Chatterpal and I understand English, the language our masters speak. I'm going to act as your interpreter and let you know what your orders are. You must exercise patience and help each other.' We all started to voice our protestations and ask questions.

'Be silent,' he said, 'the voyage will be rough. It'll be many moons before we arrive at our destination, as we have to cross many oceans. The waves will rock the ship back and forth. Many of you will be sick, but you will be given medicine. Make the best of your voyage because work and money wait for you at the end of the trip. You can make a fortune and prepare for your return home to Mother India. There's a doctor on board to take care for you.'

When I listened to Chatterpal, I decided that I, too, would learn to speak the language of our masters. That knowledge would give me power. I had no idea of what the journey would bring, but I was determined to look for opportunities. We all vowed to stick together, make our fortune, and return home. The future we'd dreamed of would happen. An uneasy peace, prevailed. Hope that our days would be better and we could create a better future for ourselves was our only choice. Something good must come from all this hardship.

On our journey to where we had no idea, there were many storms. The ship rolled from side to side. We emptied our stomachs until there was nothing left. Seasickness and other illnesses took their toll. Many people died.

Women disappeared mysteriously to the upper deck and returned in tears. We whispered among us, but knew we could do nothing to help them. At the end of our voyage, many had 'swollen' bellies.

We fought among ourselves. Uncertainty, illness, and jealousy, caused despondency and disagreement. After endless days and nights, the journey across the oceans had stolen our courage and our hope. Once again, I found myself wondering, like that day lying under the rock, whether death was the best and only way forward.

In the grips of my doubt, there was a subtle change. The ship's movements became slower and steadier. Shouts from above signaled that something was about to happen.

A very troubled bunch of Coolie labourers arrived in Georgetown, British Guiana. We'd heard that we were going to be sent to different places, and it would be the last time we would see our ship 'families.' Travel to visit other plantations was forbidden. We'd be confined to the plantations where we were being sent and would be punished if we disobeyed this rule and sought to find our friends. Our hearts trembled and our bodies shook with fear.

As we left our ship I looked beyond the river toward the horizon where the sky seemed to meet the water. The water stretched on for ever, it seemed. The water was muddy; angry waves lashed the vessels moored beside our ship as the water made its way to the shore.

We were all quickly herded into a building when we left the ship. I felt like lying down and kissing the land, but I was poked and prodded to move on. Once inside, we were told to wash and clean ourselves. We all received a bundle of new clothes. What we had worn for months were so foul and grimy, we all smiled. The future had to be better than our ship journey.

When we left the building next day, we were moved to a platform. Many White people had come to gaze and gawk at us, pointing and laughing at our clumsy walk. Several men approached us and selected some of our group. Because of my meagre condition - I was so thin with no muscle- I was left to the last. I found myself in the company of eight others, awaiting and fearful at whatever was to happen next. The sun was bright, the heat was penetrating, there was no water to drink, and flies and mosquitoes feasted on our bodies. The people who had come out to see us had all left. I was almost happy to be on dry land again despite the strangeness of this new place. My spirits had sunk lower when I learned that my shipboard 'brothers' were being sent elsewhere. I felt dejected; I'd thought the companionship we'd formed over the voyage would help us all to adapt to our new surroundings, but I'd seen them all disappear and my heart had grown heavier.

My physical condition had worsened. I was just 5 ft. tall, and I weighed under 90 lbs. The overseer who was in charge of transporting us to to Plantation Bath in Berbice County where we were being sent looked me up and down and assessed my fitness. He wondered aloud "how long will this one survive; it may be better to leave him here to die." He didn't know that I understood his words as he shook his head in disgust. I learned later than many Coolies died from overwork but this didn't matter, it was cheap enough to replace them.

'Where you taking us, Bass?' The overseer was surprised at the sound of my voice. He'd quite unexpectedly come upon an English speaking Coolie, someone who could understand orders and pass them on. He was worth a lot of money. 'You speak English?' he asked me as if he couldn't believe what he'd heard. 'Yes, Bass, I learned on the journey here. I'm good English-speaking Coolie,' I replied with pride in my voice and a smile on my face. I straightened my shoulders and drew myself up to my full height.

He patted me on the back and said, 'Jolly good. You'll make a good worker.' He smiled.

The overseer seemed happy to find I could understand English. I, on the other hand, felt a sense of despair which took root and control of my mind and body as I journeyed towards our destination.

Why did I ever trust the people who told me that I would find work which would put money in my pocket? This was worse than starvation at home in my village. People talk around me in a language they think I can't understand. I'm poked and prodded like an animal. Death would be the best way out, but I don't have the strength; even so, I didn't know how to make it happen. I fell into an uneasy sleep and only awoke when I was jabbed and told to get off the cart.

A man who I later learned was called Durga spoke to me in my dialect. He told me I was consigned to a 'gang', indicated where I would sleep, and added that I would start work in the morning.

Communicating with someone in my own language eased some of my insecurity. I was given food, and then I curled up in my space and fell asleep. Next morning, I was provided with a cutlass and taken to the cane fields. The cane had to be harvested, loaded into punts, and taken to the factory to be turned into sugar."

⊫╪ ╪⊩

Nana ended his tale at that point because it was time for him to leave to 'catch' the next ferry to Georgetown. He promised to finish his tale when he returned in a few weeks. We weren't pleased, but we knew he had to get home; our curiosity and enthusiasm had to await his return.

Nana never returned to Vreed-en-Hoop to continue the tale of Grandfather Ramesh. He contracted pneumonia and died two weeks after his return to his home in Georgetown.

We were heartbroken and wondered if we would ever know the end of our grandfather's story.

We missed our Nana, his tales, his straw hat, his cane, and the six cents coin.

I wondered how we could pick up the story that we had so ardently listened to, but something happened to me, which sent me hurtling down and shuddering into the depths.

CHAPTER EIGHT

MY CHILDHOOD DIES. It was customary in our household for the younger children to have a nap after lunch. I was vivacious and happy, always asking questions and demanding answers. My mother always said to me, "You're setting a fine example, aren't you? I say 'do this' and then you go the opposite way. What am I going to do with you?" She always chided me. I wanted to play after lunch, to run about, chase the chickens or catch a butterfly, but in the middle of it all I would hear, "It's time for the afternoon nap."

I must have been completely beside myself that day. It was a Sunday; that much I can remember. The servants always had half days off on Sunday. A distant cousin, Cyril, was visiting. He was a favorite of us children; he always paid attention to us, brought us sweets, and always eager to join us in our games. With his wavy black hair, good looks, and mannerly behaviour we were always delighted when he came to visit. After my mother's complaint about my always making trouble to have an afternoon nap, he offered to put me to bed and to see that I remained there until I fell asleep.

We went upstairs to the room we called "the Last Room" because it stood at the end of the corridor. I thought nothing of
it since we used it as a playroom and it also doubled as a guest
room when relatives and friends stayed overnight. It had a large
bed. He tickled me which brought laughter and joy, then told me
to get into bed; he then he laid down beside me. I turned on my
side as he started to stroke my back gently so I would go to sleep.
As my eyes were closing, this suddenly changed, and he began to
pull my panties down. I objected and asked what he was doing.
He told me to shush and do as he instructed. I protested and told
him I didn't like it and started to roll out of the bed. He pulled
me back, then put one hand over my mouth and said, "Shut up.
No one will hear you, or come to see why you're crying out. You
have to do what I tell you, or I'll complain to your mother and
she'll slap you and put you in the corner for lying about me, and
disobeying me."

I squiggled and squirmed, and tried to use my hands and
push with my feet to get away, but he was so strong. I was only
five years old. He was a teenager. He foiled my efforts by climbing on top of me and covering my mouth with one hand, tug-
ging my panties down with the other; then pushed his 'big thing'
into me. Pain enveloped my entire being. It was excruciating and
overwhelming.' I thought, this is what death must be like. I asked
myself 'what's happening to me, why is he doing this to me'? It
went on and on, never-ending. I fainted and lost consciousness,
because I remembered nothing more.

I was awakened by my mother. She was on her way to the
washroom and had to pass the Last Room. She looked in and
saw me lying in a pool of blood on the bed. She shook me awake.
"What happened?" she exclaimed in a voice that told me she
dreaded what she was seeing. "Where's Cyril? He was putting you
to sleep. You poor child! What did he do to you?" I remember I
started screaming. My father heard and rushed in to see what

was happening. He couldn't understand or believe what his eyes observed.

"Who did this to her?" he asked over and over again, his tone reflecting his sadness.

My mother told him to hush. "Let's look after her now, and we'll talk later."

I remember being submerged in a tub of warm water. She treated me like a baby, rubbed me down with coconut oil, dressed me in a clean white nightgown, then tucked me in my bed. I was given a glass of milk with brandy, cinnamon and nutmeg, and told to go to sleep. Through my sobbing, I cried, "Cyril hurt me, Mother. Why did he do this to me? He held me down and I couldn't run away."

She said, "Don't worry, child. Rest and we'll talk later."

I fell into a deep sleep. When I awakened, I began sobbing and screaming. My mother came and lay beside me. She said, "Cry as long as you like. I'll be here beside you. No one can hurt you."

Later that evening, both my parents came to the room to check up on me. I could see the concern in their eyes and hear the sadness in their voices. My father took me in his arms and rocked me back and forth. He started to sob. "Child, I would've given my life if it could've kept you from this. I caught Cyril as he was sneaking out of the front door, tied him to the post in the dining room and gave him a good whipping. I have written a letter of complaint to my brother. He will deal with him. I'll never speak to him again, and he is forever barred from this house. He's dead to us and he'll never hurt you again."

My mother whispered, "Hush, don't cry. It won't happen again. You must never talk about this to anyone. Your body will heal and you'll soon forget this terrible thing that happened to you. It has to be kept secret. No one can ever know what occurred; that'll only make matters worse. You can trust me to see that Cyril is punished for what he did to you and to our family."

"What is she telling me?" I asked myself. *"That I should forget and not cry out? How was this going to help me? Didn't they realize that violence had happened, my body had been destroyed and my mind torn asunder? How could I help myself when no one wanted to talk to me and explain what had occurred? Why just warn me that it was a secret never to be shared?* I was left alone to battle fear and uncertainty, adrift in a sea of disbelief, horror, pain, and sadness. My psyche, my innermost being, as well as my body had been destroyed. Did all children have to endure this? Was it a part of childhood, of growing older? I was lost. I felt shame. My body had been used and defiled in the worst possible way, and no one was willing to explain what had happened to me."

As children, we were taught to obey our elders. It was a strict code. If the older siblings complained that we were being disobedient, we were sent to the corner to repent our ways. I couldn't understand what had happened. *Sex was something I had never heard about. If this violation was a secret and I had to carry it alone, what would become of me? My body was so broken, I could barely limp. Terror filled my mind. What had Cyril done to me and why? There were many questions but no answers were forthcoming.*

The night terrors began that night. I became afraid of the dark. The candle flies (fire flies) which strayed into the house through the open jalousies, lit up the walls at night and took on a different meaning to my shattered mind. Vampires waited for me to fall asleep so they could turn into human form and suck the blood out of my body. Snakes slithered beside me. I ran screaming at the top of my lungs trying to escape them, only to find a gang of coyotes waiting to pull me apart limb by limb. I had been a happy child, full of love and adventure, and excelling in school. I was now a frightened waif, adrift in a sea of terror from which there was no escape. What had happened to me and why, I couldn't understand, and there was no answer forthcoming. Fear walked beside me and became my constant companion.

This dastardly act that had been perpetrated on my body was in reality a life sentence. It had left me adrift in a sea of darkness and disbelief, tormented by horror and suffering. I had been thrown into a dark chamber from which there was no escape. My body and soul had endured physical pain and degradation, which continued to wreak havoc with its never-ending wave of terror and desecration of mind, body, and soul,

My brain tried to find different ways of dealing with this, but the horror of this shameful attack became a part of me. The innocence of childhood was lost. Darkness invaded my being. Trust had been replaced by a world of crazy specters filled with evil, from which there was no escape. The once happy little girl had become a tortured, tormented creature.

My joy and laughter never returned. I cried at the least hurt or slight. My siblings started reciting the nursery rhyme about traits children inherited, dependent on the day of birth. I was born on a Wednesday, and Wednesday's child was cast as "full of woe." I always thought, "If you only knew?"

What does a child of five know about keeping family secrets? Why did such devastation happen to destroy my childhood? I constantly asked myself. The word 'sex' had never factored into my vocabulary. I'd never given a thought to what this meant. I knew that people got married and had babies, but what made this happen? I had no idea. I knew nothing of penises and vaginas. I recognized boys were different from girls, but at five years old, why there was this difference had never interested me. I felt that babies were magically delivered by a stork. My life had been filled with fairy tales and fun-filled games, and with trying to outdo the children at school with my prowess for reading and writing. To look up at night and see a 'star' falling in the sky had given me so much pleasure that I feared my heart would burst from happiness. But all this had changed.

Now what? I'd been told to keep a secret, one so shameful that it had completely destroyed the innocence of my young life. I couldn't talk to anyone about what happened to me. I was told it had to remain a secret because of the shame it would bring to my family. Could anyone have helped me understand what happened and why? And would this understanding have helped? I'd done nothing wrong. Why would I bring shame on the family?

My world changed that fateful Sunday. My parents never discussed the matter further with me. My father would always hug me and let me sit beside him. My mother said nothing. Her silence made me feel that I'd somehow disappointed her and she blamed me for this. In the days, months, and years that followed I evolved into two people: one, the true me, who was a shrinking violet, sad, lonely, and insecure; the other, my protector who presented herself to the world as a 'normal,' happy child. One part of me comforted the other. I talked about my fears and insecurities with my 'friend'. She understood and gave me the love and understanding I craved. We couldn't review what had happened because we both didn't know the whys and wherefores of what had taken place, and why it had happened. My two selves were always striving for dominance. I wonder if anyone ever realized that I'd developed a split personality and that there were two of me in one body!

But it's time return to my tale of Grandfather Ramesh, so that my story can achieve coherence.

CHAPTER NINE

RAMESH IMPROVES HIS STATUS. As you may recall, Nana died before he could finish his story of Grandfather Ramesh's adventures. We pleaded with Dad to continue the tale for us, but he always demurred. After several months he grew tired of our constant pleadings, and one Sunday, after a particularly sumptuous lunch, he gathered us together and continued the story.

"Ramesh, your grandfather was weak from the voyage, but he'd been given food. He'd slept on land for the first time in months, and at long last he'd been given a job that would earn him money. His spirits rose, he would work hard, save whatever money he earned, and return to India at the end of his five years of indenture.

One work battle merged into the next. One day, when he was hard at work, he saw the overseer who'd collected him from the wharf in Georgetown approaching on horseback together with another man. They rode up to the gang, and he saw the overseer pointing to him. He was ordered to stop what he was doing and join them. He felt afraid. "What's wrong, what did I do?" he asked himself. The foreman of the gang approached them. "He's a new Coolie, Sah. That's why he's slow. He will get faster when he learns." The foreman feared that your Grandfather had been singled out for punishment because he could not keep up with the others.

The overseer replied. "He speaks English. We can use him to make other Coolies understand our orders. We need faster work. Cut him from the gang. Tell him to report to the Estate office."

And that was the start of an astounding journey for Grandfather Ramesh.

Two years passed, during which he became efficient, knowledgeable, and trusted. He knew that abuse of many kinds was rampant but he did his best for both workers and their plantation owners. Quite unexpectedly, he had used his intuition and his farming knowledge to devise an easier, simpler and faster way for planting and harvesting sugar canes and transporting them to the factory to be turned into sugar, sugar bi-products, molasses, and rum.

He never did get the credit directly. Instead, his bosses presented the ideas as theirs and got big rewards. He'd earned the trust of his fellow Coolies and the respect of his masters, and he'd been promoted and given more responsibility. However, his boss continued to get the credit for his insight and acumen. It was the order of the day. He was content. His wages had increased and he'd started saving some money for his return to India. There was a new swagger in his footsteps and a confident air about him. People came to him for advice and he was generally looked up to. He knew that the treatment meted out to the Coolies was unjust, but anything he could do to make it better would only make it worse.

One day as he was returning home, his life changed. He stopped at the local corner street market, situated under a spreading tamarind tree, to buy a sweetmeat. His eyes fell upon a new seller; a young beautiful Indian girl he'd never seen before. Her lovely features, fair complexion, and charming smile took his breath away. She was small and slim, and her beauty added a glow to the open-air market. She was dressed like all the other women, but the orhni that covered her head added enchantment to her beauty.

"Where did she come from?" he asked himself. She looked up at him, their eyes held for a moment, and he was lost. Dazed and confused, he pointed to her tray where there was an assortment of treats. As she handed *him his purchase and he gave her the money, their hands touched. His heart leapt. Her touch awakened something in him. He walked away towards the "logie" (labourers' quarters) where he lived. He slowly sat down on the steps and pondered. This must be the feeling of love he'd heard about. Could he live without her? He doubted that. He had to find out more about this wonderful creature. Just looking at her and feeling her touch had transported him into a magical world.*

He promised himself that he would begin to make enquiries about this wonderful girl. His best bet would be to visit "Mussie" (Auntie) an old woman who lived alone and performed the duties of healer and midwife. Mussie was friendly, reliable, and well-liked. She would know whatever there was to know. Her face was wrinkled, perhaps by the length of her life and all she'd endured while living on the estate. She was the local 'Yenta.'

Mussie lived in an old shack just beyond the outskirts of the plantation boundaries. When she finished her indenture, she'd had no desire to return to India. Her husband, the local 'medicine' man, had died years before. His extensive knowledge of tropical medicines made him a valuable consultant to the white ruling class. She'd learned and expanded on what he'd taught her. She was also the recipient of many secrets. People usually went to seek her advice when they had problems. She delivered their babies, dispensed healing herbs, and gave unsolicited advice. She was childless but she didn't lack companionship. She was regarded as the 'universal' aunt who would always listen and give practical suggestions. Importantly, she also helped to arrange marriages.

Mussie had an ear to the ground so she knew even before he'd come to see her that Ramesh had fallen in love with Zeena, the daughter of Abdul Mohamed the Mulvi (priest) of the Muslim religion. This wasn't good. Ramesh was a just low caste Hindu boy and Zeena was Muslim. Muslims and Hindus didn't marry. The Plantation Manager whose right it was to determine what marriages could happen, didn't want to disrupt the workings of his Plantation over disagreements for such an inane subject as marriage among the Coolies. He was the sole authority in case of disagreement, but he seldom intervened.

Nana (Abdul Mohamed) cherished his only daughter and wanted an attachment with someone 'with money', steadfast in the Muslim faith. He also knew that his daughter's beauty had attracted the unwanted notice of the overseers, and he didn't want her to become the victim of one of them who would await her on the road and take "advantage" of her. He arranged protection with one of the other vendors who would walk her home at the end of the day, but he knew that if threatened by one of the overseers, the worker would flee and leave Zeena to her fate.

Mussie knew that Ramesh would seek her counsel, but what could she tell him? "Forget your love and let me find someone else?" Ramesh was not the handsomest of men, but he'd made a name for himself; she wondered if Zeena had also fallen in love with him. He had an air of authority about him and Zeena was at an impressionable age.

As the days passed, she felt she had to get the facts. Mussie didn't like going out in the midday sun because the heat distressed her and added more lines to her already wrinkled face, but there was no help for that. She wanted information. She cut a plantain leaf from one of the trees near her house to shelter her and off she went to find Zeena. Zeena was with the other sellers taking shade under the tamarind tree.

"Salaam Alaykum, …Namaste," Mussie greeted all the sellers with a sweeping wave of her hand. She pointed to Zeena. "You're the new girl everybody is talking about. Did you make these yourself?" pointing to the array of ladoo (sweet treats). "I hear you're quite the cook. Your mother is always boasting about you. What do you have to tempt your old Mussie?" She smiled as she invited a response to her many questions.

Zeena blushed. She was proud of her skills. She looked up at Mussie with a radiant smile as she pulled her orhni (head covering) closer to her face. Mussie thought 'You're beautiful, the prettiest girl I've seen in a long time; no wonder Ramesh has fallen in love with you. Your good looks and enchanting smile will get you into trouble. You're much too trusting, smiling at everyone. No good can come of this. I'd better help you and Ramesh and try to protect you from the bad things which could surely happen to you."

"*Mussie, choose some mithai. I made this today. It's different from the Hindu kind. We use cardamom and our mithai is soft and chewy.*" *Zeena offered, with an inviting smile.*

"*I hear Ramesh is a constant customer here,*" *Mussie whispered as she paid for the mithai. Zeena blushed and confided quietly, "Yes, Mussie. I always put aside a special something for him. He doesn't know this, but I like him; I've heard a lot about him.*"

"*You're playing with fire, girl,*" *Mussie chided her, her shaking head voicing the problems ahead. "This isn't good at all. Your father will punish you if he knows what you're thinking and he would raise hell and high-water here. I hope you know what you're getting into!*"

"*Mussie, these words I speak wouldn't come out of my mouth except to you. I know my secret is safe with you. What can I do? I've never met anyone like him. My Pa thinks he's worthless and has nothing good to say about him. I know Faizul wants to marry me, but I'm afraid of him. He and Pa have spoken. He's so old and fat, only a few years younger than my Pa, and so very boastful. When he's angry, he raises his voice and his hands 'fly'. He hurts women and I'm afraid of him. I hope and wish Ramesh can rescue me.*"

Mussie gave her a look that warmed caution, pointing her index finger and waved it in a gesture that indicated 'take care', "I hear your concerns, girl. Keep your secret and your feelings to yourself. This is important. Talk to no one about this. I'll ask around and see if there's anything I can do to help you and Ramesh. Your father won't give in easily. I don't think he will agree for you to marry that useless womanizer, Faizul. He loves you too much. Then again, he won't let you marry Ramesh who's just a low caste Hindu boy. You don't want people talking, so be careful and don't make eyes with Ramesh, or call attention to yourself."

Mussie walked home, the plantain leaf withering in the heat in one hand and the mithai in the other, leaving crumbs on her lips as she munched. She believed that there was nothing that could be done to prevent tragedy from unfolding. Ramesh had no one to speak for him. Abdul Mohamed was well-respected in the Muslim community, and if he wanted

Zeena to marry a Muslim boy and no one happened to be available, he would reluctantly accept Faizul in preference to Ramesh. Abdul Mohamed was fully within his rights as a father. Even the plantation management would make no objection.

Union between Hindu and Muslim would be fodder for the factions within the plantation that liked to stir up trouble. If the Coolies fought with each other, work on the plantation would come to a halt and profits would fall. No matter which side won in the ensuing fights, there would be punishment inflicted by the manager, and loss of wages as well as imposition of additional fines.

Shortly after Mussie's return home, Ramesh visited her. "Mussie, I've not slept since I met the new girl at the corner market. Have you seen her? I repeat to myself over and over again, that she's the daughter of Mulvi, Abdul Mohamed, and he's Muslim and I'm Hindu. She's on my mind day and night and I can't live without her. I think she cares for me too. When I buy my mithai, she always smiles with me and that turns my heart upside down. I know you'll advise me to forget the whole thing. Give me some different advice; help me."

Mussie berated him for creating such a disaster, waggling a crooked finger close to his face. She admonished "Don't you know that you must never look at a Muslim woman? It is forbidden. Hindus and Muslims never mix. Only trouble can come of this. Leave well alone, and I'll look for a nice Hindu girl for you."

He pleaded, "You don't understand, Mussie, if I can't marry her, it will break my heart. I'll leave this place and go with the 'bucks' (Arawak Indians) who live in the jungle. I can't live without her. My heart is filled with longing. I've never felt this way before. You make matches for both Hindus and Muslims. You must know something that can help us."

"Well, boy, you're lucky and you're stubborn. You're making me think too hard. Ask yourself, what is different about you, a low-caste Coolie? Let your brain work for you. You're a sadaar (foreman). You have your own power. Use it. Approach Abdul Mohamed. Tell him you love his daughter and want to marry her. Abdul has his eye on that plot of land

in the village where the old Dutch house still stands. Tell him that you'll speak to your boss and get permission for him to buy it. Tell him also that you've heard that Faizul has been sleeping at the house of Parvattie, the new widow, who is Hindu. Remind him that Faizul is an old man. He'll be unfaithful to Zeena and he'll beat her. Tell him, he only wants to marry Zeena so he can inherit your money. Remind him that rumour says he doesn't love Zeena, he loves your money." Her voice imposed a confidence in his mind he'd not felt before. He'd try to bargain and, hopefully, obtain the Mulvi's consent.

After some delay and a lot of permissions and gossip, Zeena and Ramesh were married in the Pilgrim Holiness Church in the nearby village. They became Christians. They had five children, three boys, Amos, me (John), and George, and two daughters Sarah and Mary. They all went to the village school, which was run by the Church.

During this time, Ramesh finished his indenture. He could have returned to India. Nana advised that he was better off where he had a good job; his children were mixed Hindu and Muslim and as Zeena and the children had been born in British Guiana, they couldn't return to India on his free ticket.

Ramesh smiled as he told Nana he'd no intention of returning to India. He planned to get a choice plot of land in exchange for the cost of of his return passage. He would build a proper house, similar to the ones the overseers lived in, for his family.

True to his word, Ramesh worked hard to build security and give his family a good life. To pay for his house, and the increasing costs of his growing family, he returned to tailoring in his spare time. He was so good at fashioning, cutting, and fitting, even the white overseers started to order their clothing from him. But this was not enough.

The only added extra income available meant that despite his best intentions, his boys would have to work on the plantation after school. When his sons returned with wounds inflicted by whips and tales of indignity and brutality, he told them "No more. I haven't suffered and worked so hard for nothing. It wasn't my plan to have my children work under the same brutal conditions. I've given up far too much to accept this now."

The brutal whipping his sons had endured rankled. He complained to the overseer who'd replaced his old boss. The overseer was young, white and quite aware that Coolies were inferior human beings. In addition, he had sadistic tendencies. He swished the whip in his hand against his own feet. "Whipping is the only things you Coolies know. Without it you slack off and chatter among yourselves. Things have gotten slack. Animals move faster when they feel the whip. You're all the same."

Ramesh felt rage and hatred rise up inside him as he heard the overseer speak. "I can't work on the sugar estate. You take advantage of us. We aren't animals; we're just as human as you are."

The overseer raised his whip. Ramesh stared at him defiantly daring him to strike. None of the coolies had ever looked at him like this. The look interrupted the overseer's motion. He lowered his whip. Ramesh turned and walked away with the stride of a man who knew he'd just set his life on a new course.

[At this point, my dad had no choice but to interrupt his story as we kids were clapping our hands, yelling and cheering. Smiling he said, "There's more, let me continue."]

My father knew he would have to start all over again. He gathered Ma and us together, "I'll make my tailoring business bigger and train young men to work for me."

Ma added, "I'll make sweetmeats and other delicacies and sell them in the village. We'll get by."

Ma became so good at turning out tasty food, her sweetmeats became famous in the village. She distributed recipes freely, and catered weddings and celebrations informally in good community spirit.

A few years later, as our family prospered we were blessed again. Amos was awarded a scholarship to Harvard University in the United States of America! We couldn't believe our good fortune. Although education, boarding and lodging at the University would be paid for, we would have to defray other expenses. The Church promised its help as it had been instrumental in preparing the scholarship application. That Amos had been granted a scholarship was an honour for them also.

Pa wondered how all this good fortune had happened. He rejoiced in the karma which had urged him to follow his dreams. He told Amos, "Son, learn everything they have to teach you. Your brother, John will follow in your footsteps, and after you will both assist George. He will be older, but learning can take place any time. Look after and care for one another"

Pa was the proudest man in the village. His heart swelled. No Coolie had never before achieved such an honour. One sunny day, we all went down to Georgetown to bid Amos goodbye as he sailed away. Pa remembered his own voyage across the oceans. He couldn't help the tears that flowed freely. Nana turned to him and whispered, "Don't cry Bhia (brother), we make progress."

We were all emotionally drained when Dad finished the story of our grandfather Ramesh. We thought how lucky we were to be living in the lap of luxury, so to speak quite a far cry from our father's childhood.

"Dad you, also, have travelled far. Tell us your story," I pleaded.

"You should ask your Tata (Mother's father) to tell you my story. I told him all of it when I asked him for your mother's hand in marriage."

Despite our pleas, he wouldn't budge. His excuse was always that he was too busy with business dealings.

I vowed to myself that I would get to the bottom of everything, and piece together the balance of the story myself.

CHAPTER TEN

D AD'S EARLY STRUGGLES. Dad missed Amos. He tried to follow his example and study diligently while at the same time doing odd jobs to supplement the family income. At fifteen years old, he completed his School Leaving certificate, and travelled westwards to find work. He didn't know exactly what type of employment he wanted; he only knew that he was looking for work where he could use his education and his skills, and earn money. He didn't want to be a disappointment to his father. People he met sometimes offered help but he didn't trust them. When the right opportunity came along, he felt he would recognize it and seize it.

He trudged from village to village throughout Berbice county and into Demerara county. Sometimes he was lucky enough to hitch a ride on a donkey cart. Every village on his journey seemed to be the same. There were no factories and no employment opportunities. Villagers were all farmers eking a living from the land. Some villagers had cows, but most existed on money earned from farming the land around their homes. When tiredness and hunger became supreme detriments in his search, he began to doubt himself. He'd started out with a few dollars, hoarding this as a miser hoards his treasure, and spending as little as possible. He slept wherever he could find a safe spot.

One sunny day he was awakened by the chirping of a bird nesting in a tree above. For reasons unknown, the sound filled him with a sense of optimism. He wished for bread and was overjoyed when he spied a little shop ahead. It was the first he had seen in days. *"The bird must have been a good omen,"* he said to himself.

As he entered the shop, the aroma of ginger, garlic, and onion, cooking smells he associated with his mother's dishes, made his empty belly roar with anticipation. Saliva filled his mouth; he realized continued hunger had made him weak. The owners were Chinese. He had heard that people from distant lands like China had settled in British Guiana, but he'd never come in contact with them. He tried to speak to the two middle-aged men, but they replied in a mixture of Mandarin (their mother tongue) and 'broken' English, as they pointed to the shelves. He wondered how they could manage the shop and deal with customers when they could barely understand what was being said? He pointed to the case where they kept bread. They shook their heads. They looked at him and felt his need. They offered him rice. He understood that they would feed him in return for cleaning the rubbish from the front of the shop, and stacking the flour, rice, and barrels of salted fish in the front.

John was weary, but the thought of food energized him. In no time he finished these tasks. They invited him into the shop and took him around to their living quarters in the back. It was a meagre place with only two beds, a table, and two chairs. The kitchen was a shed erected at the back. It was no more than zinc held aloft by two posts, providing a roof over a fire pit. They indicated he should sit down. He consumed one bowl of rice covered with stew. He couldn't truly register the taste as hunger caused him to wolf it down. A second bowl appeared as if by magic. The two men liked the way my father worked and they wanted to entice him to stay with them. With many hand gestures, much head shaking to indicate yes or no, words in their their mother tongue, and the few words of English they knew, they offered him a third bowl to encourage him to stay. He understood through their gesturing, they were offering him a job. He would have to keep the premises clean and serve the customers.

He indicated with the use of his hands, one finger drawing letters on the palm of the other hand, that he could read, write, and do sums. Their mouths dropped in wonder. They could read and write Mandarin, but could barely speak a kind of Pidgin English. They offered him a wage of two shillings every month, and further if he kept their books, they would give him more.

Merchandising was not entirely new to him. When he'd delivered finished garments for his dad, he'd collected payment. He'd also helped his mother balance her accounts from her wayside stand. The men told him he could live with them at the back of the shop, and they would give him food when they made it for themselves. He looked around. This was a far cry from the office job he had hoped for, but it was the only job offer he'd received. He would stay for a while and learn.

John learned how to deal with customers and suppliers. Everyone deferred to him because he spoke English and Hindi, he could read and write, and he was fair. He soon became the accountant with all financial responsibility. Customers paid promptly, and he settled with suppliers as soon as goods were delivered. Suppliers taught him it was better to shop for large quantities. Goods could be bought at lower prices. Lower prices attracted more customers from the surrounding villages, and soon the shop expanded. People were willing to trudge a few extra miles to save a few cents. Money was scarce and difficult to obtain.

The owners were happy because of their new prosperity. They began to gamble with their friends in Georgetown, leaving everything to John. He complained about this, but they were so deep into gambling, his complaints went unheeded. Time passed and he hired someone from the village to help him. The shop had become twice the size with only modest improvement in his own circumstances.

One day, after completing the ledger, the thought occurred, "What am I doing? I run this shop. I make money for other people, the same way my Pa made profit for the owners on the plantation. Where is the future for me! This isn't why I left my father's home three years ago."

He questioned his suppliers about the availability of similar jobs in the city of Georgetown. He learned that one of the rich Indian merchants in Georgetown, was looking for a bookkeeper and recommended he should try his luck there as prospects were better in the city for an up and coming young man like him. John had his shop duties to fulfill. He felt the only time he could go to the city was on a Sunday but even on Sundays, when the shop was closed, people came knocking at the back door and he had to serve them. Going to the city presented a quandary.

He told the shop owners he needed to travel to Georgetown on business. They shook their heads as they refused his request. Regretfully, he decided he would have to make a clean break. They had begun to smoke marijuana and the entire business, buying and selling commodities, was left up to him. John knew he could have cheated them because they would hardly have recognized what was happening, but his ethics prevented this. He waited until the end of the week when they paid him, then he packed his few belongings, and bade them a tearful goodbye. They were full of recriminations and promises, but he didn't look back. Their shop lasted for another six months, then they closed it and went into the city. John never saw them again.

He had learned a valuable lesson from their behaviour: *Never take money or good fortune for granted. If things are good today, you must take care of tomorrow by building on what you have.*

John was approaching his nineteenth birthday and he felt it was time for him to earn enough money to assure his independence. He needed to find a job, look for a wife, get married, and settle down. He didn't want to wait until Amos graduated and returned home to begin his life afresh. He would make sure that when he had children, his sons would go to university and become lawyers and doctors. Higher education was lost to him. Now he needed roots, his own home, a wife and family.

He headed for Georgetown, getting a ride from traders partway and walking the rest. Securing a place to sleep was difficult. He spent his first night in the city under a huge tamarind tree. Next morning, he set off to find the shop of Resul Maraj, the man who was looking for a book-keeper. He asked for directions, and on his way there stopped to admire the huge buildings, the markets, the hustle and bustle of people, and the horse drawn vehicles.

It was the beginning of the 20th century, and Georgetown had become a metropolis, the likes of which he had never seen before. He looked around. He was in awe. He promised himself that one day he would be recognized in this large city because of his own accomplishments.

The Stabroek Market with its huge clock tower was an inspiration. Different shops were housed under one roof. He ventured inside to investigate further. His reflections were overwhelmed by the many different shops, side by side, offering a variety of goods he had never seen before for sale. At the back of the market, he saw all the boats transporting produce from farms along the Demerara River. Large and small, all floated on the water, until they could get moorings on the market wharf. Hucksters bought complete boatloads and offered vegetables and fruit for sale to the people who came to the market. The array of fruit and vegetables was dizzying. He was impressed. There were many ways money could be earned.

He stood and looked at the Demerara River, and thought about Ramesh, his dad, who had landed there so many years before and had gazed out at the city with fear in his heart.

Time had stood still on the sugar plantations, where the production of sugar was king and all efforts were always centred on planting and reaping the canes when they were ripe. Time had marched on in the city and had brought many changes. He was overwhelmed by his surroundings, but he was more elated at the thought that he could prosper here because opportunity abounded.

He had education, he was literate, a bookkeeper with experience in shop keeping, and he had the drive and desire to succeed. Moreover, he wasn't afraid of hard work. He would follow his father's example and give this opportunity his all, everything he felt in his being. He had kept in touch with his family through messages brought and sent, but hadn't returned home to see them. He missed them. Sometimes nostalgia had almost made him give up and return home. To still this feeling, he promised himself that once he was settled, he would return to narrate his adventures and the wonders he'd seen in Georgetown.

He eventually found himself at the establishment of Resul Maraj around midday. It was quite a large establishment, retailing foodstuffs to merchants with established businesses up and down the coast and across the river. Clerks bustled to fill orders for bags of flour, sugar, salt, Indian spices, drums of oil, barrels of salted fish, boxes of herrings and items, the likes of which he was seeing for the first time. As orders were taken and paid for, goods were laden on to huge dray carts (pulled by donkeys) for transportation across the country. He thought, *this man has vision. He sells goods from all over the world all across British Guiana.*

He approached a clerk and hesitantly asked him to direct him to the Manager. The Manager was brown, well-dressed, and sported a precisely trimmed beard. As he approached, the Manager looked up and asked in Hindi, "Why do you want to speak to me?" John explained in correct English that he was looking for a job.

"What can you do?" the Manager replied in English, in a tone which suggested he was annoyed at the interruption and resented the intruder who had intercepted his thoughts.

John was nervous. His future lay in landing a clerical job. He had never before seen an Indian man so well dressed and in control of his own business. He explained, "I've been working for two Chinese men on the East Coast, running their shop and keeping the books for the past three years."

"Oh," the Manager interrupted, "I've heard of you. What's taken you so long to get here, and why is your name John?" His eyes questioned what seemed to be an anomaly. Indian people had Indian names.

John replied, "My family joined the Pilgrim Holiness Church back home in Bath, Berbice, so we were given Christian names when we were baptized."

The Manager laughed. "They don't want you to go back to India, so they make you convert to Christianity and speak their language. Yes, we want a good bookkeeper, and as you appear to be fluent in English and Hindi, and I've heard good reports about you, I'll hire you. You can start now." Pointing to a desk in the corner, he continued "There's that desk over there. It's yours, and all the work you find there is yours too."

John didn't want to ask about payment, but he hesitated, "Can you tell me where I can get lodgings?"

The Manager directed him to a rooming house near the Stabroek Market. "You can get temporary lodgings there and later rent a room nearby." He quieted John's heart by adding, "Based on your work for the balance of the week, we'll let you know what we'll pay you. Keep your money safe in a bag tied around your waist hidden under your pants. You're in the City now."

John worked diligently getting invoices and payments organized, even helping to take orders from the many people who came into the shop. He bought his meals from the sellers around and at the end of the week smiled happily when he was paid. He would be able to save some money and in a few months, he could make the trip home to see his parents.

Six months later, he was on his way to Bath. He found that father Ramesh was not doing as well as expected. His eyesight was failing, and he couldn't manage his tailoring shop any longer. His mother's income wasn't enough to sustain them. His two sisters were still at home, and so was his younger brother, George. John cared deeply for his family. He couldn't leave them to continue life under such conditions. Amos had graduated from Harvard, but decided not to return home. He had settled down to life in Chicago and reportedly met a young lady he wished to marry. The news had been a big disappointment to Ramesh and Zeena, but their bigger worries now, were how would they face the future without the money earned from tailoring.

John quietened their fears. His smiling face and air of authority gave them hope. "I've heard that houses are cheaper across the Demerara River at a place called Vreed-en-Hoop, a village cross the river from Georgetown, I have a good job and I make good money. I'll visit the village and see what's for sale. We can all settle there when I find a place to accommodate us. Getting to work in Georgetown will take me longer because I'll have to use the ferry, but I can manage. Meantime, I'll send you some money each week to tide you over."

He left Bath with a heavy heart. He'd thought about getting married and starting a family, but this would have to wait. His mother, father, sisters, and brother required his help.

Six months later, he found a plot of land with two small cottages in Vreed-en-Hoop. Buying it was a huge undertaking, but the place was ideal, close enough to the ferry stelling and enough land for expansion later if he wished. Meantime, his father had sold his house to settle his debts, and there was little money in the kitty. His mother promised that in their new home, she and his sisters would make sweetmeats and sell them on the weekend to supplement their income.

The move from Bath to Vreed-en-Hoop was heart-wrenching for his parents. This place was all they had ever known. "I'll take care of you," comforted John, "Times are changing. You're all no longer required to remain close to the plantation. Moving will be a welcome change. The girls and George will be with you too, and having you all close is very important to me. I'll take care of you. I'm the eldest now that Amos is away. Don't worry. You've done enough for us. It's time for you to rest."

They all worked together to make their new home comfortable and everything seemed to be falling into place. All went well for two years, but change is ever constant. A new girl came to work at Resul Maraj's shop and John lost his heart.

"*A fine kettle of fish*", he thought. "*My family are still getting used to their surroundings, so how can I tell them now that I've seen a girl I like? They might feel that they'd be displaced by the new bride. Then again, this girl may not want to come and live with her husband's family. These Georgetown girls have strange ideas.*"

His heart told him, "*Where there's a will you'll find a way. First things first, see if the girl has feelings for you, then you can make plans.*"

CHAPTER ELEVEN

M Y MOTHER. Dolores Indira was the eldest child of Joseph and Leila Ramsammy, my maternal grandparents. We called our grandfather Tata, and our grandmother Pahti, according to Tamil (Madras) customs.

My Tata and Pahti hadn't come to British Guiana as Bound Coolies. Tata's father was an early recruit of Government agencies in need of interpreters to deal with complaints from Bound Coolies. Buoyed by hope and enthusiasm, as he listened to the glowing picture of life in the new country, he decided to make this new land his home. Tata was tutored by his own father. He also had the privilege of education in the local school set up for children of white overseers. My grandfather was a handsome man, tall and stately; he reminded me of Maurice Chevalier, both for his good looks and the way in which he dressed and carried himself. He always wore a straw boater (hat), and had a flower in the buttonhole of his jacket.

Pahti could neither read nor write. She was the daughter of another professor and while she spoke several dialects, as was customary, she had never learned to read nor write. Her fine features, beautiful brown eyes, and heart-shaped face had attracted many admirers in her younger days. Her head was always covered with a "Madras" head kerchief, which hid her beautiful tress of hair.

One of the requirements of a government job was conversion to Christianity. The Missionary Churches worked tirelessly, and Christianity flourished. Tata and Pahti had both converted to Christianity and they had also adopted English ways. However, they still clung to some of their old Indian traditions, and of course, Indian food.

When he was eighteen, my grandfather obtained employment in the Indian Affairs Department. This was a good job with a bright future and a secure pension. Life had gone well for my maternal grandparents. They were highly respected and loved in their community in Georgetown, the capital city, where middle class people of all races had houses, some owned, others rentals.

Pahti was an exceptional cook. She could turn the simplest dishes into a feast. My mother was always jealous of her culinary reputation, and the way we all were devoted to her. She was our friend and confidante, always lavishing us with attention. She held us tight and tickled us to make us laugh and squeal. We loved to play games with her, thinking we could come out winners in the end, now knowing that was her plan.

Tata wrote letters for his neighbours and led event discussions about happenings in Georgetown and the country as a whole. His reputation as a speechmaker and an 'emcee' added distinction to his bearing and stature. My maternal uncles were police officers and civil servants; the family was highly respected and regarded. My uncles were good-looking men, wooed by girls of every race and regarded as good 'catches.' The girls in the family had beautiful features; they were proficient in English, dressed fashionably and carried themselves with an air of confidence.

My mother Dolores was born and raised in the City of Georgetown. She graduated school at age fourteen. The law required that all children went to public school, until graduation or age sixteen; parents could be charged for breaking this law if this was not followed. Middle class children of all races attended public schools in Georgetown. Teachers were mainly negro or mulattoes. The attempt to teach Hindi in school died a natural death because of lack of interest.

After graduation, my mother found a job as governess to the daughter of a distant cousin, Maya, who was legally married to Henry Muir, a white overseer. Marriage between Whites and Indians was the exception, not the rule. It was usual for white overseers to 'set up house' with Indian women, but when they returned to England their family was forgotten.

My mother was required to undergo rigorous training in English ways and behaviour. Speaking and acting like an English woman was a job requirement. She took her education a step further. She learned to cook English dishes, refined her knowledge of English clothing, customs and behaviour patterns, and walked and talked with confidence. She was considered a 'good catch.'

As was the custom in those days, Indian girls were married at the age of sixteen. A match maker had found a suitable boy for my mother. My grandparents visited with the family and approved the match. My mother didn't have a say in the matter. Reluctantly, she left her post and returned to the city.

The wedding took place amid pomp, ceremony, and grand celebrations, and then she was whisked off into the country to live. Unbeknownst to the family, her husband, Patrick Viapree, was a roué (sweet boy as the locals referred to him) who'd been carrying on an affair with an older woman in the adjoining village. The woman, Sarah Menize, was the owner of a large coconut estate she had inherited on the death of her elderly husband. She was independently wealthy.

When Patrick saw my mother for the first time, he lusted after her. Sarah advised him not to go through with the wedding. His excuse to her was that he couldn't go against the wishes of his family. After his lust was satisfied Patrick began to ill treat my mother. Soon he left her alone for days at a time without food or money. When he found out she was pregnant with his child, he moved out of the matrimonial home and went to live with his mistress.

Sarah Menize had pressured him, it was true, but life with her was easy because he had become a kept man, waited and fawned upon, and money was not a problem.

My grandparents were bereft when they heard that their cherished daughter had been abandoned. The family visited her and my mother returned to Georgetown with them. The child, a bouncing baby boy, was bon in his grandparents' home. He was welcomed with joy and love.

When Patrick learned that he had a baby son, he preened like a peacock. Sarah was envious. She was much older than Patrick, and was beginning to show the ravages of age and good living.

She was childless, despite her many romances during her marriage and following her husband's death. After six weeks, she and Patrick concocted a plot to have him claim the child. She promised that they would raise him together and she would make him and Patrick the beneficiaries of her estate.

Armed with this information, Patrick arrived at my grandparents' home and demanded to see the child. Pahti was alone at home with my mother. When she opened the door in response to his knock, he pushed her out of the way and ran to the bedroom where he could hear a baby crying. My mother was alarmed at the sight of him, and gathered the child to her breast.

"I'm taking my child," he shouted, his face like a thunder cloud. "He's mine. Give him here," he commanded with arms outstretched, "and I promise you'll never see me again. He'll have the best of everything. Sarah will make him her heir. You can't compare what you have with that offer."

My mother screamed, clutching the baby to her breast, "No. You left us both to starve. You don't deserve a child. I won't give him to you and your 'fancy' woman". Her look of hatred stopped him for a moment, but this did not deter him. He advanced toward her, intent on forcibly grabbing the child and escaping.

Vincent, my grandmother's neighbour was tending the guava trees in his yard when he saw Patrick rushing out of a car. He felt no good was about to happen. When he heard the shouts and heated conversations between my mother and Patrick, he realized his intuition was correct. He rushed next door to help. Pahti was standing with her back towards her open front door listening to the voices from the bedroom. Vincent placed a hand on her shoulder and they moved together toward the room.

Vincent saw Dolores in the corner of the room shielding the child with her body as Patrick advanced toward them. He raised his voice, a look of displeasure on his face, "What's all this shouting about, Dolores? You should be resting." Turning to Patrick, he admonished, "I guess you've come to visit Dolores at last, but the noise you're making isn't good for the child."

"Keep out of this, man. You've no right to interfere," Patrick rejoined. "This is none of your business."

"Yeah it is," Vincent replied. "Mr. Sammy asked me to keep an eye out in case you should come by. He's worried about Dolores. All this ruckus you're making ain't good for the child or for her. Get out and come back only when Mr. Sammy's home."

"This child is mine, and I'm taking him. If they want him, they'll have to 'take me to the Magistrate'," Patrick shouted as he grabbed at Dolores' arms.

Vincent was much older than Patrick, but much stronger. He felt the bile rising in his throat and heard only the sound of the blood rushing in his ears. He took two large steps across the room, put his arms around Patrick and propelled him out of the room, out of the house and on to the street.

"Don't forget Mr. Sammy knows the police. Don't come back. If you think the Magistrate will give you the child, see him. I'll tell how you tried to kidnap the child". By this time, many neighbours had gathered outside. Upon hearing Vincent's words, they hurled curses at Patrick. Defeated, he got into the car and left.

Everyone breathed a sigh of relief. Vincent was the recipient of a special cake from Dolores. Even when she eventually moved away, the cake always appeared. Tata reported the matter to the police. Patrick received a visit from the Sergeant in his district, and was warned that if he bothered the family again, he would be arrested as he had no claim to the child. There were three levels of 'justice' at the time, one for the 'whites' and higher-ups, one for the middle class who held good jobs, and another for the lower class. My grandfather fell into the middle class.

Despite the love and protection given to the small baby, nothing could save him from the diseases of the day. He developed croup a few months later. Family and neighbours rallied around, but there was no medication available and he died.

CHAPTER TWELVE

DOLORES INDIRA EMBRACES HER FUTURE. My mother was just 18 years old. Her future was dim. She was at the prime of her good looks, and cut a nice figure as she also dressed well. Divorce was the exception not the rule in those days. She couldn't get married again legally without this. The options of living with someone without the bonds of marriage, or being a financial burden to her parents, were unappealing. She needed a job.

Jobs were few and far between for Indian girls. She felt lucky even to hear of a vacancy at the Salvation Army Tea Shoppe on the High Street. The manager needed an assistant to bake cakes and serve tea in their tea rooms. She applied. The interviewer was impressed by her personality and good looks, and asked her to bake a 'pound cake'. She hadn't brought her recipe book, and making it from memory was somewhat chancy, but she decided to make the most of her opportunity. The cake was perfect and she was hired.

It was her first job and wages were small. In the three months that followed, there was a steady increase in the numbers who came in for tea or placed orders for cakes. She asked for an increase in salary but was told that while the 'Army' respected the work she was doing, they were a charitable organization and didn't have the funds to pay her more. They would miss her if she left as her baking had resulted in increased patronage and the Tea Shoppe was at last paying its way.

After eighteen months she decided she needed to look out for herself and find another job with better wages. It was uncommon for an Indian girl to be working in any establishment. Indian girls got married; they didn't go out to work. She decided to take her courage in her hands and apply for a job as a shop assistant at the firm of Resul Maraj. He was the only Indian merchant in the country, and she felt her chances there would be better. She had nothing to lose and was optimistic enough to summon her courage and present herself for an interview.

Chetty Singh, Manager at Resul Mara's business was impressed by her confidence and her good looks. He decided to give her a chance as she was 'nice on the eye,' knowledgeable, and confident for a girl. Truthfully, he had fallen in love with her and hoped somehow he could succeed in getting her to agree to live with him in a second home.

He was more than twice her age, with children older than her. Having a second home with a younger woman was common practice at the time and gave men a boost in their community. Men could have as many homes as they wished. Children from their second and third wives were branded 'illegitimate', had no claim on their fathers, and most men seldom cared.

Chetty tried to make approaches to Dolores, but she was firm in her refusals. He approached Tata but here, too, he met with resistance. Tata felt Dolores was meant for someone her own age.

When my father met my mother, it was love at first sight. He thought *'this is the woman of my dreams'*. Of course he was charmed by good looks, but when he saw how quickly she was learning the ropes of merchandising, he was determined to make her his wife.

She was also secretly attracted to him. He was handsome, had beautiful kind eyes, was well-dressed and carried himself with purpose and confidence. Given her experience with the indolent Patrick, John was appealing on an entirely different level. He was popular and his progress at the shop was well-known. But sadly, marriage was out of the question for her. Divorce was for the upper classes, and unaffordable anyway. She consoled herself that he wouldn't want her. He was single, an eligible bachelor, and probably looking for someone he could marry.

Despite her not wanting to get involved with him, my father wooed her diligently. He was a new 'house and land owner'. He was reliable. He'd given a home to his aging parents and three siblings. He was a good 'catch'.

He made plans and talked to her about them. There were two small cottages on his land. He could extend one to accommodate his parents and family, and he and Dolores could live in the other. He dangled land ownership before her, telling her she would be his heir if he died before her, but she still held firm. Dolores had no desire to be abandoned again. She would make her way, earn her own money, and become independent.

Alas, she had forgotten the dreams of youth, the attraction that one sex could have for the other, that there was something called love, which drew people together. My father played his cards well. The Manager, Chetty Singh, still desired my mother. He approached my grandfather Tata, promising to give her a house with land, and to provide for her. My grandparents wanted to see her settled and thought that in the circumstances, the arrangements with Chetty Singh would work well.

They started to encourage her to look favorably at this opportunity. Promises between a man and a woman with regard to money and property held no value. If Chetty wanted her to be his second wife, they would tell him he needed to deed title to the land and house to Dolores legally, and set up an account for her with the bank. When Chetty met with my grandfather again, he said, "Sir, I'll take care of her. She'll have house and land, and in addition, money each month, I promise you". He knew that his words were just idle talk to gain what he desired.

Tata made a counter proposal. "I've been discussing your proposal with a senior colleague at work. He advised me that it would be a good union, and we should consider your proposal. However, having worked in the Indian Affairs Department for some time, in order to complete the proposal, you'll have to go to the lawyers at Haynes and Johnson, and have them draw up the documents. Even if you live together, and she had children, if you die without this legal formality, she and her children fathered by you stand to lose everything. I cannot allow this." Tata added, "Think about it. I'm not pressing you. These are my conditions. Dolores doesn't fancy anyone now, so take your time."

Chetty Singh was astounded at the proposal. He'd never heard anything like this in his life. Give a woman property and money legally! Promises were just words which could be made, then forgotten. Legal documents were binding. No woman was worth that. He would forget her. However, when he saw Dolores in the shop the following day, all his good resolutions fled. He decided that he would have her by fair means or foul. He would deal with the consequences later if there were any.

My father heard the rumblings about Chetty's serious infatuation with Dolores. He was worried. He decided to seek her out alone and ask her to visit his house in Vreed-en-Hoop, with her two brothers and meet his family. "Dolores." he entreated, "You're a popular girl here. The rumour mongers are saying that Chetty wants to make you his second wife. He's wealthy. I'm young but ambitious. You'll be my only wife. With you by my side, we'll succeed, and we'll be happy. Come to Vreed-en-Hoop and meet my family. Bring your brothers. I know I should visit your parents first, but they want you to go with Chetty and they won't listen to me. Let's take matters into our own hands. You have a choice. I love you, and we're young together. Come over to Vreed-en-Hoop and see for yourself."

Two Sunday's later, my mother and her two brothers, Jacob and Norman, crossed the Demerara River by ferry and walked to my father's house. The house was rude and bare, but clean. Lunch had been prepared and the family were all waiting. Everyone was in awe of this strange beauty from the city. The girls hung onto her words and followed her everywhere. My grandmother, Zeena, took her aside and whispered, "He loves you. I married his father because I loved him. We've been happy. Life's easier when you love the man you're with. My son has big ideas. He'll make you happy. His sisters already love you. They're calling you Bhowjie (big sister-in-law). Make me happy too and say yes."

John took her outside to see his "holdings." The land appeared enormous. Two acres of land seemed to stretch forever. "This is the foundation of my dreams," said John, arms outstretched in a sweeping motion, "Here, will stand a big house. Our sons will be doctors and lawyers. Our daughters will marry well. We'll grow old together, have many grandchildren, and I'll make you happy."

Her brothers were impressed and so was she. What could they not do with all that land? This is wealth beyond dreams. Her thoughts raced on. As they walked, they came to a massive trunk of a coconut tree that had fallen blocking the path. John offered his hand. She was lost at his touch. They paused, and still holding her hand he whispered, "Do you think we can?"

With a smile on her face and joy in her heart, she replied, "Yes, we can, John; yes, we can." And so on the land that would eventually see my birth, their courtship began.

Dolores still couldn't be married legally. My grandparents held a private 'Madrs' wedding ceremony in their home. John and Dolores were married according to Madrasi rites. She had no legal protection, but my grandparents respected my father and trusted him, and they felt, somehow, that God would bless the union.

Dolores left Resul Maraj's business to marry John. Unbeknownst to her, her joining the workforce would encourage change in the lives of Indian women. Following her example, many decided to seek jobs so they could earn money and become independent. A new window of opportunity had begun to open. They could become financially independent and not have to rely solely on parents or husbands, or settle for jobs as maids, cooks or nannies.

CHAPTER THIRTEEN

C HANGES IN THE COLONIAL SYSTEM (MID 19th CENTURY). Development transformed the country on which Grandfather Ramesh disembarked but it couldn't erase the impact of history. Abolition of slavery freed the Africans. Indentureship continued the abuse of Indians.

Coolies remained the main workforce on the sugar plantations despite the harsh treatment meted out to them. The laws under which they lived and worked tied them to the sugar plantations. They couldn't afford the cost of housing away from the plantations; the wages they received kept them in poverty. They were tied to rules and regulations which were enacted to ensure that labour was available to keep the sugar industry alive and profitable. Their ancestors had put their thumb print on a piece of paper because they had no understanding of what they were doing; their descendants couldn't return to India.

After abolition of slavery, Negroes fared better. They found work in different arms of government institutions – maintenance of Law and Order, the Civil Service, Hospitals, and Education.

Conditions of employment for Coolies changed gradually, but still revolved around the sugar plantations. Many Indians sought a better life. When they became proficient, they saved their money and moved away.

Civil unrest from time to time gave birth to the Guyanese labour movement. Unity was strength; disagreements gave the movement a podium. A labour department was created to settle the tribulations, but workers seldom won. Justice never happened.

The Second World War opened new areas of thinking. Labour awoke to the realization that education and knowledge were powerful tools in the fight for equality. Everyone wanted peace, progress, and prosperity, and a future better than the past. Knowledge created power. Schools offering secondary education sprung up, mainly in Georgetown, the capital.

Aside from the Sugar plantations, British Guiana itself was a developing country. There was a flood of businesses from England seeking to extend their holdings and benefit from the country's many resources. Other than managerial jobs, which were kept for the expatriates, this opened new avenues of employment.

Transportation across the country was facilitated by the construction of two railways. Ships sailed up and down the coasts and across rivers providing access to villages. New roads provided ingress and egress. New houses sprang up. Georgetown, the capital, was the hub of development and became a diverse metropolis. Sugar plantations belonged to wealthy companies in England and were operated for wealth generation. Cities and villages beyond were ruled by the government and generated income through taxation for the British Crown.

Amerindians, the indigenous population, remained in the interior. Long communal houses were crafted for them in the capital cities of the three counties probably to help them gain an insight into the rest of the country. They never integrated with the general population, but could be glimpsed from time to time when they visited the cities. Little attention was paid to their wants and needs. They lived in the interior and seemed an entity onto themselves. Although there was a Commissioner, who was responsible for them, they didn't appear to have any rights. The local police stationed to preserve law and order among them in the interior dispensed justice. Rape and violence led to complaints, but the general population were seldom, if ever, made aware of their circumstances. They were the original owners carrying on life as it had been handed down to them. Their land had been seized by foreigners, who had little or no concern for their welfare.

Fashion and clothing had also changed. European clothing was worn by all. Women of Indian descent covered their heads with an orhni or head kerchief but this practice slowly declined. Only the very poor walked without shoes or yachtings (sneakers).

Hindi as a language was quickly forgotten by the mainstream except for the few religious centres in the mostly Indian villages. Ability to speak and understand the language was pointless.

Food tastes had also diversified. Curries, stews, roti, cassava bread, metagee (root vegetables, plantain cooked in coconut milk), pepper pot (stew made with casareep), Chinese roast pork, chow mien and noodles, to name a few, became recognized as "Guyanese" cuisine

Christianity flourished. Slavery was a 'thing' of the past; 'Coolie' and 'Nigger' were used only as derogatory terms when quarrels arose between Indians and Blacks.

The economy flourished. The Kaieteur Falls had been discovered. British Guiana was a great place to live. There was pride in the land. "Born in the Land of the Mighty Roraima" was an anthem that said it all. Pride in our country had taken root and begun to flourish. But the past wasn't easily forgotten.

CHAPTER FOURTEEN

NEW BEGINNINGS (20TH CENTURY). I get carried away by the bitterness of memories when I look back to the time when inhumanity overpowered justice. However, I must return to chronicle the story of John and Dolores, my parents. They had come from different backgrounds. He had grown up within an arena of cruelty where people dependent on employment to provide food and shelter for survival, suffered under the whims of their masters. She had grown up within a middle class society, her parents and family held in high esteem because of civil service jobs.

Her race was pure "Madras," his, a mixture of Hindu and Muslim. They were both Christians.

Although he had been raised in the Pilgrim Holiness brand of Christianity and she in the Anglican Church, they both believed in the same God. Divisions within the Church removed their ability to worship their God together.

When they attempted to become members of the Anglican Church in Vreed-en-Hoop, they were turned away because their marriage was not legal. They were told, "You're living in a sinful relationship, which God can't condone." Dispiritedly, they returned home. The worship of God was important to both of them and to their families.

Ramesh consoled them as best he could, while recounting his own experience of life. He reminded them, "I came to this country as a Bound Coolie. I found God. He brought Zeena into my life. I prayed to Him and He showed me the way to make everything work. We brought up dutiful sons and daughters, and now you, John, are good to us when I can no longer provide. Find another Church who will accept your promises and pledges to each other. We'll all join with you, God is ever merciful and He will shower us with his love."

The Canadian Mission had established a church in the neighbouring village of Plantain Walk. John and Dolores were welcomed with open arms. The entire family became members. It was not unusual to see them in their Sunday best clothing, shoes cleaned and polished, all riding in the donkey cart on Sunday mornings on their way to Plantain Walk to worship their maker.

Meantime, John continued to work in the city. The family at home in Vreed-en-Hoop decided to start a small business to increase the family earnings. They were all enchanted by Dolores and regarded her as their leader and mentor. Grandmother Zeena expressed her desire to start selling sweet meats and Indian delicacies on the weekends. They brainstormed and came up with the idea of building a kiosk on the vacant land in front of their house. Certain items would be provided for sale during the week. A bigger variety would be available only at the end of the week. Weekends would yield the greatest revenue because people received their 'pay' and ready cash was available.

Bread for the village came from the city. It was not as fresh and tasty as it could be because it took time to get it packaged and shipped across the river. Getting bread also meant a constant trek and a purchase to last for at least two days. Zeena and Dolores discussed a bread source with John. If they had ovens they could provide a supply of this much-needed staple, and this could result in a profitable source of income.

With the help of Henry Langedevine, a Negro childhood friend of my father, an oven was designed and built on land behind the houses. They ran several tests, and when they were satisfied with the results, decided to advertise their new product. The Bell Ringer ran through three villages announcing that fresh bread would be available locally. There was much excitement as demand was more than supply. The bakery was successful. They were in business.

It was time to plan for the future. John was ambitious. His dream of a Big House, and his own grocery shop could be set aside no longer. Plans were drawn and redrawn. There was talk of running water in the house, a septic tank so there could be toilets, and wonder of all wonders, electricity. There would be a wood burning stove in the kitchen, furnishings the like of which had never been seen before, chandeliers to grace the drawing (sitting and entertainment) rooms and furniture designed and built by the best local craftsmen. The dream began to unfold. Somehow my father came upon a catalogue from Montgomery Ward in the USA. This catalogue was a source of new items, which were still foreign to British Guiana. Moreover, they were unique. The village was agog with excitement. The splendour of the city would be reflected in Vreed-en-Hoop.

Henry Langedevine, the friend who helped design and build the bakery ovens was summoned to help. Plans for an enormous wooden home with six bedrooms on the top floor, a huge sitting room and dining room, a music room, a library, and front and back galleries were drawn and redrawn. The kitchen was large enough for an an eating area for the many servants who would be employed.

The ground level was designed to accommodate a grocery on one side and a rum shop on the other. A separate area was incorporated for the sale of baked goods and ultimately became part of the grocery.

During the eighteen months it took them to design and build the Big House, they raised the height of the front cottage in which John and Dolores lived, to create space for a small grocery store. My father had developed a wizardry for commerce and he was able to buy supplies at optimum prices. He transferred the savings he made into lower prices for goods he sold. Villagers found it more economical to make their purchases at his shop. Wholesalers found it was better to do business with him, and he soon decided to build another shop further down the coast.

It took them five long years to establish their thriving business ventures. Good fortune and hard work contributed to their success. Their union was also blessed with three children, two boys and one girl.

Sadly, Grandfather Ramesh never lived to see the big house. He showed his pride in my dad's accomplishments by regaling Dad's exploits as a young lad to all who would listen. There were always people willing to hear his tales and he developed many friendships among the villagers. He had laid the foundation for his family when he realized the value of knowing how to speak English. He had begun to understand the glimmerings of commerce, to ask questions and find solutions which improved efficiency for the many different jobs on the sugar estate.

Being proficient in English helped him spot opportunities and make use of them, a talent he saw in John. He always marveled at the difference between his life in India and his life in British Guiana. Unhappy after he learned that his choice to sign on as a Bound Coolie was fraught with uncertainty, he had turned disappointment around and made the best of a bad situation. His son would be wealthy and he knew his grandchildren would rise to become respected lawyers, doctors, and other professionals. He left this world a contented man.

Grandmother Zeena also died during the construction. She never recovered from Ramesh's death and felt lonely without him. She lost her verve for life. They had forged their lives together, had seen a son leave to attend Harvard University but he'd never returned home. Her son John would fight with the future. She felt it would be bright and happy. Grief made her weak and she contracted whooping cough. The best medications couldn't save her. The entire village attended her funeral.

Her two daughters found suitable husbands and moved to different villages, but her youngest son remained with John and became manager of the grocery store.

My father never forgot his promise to my mother to get a legal divorce. He engaged a firm of lawyers who could pursue the matter and free my mother from the bonds of an unhappy marriage, so she could become his legal wife. He knew Dolores missed the Anglican Church, and a legal marriage would allow her to return.

The divorce was long and drawn out. First they had to find Patrick, her legal husband, then persuade him not to contest it. He was living with another woman and had fathered three children. He was jealous because my mother had found someone else, and their rapid rise in money and status was difficult for him to accept. He asked for a sum of money in return for signing any papers, but the lawyers were too clever for him and they went to Court.

The judge was harsh in his condemnation of my mother's ex-husband, and ruled in favour of my mother. The divorce was final after a year and they were quietly married by a Justice of the Peace the following day.

There had always been a little jealousy shown to my mother by some of the village ladies, who had once 'set their caps' on my father. He was a handsome man then, a young bachelor with a good job. He had bought land and the presumed, quite correctly as it turned out, that his fortunes were on the way up. Seeing him with a girl from the city put their noses out of joint. That she could bake excellent cakes and was recognized for her culinary skills made them envious. She never became part of that village group or even attempted to get to know them better. She had quietly accepted friendship from others, some not so fortunate, and was very popular and well-respected.

The new house signified new beginnings.

CHAPTER FIFTEEN

PROGRESS AND SUCCESS. The modern (for its time) grocery store under the Big House was an instant winner. My father had successfully gauged the tremor of the village population. It was easier, cheaper, and more efficient for the villagers to get their groceries just outside their doors, so to speak, without having to deal with the ferry crossing. Following this success, Dad started to blend his own rums, and this was also an instant success. The Rum Shop provided a space for villagers to unwind. Something in the nature of the English pub, people could buy a shot of rum and spend time easing the cares of the day.

Rum is a by-product of sugar. The rum is extracted from molasses in processes used by distilleries. Each sugar plantation had its own distillery. The quality of the rum was dependent on the acids used in the distillation process. My father never disclosed the recipe for his rums. He blended and matured high wine (over proof rum), fruit cured rum, and white rum. The rum was aged in oak barrels, and the dark rum was coloured with burnt sugar and matured with pureed raisins, currants, and prunes. The white rum was pure, aged only in oak barrels. As his patrons always remarked, "Good stuff, chief. Hits the spot."

The rum shop always showed a profit. Like a good bartender my father could be depended on to lend an ear to the ramblings of his patrons. He offered advice and encouragement, admonished them when they were wrong, and never turned away someone in trouble.

It seemed he could do no wrong. The Midas touch was his. His businesses were all flourishing. He acquired more land across the road from where we lived and erected a large hall, which he rented out for dances and vaudeville shows. A few years later, he saw the opportunity to turn the dance hall into a cinema. He did his research, learned the ins and outs of exhibiting films, imported his equipment from the United States, and he was in business.

I admit that I was born in the lap of luxury. What we had was luxury compared to our neighbours in the village. We even had servants, a cook and an undercook, several housemaids, and a nursemaid and nanny to look after our needs.

Childbirth was difficult for my mother when I was about to be born. Doubly so, perhaps, because I was born on her birthday. In the midst of her birthday party, labour began. The birthing time was long, and the next day she developed an ache in her ears. The Doctor could find no reason for this, but consoled my father by telling him that the malady would disappear with time. It never did and unfortunately I felt she blamed me for her deafness.

Nonetheless my mother was complimented at having a child as a gift for her birthday, but as I grew older I found this was no compensation for me. I grew up hearing, "Where's that child? I left her here a minute ago, where can she be?" I was never where she wanted me to be. I loved being with my father and he loved my being with him. I was chatty and engaging. I only had to hear something once and I repeated it parrot-like. I was spoiled. But one thing I remember is the disappointment when I felt I couldn't run into my mother's arms because they were never outstretched for me.

I cried when my older siblings left for school. I didn't want to be left out. I wanted to go with them. I wanted to learn and be a part of what they were learning. I was told I was bright and promising, but then there was the incident in The Last Room that disintegrated my world and changed me, forever.

There came that fateful day when my fledgling innocence was torn apart ... when plague and pestilence entered my soul ... when I experienced violence and terror, which changed my life and burdened my soul. No one ever offered an explanation. It was treated as if it never happened, as if there was no need to question why and somehow I had to manage whatever the fallout was on my own.

Memories never leave you. How could I live with that? I looked around for help, for arms to hold me tight and protect me. There were none. Like every day happenings, it appeared to have disappeared into the dust. I longed to ask someone why this happened to me, to talk about it, to hug me, let me shed tears, and love me. I'd been left to find my own way out. I asked myself again "*Is this something that happens to all children?*" I didn't dare start a discussion about this, to bring it into the open, ever fearful that I'd be doing something irreparable. I needed to escape, but how could I do this? The mind of a five-year old is limited as to how you perceive the world. 'Questions, always with no answers'. The way out was closed.

I felt I was targeted and the devil was waiting to get me, and worst of all "I'd developed two personalities."

CHAPTER SIXTEEN

THE WICKED NEVER REST. Two years rolled by. In the intervening years, seven-year-old (me) lived vicariously through fairy tales. I imagined myself the heroine who conquered every obstacle in her path to happiness. I stilled the angst in my heart by replacing trauma with flights of fantasy. When my imagination was channeled into the genre of storybook fiction, I felt a sense of peace, but I could still spiral downwards into moments when death courted me and embracing it seemed a pleasant alternative. Concentrating on the always pleasant outcomes temporarily stilled the voices that reached out to me from the darkness.

And then it happened again. Satan laid claim to me.

As younger children, my mother always insisted that we listened to and obeyed our older siblings. One quiet afternoon when everybody seemed to be elsewhere, I was summoned by my older brother Henry, who said he needed my help to find a tie clip he'd misplaced. As I entered his room, he closed the door. The look he gave made me feel uneasy. His face had taken on a cunning look which made me distrustful. He took my hand and held it so tightly I couldn't run away. "Tab, you have to help me, you're the only one who can. I'm suffering from an illness in my thing" (pointing to his penis). "It keeps swelling and won't go down. You have to help me or I'll die". Fear filled me, I was terror stricken, but I summoned my courage. "Why don't you tell Dad?" I said in a trembling voice, "He'll know what to do or maybe send you to the District Doctor." I moved quickly and managed to get him to loosen his grip of my hand, but I was no match for him. He put his hand over my mouth and pulled me back into the room.

Despite my terror and fear, I still struggled. He quickly subdued me. Henry was seventeen. I was not yet eight. He overpowered me. Then came the physical pain of contact. When it was over, he pulled his pants on and removed his belt. He raised it over his head. It sliced through the air and the buckle slammed onto the mattress making a sound similar to a hammer on concrete. "You'll feel this," he hissed looking at me like a cat toying with a mouse. "If you ever say anything, you'll feel this belt on you. Mark my words, whenever I call, you come at once or you'll get two straps from me, and I'll tell Mother and Dad you were being disobedient. Who do you think they'll believe, me or you?"

Tears flowed freely as he left the room. I was totally demoralized and devastated. I felt ashamed and unclean. The world had crashed around me again. What could I do? I could cry and scream, but what would that achieve? There was no escape. My mother had told me that what happened to me before could never be revealed. I couldn't expect a different answer. Henry knew his secret was safe. I was shackled by unbreakable chains. The beautiful home I lived in had become a prison filled with terror and unknown menaces. I knew I had to escape, but how or when I couldn't fathom. My world was dark. Everything was hopeless. I considered death. If I had known how to commit the deed, my life would have ended then.

Our servants always gossiped among themselves about happenings in the village during their lunch break. Quite unexpectedly I learned that Jason, a young man from the village had jumped into the river on purpose to kill himself; he couldn't swim, so he was certain death would be his. I listened carefully and with increasing interest. A walk to the river was impractical. How else could I end my life? It was a good idea, it seemed, but how could I make it happen?

We lived in a three level home. The bedrooms were on the top floor. The top floor towered over the tallest coconut tree. I could climb through a window in the Last Room, get on the rooftop outside, roll off the roof which was slanted, and fall to the ground. Death would happen, and I'd find peace.

I told myself the following Saturday, when everything was calm, would be the best time for me. No one would miss me and that would be the end of my unhappiness. I'd found the solution to the answer I was seeking. I had a plan. It felt good.

Saturday arrived quickly. When the house settled down after breakfast, I looked around until everybody was elsewhere. I went into the Last Room, pulled a chair towards the window, climbed on to the sill, and opened the window shutter with a stick. I braced the stick against the sill to keep the window open, then I climbed out. I sat down to calm myself from my exertions, and gazed at the scenery stretched out before me. Unbeknownst to me, my aunt who owned a cake shop across the road, had seen me climbing out the window. She rushed over to alert my parents. While I was still daydreaming about my death, I heard a sound. My father had jumped through another window and was coming toward me.

"Stay still. I'm coming." I looked at him with dismay in my heart. He pulled me into his arms and whispered, "What are you doing, child? Don't you know this is dangerous and you could fall down and die? Your poor father would die himself if that happened." He brushed the hair from my forehead and carefully handed me over to my mother and the maids who were at the window, through which I had jumped. Bars were subsequently erected over the windows. I was questioned, "Why did you do something so foolish?" I was silent. No words came from my mouth. There were only tears of frustration. "*If you only knew?*"

Fear redoubled its efforts to consume me and walked side by side with me; it assumed the role of constant companion. I became more afraid of the dark. Darkness meant that evil was at work. The devil had found me and there was no escape. The 'Headless Horseman' who patrolled the street in Vreed-en-Hoop on his white horse, chased me with sword in hand to kill me. The 'Ole Haigue' who sucked the blood of children, vampire-like at night, was waiting for me.

I often asked myself, "*Does this happen to all children, or have I done something wrong and this is my punishment?*" I began to tell lies and make up stories to gain attention. No one bothered with me; they just labelled me as "mischievous" or "attention seeking." My fairy tale world crumbled. I was always in tears, crying because of the occurrence of some imagined frightening event occurring, or more likely a really terrifying event – the memory of what had transpired almost three years ago, and the ongoing torment of Henry.

Three years passed in a blur. I went to school and learned nothing. I was told that I wasn't keeping up the tradition of my family, and that I was letting everybody down. I wished I could do otherwise, but I lacked the will. My passage through those years was spent in a 'zombie-like' daze. I lost the part of me which had helped me to bolster my courage. I succumbed to the fears at night, no longer trying to escape them. The terrors had their way with me. Snakes always caught me. I was again entangled in a web of fear from which I could find no escape.

I told my grandmother, Pahti about these dreams. She believed that evil spirits had invaded my mind and discussed the problem with my mother. They decided that I needed to have a bracelet of asafetida—devil's dung—to guard against the evil spirits which she believed were following me. I knew this was useless but didn't protest despite the sickening smell of the asafetida. There was no escape for me.

On Sunday afternoons, it was usual for residents of Vreed-en-Hoop to visit the sea wall, which had been erected to reduce the impact of tidal currents on the coastal lands. A concrete walkway had also been constructed to join the lighthouse to the original jetty built by the Dutch. This walkway provided an ideal place for a Sunday afternoon stroll. We always pleaded with our Nanny to be allowed to walk out to the lighthouse on the "floating" walkway. This gave us a sense of adventure and to our young minds, was a daring feat. The Demerara river flowed on either side, waves lapped against the wall, and as children we could pretend to be whoever and whatever we wished. I always loved sitting on the wooden supports of the lighthouse, listening to the sound of the waves as they encountered the resistance of the structure.

Georgetown, the capital, lay on the other side of the riverbank. Looking across the river to the façade of buildings and ships anchored on various wharves, was amazing. Seagulls, always in search of their next meal, were in constant flight. I would gaze at them, with my chin in my hands, and wish I could have the magic of their wings. I could flee this awful life and be transported to a magical land far away, where fear and torment were non-existent. Nanny always called time, too soon, and my respite was ended.

In my tenth year, my period arrived. My mother scolded me and told me that this wasn't normal. She seemed angry with me, as if I was at fault. My older sister explained to me the nature of how and why I would bleed once a month. *Loss of childhood*, I thought. *But did I have a childhood? I know I'd had a horrible five years of life. I didn't care about whatever followed, or whatever became of me.* I continued to have a morbid interest in death. I could confide in no one. After all, who would believe a ten-year-old? I would be punished for telling untruths. Believe it or not, however, my period gave me freedom from my attacker. Something changed. Periods were related to childbirth. What Henry was doing could result in pregnancy and a ten-year-old couldn't be blamed for that! Escape was mine at long, long, last.

I was ready the next time Henry cornered me. I took an attack stance and readied myself for battle. "No way. Not again." My head was held high, making room for my heart, which had found itself thumping loudly in my throat. "There's no way you'll touch me again. My period started. Mother can't understand why. I'll tell her you did it." My voice showed my triumph. I was free of him and he knew it.

"She won't believe you," Henry replied, putting his hands to his belt and giving me a look which threatened me and was supposed to reduce me to fear.

I dared him, fury in my face, "Try it and I'll scream SO loudly that everyone will come. YOU'LL BE CAUGHT!" I was shaking and losing control quickly, "Think of what you've done to me. I HATE YOU!"

"I'll tell them that you started it and encouraged me," he stupidly retorted, trying to quell the hate in my eyes, and foolishly referring to my previous encounter with another devil. "Don't you think I know that you did this with Cyril when you were only five years old? Who do you think they'll believe, a schemer and a liar like you, or me, their older son and heir?"

I shrugged my shoulders and smiled triumphantly, "I don't care what they believe. What will happen is that they'll watch you carefully, and you'll never be able to hurt me again, so I'd win." I shrugged my shoulders. "God knows everything. He knows I've suffered. He will help me, and you'll be punished."

"Okay missy, you can have your own way," he smiled derisively, backing out of the room. Whether it was the wildness of my voice or the realization that he could be found out if I became pregnant, he left!

"Whew, I whistled through my mouth, which was pursed in victory. *Somehow my anger and my tone must have gotten through to the bastard. Maybe I'd indeed put a wrench in his evil doings, or he'd felt on shaky ground with my parents, because of his poor school performance. He left. He actually left! I felt a thrill of victory coursing through my body; However, it wasn't the end of what I felt about myself: used, abused, not good enough, spoilt goods, utterly humiliated.*

Even in victory, I blamed myself, chastised myself, and descended into a horrible pit from which I couldn't climb out. My optimistic self tried to help, told me to look on the bright side of life, to forgive myself for happenings I couldn't have prevented. I tried to look beyond what had happened to me, to count my blessings and to believe that life had good things in store for me, but the past had left its mark. The past always returned, it seemed. I had been branded me for life.

When I continued not to do well with my education in the village school, my parents thought it was time for them to try another avenue of education. My older siblings were attending "Modern High School" in Georgetown. My older sister and a brother were doing well. They felt removal from the village school might work. My father broached the subject with the Principal, Mr. Claremont. He was mulato of mixed races, African and European.

I was ten years old, going on eleven, below the age for admission to secondary school, but in their minds there was no alternative. Something had to be done. They questioned the change that had caused the disappearance of the bright youngster who had revealed such a thirst for knowledge. I wondered whether they ever associated this change with what my cousin had done to me, or even questioned what had caused this. They hoped the difference in schools would awaken some response to learning again.

"What's Henry doing now?" Mr. Claremont enquired when we went for an interview at the school. "I consider him one of our failures. He never tried very hard to assimilate what we're teaching here."

My father replied, "He's working at Sprostons in the Foundry, learning ironworking. He said he had no further interest in education, and I couldn't convince him otherwise. He seems to flit from one thing to another, unable or unwilling to settle down. He has big ideas, but doesn't seem to recognize that hard work is a necessary element if you wish to accomplish anything."

They laughed as Mr. Claremont said, "He'll come to the realization that he has to put his shoulder to the wheel if he ever wants to succeed. Give him time." As I heard this I wondered whether the words I'd said to him were having an effect on him. I certainly hoped so.

Mr. Claremont continued, "Tell me about Tabitha. How is she doing in school?"

Dad replied, "She was a bright and intelligent child, always seeking to find out everything about anything. But this changed a few years ago. She became withdrawn, cried when we spoke to her, and was disinterested in everything except when she was running about the yard seemingly caught up in her own fantasies.

"The Headmaster at the local school told her to hold out her hands and he used his cane to punish her when she couldn't do her sums or give the correct answers to the questions. His flogging caused blisters on her hand. I've complained to Rev. Wight, the priest in charge. I don't want her to return there. I think she can do better with you. Look at what you've done for the other two," he added.

Mr. Claremont considered his problem. "Has she completed the sixth standard?" he asked.

"Yes," my father replied. "She took the county scholarship examination, but failed. I don't think she really knew what she was about. I'm not sure about the teaching she received either."

"What do we have to lose?" Mr. Claremont asked himself. "She comes from a family who seems anxious to learn. Everyone should have a chance." He smiled and said, "I'll enroll her in Form 2 with two other students, and we'll take it from there."

This was the start in a new period of education and knowledge for me. Life slowly changed. I found I was being challenged to learn.

An innate desire within me impelled me to show I was intelligent. What I couldn't understand, I questioned. Excitement at gaining an understanding of the nature of things, what and why certain things happened, of history, of foreign languages like French and Latin, opened my horizons. Learning provided a new challenge for my mind and a respite from the tortuous thoughts that lived within me.

Reading was therapy. It allowed me to tap into a reservoir of knowledge, interesting ideas, beliefs, and customs that made me wiser beyond my years. I delved into worlds that were vastly different from mine; worlds which offered temporary relief from my own, unhappy, wretched life.

Sometimes I would sit outside on the back steps of my home, gazing up into a sky dotted with stars and bright with starlight. I always wished to see a falling star, then I could make a wish that would certainly be fulfilled. *Occasionally I wished for alien beings to descend from the universe and rescue me, for knowledge that would make me the top student in the country, for someone to hug me and comfort me, and oh so much to make me whole again, to wipe away the rape and continued violation, and to return me to that period in my life when all was well with my world.*

My imaginings would sometimes take a different turn. Death came for me and angels journeyed down with winged escort to bear me up to Heaven. The music following my demise provoked tears of sorrow and recrimination. I was vindicated. There was regret that this "thing" had happened to me and spoiled my life, and nothing had been done to safeguard me. I would feel utterly triumphant and happy at last. But then I had to return to Earth and the reality of life.

I concluded that I needed to rid myself of the slough of despondency of past years. A new road was opening for me to explore. There were theories and concepts I could latch onto. Life could offer opportunities. If it was to be, it was up to me. There was nothing wrong with me; wrong had been done to me. My psyche was damaged, but what about my intellect?

The darkness of the night would abate somewhat, but my dreams continued to be tortured. My grandmother, Pahti, told me I had to learn to fight, always to try to overcome the demons which ravaged my dreams at night, and become the victor. "You have to fight them, reprimand them, and be confident and in control." Somehow I remembered this, and was always happy the mornings after I'd managed to conquer the night terrors which attacked me.

CHAPTER SEVENTEEN

T HE POWER OF KNOWLEDGE. During the next five years I used learning and knowledge as a panacea. When I felt hurt and despondent, I opened a book. These weren't always novels. I delved into mathematical problems or translated Latin passages. Caesar, Cicero, Hannibal, the Mogul emperors, and the Greek philosophers dwelled in my thoughts. Darwin's theory of evolution and the fact that humanoids were once apes sounded so logical, I always got into trouble at Sunday School where only the Gospel and the word of God were understood. The Sunday School teacher needed to convert me. She did this by being kind to me and making me feel she valued my input when she was teaching the precepts and concepts of the Bible.

I attended church regularly and became a devoted servant of God. I even believed I heard God speak to me one Sunday morning when I was at the altar for the sacrament of Holy Communion. A study of the Bible and the New Testament increased my knowledge and understanding about the spread of Christianity. The Beatitudes in the New Testament were always a source of comfort, but I questioned the significance and interpretation of what

I was learning. A vast leap of faith was required and no one could give me an answer. I was filled with restlessness.

One day, we had an interesting discussion at school about the Greek philosophers and their concept of philosophy and Gods. The philosophical dissertation of Socrates as to why humans created "Gods," and why we believed that we were accountable to them for our actions was of particular interest. I stopped to chat with a former school friend from the village school, about this new direction in my thoughts and this delayed my return home at the expected time.

When my mother questioned me as to the reason for my late arrival, I told her, "I was visiting with Socrates at the Agora to get to the bottom of his philosophy about why we worship the deities and gods".

My poor mother was confused. She had never heard of Socrates or the Agora. This was probably the work of Satan. She raised the alarm. "Evil spirits have gotten into this child." She hastily summoned Pahti from the city. Once again, they cleansed my outer body with a bath of special 'neem' bushes, then purified my mind with a 'jareh,' a ritual of incense made from certain herbs and spices and carried out when the sun was setting.

After all this 'set to,' I was determined never to divulge my true thoughts and so avoid misinterpretation and its consequences. My beliefs were my secrets. I perfected the art of listening while being absorbed in my own thoughts and flights of fantasy. This has stood me in good stead throughout my life. There were two simultaneous parts to my mind: The Listener and The Thinker.

Food preparation also held my fascination. I learned the art of making tasty dishes, cake baking and decorating. The cooks who worked in our kitchen told me, "Girl, you are brown, not black like us, but not fair like your sister. No man is going to look twice at you. 'White' is what matters. If you were fair like your sister, you'd find a nice wealthy professional doctor or lawyer for your husband. Learn to cook. Men like food. You can't go wrong."

I laughed as replied with a smiling face, "A husband is far from my thoughts. I don't need a husband. I'll work, earn my own money, and be independent."

They replied with wagging fingers and stern expressions, "Don't let the Mistress hear you speak like that. You'll get into trouble. "All girls must get married and have children. We want to dance and celebrate with you at your wedding. We'll all come and work for you and 'mind' your babies."

They were so eager to help me; I didn't want to hurt their feelings. I learned to cook roti, to bake bread and cakes, and make fudge. I experimented with curries and different masalas and stews. I could make coconut oil and ghee (clarified butter) from scratch. I kept asking for recipes and became such a nuisance, my piano teacher gave me a cook book for Christmas. This experience was a great addition to my culinary skills. At that time I had no idea this would turn out to be one of the most valuable learning experiences of my life.

Time passed and I learned to deal with the horror of my childhood. I studied diligently and passed the Senior Cambridge Examination with an exemption from the London Matriculation; this would have allowed me entry into an English University of my choice. I was just fifteen years old.

I began to feel proud of my accomplishments and asked myself, "What can't I do?". Thoughts always came back. *"No matter how hard you try, you cannot erase the past and that will always distinguish you"*. I reiterated, *"Then, must I always live a lie? What if I were found out? What would the consequences be?"* I always blamed and tortured myself with thoughts of how I could have avoided what had happened to me. *"If only, if only,"* I would berate myself. "If only" became a habit I cannot shake. When things go wrong "if only" always consumes my thoughts.

Despite everything I accomplished, black thoughts still seeped into my consciousness, creating cataclysmic vortexes in my soul. Getting away from them always left me weak and melancholy. I always questioned, "Isn't death better than this?" Humiliation was rife within my very being. I was easily hurt. Criticism made me anxious and ashamed. I felt the whole world was looking at me and judging me. I was blame-worthy and should accept that as a flaw in my character. But then I'd ask myself, *"Why should I be blamed for being a victim?"* The answer always was, *"You should have tried harder."*

The Lighthouse still presented me with an avenue of escape from my thoughts. Who knew? Miracles could happen. Sometimes on a Sunday afternoon, as was my custom, I would gaze at the skies and ponder my fate. Will my thought processes ever change? Could I erase the past? Could I ever be free as the seagulls whose only contemplations were satisfying their hunger? Could my fairy godmother suddenly appear, wave her wand, and remake me into a new person. I could soar afar from the "Hell" that was my life, travel to foreign lands, and explore the world. I would wipe a tear from my eye, feel the weight of the burden on my soul, and trudge home with leaden footsteps. *Was I never going to escape?*

Friendships with school chums weren't encouraged by my parents. One male chum started writing to me during the school holidays. My mother opened all mail that I received and demanded *"Show me every reply you're sending."* I'd made a few pen pals locally and abroad, just people who had contacted me or whom I'd contacted because I was interested in their world. I was most irritated at this intrusion into what I considered my 'private' life. *"Why weren't you more careful with my safety when I was young? Why did you allow all those awful things to happen to me? Why do you always humiliate me?"* When the criticism became too much, I would run away and cry. Then I'd find something to eat. Eating always seemed to bring some sweetness into my life. It did something to my brain. It offered me solace and comfort.

Days turned into nights and nights heralded the approach of new days. Time didn't stand still for me. The years had seen me grow from childhood into adolescence. I always had a smile and a kind work for everyone. I was popular. I was even referred to as a "blue stocking" because of my accomplishments and my love of books. Had I been a boy, my father would have been seeking my admission to a university in England so I could become a doctor or a lawyer or some other professional. To me, it seemed I was only nuisance value. I had no deep insight into why I had been born in the first place and what I was supposed to accomplish. I was just a blot on the landscape.

I looked upon myself as being a captive locked away in a turret because of what I'd let happen to me. I was shackled by the acts of violence perpetrated against me, a prisoner for all time.

CHAPTER EIGHTEEN

T HE MAGIC OF MOVIES. Time didn't stand still for my father. He'd built and operated three cinemas during this time. He'd also turned his prosperity into grocery shops, property holdings, money lending, and cinemas. He had little competition. His cinemas in the rural villages on the West Bank and West Coast of the Demerara River were the first in this field. He exhibited both English and Indian films. Indian films were very popular. Even though the Indian population couldn't understand the language and there were few or no subtitles, these films were always sold-out performances. Chartered buses brought people from all the surrounding villages and sugar plantations. Going to the cinema was a major social event.

I became an avid movie fan. Movies with happy endings were my favourites. Musicals always made me try harder to master the piano. Happy endings provoked feelings of content and emotional well-being. I often whispered to myself at the end of a movie, "Will happiness ever be mine?"

Movies also enriched my knowledge. It was astonishing that a leisure activity, which was pleasurable, could also become a method of learning. I learned to interpret behaviour patterns, to read facial expressions, and guess at outcomes with some truths, simply by watching movies. Every movie seemed to convey a message or affirm a truth. Movies with sad endings made me realize I wasn't alone in the battle for survival.

Without the magic of movies and the wizardry of words, which left me spellbound and longing for happy endings to fall upon and embrace me, I wouldn't have survived.

I became selective and tried to choose my friends wisely, but hard luck stories always grabbed me and I never had it in my heart to turn someone away. Truth to tell, I was so needy; I couldn't move away from the slightest approach at inclusion.

Family honour was the doctrine which permeated life in Vreed-en-Hoop. The individual was judged by the family's standing in the community. Family secrets were therefore sacrosanct and closely guarded. The mere whisper of scandal could cause a family to fall from grace. My parents had their own secret which they wanted to keep. Few people remembered they hadn't been legally married when they started their lives together. They were now wealthy and respected. Reputations had been built by accomplishments. Over the years, whispers about their relationship had died, but any rumour now could tarnish their hard won standing and that of the family.

My success at examinations, my prowess with home economics, and the fact that I discoursed with everyone added to the mystique of what and who I was, and this made me a person of interest and a prime target for the gossip mongers.

Gossip ruins lives but it provides a hubbub of interest and stimulating conversation. It was more interesting than the humdrum pace of village life. Secrets were the best fodder. Wormed out of reluctant sources under the guise of friendship, only to be revealed at the right time, could enhance popularity and standing. Truth was of no consequence. The harm done to people didn't matter.

The ferry crossing from Vreed-en-Hoop to Georgetown was a great hot-place of gossip. Many a reputation had been tarnished by idle speculation, which had its early beginnings here. Gossip about Ismay, a young woman school friend, about to get married, caused the parents of her betrothed to withdraw their consent. She had been seen talking and laughing with an old school friend, Leonard Bart, a mulato boy, outside a local hotel. Rumours spread like wild fire. Speculation about her 'innocence' went out of control. Raised eyebrows and facial expressions asked '*what else happened?*'

The bridegroom's parents intervened; they withdrew permission for their son to get married to 'a girl of ill repute'. After the wedding was called off, her family fell from grace. Ismay's life was in tatters and all because of harmless banter with a male friend. Her future ruined, she moved to Georgetown to live with relatives to avoid the shame of gossip gone out of control. No one showed any remorse. She was tarnished for something she had never done; a lie told by the irresponsible to gain the spotlight.

I commanded a certain status in the community because of my parents' wealth so I was an ideal person to gossip about. Whatever I did gave rise to endless speculation and gossip. If I laughed with a young man, I was "carrying on" with him. I soon got the reputation of being a flirt because I laughed and talked with everyone. It seemed my boyfriends changed from day to day because every time I chatted with some boy, the gossip was, "There she goes again, another beau in tow." I longed for friendship, but feared it. I had secrets to keep and didn't want to risk exposing them. I didn't need the Gossip Gang to come after me.

Gossip is like a seven-headed dragon, easy to give life to, but difficult to kill. Everything I did was reported to my mother, and it drove her crazy. My father told her not to worry, but she felt I was letting the family down. Somehow, I think she believed what she heard had some truth to it. I couldn't defend myself, so it was better to be silent.

While there was much gossip and speculation, in reality, it made little difference to my ability at commercial classes. I took to shorthand and typewriting like a duck to water. I hoped to get a job in the Civil Service when I reached the age of eighteen and again, hopefully, could work towards freedom from parental jurisdiction. Jobs outside the Civil Service were usually reserved for white or fair-skinned mulato women. The pay was far better than in the Civil Service and perks were also better, but because of my colour and despite my father's prominence, I knew I had little chance of a job in that market.

I was ambitious. I wanted to do something more than being just a stenographer, so I decided to take a chance and ask my father whether he wouldn't consider sponsoring and financing my education at a university in England where I could study medicine and become a doctor. I promised to repay him whatever he spent. His reply was, "As much as I love you, I must be honest. Your competence will never be recognized. You'll be fighting a losing battle. A woman's place is in the home, rearing children. It's a man's duty to earn the money. Rest assured, I'll not permit you to marry an unsuitable man."

This was a big blow to my hopes. I protested, "But look at what I did. I took the Senior Cambridge Exam, and passed with honours. I don't have to write the London Matriculation. This means I can get admission to an English university."

He replied, "You'll break your heart trying to gain a foothold in a man's world. Be content with a clerical job until you get married. Save your energies for your children. They'll get you where you want to go. Times are changing, and this isn't yet the time for you. Women will get equality, but it'll take time."

I was dissatisfied, disheartened, and very unhappy. I felt humiliated and cheated, boxed into a corner from which there was no escape. I'd scored top marks in my examinations, far better than my brothers had ever done. No matter what I did, some rationale I couldn't understand seemed to withhold from me what

I really desired. My hopes were dashed; my fate sealed. I'd never be independent, never be allowed to think for myself, but would always have to defer to a man and do his bidding.

The disappointment was unbearable. I queried, "*What is there in life for me? Would I always have to be dependent on the whims and fancies of a man, and did such dependency mean being subservient?*" I had changed, my horizons had widened, but I lived in a world which didn't respect the fact that a woman had brains and could even think for herself. In a different way, I felt I had been raped again. Death, it seemed to me, would be far preferable to subservience in a relationship.

"Don't worry, child. You're only sixteen years old. Your parents know what's best for you. You'll find happiness in marriage and children, you'll see," was always my father's confident reply.

I thought of getting a job and leaving home immediately, but parental control until the age of twenty-one didn't even allow this. It was the law.

CHAPTER NINETEEN

B RITISH GUIANA'S GROWING ECONOMY. It seemed that before I could collect my thoughts, the Second World War, which had been a backdrop to life in the Colony for the past seven plus years, was over at last. The powers of Axis had been vanquished. In the midst of all the changes occurring in the wake of peace, my thoughts took flight from my own circumstances. New winds were blowing away old ideas. The world was evolving, the environment was changing, and new beliefs and ideas prevailed. Hope for change had spread like wild fire throughout the world. Colonial empires were facing demands for self-rule and independence. Perhaps there might yet be opportunity for me.

British Guiana was also evolving. In the early stages of its birth and growth, the sugar plantation owners called the shots. The colony existed for their gain, wealth and prominence and the likelihood of their releasing their grip on power was slim. Any shrinking of their foothold would be a sign of weakness, and any weakness could result in defeat and total loss of their prominence and prestige.

Change in relaxation of rules and regulations was gradual but it was hard won. People were more determined and relentless in their efforts to fight for justice. Some had literally fought and died for it. The normal remedies to solve grievances were strikes and riots, and these avenues almost always resulted in death. Their battles always left hatred and hard feelings. Sometimes it seemed that the cost was not worth the suffering which ensued, but the descendants of the slaves and coolies wanted reform to the justice system. Injustice had removed them from their homeland and condemned them to labour under harsh and brutal jurisdictions at little cost. They still laboured and strived to obtain a fair wage, while those who had virtually enslaved them had grown fat and wealthy.

The passage of time had not gone easily for either the sugar plantation owners or their labouring workforce. Their dominance of ownership was slowly evaporating. Education and information were raising people's expectations, and labour was no longer content to accept the 'slave' wages doled out to them. They wanted fairness and equality, better wages, and better working conditions.

Information was power and so was education. The labouring classes were not as 'caged' and isolated as they had been in the past. They could travel, read, and write. Education had played its part. Political gains which guaranteed change elsewhere in the world, if people were prepared to battle for them, hadn't gone unnoticed. Trade unions offered a way to fight for a fair wage. Labour found a way to achieve justice. Their value had to be recognized and rewarded. New thinking permeated the world of the working class, and they were prepared to lay down their lives for better wages, beliefs in justice, fair play and a better life for their families.

The common man had little faith in the government of the day. It was no secret that government existed solely for the benefit of sugar plantation owners and foreign companies, and labouring classes were merely glorified slaves who had to be kept in check to continue this pattern. Top positions were usually "grace and favour" appointments made by people in power. It didn't help that "colour" not ability determined the result.

Looking back, it was ludicrous that in order to preserve the supremacy of colour and race, the British and Dutch citizens tried to veto recognition of the Portuguese inhabitants as equal, even though they were Europeans, born with the correct colour. The government sought a new classification, "aliens," for them. The Portuguese were smarter. They aligned themselves with the rising middle class comprised of all races, and the veto was denied.

The government was slowly coming to the realization that dominance and control of the political, social, and economic systems by the white ruling classes was marching inexorably towards its end but their intention was to stave it off as long as possible.

The impact of the Second World War on Britain was the loss of its hold and influence on its colonies and the continued internal growth, of the aspirations and hopes of its colonial peoples. The granting of independence to India, had flung the doors wide open for all colonies.

This was the beginning of the dissolution of the British Empire and the dominance of rule by a Parliament, which lay thousands of miles away, having little knowledge of the countries they ruled, or of their inhabitants. They were sticking a pin of ownership on an outdated map.

British Guiana was becoming prosperous. Its exports of Demerara sugar, rice, bauxite, timber, gold, and diamonds were reflected in the standard of living of its people. New developments, new businesses, and commercial enterprises sprung up throughout the coastland. Increase in disposable income among the inhabitants led to better education, better living conditions, and better sanitation. There were more hospitals and doctors to care for the sick. More importantly, there were now new private high schools, which offered further education to all who could afford to pay for it.

The races had learned to live together. Although there may have been underlying negativities, intermarriage, though it happened from time to time, was not general, except among the mixed races.

In Vreed-en-Hoop where I lived, we respected one another. We'd all attended the same school and friendships bonded us. Both my parents had friends of all races. In my father's case, he was very friendly with a group of black and mixed-race musicians who were members of an orchestra. They came over from Georgetown to Vreed-en-Hoop on the ferry to visit once a month and enjoyed the day 'jamming' together.

The piano in the living room was a drawing point; my father was an avid musician and a good guitarist, and my mother, who was renowned for her culinary abilities, usually prepared a sumptuous curry and roti lunch.

CHAPTER TWENTY

U NSEEN CONSEQUENCES. History is always drab, but it's important to understand the turbulences that moved back and forth during this period. Despite the fact that I was a successful scholar, my accomplishments were satisfactory to both teachers and parents, and I was popular, my original fears and unhappiness began to surface. Night terrors returned. I constantly looked around for some avenue of escape but could find none.

After a particularly gruesome night, the following day when I was traveling to Georgetown on the ferry, I stood at the back of the boat watching the churning of the river water as the propeller turned round and round. I thought I could jump from the back of the ship into the water and that would be the end of my unhappiness. The water seemed to call me and I thought I heard the engines repeating "jump, jump."

I was hypnotized. The call was urgent and carried with it a guarantee of 'peace.' I looked about for a bench or chair I could drag to the side of the ship to facilitate my climbing over the rails. But there was nothing there to help me. "Jump, jump," I heard. I put my hands to my ears, but I could still hear the voices.

Suddenly there was a shout. Someone had sighted a three-masted sloop sailing into Port Georgetown. I looked up and there it was. Everyone rushed to the back of the boat. I was surrounded by people. There was no way out.

I wept, quiet tears, as I walked along the streets teeming with people going into the Stabroek market. There was chatter as they hailed out to each other, little crowds forming here and there. Everyone seemed so happy, their purpose in life clear to them. Just then I felt a hand on my breast. A negro man had fondled my breast and he was quickly disappearing into the crowd. I felt so ashamed and humiliated that instead of raising an alarm, I lowered my head and hoped and prayed no one had seen what happened to me.

I stopped to calm my shock and terror and pretended to look at the displays in the show window of Brodie & Rainer, one of the huge drug stores in the city, to catch my breath and assess what had just happened to me. Stacks of biscuits, jars of candies, candied fruit, boxes of nuts, in fact everything that could excite the senses and tickle the palate caught my eye. These goodies were imported from England, and this took on special meaning. We'd been taught that England was the centre of the universe and everything English was top notch. I couldn't escape and go to England to study, where I reflected I was safe from harm, but I could at least taste these treats. They beckoned. I entered the store and bought a packet of bourbon creams. I opened the packet and started eating. My fears and hurt were soothed. I had found another avenue of escape and comfort.

I didn't realize I was starting down the slippery slope of binge eating where food consumption would become the means of solace when the "heebie jeebies" surfaced.

Occasionally, I wished I could talk to someone about the terrible things that were done to me and the misery of my life. But I found to my chagrin that though people invited your confidence, if you let go and spilled the beans, sharing your confidence always turned into a weapon that could be used to hurt you. That afternoon I felt so desperate after my return home, I thought my heart would burst if I couldn't relate the trauma I experienced to someone I could trust.

It seemed a godsend when my cousin who lived across the road came over to visit. We sat down together on the porch. The Hoya, which seemed to wind its vine up and around the structure, was covered with blossoms. It was my mother's pride and joy as it turned the porch into a bower. I'll always remember the perfume of the flowers and the beauty of these blossoms. "Nice of you to come over, Elaine. What's happening?" I asked. Elaine was my own age, a little browner than me, not a beauty, but certainly not hard on the eyes, with long straight black hair down to her waist, which we all envied. We had always been friends, holding hands walking to the village school, laughing at silly things, stretching our imagination about the world.

"We haven't chatted for a long time. You're always so busy. I just thought you could spare some time and we could chat for a bit," she replied. "You don't seem yourself. What's up?"

I don't know why, but I burst into tears, and told her what happened to me that morning. She was someone I could trust.

She asked, "Did anyone see?"

I replied, "No, he just squeezed my breast and walked on without stopping."

The triumphant look on her face and her reply stunned me. She folded her arms and hugged herself. She looked at me without a smile on her face but satisfaction in her voice "Well, you brought that on yourself, didn't you? You always wear the very best and are all dolled up, as if you're a film star. You always want to outshine everyone. You even wear make-up. You deserved that." I couldn't believe what I was hearing. She'd pulled the carpet from under my feet and dragged me down. At last she'd found something to shame me.

I couldn't understand. My alter ego came to my rescue, as it answered me *"You'll never learn. You have to be tough and never share your thoughts. No one wants to listen to you. They all envy you, and want to take you down a peg. She had no right to say such cruel things. It's true you were given the opportunity to attend a school for higher education and she wasn't, but you've always shared what you had with her. Button your lips. Remember, sealed lips prevent further hurt. Always remember that look on her face when you feel you must share your feelings with someone you trust."*

I understood then, that my attainments had turned me into an "object" and somehow set me apart. My future would be different because I was learning skills that would help me to get a good job and earn money, possibly be independent. My cousin, Elaine, felt that our friendship was threatened because of my education and she needed to even the score. That was wrong. She disrespected the value of our friendship. We were both losers.

My mother joined us to water her prized Hoya. Elaine couldn't wait to divulge the incident and my sharing it with her. My mother became annoyed with me for not disclosing the incident to her. This turned into a big showdown at the dinner table that evening. My father was flabbergasted that something like this could occur, but we all knew that because I hadn't screamed and brought attention to the perpetrator, nothing could be done. Even then, I realized if I were to reveal it, such a happening would only bring undue attention to myself and proclaim to the world that someone had violated me.

My mother vented her frustrations by altering my dresses so they hung like bags around my body. I felt so ashamed, so disillusioned, so alone, so humiliated! My siblings teased me. Henry, the brother who had violated me, caught me when I was alone and said, "You see what happens when you talk about things like that. You got exactly what you deserve. Even that man in the street realized that you were nothing but a "bad girl." 'Bad girl' was the local terminology for whore.

"Will there ever be an end to this?" My lips were sealed forever. Something was indeed wrong with me. Why would people want to hurt me? What was the cause of their envy? I was brown, not fair. I'd never thought I was beautiful. And even if this was so, why would they want to hurt me? I never talked down to or decried anyone, I always comforted, kept my promises, and went out of my way to help. That's how I saw myself, but it had suddenly dawned on me that for some reason, it was necessary to keep my own counsel. Listen to others, but never reveal much about myself. This was a salutary lesson.

Sometimes a rainbow appears at the end of the road. Two weeks later, Mother St. James, my shorthand and typing teacher at the Ursuline Convent, told me that she had managed to get me an interview for a job with a local firm of importers and traders. They also represented a local life insurance company. I was elated. It was most unusual for private firms to offer employment to Indian girls. I had to do my best.

I was given a very simple test. The Managing Director dictated a letter to me and I needed to transcribe it and get it ready for signature. This was a 'piece of cake', especially as I corrected a grammatical error, which I felt had been made to test me.

My interview also included being vetted by two other members of the firm. While I waited, they had a quick confab; the Managing Director came over to me, shook my hand, and told me that I was hired. They would expect me to start work on Monday of the following week, and best of all, I would earn $50.00 a month. I was elated. The starting salary in the Civil Service at that time was $35.00 per month. Even though a job there hadn't been my goal, I couldn't start work, even if I wanted to, until I was 18 years.

I was overjoyed. Good things did happen to me. I stopped at the local Salvation Army tea room and rewarded myself with a meat pie and tea, not even realizing that food had become my 'friend,' my solace and my comfort.

People I met on the way to the ferry stelling asked me why I was smiling, but I kept my counsel. At home, I rushed into the shop, threw myself at my father, and told him the good news. He was very pleased. His advice was, "Always do your best. They're paying you $50.00 a month, give them $60.00 worth of work."

I heard him telling my mother later, "You see, someone recognizes her intelligence and respects her training. She'll make good". My mother made a sound, which we called a "suck teeth." she seemed troubled but not pleased. I never knew why. I could only speculate and come up with a number of reasons, but could never pinpoint the truth. However, I consoled myself by saying, "She only wants you to get married and out of the house safely and be someone else's responsibility".

Afterwards, I learned that her friends had told her about all the gossip circulating about me. When I smiled and talked to a male friend, the report was that I was flirting and throwing myself at him. One small event would be tarnished with lots of meanings. Everything I did was news.

As I write this, I think, *"I must have been a tremendous burden to her. She should have been bright with happiness about the accomplishments of her daughter but the daughter seemed to be bringing her nothing but shame".*

Someone did seem to love me, though. A week later, my father asked me to remain at the dining table after dinner. He told me that he'd received a letter asking for my hand in marriage. "It's a good offer from a respectable professional gentleman, a doctor; in fact, our local doctor Dr. Imran Sankar," he smiled. "You'll be set for life. He promises to give you a car and an allowance. You won't have to go out to work."

I struggled with my thoughts. "Why is he bringing this up now? What's wrong? Marriage is not for me. I'm not yet eighteen years old. I need to expand my knowledge of world events and how this effects us. I'm not even interested in knowing whose wish it is to marry me. Dr. Sankar is much older that I am."

In those days, the local District Doctor travelled through the village on different days dispensing aid and medication. He was "flagged" down through use of a stick with a flag on the roadside in front of the house; this signaled that medical attention was needed. Dr. Sankar had become a family friend. As a doctor he was very highly regarded. Marriage to him would be a feather in my cap.

I said, "No, Dad. I don't want to get married, and when I do, it'll be to someone I choose." He looked at me, but I didn't like the smile on his face.

I later found out that the offer of marriage was the doing of a friend of my mother's who was the local Yenta, and matchmaker. I was angry, but didn't show it. I bought a small bottle of Mitchum's Lavender water and gave it to her later. I thanked her for the efforts she'd made on my behalf. I explained that I wanted to be part of the working world. I wished to be independent for a while, to savor the aspects of earning my own money, and spending it without having to explain my every action. She shook her head, and told me to be careful lest I be left on the shelf. An unmarried woman who lived alone and earned a living was always looked at as someone to be pitied. Poor creature! No man wanted her to share his life.

I hoped that this would put an end to her match-making.

My mother talked to me about the offer and tried to convince me that marriage would be fine and that love would follow. She was hurt when I told her I wanted freedom first and foremost. I wanted to understand how the business world operated, and marriage would hopefully follow sometime in the future when I fell in love.

She was not convinced that this was a workable plan, but she didn't press me further.

CHAPTER TWENTY-ONE

JOB RELATED STRESS. I was off to my very first job, excited, enervated, and as proud as a peacock. Everything was new, and everything was a challenge. I decided I would be smart enough to listen and learn. I was the new kid on the block. I had to make my mark. Common sense would have to be my guide and I had to learn as much as I could about business, job related or not. I volunteered for tasks no one seemed to want, and pretty soon my enthusiasm helped me find my place in this establishment.

Dedication to business was not on everyone's minds. People worked at their leisure. The office was a comfortable place to pass the working hours. More attention was paid to the news, personal happenings, and plain gossip, which I labelled idle conversation. Personal business was conducted over the phone. In my mind I questioned the ethics of my fellow workers. I concluded that our bosses were to blame. But that was the order of the day. Employees were all given a certain amount of work to get through and this was what they did. Their work was always up to date. In their minds, they had completed their contract. As the newest addition to the office, I considered I had to conform, but I was bored out of my mind. The salary was great and this was my first job. I would expand my knowledge into the realm of life insurance.

Insurance was a new concept for me. Fire insurance meant protection against loss by fire. Life insurance was marketed as a means of "savings for old age" or in the unlikely event of early death, a payout to defray expenses and provide for the future. My view at the time was that savings were better. Weekly or monthly savings in the bank would grow into enormous profits over a period. Best of all, savings were available at any time money was needed. Death before old age was just a chancy occurrence.

When I voiced this argument, I was told that death could not be relied upon to wait for old age. Our life span wasn't a written agreement and death could happen at any time to young and old alike. Insurance was the only sure road to security. This couldn't convince me that life insurance was a must for everyone.

Coincidentally, the death of a young man in his early thirties helped me to understand the concept of risk. He had been killed in an accident while at work, leaving his wife and young child penniless, except for the insurance policy pay out. At that time, worker's compensation was an unknown element in conditions of employment. His widow came to the office to collect the cheque and was very grateful for the payout. I had second thoughts about life insurance. It wasn't that bad after all. It gave reassurance.

I asked about calculation of premiums. I learned that actuaries computed premiums for life insurance based on family history. The medical record of a prospective client, his parents and siblings determined his life expectancy and his risk factor. If he died accidentally before his time, then his family would be protected. Actuarial science was also a new concept for me.

Commission for work done was also a new element in the scheme of things. Local companies researched products made in Britain, Canada, and the U.S., which they thought would have a market in British Guiana. Sole agency status from companies which manufactured and sold those products earned huge profits. Agencies received a commission for placing orders for goods bought abroad and sold locally,

Sole agency companies were lucrative. Business boomed as demands for goods, hitherto available only in major stores became available through increased sources of distribution country wide. My world and my knowledge were exploding with new ideas. If you dig below the surface of the rainbow, you can often find myriads of possibilities.

When I discussed this with my father he encouraged my thought processes, but laughed at the idea of my ever going into business on my own. I looked at him and smiled "You never know, Dad!"

At the office I offered to pick up the slack in other departments when I had time. At the end of six months I was told that they didn't know how they had functioned without me. I received a Christmas bonus of $50.00 and felt very proud of myself. "This is a good place to be," I congratulated myself. My eating binges were not so many now because there was little time for them. I walked both ways – to my home and back after, and felt exhausted at the close of day.

It seemed a good idea to continue piano lessons, which I had begun with much indifference, and only to please my parents. It was the "thing" to do. It signified "culture" and status. Bus service was limited. With great pride, I bought a new Raleigh bicycle, all paid for by myself. This solved my transportation problems. Life was good. I had done what none of my siblings before me had accomplished. I'd spent money I earned on something tangible, a bicycle.

Buoyed up by this improvement in my circumstances, I enrolled in dress making classes offered by the Singer Sewing Machine

Company. With a trim figure, dressmaking was a breeze. I bought a sewing machine as a gift to myself.

Life was busy and I was happy. I fell asleep easily at night, and peace seemed to return to my soul. Whenever bad thoughts surfaced, I told myself "close the door and activate the lock." I hoped the demons who persecuted me in my dreams were disappearing within their prison walls. Somehow, for whatever reason, they seemed to be receding into the past. I was content.

Just before my eighteenth birthday, I received a letter from the Chief Employment Officer in the Civil Service inviting me to attend an interview with the possibility of an employment opportunity with the Government.

I was torn. I was happy in my present position and didn't think I should waste my time attending an interview for a job I no longer desired.

Coincidentally, Alan James, Chief Life Insurance Underwriter, told me he wanted to have a few words with me before I left for home that evening. I wanted to catch the early ferry that evening and I told him this wasn't possible. We arranged to meet at 3.30 the next day. Alan was a handsome man, a mulato (mixed race). He was always well-dressed, always approachable, and had never turned me down when I asked for explanations about anything and everything. I liked and trusted him.

He opened the discussion with his customary smile. "Tabitha, there's something I've been wanting to talk to you about before, but I hesitated. Now it has become urgent and I hope you'll hear me out."

I nodded, "Go ahead, I'm listening." He smiled as he patted my hand, "The Agency is about to write a huge account with an aspiring young coloured (mixed race) guy. He's going to make it big in business and we don't want him to take his business elsewhere. This'll be a coup for me. He has always admired you and wants to take you up to Bel Air for a ride in his car to get to know you better."

"What has this to do with underwriting?" I queried, my face registering my shock at the innuendos in his request. "I don't accept rides from people I know, much less with people I don't. My parents taught me better. Going up to Bel Air in a car signifies consent to endless possibilities, chief of which is to have sexual encounters. What made you think that I would be agreeable to something like that?"

He smiled reassuringly and in a conciliatory tone, pleaded "You'll be doing the Company and me a great favour, Barbados Mutual, our competitors, are hot on his tracks. You'll give us the edge on this one. Don't lose it for us. He only wants to get to know you. He's quite smitten with you."

My head was spinning. I asked myself *"What is it with these men? Does everything have to revolve around sex? Do I have to sell my body in return for my job?"*

Humiliation filled my heart, my stomach grew bitter with bile, and I felt a great sense of unease. *This is the reason why young ladies do not seek employment but prefer to get married?* I concluded.

"Are you asking me to prostitute myself so that you can 'sweeten the pot' for the company to get his business?" My voice was filled with disgust and anger.

"It's just a little favour, you know. Just a little joy ride. Everyone does it."

"But not me," I quietly replied with a shake of my head. *What had I done to incur the belief that I wouldn't care that my reputation would be sullied? Did he think I was foolish enough not to realize the consequences of such a senseless act for any young woman?*

I got up, glared at him, my face reflecting my contempt at his suggestion. In a tone of voice which indicated that he had fallen in my estimation, I said quietly "I go nowhere with no man, for love, money or otherwise. Any man who wants me to go out with him must first earn the right to put a ring on my finger. That means he has to match my standards and I have to be in love with him. If you wanted to humiliate me by propositioning me, you've succeeded. The resulting effect is to make me walk away from this firm today and never show my face here again. However, I'm reasonable and I won't leave the company in the lurch. I'll be quitting four weeks from today. I do not sell sexual favours."

I got up, but turned back after a few steps. *"Would you have asked a 'white' girl to do this 'favour', or do you think I'm cheap and easy because I'm not white?"* I glared at him. He looked crestfallen. He'd obviously miscalculated in his opinion of me and thought that an Indian woman would do anything to keep a job that should not have have been given to hers in the first place.

Holding my head high, I picked up my handbag, imagined I was Queen Victoria, and sailed out of the office.

I fumed all the way to the ferry. I had grown up. Previously I would have sobbed at the humiliation, but now I fumed. On the ferry, I avoided all calls to join people who were keeping a seat for me. I went to the back of the boat. This was almost always deserted. I was outraged. There was nothing I could do. And then a thought occurred. *Mother St. James, commercial teacher at the Ursuline Convent had referred me for the job opening. I would report these happenings to her. She had to know where she sent her students to work and what was required of employees. That would teach them. "Vengeance is mine' God is reported to have said.* I smiled. *I'd give Him a helping hand.*

By the time I arrived home that evening, I was calm. Czerny exercises on the piano always promoted a sense of calm within my mind. They stimulated dexterity in my fingers and the music they engendered required total concentration. Immoral thoughts or disillusionment couldn't linger here. The exercise restored my equilibrium.

I attended the interview for the Civil Service position. Despite the fact that I would only be 18 years of age when I started work, but due to my previous work experience, I was told I would be assigned to the Deeds Registry as Secretary to the Chief Justice. The Personnel Director informed me that the secretary I would be replacing didn't have my shorthand and typewriting skills, and they were having trouble filling the position.

On my return to work following the interview, my soon to be ex-boss apologized to me on behalf of his underwriter and asked me to reconsider leaving. "Tabitha, you're the first person who started here as a secretary and undertook responsibility for so many things and did them so well, you created a position we never thought we needed. You've a great future here. Don't leave us now. To show how much we think of you, and need you, I'll give you an immediate increase of $10.00 a month". The smile on his face pleaded for my acceptance, but it couldn't remove the 'stone' blocking my heart.

"Thank you, sir," I said. "I've enjoyed working here and I've learned a lot. I've accepted a great opportunity and I can't pass it up. It just fell into my hands, so to speak.

I thanked him for this courtesy and we ended on good terms, but I was quite determined that I would never ever return to that office. This was a salutary lesson. *Did they think less of me because of race? Would they have acted in the same way if I'd been Portuguese or white? What did they really think? That I could be exploited, and wouldn't create a problem. Being born white was indeed a privilege. As I was brown, I would always be excluded. Had I been white, they would never have asked me to prostitute myself to advance their business. Who I was and what I could do had no value in their opinions despite the fact that I had exceeded their expectations at work."*

The rumour mill was in full operation following my abrupt departure from my job. Everyone made an effort to chat with me or to reserve a seat for me on the ferry. I was silent on the subject of why I had chosen to leave and join the Civil Service. Everyone seemed intent on finding out why I was giving up a job that paid me so much more, and also rewarded me with Christmas bonuses, to accept a lower paid position in the Civil Service, despite the prestige and importance of that job. They all told me I was foolish, then added, "We forgot, you don't have to worry about money, as your father is rich. He'll take care of you."

"Phooey," I thought, *"Little you know. My father will give me a good wedding, but I must pay my way until then. I was born the wrong sex. Doesn't matter. I'll do the best I can with what I have. What I want and gain from life will be what makes me happy, and they can put that in their pipes and smoke them."*

I was determined to look my best on my first day at work. Secretary to the Chief Justice of British Guiana was an important job. It bespoke my ability and my education in a nutshell.

I researched various fashion magazines, chose designs I liked, bought material, and made myself a new wardrobe. Ready-made clothing was not available locally. Dressmakers plied their trade, but I felt I could do just as good a job as they did. I was pleased with the results.

I wanted my dress and decorum to match the importance of the job, to reflect the image that the heroines in movies conveyed. I could walk like the stars, talk like them, and be great at my job. I had every confidence in my ability to succeed.

This was all grist for the rumour mill. At the time I thought, "Why don't you get a life?" Now I realize that rumour was a primary means of communication in the village. Those who could add a new tidbit of gossip gained notoriety and prestige. They were leaders because they had a nose for interesting happenings and an ear to the ground. They heralded the information age. Sometimes I smiled when I thought, "If you only knew my secrets!"

CHAPTER TWENTY-TWO

M URDER AND MAYHEM. Vreed-en-Hoop was the centre of my universe. We lived there, we loved it, and because of my father's commercial enterprises, we had a special place in the community. Everyone expected the children who had grown up in such a comfortable environment to be successful, and to carry on the traditions of their parents. It was a small village, important because the ferry docked there, the trains left for other parts of the coast, and buses supplied transport to the villages on the river bank. It was the hub of transportation along the coast and river bank. In addition, a 'match factory' provided employment. This was one of the the first manufacturing companies that offered alternate employment to unskilled labour.

Because of foresight of the early Dutch settlers, kokers were constructed to prevent flooding at high tides when the river currents changed. The early settlers knew they had to eliminate flooding. A small canal was created under the road to channel the river water into a drainage trench during high tides. Part of the village lure was that mermaids lived under this bridge. When I was a child, we were cautioned that unwary children on their way to and from school, could be captured and taken far down into the depths of the river where they would be turned into mermaids. Children quickly hurried over the road and drew breaths of relief as they passed safely across. This wasn't the only hurdle in our lives.

Getting past the graveyard of the first Dutch sugar plantation owners and the Headless Horseman was another challenge. We were warned that ghosts claimed that terrain at their own and were anxious to recruit the unwary into their universe. As the darkness of night descended, their objective was to frighten to death all children caught lingering on the bridge; as their souls left their bodies to travel to heaven, they would intercept and claim them for their own.

There was also the legend of the Headless Horseman. Someone could always be found who attested to the fact that he travelled down the road on his white horse after midnight, carrying his head in one hand, fire flying from his piercing blue eyes, and brandishing his sword with the other hand, as he searched for victims. Any person who had the misfortune to see him, would lose his memory and become a lost wanderer, or some other bad event would occur in his life. People didn't often wander at night. No one wanted to see the ghosts, but we often heard tales from people who whispered, as they looked around to ensure there were no eavesdroppers, that they'd had the misfortune to pass the gravesite at night and witnessed the event.

Growing up with these 'mythologies' made Vreed-en-Hoop an exciting place to live. School friends gathered at the main corner on our way home, some going south, others going west. We exchanged knitting and crochet patterns, oohed over one another's finished work, despite the closeness of evening darkness. When we were tardy, we ran all the way home over the bridge.

Crime wasn't a big event here. The local constabulary usually settled the problem by talking to the people involved. The magistrate held court for repeat offenders and resolved the matter at issue quickly.

The week before I was to start my new job, local fishermen discovered the body of a young lad on the seashore. He was identified as Balram Singh, a youth from Windsor Forest, a village further down the coast. His family had reported him missing over the weekend. He had not returned home from school as usual on Friday. This added a chill to an otherwise peaceful village. There was speculation as to why he had gone to the seashore in the first place. Mother and Dad were respected members of the community. Their opinions were valued and people always sought advice when there was a problem. We discussed the ramifications of this event, and were warned not to go the Sea Wall until the culprit was found.

Balram's body had been discovered on the Vreed-en-Hoop seashore by children playing there after school. Cause of death was attributed to a blow on the head and a knife driven through his heart.

Rumour lost no time coming to the forefront. No one was immediately apprehended for the murder. Mounting speculation circulated. Balram was courting Leila Ramessar, the daughter of a wealthy merchant who lived in Windsor Forest, a village situated further down the coast. Her parents considered him unsuitable, as his family was poor. Neither had given in to pressure. After finishing secondary school, he intended to study medicine at an English University. He and Leila had planned a future together, despite parental disapproval.

Speculation was rife that her family was involved in his death.

The gullible among us wondered whether the Headless Horseman had at last found a victim, and he would now rest peacefully. Others suggested that 'obeah' (black magic) had been used to procure someone to do the job, and that the person who had committed the crime would have forgotten all about it.

These theories provided endless conversation and gave rise to many other speculations.

One rumour, in particular, was that Balram had been cut down in the flower of his youth because of jealousy. He had been a promising student, rumoured to become the next Guiana scholar. This would have meant that his university education would be paid by the Government and his future assured. Jealousy attracts strange bedfellows.

As the son of parents who were poor, Leila's family felt Balram wasn't *up to snuff*. She was their only child. Her future had been mapped out for her. She could attract a much better prospective suitor and live in the lap of luxury.

Balram was such a good-looking lad, we all likened him to a movie star and always described him as the brown version of the "tall, dark and handsome Errol Flynn." We'd all asked "Did parents ever realize that we had opinions that not always coincided with theirs?"

What a waste of a life, I thought and hoped that the murderer would be found and brought to justice. Life wasn't fair. We had to live before we died. Balram had been robbed. His dream would never be fulfilled.

My chief source of reading at this period of my own life was Rex Stout, Ellery Queen and Agatha Christie. These "Who Dunits" were my favourites. They challenged both the imagination and the mind while provoking endless thought. Without evidence, there was only speculation and gossip.

In a world where communication was restricted to the newspaper and limited radio broadcasts, the exchange of gossip and news played an important role. When it became malicious and gave rise to fabled events, which would damage people's character and reputation, it became dangerous.

I was sorry to learn that the Police couldn't find the culprits, but felt that they were just policemen and the case warranted the use of detectives who could pursue clues and track them back to the perpetrator. Policeman were there to make sure the law was obeyed.

Balram had been a school friend. We'd exchanged thoughts and ideas, and been competitive at passing exams. I would miss him. His murder was a sad element in the otherwise exciting thought of my new job.

CHAPTER TWENTY-THREE

T HE FAR REACHING ARMS OF JUSTICE. Work in the civil service was very challenging. I was also intimidated by my new surroundings.

Being Secretary to Chief Justice Sir Thomas Bingham, a man who had been knighted by the Queen, placed me in a category all by myself. I was told that my boss was subject to tantrums, that I had to be very careful how I approached him and how I addressed him. What I did was also very confidential that I was again warned that if there was any leakage of information, there would be an investigation. If it was proven that I had been involved I would be prosecuted. I was going to be privy to many secrets and many judgments before they were delivered in court. "Could I be trusted?" I was young and could neither understand nor comprehend the many responsibilities of my situation and the resulting dangers from knowledge. It was generally felt in the department that the position should have gone to an older and wiser person.

This eroded my confidence and made me fearful. I became very circumspect in my dealings with colleagues and people I met when I walked along the hallways of justice to get to the various courts. I felt a thrill and an importance. I was someone who mattered. I had gained recognition because I had been selected and trusted to fulfill the responsibilities of this very important post.

The Victoria Law Courts was an awe-inspiring structure; the imposing statue of Queen Victoria dominated the landscape and gave it a regal aura. I felt that "these hallowed halls" were the home of dispensation of justice, and equated with living by the Ten Commandments and worshipping in church. I was proud, honored, and very humble.

It would have been easy to let this position get to my head and not work as hard and as diligently as before. My father had felt his sons would bring him honour. I would show him that his daughter was just as capable. I had inherited his will and determination.

I took my job seriously. I became acquainted with the workings of the Courts and the Deeds Registry. I asked questions about the law and read the law reports. It took me about eighteen months to fully understand the various procedures the law required, and I was also placed in charge of preparing routine, but important legal documents.

Those two years were idyllic. I felt pride in my accomplishments. Perhaps with my background, one day I could become a lawyer. If I saved enough money to get to England, I was sure that with recommendations I was sure to receive from the Chief Justice, I would be admitted to Middle Temple to study law. Being a doctor faded by comparison.

Sometimes I attended court to observe the proceedings. Justice seemed perverse at times, but dispensation of it according to the law was meted out fairly. There would always be winners and losers, the Crown versus the alleged criminal, and the plaintiff versus the defendant. In criminal trials there was always a jury. Jury service wasn't popular with those summoned to fulfill this duty but it was indispensable to the preservation of justice.

In civil trials 'wins' or 'losses' rested with the lawyers and the cases they presented or defended before the Court. In criminal cases, juries decided 'innocent' or 'guilty.'

One case that interested me particularly was the case of the Crown versus Johnson & Crabbe. The alleged culprits had finally been caught and brought to face justice, for the murder of Balram Singh, the young student who had been in love with Leila Ramessar. I was wrong after all. The police had monitored the evidence doggedly. It had taken them several months to follow the clues and gather proof to charge them with murder. Murder was a capital offence, conviction for such was *'hanging by the neck until you were dead.'*

The murder scene was placed at the Vreed-en-Hoop jetty.

You will recall my earlier description of the jetty and the lighthouse, the part these places played in my own life and that it was a favourite strolling place on Sundays for people who lived in the village.

Fishermen also used the base of the jetty to catch the "Paku" fish, which were plentiful in the area, the rocks in the water providing a good habitat for them. The fish was considered a delicacy and much sought after locally. Johnson and Crabbe were local fishermen. That fateful Friday afternoon they were out to net fish for sale at the Saturday market.

Balram had taken the earlier ferry from Georgetown at 2 o'clock. He and Leila had made a trice to travel together and spend some time on the seawall, visiting the Lighthouse and Jetty. He'd looked around the ferryboat in vain for her, and when the boat docked at Vreed-en-Hoop, he'd disembarked disconsolately. He didn't want to arrive home early and be required to answer the questions which would follow, so he decided to take the walk alone and travel home by a later bus.

He had seen Johnson and Crabbe fishing and stopped to talk to them. They were obviously poor and seemed to be barely able to eke out an existence. Their faces were old and worn and spoke of a lifestyle that had left them dissolute and penniless. Their feet were bare, two old felt hats covered their heads and their clothing was tattered, unwashed and smelly. They were toothless and as life follows, penniless.

They felt that as Balram was alone they could con him into giving them some money. He was obviously alone for some reason he didn't want made known, and they could take advantage of this. At the very least, they could take his watch. He would not dare make a complaint because his parents would find out that he had skipped school. He was easy prey.

"Johnson stared the ball rolling hoping to coax the truth from Balram, and use it to his advantage. You're 'sculting' (absent from school without parental knowledge), aren't you, and the girl let you down and didn't show up?" Johnson asked him. His tone of voice made Balram fearful. He believed they were planning to rob him. He wanted to runback to the shore line but hoped to sidetrack them by being polite and confident.

Balram laughed. "I'm waiting for the 4 o'clock ferry because my parents are on it and we can all travel home together. The ocean breezes are fresh here and they help to eliminate the heat of the sun. It's a humid day and more pleasant taking a walk here than waiting on the stelling. It's been nice chatting with you, but I must hurry. Do you think I can get to the Lighthouse and back in time to meet the next ferry?"

In an instant, Crabbe jumped up from the rocks below, grabbed Balram's hands, pulled them together and placed them behind his back. He said to Johnson, "Search his pockets. He must have some money. I'll take his watch. That'll teach him not to scult from school."

One held him while the other searched his pockets. He tried to fight them off, but they restrained him with a tight hold on his arms and legs. He managed to push them off and ran away but they caught him. A blow from one landed on his chin. He fell backwards and hit his head on the stone surface of the walkway. When he didn't get up, they became afraid. They decided to conceal their actions by finishing the job. One of them plunged the knife they used to kill the fish into his heart as he lay unconscious. They'd looked around. They were still alone. They needed to conceal his his body and so avoid any disclosure of their presence. They dragged it back to the shoreline and camouflaged it among the bushes. It was unclear which one landed the blow to the chin or who had plunged the knife into Balram's heart.

They washed the blood off the jetty with buckets of water from the river, packed up shortly after that, and returned to their home. As far as they were aware, no one had witnessed their actions and no one would connect them with the murder. To avoid any connection with the murder, they stopped fishing on the jetty. When they were asked why no "paku" fish was available, they replied that the fish had 'stopped running'.

Sergeant Blackmore, locally called Sergeant 'Man-O-War,' hadn't really given up on solving the crime. A word here and there led to suspicion. While drinking at one of the local rum shops, someone asked "What's happened to the paku fish, we haven't seen any in months." Crabbe's answer "We can't go back to the jetty because the ghost of that chap Balram, haunts the place," was repeated to Sergeant Blackmore. He interviewed them separately. One blamed the other. They were both charged.

I was glad they were apprehended. I decided to try and snatch a few minutes now and then to observe the trial proceedings and listen to the evidence.

The trial lasted five days. They were convicted.

I shuddered when the Judge read the verdict. *"Henry Johnson and Joseph Crabbe, you've both been convicted of the murder of Balram Singh. It is the sentence of this Court that you be taken from this place to a lawful place of execution and hanged by the neck until you are dead."*

I couldn't control the shakes my body made of its own voli-
tion. The shock of it all had taken control of my subconscious. I
was sad. Three lives had ended needlessly, and all for what? The
sensation created by the trial and conviction took a little while to
die down, but true to itself, life returned to normal.

CHAPTER TWENTY-FOUR

S EALED LIPS SAVE SHIPS. I tripped up. Looking back, I can still kick myself. The shell I created to keep me safe and protect me, must have cracked. Was it destiny? I don't know, but here is how it happened.

I accepted an invitation to lunch at the Brown Betty, a local ice cream shoppe/restaurant, from Michael Jagdeo, a friend who also lived in Vreed-en-Hoop. Mike was a flashy dresser. He wasn't handsome, had a medium build, was dark-skinned with nice brown eyes and a good reputation. He was popular with the Vreed-en-Hoop crowd. I knew he was keen on me, but as far as I was concerned, he was just a trusted friend. Our mothers were friends, but beyond this, it was a casual relationship. He had invited me out before, but I always turned him down.

This time, he explained he wanted me to meet his friend, Mohan Bahadur, a famous Guyanese reporter who wrote under the pen name of Sinclair Jonas for the local newspapers. He was also the English correspondent for '*The Daily Express*' of London and sometimes supplied news on British Guiana to '*Reuters.*' I'd heard of him before and thought it would be nice to meet him.

His articles were challenging and his news sources always seemed reliable and believable.

Lunch was pleasant. Mohan had an intriguing personality. He was of Indian descent, a Brahmin, (Upper class Hindu) chatty, informative, and challenging. He seemed to want to make a good impression and made me the centre of conversation during lunch. I wondered how much of this was due to the responsible position I held and felt that perhaps he might be "buttering" me up so he could obtain confidential information from me but I was intrigued.

Mohan was in his mid-forties. He wasn't a snappy dresser, almost nondescript in looks, neither dashing nor handsome, but possessing a magnetism which gave him a certain charisma.

The following week I received a telephone call from him inviting me to lunch, at a different location. I wondered what this was all about. I thought, *it couldn't be that he's smitten with me.* He was so much older than I was, in fact twice my age, plus another year or two. I questioned the wherefores's and why's but I accepted. Lunch was great. I enjoyed my conversation with him, his world knowledge, his knowledge of local affairs, and his friendship with local politicians. He was charming and interesting.

And so began a friendship I thought was platonic. I guess something inside must have needed me to relieve the stricture around my heart by confiding in someone. One day, I told him of the childhood rape and sexual abuse, and the mental torture I had endured. Tears settled in his eyes. He hugged me after, but there seemed to be a subtle change in attitude, something I couldn't quite fathom.

Mike wasn't happy with the friendship developing between Mohan and me. While walking home from the ferry stelling, he warned me that I was the centre of gossip, and my reputation was being sullied. "I wanted to develop my friendship with you and that's why I introduced you to Mohan and our circle of friends.

He's much older than you, in fact more than twice your age. What do you see in him? Tab, be careful. You know how people talk?" he warned. I was bemused by his thoughts.

I smiled. "He's just a friend, and there's no romanticism in it. He's so knowledgeable about people. He stretches my imagination. Our conversations are always interesting. We meet for lunch, we talk. Sometimes I catch the later ferry and we spend time in his office, just talking and reading. What's this all about, Mike?"

"I can't understand what you have in common. He doesn't go to the movies, won't take you dancing. Why are you spending so much time with him? He's from a different generation. He's never had a girlfriend before, or even been interested in anyone. You've nothing in common. He's Hindu and you're Christian."

"I don't quite know myself, Mike. I certainly don't love him. I like the challenge of talking to him, tapping into his knowledge and his intelligence. He's the friend I never had."

"You're playing with fire. I blame myself. I should never have introduced you two. Take my advice, break it off. Spend time with people your own age" he advised.

"We'll see how it goes, Mike. I can take care of myself. You're still my friend, you know, but I'm not ready to settle down to marriage and children. I want to go abroad to study, make something of myself. I'm truly not interested in getting married or having a special boyfriend."

He wasn't convinced, but I guess he felt he couldn't persuade me to drop the friendship without antagonizing his relationship with me.

Life settled down, but it seems I am always the one to blame. I again became an overnight news item. Everybody in the office was talking about me. I was summoned to the Registrar's office and told that I was placing my job in jeopardy because I was associating with a news reporter.

The Registrar ended the interview by reminding me, "You're a valuable person here and you don't want suspicion if there's a leak. I'm advising you to break off your association with him."

I countered by saying, "You have to trust my integrity and my judgement. I know that everything I do here is confidential. I leave my knowledge of whatever transpires here at the doors when I pass through them. You have to believe me. I love my job here and the confidence entrusted in me."

He shook his head and murmured, "I don't know what you see in a man who is so obviously below your standing in society and twice your age. I've told you how I feel and what this is doing to your career. It's up to you."

I thanked him and left. I pondered the advice I was receiving, but decided I was the better assessor of people and everyone was wrong in their judgement of my friendship with Mohan.

The following Sunday morning as I was reading *The Daily Chronicle* I was shocked to discover that something I thought was confidential had become headline news. The judgement in a land dispute case was scheduled for Monday. I had typed the document and given it to the Clerk of the Court. All copies had been included in the file folder including the rough draft in the Judge's handwriting. I wondered what had happened. How had the press gotten a hold of it? Somehow, I knew blame would fall on me. My heart felt heavy. How was I going to prove my innocence? I was the friend of the news reporter who'd told the story.

On Monday morning, I arrived to a buzz in the office. Everyone turned to look at me. I said, "Cool it, guys. I'm the innocent party here. No word of this has ever left my lips and no part of the judgement was transferred by me to another person."

Of course, the Registrar was waiting for me. He beckoned me to his office and proceeded to upbraid me. He said he would discuss the matter with the Chief Justice and ask for my suspension until the matter was investigated.

"*Would I be condemned without a hearing?*" I asked myself. "*It seems that suspicion has turned to judgement.*"

The Clerk of Court to the Chief Justice, Kenneth Brigham, was new to the Georgetown office. He had been transferred from New Amsterdam. I stopped at his desk and glared at him, my body shaking with anger. "I need to see you now. We have to get to the bottom of this. I'm not going to take the fall for anyone. You're the only person besides me with access to this document. I advised all documents were to be locked in the safe, along with any handmade notes. If you made a mistake and left every thing carelessly on your desk, then that's your fault, not mine. This is an important matter which can only be discussed in private. I didn't want the whole office gawking at us and trying to eavesdrop.'

He wished to, but couldn't disagree with me. We ascended the stairs to one of the empty courtrooms where privacy was assured.

With daggers in my eyes, I questioned, "What did you do with the judgement and the files when I handed everything to you on Friday? I checked the number of copies and the draft with you. You acknowledged that I'd given you all notes and the handwritten copy. I reminded you to lock everything in the safe. What happened? Who got to you? You're the only one who could have leaked the news."

He 'hemmed and hawed' for a while, and when he could no longer truthfully answer the barrage of questions I was putting to him, replied, "I hoped this would go away. I made a mistake. Can't you cover for me? Don't throw me to the wolves. I was indiscreet on Friday when I was having a beer with friends at the local bar and the decision slipped out. I was stupid, I only wanted to show off. I didn't think the information would be leaked to the press. Can't you just forget it, and let it all die down? I can't afford to lose my job or my reputation."

I thought, how foolish do you think I am? Is my own reputation not important? Is this because I'm a woman? I scowled as I asked "What about my standing and my own career? The Registrar is waiting to see the Chief Justice because he feels I should be suspended for leaking the news to the press. He puts the blame squarely on my shoulders. Why does blame fall on me and not you? I don't want to lose my job either, and I also don't want to lose my standing with the Chief Justice. It was your fault, and you have to make it right. If you don't, I will."

As we were heading back to the Registry offices, the Chief Justice arrived. He indicated that he would like to speak to me and asked me to join him in his Chambers in ten minutes.

When I returned, the Registrar was waiting outside. He glowered at me and asked, "What are you doing here?"

Before I could reply, Lloyd, the Chief Justice's orderly came through the door and said, "Miss Rajnarain, His Lordship will see you now; Mr. Hinds, His Lordship knows you want to talk to him. He'll see you after he's finished his meeting with Miss Rajnarain."

I was shaking when I entered his Chambers, but the Chief Justice calmed my fears and smiled, "I have complete confidence in you, Miss Rajnarain. Your work here has gained my esteem. I know that you aren't responsible for the leak of information to the press; I'm concerned and will get to the bottom of it. The Registrar deals with these problems. He has to set his house in order." He stood up, shook my hand and I left his chambers. I was so relieved that I'd been vindicated without being asked to tell my story, I needed to stop for a while and regain my equilibrium. My guess was that Chief Justice would dismiss the Registrar's suspicions and direct him to find the real culprit.

The matter was settled when the Registrar learned that Kenneth Bingham was indiscreet and had discussed the case with friends at the Bar. No apology was ever given to me by the Registrar. Kenneth was transferred to another department. He was lucky not to have been dismissed.

I recognized at that time women were never safe from the advances of men. Men controlled the office and felt that if women wanted to remain in their jobs, they were fair game for predators.

The Registrar had asked me out on a date before this happening. I'd refused with the excuse that I didn't date men who were married and had children almost as old as I was. He'd persisted and confessed that he'd fallen in love with me and couldn't live without me. He would set me up in a home and give me everything I wanted. He'd travel over to Vreed-en-Hoop, speak to my father and ask for his consent.

I queried, "What happens to me when your lust is satisfied?" He'd just smiled and assured me that could never happen. He'd pursued me for a while with gifts and flowers, but dropped the matter when I told him with finality that he was wasting his time and only tarnishing my reputation.

Work settled back to normal. I began to think of my future and studying law at Middle Temple. I didn't know this was a dream never to be realized.

CHAPTER TWENTY-FIVE

THE AXE FALLS. One fateful Friday afternoon, as I left work, I found Mohan waiting for me on the street. He was dressed differently and my face registered my surprise. For the first time since we had met, he was well-dressed, sporting a jacket and tie. He saw my questioning look and explained that he wanted to speak to me on a personal matter and thought it best for us to find a quiet place where we wouldn't be disturbed. I was tired. It had been a week where everything was urgent and important. I longed to get home, have supper, and get into a good book. I thought *this must be something important, and as a friend, I needed to listen.*

"Let's walk up Main Street, there are benches there, and the few who pass by wouldn't recognize us." I indicated the direction. The sun was slowly moving down in the heavens, and cool breezes turned the avenues into inviting places. We stopped at a bench under the shade of a flamboyant tree ablaze with red blossoms. The leaves rustled as the winds swept through the branches. It was a peaceful setting for the end of the week.

Thoughts kept repeating themselves in my head as I wondered what this was all about. I hoped he wasn't going to try to have me reveal any confidential information or perhaps borrow some money, which I didn't have to lend.

We sat down. He reached out and took my hand, and with a look I couldn't fathom said, "Tabitha, "Will you marry me?" I was astounded and bowled over. I pulled my hand away, my face registering the astonishment and dismay I felt. "Why would we want to get married? We don't love each other, we're just good friends, and I have other plans for my future. Our friendship has never followed that path. I was under the impression that you understood what we had together was simply a platonic relationship. You've bowled me over with this sudden proposal. It's like a bolt from the blue. Marriage is of no interest to me at this time."

"I know this is sudden and unexpected to you" he replied in a conciliatory manner, "But we have a good relationship and your love will follow in time. I fell in love with you the first time I saw you." He took hold of my hand again and whispered, "Didn't you realize that I was smitten. Your beauty and intelligence awakened desires. I know I'm much older than you, but I'll care for you and cherish you."

"You know I'm not in love with you; then why the rush?" I questioned with a shrug of my shoulders. "We could just wait and see if love develops." I shook my head in exasperation.

"This is important to me," he pleaded, "and I need an answer from you now."

In a dismissive tone I retorted, "If that's the case," and I started to rise, "the answer is no. I'm not yet ready for marriage. I want to study law, and after I return home, if the opportunity arises, I may decide to get married." I shook my head negatively, and with a questioning look asked, "What's brought this on? Our friendship is platonic. There was no talk of love. We've had lunch, it's true and I've spent time after work discussing different events in your office. You've never even held my hand or given me any indication that I was the object of your love."

"Hear me out," he begged, trying to placate me "I don't want to upset you, but if the answer isn't 'yes,' you'll force me to take an action that would pain me. I'll expose your family to ridicule. I'll write a story about you for the newspaper and expose the rape and sexual abuse by your cousin and your brother. This will destroy them and you. Do you think you'd be allowed to keep your job as Secretary to the Chief Justice, or that your family will ever be able to be hoity toity again? Your brothers' careers would never take off. People will look at your family differently."

"Are you blackmailing me into a loveless marriage with you, Mohan? What's in this for you?" I questioned angrily, my face showing the shock of the stricture around my heart. What about my own feelings? If you truly loved me, that should be part of your consideration. An unwilling bride can bring you nothing but unhappiness."

"I love you, and I can't live without you. I'll do anything to make you my wife. You do care for me as a friend, and this will grow into love," he smiled.

I was reeling from the shocking events unfolding in my life. Something I least expected had exploded around me, and now what? "You've given me a migraine," I replied. "I just want to be left alone." I got up. He said, "Take your time. I can wait until Monday for your answer. The future of your family rests with you. I love you and thought you loved me, too. I never imagined I'd have to threaten you, but that'll only tell you how much I love you." *His look of guile and cunning caused me to think "you can't trust him. Run away while you can."*

My head was ready to burst. This was unbelievable. What had I done to have something like this happen to me? I must be truly cursed. I was being raped and violated once again. I could see no way out. Even if I complained to someone, Mohan held the bomb which could destroy my family. The mere whisper of rape and incest could mean that my family would be ostracized. What would happen to their lives? I couldn't bear the thought. During the war, there were many posters which said "sealed lips saved ships." My lips had been sealed for such a long time, why did I believe I could confide in anyone and allow the floodgates to open?

I grabbed on to the bench for support. My heart was heavy and I was in shock. "I don't know what you hope to achieve by this blackmail. My father won't die soon and he won't give you money. I hope things happen to you that'll make you regret you ever tangled with me. I may look easygoing but I'm no fool. It will take time, but my life will sort itself."

He smiled sardonically, like a snake who had me in his coils.

I asked for help from someone I trusted. Dear God in Heaven. How can I get out of this mess? If the newspapers print the story, my family would be ruined. The public would destroy them. I remembered the saying 'Coolies are like crabs. Confined after capture, those who reached the top are quickly pulled back to the bottom.' This would be the fate of my family.

I reminded myself, You've gone through worse. You'll marry him and deal with whatever the future brings. Rape and incest have taken on a life of their own and there is no escape.

I pondered the situation over the weekend. I would have to resign my job at the Deeds Registry. Employment regulations in the civil service forbade the hiring of 'married' women, and even so, he was a newspaper reporter.

Worst of all, no matter how I thought of it, sex with Mohan would be a continuous nightmare. *Could I do it?* I asked myself. I had endured violation in my childhood. Would my nightmares return? The whole thing felt so repugnant, I felt the bile rise in my stomach.

Could I tell my parents the truth and ask them to help? I couldn't make that request. I had disobeyed my mother. She had warned me that I had to keep the rape I'd endured as a child, a secret. My parents had worked diligently to ensure better lives for their children. I longed to discuss the matter with someone, but there was no one I could trust ever again. This was a job I would have to do on my own. I was being blackmailed into marriage and shackled for the rest of my life.

Where the strength came from, I didn't know. I knew my future was up to me. I hoped for Divine intervention, but realized no one could help me. If I needed help, it had to come from me. If I made the wrong decision, I must be prepared to live with it.

On Sunday, after dinner, I spoke to my parents. "Mother and Dad, Mohan has asked me to marry him and I've agreed. He'll come over to Vreed-en-Hoop to ask your consent. This is my wish, so please don't say no."

"This is very sudden," my father replied. "What's all the rush about?"

My mother intervened. "Are you pregnant?'

Pregnancy without marriage was something all parents feared. Women who had children outside of marriage were stigmatized for life. It was one of the ten commandments. *(Thou should not commit adultery).* I felt sorry for my mother. She knew what this was all about because she and Dad had lived together and illegitimate children were born out of wedlock. These children had been 'legitimized' after they'd gotten married, but she still felt the stigma.

"No, Mother," I replied. "We just want to start on a new phase of our lives. We care for each other. He isn't getting any younger, and we feel this is a good time."

"Can't we talk you out of this?" my father replied. "I thought you, for one, would understand the unsuitability of what you're proposing. I have a proposition for you. You've always wanted to further your education. Instead of getting married, take the trip to England and enroll in Middle Temple. Become a lawyer. You'll make me proud. Don't throw away your life."

"Dad," I replied, "the time for studying has passed me by. I've given Mohan my word and I can't go back on that. We'll get married in Barbados. This'll make it easier for you. You've warned me time and time again that my friendship with Mohan will only lead to heartache, and I know you think I'm taking a wrong step, but this is what I wish. I'll resign from the Civil Service after I've completed four years' employment. I'll then be eligible for six months' leave of absence with pay". After I'm married I'll have to find a job outside the Civil Service. I know you both think this is wrong, but you have to trust me."

My Dad asked, "Does this man have some hold on you? Is he blackmailing you into this marriage? I can't believe that someone as sensible as you can be making such a foolish decision."

They both tried to dissuade me, but I told them my mind was made up. I wanted to get married and have children and this was my motivation.

"Surely, there are many younger men you can marry. Why this one?"

"Dad, he's an intelligent human being. We're on the same plane in our thoughts. Our discussions are challenging. I don't find the same intellectual conversations with men my own age."

They shook their heads, but I know they secretly hoped I would come to my senses and forget the whole thing.

Time passed. I paid extra attention to my duties at work and volunteered for tasks usually done by the legal clerical staff. Knowledge was power, and I could apply for a job in one of the many legal firms after I was married.

When I told the Chief Justice that I wouldn't be returning to work at the end of my vacation leave, but getting married, he said he was very sorry to see me go, but wished me well.

I asked whether he would give me a reference. He smiled and said, "Of course I will, and if you ever decide to go to university to study law, just let me know, and I'll endorse your application.

He gave me the reference when I said goodbye. I was touched when I read the following: "She brings her intelligence to bear upon the tasks assigned to her. She is leaving the service at her own request and to my regret."

When he was transferred to another posting a year later, in his farewell speech to the Bar, he also mentioned me and was very complimentary about my secretarial skills, integrity, attention to detail, and my considerable knowledge of the law library.

Looking back, this period in my life had been idyllic. I had worked hard, applied myself, and asked, "If I held such a position as Chief Justice, what would make my life easier?" My response was easy. "Someone I would trust and rely on, someone who would anticipate and provide the research I needed, a true assistant." I'd made that my role and scoured the shelves of the law library, and like a librarian, gleaned an overview of the content in the many volumes. It became easy for me to research particular cases quoted as precedents. I had not only added to my duties but also increased my knowledge.

The work was challenging and inspiring. It made me think. I'd expanded my capabilities beyond the demands of the job and excelled. It was indeed a pity that I couldn't have gone on to study the law and become a qualified barrister, but destiny had determined otherwise. It was no use fighting it. I would follow the direction it provided, and who knew, perhaps it would lead to happiness one day?

As I said goodbye to my colleagues and walked away from the Victoria Law Courts, I felt a chill of foreboding. *Why hadn't I tried harder to escape the yoke fastened around my neck since childhood?*

Shouldn't I have put myself first? I'd saved some money. My skill set were many and varied. Surely I could find a job somewhere in the world, in England perhaps, where my qualifications would be recognized, or in New York, renowned as the place where dreams could be fulfilled.

Women of these times lived within the boundaries of convention. I had little knowledge of the outside world and would have needed help and advice; who would have heeded my needs with such an improbable task? I had thought it would be easier to 'bear my chafe', rather than expose the wrongs done to me.

I argued with myself but had to accept the fact that I had been taught since childhood that a promise was a binding commitment. Other people made promises, broke them or forgot about them. But it all centered on what my father had instilled in us: "*Who you are and what you do*" define you. *You must be true to yourself. There are reactions to every action. Once you break a promise, you're not true to yourself and you'll fail as a human being.*

Unknown to myself, those words found roots in my soul. I had promised because I was being blackmailed. I would keep my promise, endure whatever happened, and hope that as the world turns everything would 'right itself.'

Now I recognize that I didn't think enough of myself. I had learned to put the needs of others before my own. I had become a willing dupe.

It was easier to concentrate on the happenings within my country than deal with my own chaos.

CHAPTER TWENTY-SIX

B RITISH GUIANA AT THE THRESHOLD (The 40's). This is an opportune moment to give you an insight into the 'categorization' of racial equality.

The Colony of British Guiana evolved from Britain's rush to expand its empire. It became a British Crown Colony through settlement and annexation and was therefore subject to the rules and regulations of Parliament. A class system was necessary to create a workable structure to ensure that British laws and customs prevailed. According to the prevailing belief at the time, colour denoted mental perspicacity. European nations controlled the world and they were all white. White people would naturally belong to the first class.

In defining who would fall into the next classes, consideration was given to the the traits of Indians and Negroes. Indians were described as industrious and hardworking, thrifty to the point of greed. Negroes were characterized as physically strong, but lazy, carefree, irresponsible, financially incompetent, and intellectually dim. The Middle Class would comprise Negroes and people of mixed race, who were educated under the British system. These would be employed in lower middle-class Civil

Service positions. Indians who were businessmen, landlords, money lenders, and rice millers would also fall into the Middle Class. A serious restriction in the case of Indians was that they didn't believe in Christianity and worshipped pagan gods.

This labouring class was uneducated; they could neither read nor write. They communicated in a jargon called creolese. This dialect was developed over the years by Negroes and Coolies who wanted to hide their thoughts and conversations from their masters. Overseers recruited from England couldn't understand what they were talking about, and labeled them 'unintelligent.' It is true that labourers could neither read nor write, but lacking intelligence was just balderdash. They were classified 'lower class'. *('Indenture & Exile' by Frank Birbalsingh)*.

The Class system created hidden animosity with Negroes when Indians realized that education was key to progress, and sent their children to school. Eventually, educated Indians began to vie for jobs in Civil Service positions. This was bothersome because jobs which Negroes previously considered were their bailiwick were now being usurped by Indians.

Sugar workers also had their own problems. They very seldom received an increase in wages, and what they earned could barely support them. Families could just eke out an existence; children were sent to work in fields and consequently denied an education. Even though they worked hard, labourers were always on the edge of poverty and starvation. When they protested, they were fired.

British Guiana was at the peak of prosperity, but none of this had filtered down to labour. Conditions were designed to keep them in poverty and ignorance to ensure labouring jobs were their only source of income. They would eventually learn that unity gave them strength and power, and they could fight for their rights.

Negro workers who flocked to the Cities in search of work were also disenchanted. Harsh working conditions and long working hours provided weekly earnings which were never enough to pay their rent and feed their family; they also felt disenfranchised. When they protested and went on strike, scabs replaced them. Some resorted to robbery and violence, but this proved to be impractical as they were quickly apprehended and punished. Trade Unions were formed, but solutions were also unsatisfactory. An uneasy peace prevailed.

Strikes threatened the economy but they were the only solutions to creating better working conditions and fairer wages for labouring classes. On one occasion, Indians on strike on a sugar estate formed a blockade to prevent scabs from accessing the cane fields. Authorities ordered the driver of a tractor to propel his vehicle into the group to disperse them. Strikers held their ground. Workers were injured and an Indian woman was mowed down and killed. This triggered an investigation by the British Parliament into labour and working conditions on the sugar estates.

Change came too late to quell hatred of the 'White' ruling class. A quiet revolution was born in the minds and hearts of people of colour. British Guiana was a country created by their labour. The feeling grew that it was time for white people to return to England and give up possession of the country to the people whose labour had made it prosperous.

Much like my own life, British Guiana was at the crossroads. Changes that followed would cause major disruption.

CHAPTER TWENTY-SEVEN

PITFALLS (THE 50's). Now I must return to my own chronicle. Mohan and I agreed a date for our marriage. I spoke to my parents. They were still adamant that this marriage was an error, but soon realized this was something they couldn't change. I presented a happy face outside, but I needed some 'alone' time to come to grips with what was a life changing decision over which I felt I had no control. Truth to tell I wished for some intervention but nothing was forthcoming.

I concluded that being by myself in Barbados for two weeks, would be a sojourn in paradise. Mohan could join me for a week after, and arrangements for our wedding could proceed. My mother decided my decision was something she could not change no matter how hard she tried. She corresponded with Joanna Philips, a friend she'd made on a previous visit to Barbados and asked her to provide accommodation for my stay. Joanna owned and operated a guest house.

When I booked my passage to Bridgetown, I was more excited at the changes happening in British Guiana than with my approaching nuptials. Whatever happened in my life would be dealt with as best I could. I didn't realize that marriage was a life-changing event where happenings beyond my control awaited me.

The two weeks before Mohan arrived in Barbados were happy ones. Two Trinidadian (Indian) girls were at the guest house, and they included me in their rounds of merriment. We swam, we laughed, we danced and sang, and I was happier than I'd ever been before. *This is life*, ran through my mind. *Stop and reconsider before it's too late. Leave Barbados and go anywhere. Mohan can't follow you.* Somehow I knew I couldn't do this. I had detected a streak in him I didn't trust. He was vengeful. He would do his best to hurt my family and then follow me and destroy me also. I wondered why men always seemed to have so much power over women. I hoped the day would come when I could hold my own. I shook my head and dismissed these thoughts with flights of fantasy which somehow always seemed to end with, *what's to be, will be.*

I felt alone when the girls left for Trinidad. I elevated my thoughts and raised my spirits by going into Bridgetown to shop. Bookstores were my favorite places. Fortune favoured me. I came upon a bookshop on the main street with such a display of new titles by my favourite authors, I was motivated to enter. While browsing I saw a title which said 'Sexuality Explained'. This was the first of its kind I had come across. I turned the pages and realized it was filled with important information about sex and sexuality, especially for a new bride.

I abandoned the books I'd selected and took 'Sexuality Explained' to the clerk at the counter. He said, "You'll want this wrapped, of course." His face lit up with quiet anticipation and I guessed he'd also browsed the contents or even read the book. His brown face had an eager smile. "You'll find it knowledgeable. You have no ring on your finger. I guess you're unmarried. Do you have a boyfriend?"

"I'm getting married in a week, and yes indeed, this book will be helpful." I thought there was regret in his smile. He'd found me attractive and perhaps had 'hopes' of friendship.

When I arrived home Joanna was busy baking my wedding cake and preparing supper. She'd planned a small reception to celebrate the wedding. I gave her a hug and a kiss and told her I was going up to my room to do some reading. The book was an 'eye opener' for me and I couldn't put it down. At dinner, wedding plans filtered into the conversation. I mentioned the book I'd bought and wondered aloud "Why haven't I come across a similar book in Georgetown?" This was just greeted by knowing smiles. *"Would the information it contained have made a difference to my life?"* I asked myself.

Mohan arrived a week later. Joanna looked at him with raised eyebrows. I could see and hear by the questions in her voice that she didn't think he was 'Mr. Right.' "He's too old, too brash, unsuitable in every way." Her thoughts were reflected in her facial expressions.

Nothing was said to me. With a false smile on her face she told him, "You're a lucky man. Look after her."

We were married the following week in the local Anglican Church.

After the wedding reception, we drove to Bathsheba (holiday resort in Barbados) to spend two nights. We slowly went up to our room, both uncomfortable and uneasy in our new relationship as man and wife. When it was time for bed, we undressed carefully, avoiding each other, and climbed into bed. "Could I endure this sexual act with this man? Would I scream and groan? I'd be reliving my brutal past. I don't love Mohan, what am I doing here? What have I done to myself?" I sighed "Perhaps, like the tales in the novels I read I could imagine this act was happening to someone else, and grin and bear it. 'Better get it over and be done with it."

When Mohan lay beside me, I rolled towards him. He put his arms around me and slowly fondled my breasts. That was distasteful and I forced myself to stop from cringing. He then climbed on top of me and tried to stuff his penis into my vagina, but nothing happened. After fumbling anxiously with this for a while he turned over and said, "We're both tired; this will have to wait."

This is strange, I told myself. *"He didn't get an erection. He knew about my rape and sexual abuse. If anything I should have been the reluctant person. I'll have a frank discussion with him in the morning. I felt relief when he turned away and postponed the "inevitable" evil deed. A strange wedding night indeed, quite different from what I expected after reading and understanding 'Sexuality Explained.' Here we were in the best room of the hotel, newlyweds with a sexual problem. Was I responsible? I was 'tarnished goods,' and this man had pursued me and blackmailed me into marriage. Now he couldn't have an erection. This is good. He's hiding something and I'll get to the bottom of it.*

The next morning when I awoke, I saw Mohan sitting in a chair, staring at me. He had a threatening look as if something was askew and it was my fault. *What the devil was he thinking?* I greeted him in a falsely cheerful tone "Hi, happy honeymooner, you're up and dressed and I'm in bed, like the lazybones I am. Come to bed and hold me tight. Let's finish what we started." I hid the shudder that was going through my body as these words were spoken.

"We have to talk," he answered in an accusatory manner, almost as if he was chastising me for what never happened. "Get dressed and we'll go for a walk on the beach. We have to get some things straightened out. When we're finished, you can decide whether you want to go back to Bridgetown, or spend another night here." I didn't like the tone of his voice. *Was he trying to blame me? It was time to take the leading role in this farce.*

"Why can't we talk about it now?" I demanded. "I'm feeling lazy and tired after our big day, and don't feel like taking a long walk. Do we have a problem?"

He gave me a look I couldn't fathom, "I love you dearly, but you've had sex with other people and that is a turn off. I wanted to be the first with the woman I married."

I laughed "I'm not stupid, Mohan. Get this straight. I never wanted to marry you. You blackmailed me. But why, I asked myself? I concluded that you had eyes on my father's money even though I told you I was not one of his beneficiaries. His money is for his sons. That's Indian tradition. Now you say that you can't have sex with me because I'm not a virgin and have had sex with other people? Why didn't you just tell me that you're impotent? Now I understand the reason why you're still single." I was outraged and it showed in my manner and tone of voice.

"I'm not impotent," he interrupted me, "the fault is not mine, it's yours. I thought I could manage, but last night when I saw you lying there, it turned me off."

"Don't try to blame me, Mohan. You knew all about my childhood. Now you say I turn you off. You've destroyed my life and turned me into a laughing stock. You can't even acknowledge your own problem! I left everything behind because of you – my family, the job I loved, my friends." I laughed, "what'll people say about you when we return home? You'll be the laughing stock then?"

"Don't threaten me, Tab. I'll tell them the truth. I can't have sex with you because you're damaged goods. We'll be living together, as a happy couple who eloped to get married, and that's all that matters."

"What do you expect to gain from this farce? YOU *will* be the laughing stock. You had me in bed, that's a turn on for normal men."

He became more conciliatory, "You're the daughter of wealthy parents. Your brothers will become professionals and some of that will rub off on me. We'll have a good life together. I'll provide for you and give you anything you wish except a divorce. You wouldn't want to be a divorced woman anyway."

"I don't understand you. Nothing good can come from this. I've never loved you. Suppose I fall in love with someone else. What then?"

My disgust at the situation and the disdain in my eyes displayed my feelings, but didn't deter him. "I don't really care, because I know you won't do anything stupid. You've too much to lose."

"I want to return to Bridgetown, now." I replied as I took command of the situation. The sooner we end this farce, the better."

Lordy, Lordy, ran my thoughts. *You're really and truly 'in the fire.' What are you going to do? How are you going to face the gossip back home, and your family? Is there no end to this? And then another thought interrupted, "I wonder if he's gay. It's strange that he's in his mid-forties and still unmarried. I'm young, good looking and have attracted many a young man who would have been happy to get into bed with me. Why couldn't my new husband have sex with me? There's more here than meets the eye."*

We returned to Bridgetown to the surprise of everyone at the Guest House. Joanna Philips told me I looked in need of some fresh sea breezes, and asked me to go for an afternoon walk with her on the beach. I was drained and profoundly unhappy. The bottom had gone out of my ship and I felt I was treading water.

The sun was shining, the beach of white sand and ocean blue water, resplendent. The lapping sound of waves meeting the sand seemed to offer a measure of calm. I demurred when Joanna asked, "What's wrong, Tabitha? I told your mother I'd look after you. You seemed devastated on your return here today. You're a new bride. New brides are radiant. You look as if the devil is after you. What happened to you? Sex can't have been so terrible."

I laughed. "You're right. I found myself in bed with the devil. I'm chained to the bedposts, and there's no escape."

"You speak in riddles, girl. What went wrong? Have you been promiscuous? Is that the cause for all this drama?"

"Wish I had." I replied. "Men always asked me out, seemingly for a drive, but I knew that their ultimate goal was 'sex in the back seat'. I've had many propositions but I always chuckled and said 'not for me.' One prominent guy who was married even offered me a home and wealth beyond my dreams, but I laughed heartily when I refused his offer. I couldn't be worse off now than if I'd become the 'other' woman and accepted his offer."

"What's wrong, tell me? We can work things out. Sometimes compromises become happy solutions."

I decided this was the moment of truth, the moment to lay bare the turmoil in my soul. I allowed it all to spew out... the hurt, the horror of my body being used against my will, the physical and mental agony, the silence that had to be, and how this affected me psychologically and physically... The compromises I'd been forced to make and the behaviour patterns that resulted... How I always felt myself standing on the brink of disaster and how I blamed myself for everything that had happened to me... I mourned the loss of childhood happiness and joy, the change in my personality from the horror that was part of my life that turned me into an empty shell. My only recourse was that part of me, which gave rise to my second self, who urged me on and comforted me during my troubles; without this I would have turned to the comfort of death by suicide... I rattled on, and on, unable to control the floodgates.

She put her arms around me, holding me tightly. "Hush, child, hush. You took it on yourself to protect your family when they should have protected you. You kept quiet because you craved the love of your parents, but you were afraid that what happened made you unlovable. Through no fault of your own you've become a broken piece of china. What a heavy weight! It's a miracle you've been silent for so long. Despite it all, you're a beautiful young woman standing on the brink. Dry your tears and let's sit for a while. The waves may calm us both.

After a while, I voiced the question in my mind. "Joanna, do you think he's gay? I read about this in the book on sex I got in Bridgetown." She put both hands on my shoulder and turned my head to face hers. If that's the truth, he's a horrible man. You're a very attractive young woman. I've seen men here ogling you. There's nothing wrong with you. Perish that thought. He's at fault. He had no right to force you into marriage. He has something planned that he feels marriage to you will get him. You should talk to your parents. Blame always rests with the man in a case like yours. He's after something. Take care."

The sun had begun its journey down the horizon and was slowly setting. Light would soon turn to darkness. Questions still dominated my mind, but solutions escaped me. However, I felt a sense of calm and peace. *I'd unburdened myself. And the world had still kept on turning! Realization dawned; decisions made aren't carved in stone. They could be changed.'*

When we returned, Mohan met us. He tried to take command of the situation, saying he'd been cheated of his conjugal rights and I was in his clutches because the fault was mine. Joanna gave him a look of condemnation, her usual smiling face, stern, and forbidding.

She squashed his attempt at bravado "Tabitha confided in me. I know everything. You're to blame, not her. Your actions were not that of a normal man. We'll talk about it tonight after dinner." Her stern look and forbidding manner boded no rebuttal.

Joanna accompanied me to my old room. She removed Mohan's suitcase. "I'll transfer this to the room he had before. If you're to sleep apart, we can start this now. Turn the key in the lock, so you won't be disturbed. Lie in bed, close your eyes, and tell yourself, 'all things right themselves; happiness will be mine one day.'

Dinner was held in an uneasy silence. Afterward, Joanna chided Mohan. "You blackmailed a beautiful girl, less than half your age, and tricked her into a marriage you can't even fulfil. Despite my advice, she's determined to return home, keep silent, and live with you under her own terms, she's the wronged party here, not you. If you leak one word about her or the Rajnarain family, I'll tell them about this farcical attempt to lure her into a marriage you couldn't consummate. You're in my hands. You've given me a weapon. You're impotent, you have no manhood". She shook her head from side to side, stern and forbidding, disdain radiating in her voice and manner.

Still sitting at the table, I sighed with relief. *I'll have myself all to myself, and I'll remain here for another two weeks. I'll have my own room when I return home and be solely responsible for my own actions. Mohan and I will become just people sharing living quarters. I'll look for another job, save some money, and go to London to study law. If Mohan didn't agree to this, then I'd remain in Barbados and find a job here. Joanna will help me.*

Mohan returned to Georgetown alone after Joanna told him my conditions for living with him. He was upset that I was spending another two weeks in Barbados and he couldn't start bullying me into subjection to his will. I would have liked remain in Barbados a little longer and research opportunities for employment, but I needed to make peace with Mother and Dad and face all the gossip and snide comments about my 'run-away' marriage.'

Two weeks went by quickly, but they were 'blissful.' I put aside all my forebodings and decided to seek happiness by becoming 'independent.' I'd earn money and be able to pay my own way. Mohan and I would be house mates, not man and wife.

I sent Mohan a telegram advising date and time of my return. Saying goodbye to Joanna had been difficult, but I consoled myself by thinking there would always be a home here for me.

Mohan met me at the airport. During our ride home, he told me he'd rented a small cottage in a good neighborhood. "I've bought some furniture and a bed. You can choose whatever else you think we need, and I'll pay for it." He was like a cock on the rock, crowing after a successful marital adventure.

At home the silence continued. When I could stand it no longer, I cleared my throat. "You've got something wrong. You said 'a bed', not two beds. We're married in name only. To clarify your understanding, this means we don't sleep in the same room, or share a bed. This is an unbreakable condition, a separate bedroom, and ownership of my future."

To my surprise, he said, "I don't recall your saying anything about your future; you mentioned getting a job and going abroad to study, but I didn't know that that meant your future."

"You can be truly obtuse when you want to be, Mohan." My voice brooked no disagreement. Getting a job, saving my money, and going abroad to study **is** my future. Joanna spoke to you about this, and you agreed. Now that you have me here alone, don't think this is going to change."

I walked into the main bedroom and saw that he had stored his clothing inside the closet. I felt like moving everything out, throwing it on the floor, and stomping on it. I resisted and said firmly, "Mohan, take your clothes out of my closet and store them where you may. This is my room, not yours, not ours. I'll get a carpenter to install some locks and bolts to ensure you've no doubt about this."

He attempted to protest but I was firm. "We're two people with an arrangement. One good thing about being a woman is that I'm the receiver not the giver, so there's no reason for my not being able to take part in the act of sex. We're married; we tried to have sexual relations and you're impotent. You couldn't get an erection. I believe you've tried to remedy that situation before, but without success. This bears out why you're still single at age forty-eight. I became the unwitting pawn in your scheme to better your future. All that's changed. I am legally your wife, but I can soon remedy that."

He seemed aghast at the change in me but recognized he could do nothing about it. In truth, I surprised myself. I had exhibited a side of my personality that was new to me. I retired to my room, shut the door, and went to bed.

The next day he asked about housekeeping. We agreed that I would buy the groceries and make dinner. We would hire someone to take care of all other duties, fund everything and he'd give me an allowance to pay for this. He suggested that I shouldn't look for a job. I told him this wasn't an option. I would begin job searching immediately. Further, I would be going over to Vreed-en-Hoop to visit my parents the following day.

"Will you be moving your belongings to our new home?" He foolishly asked.

I glared at him and sneered "Perish the thought, this isn't your concern."

He sensed that things were not going his way, but didn't want to provoke further argument. My attitude wasn't one of compliance. He had lost control.

To my surprise, I returned home to Vreed-en-Hoop to find myself the guest at a small wedding reception to welcome the Bride. The absence of the new bridegroom caused questions, but snide remarks went unspoken. Everyone wanted to meet my 'new husband'. I fobbed them off by saying that he was following some breaking news, very important to the future of our country. I saw raised eyebrows, but made no effort to answer questions or allay suspicions. Of course, I was examined from head to toe with particular concentration on my belly for signs of pregnancy. Any difference would provide fodder for the gossip mongers.

This was the age where women were always blamed for pregnancy outside wedlock; men got off with a nudge and a wink. This was so unfair! Women didn't seduce men. It was the opposite. 'Pregnancy' outside marriage meant disgrace to mother and child. The future of children was always clouded. They grew up with the word 'illegitimate' like a load on their shoulders. In most cases, child support was never paid. However, if the child did well in life, men were quick to compliment themselves on their child's success and 'prance like peacocks' with the glory of it all.

Mother and Dad welcomed me with open arms. "Is everything all right? Where's Mohan? You don't seem as happy as we expected. I heard from Joanna. She had only praises for you. How did everything go? Tell us about the wedding. She said she'd baked you a cake and held a small reception?"

"She's a lovely woman, Mother. She did everything she could and more. She made me feel very special and I'll always be grateful for her loving kindness. It's good to have friends like her. She has the greatest respect for you and Dad."

My father looked at me with questions in his eyes, but said nothing to press the conversation further.

Next morning, I travelled back to Georgetown. Mohan hadn't left for his office when I arrived at our home. He greeted me, "Next time you plan to remain away, let me know in advance. Don't tell me later."

"Get this straight, Mohan," I replied. "We're house mates. You don't own me. I was at my parents' home, and that should be enough for you." I went to my room, slammed the door, and bolted it. I thought, *this cannot go on for long. I've got to make plans, but what am I to do?* No answer was forthcoming.

I decided I needed to go job hunting. Next day, I completed applications at commercial houses I thought could use a secretary. I hoped against hope that even though I was brown, my experience would entice them to hire me.

Luck was on my side when I met an old school friend who greeted me with a hug and a smile. She asked, "What are you doing here?"

"Job hunting, of course," I replied with a laugh. She seemed surprised, but held back. Her reply was like a ray of sunlight. "Why don't you phone the personnel office at the Public Service Commission? I heard they were asking if anyone had heard from you. I understand the Manager of the Transport & Harbours Department is a very demanding expat, (ex Colonel in the British Army) and they can't find him a secretary." I thanked her, and arranged to meet later for an ice cream soda.

No time like the present, I thought, as I walked over to the office of the Public Service Commission. I asked to see Harry Jones, the Head. His secretary said, "He's been asking for you so I'm sure he'll see you. You'll have to wait a bit though, as he's with someone. I hope you don't mind."

I sat down and waited, twiddling my thumbs hopefully. *Such a job should pay me about the same as when I left the Civil Service. I'd be able to add to my savings and in about two years could travel to London to become a Barrister.* I refused to let despair enter my thoughts. Inside, I was the quivering shell of an abused woman with very little self-respect or self-esteem, and on the outside, a confident woman who knew what she was about. Self-doubt always hovered, but I made an effort to keep it hidden.

Time ran on. Opportunities once lost can never be regained. This discussion must be important, but it can't last forever. I'm going to wait.

Shortly after, when I looked up, I saw the Registrar leaving the office. He stopped short when he saw me. "Hello, Tabitha, fancy seeing you here. Are you going to rejoin the Civil Service? If so, tell Harry to talk to me. We can get around the regulations somehow and get you working for us again."

Wonders never cease, I thought. Did he still hanker after me?

I always felt at ease with Harry Jones and hoped he would help me find a job. *Why didn't I think to call him in the first place?* I wondered. When he heard I'd been waiting to see him, he had called the Transport & Harbours Department and arranged an interview for me for 9.00 a.m. the next morning. I was somewhat hesitant about asking about salary. This was important but I decided to bide my time.

I returned to Mohan's home on winged feet. I felt gracious and happy. Life seemed to be opening doors for me. My stars were aligning, and I was hopeful.

We had a pleasant dinner together. I told him about my prospects and was only mildly irritated when he "pooh poohed" the idea of my thinking of going back to work, and even of my landing a job. "We'll see," I said. "This will give me something to do instead of lounging around. I won't get bored with life and besides I'll be my own wage earner." I was thinking about my freedom.

My bicycle helped my independence. I had collected mine from Vreed-en-Hoop and stored it in the room below the house. Bicycles were the main means of transportation to work for most people. Car ownership for the general population was restricted to the wealthy and the holders of major civil service positions. Mohan owned neither car, nor bicycle. He used taxis to get to and from work, and sometimes he rode the bus.

I saw what I interpreted as a funny look on Mohan's face. It gave me the feeling that my bicycle was in trouble. I needed that bicycle to get to the interview. I said, "Talking about my interview tomorrow, I need to make sure my bicycle tires are inflated and okay." I went down to the storage room. Fortune smiled again. I found a padlock on one of the shelves, probably left by the previous renter. I locked the room, pocketed the key, and returned upstairs.

"I have to make an early start tomorrow, Mohan. Must get to bed." I closed my door and prayed that everything would work favorably. If they didn't, what then? "Wait and see." my alter ego whispered. Positive thinking will see you through."

CHAPTER TWENTY-EIGHT

N EW BEGINNINGS (THE 50'S). As I walked through the general office of the Transport & Harbours Department next morning, work seemed to come to a halt. Disquiet filled my mind. I felt all eyes were on me, but managed to smile as my eyes connected with the eyes of some of the staff. I smiled as I climbed the stairs to the second floor. As soon as I disappeared from view, I heard questioning murmurs. *"What are they whispering about me?"* my mind asked. *Georgetown is a small place and I'm sure someone in the general office knows me, and is relating tales of my life.* I thought I had indeed recognized someone from Vreed-en-Hoop, so I guessed the fat was in the fire.

My interview went well, the letter of recommendation from the Chief Justice seeming to have the most impact. I was offered the job at a salary beyond my expectations, and advised I could commence work as soon as possible. "I'm anxious to get back to work," I smiled. "I could start tomorrow." This was greeted with a wide smile. "You can start today, if you like. I'll get the office manager to show you around after he has confirmed your appointment."

I rejoiced. I had the 'wherewithal' to be free again, and a job to distract me from the mess I'd made of my life. The Fates were in my corner after all.

The day passed by in a flurry of activity. Stenography was the least of my problems. I had to learn the nature of the business in which I was to be employed, the responsibilities of my boss, the General Manager, and where I could be of best use.

I telephoned Harry Jones to give him the good news and thank him for his help. He said, "Good news flies fast. They've already called and thanked me." *Well*, I thought, *responsibility rests with me*. I remembered my father's advice whenever I complained. "You can change it all by the way you respond. Always remember, 'if it is to be, it's up to me,' stop complaining now."

Mohan was, of course, displeased. He told me that two journalists were visiting from England, and he wanted me to prepare dinner for them, and entertain them at home. I replied, "Mohan, this place is still unfurnished. Entertainment at home will have to wait. Why not meet them at "The Blue Ribbon" restaurant? Fix the date and time and let me know." I felt that meeting people from England would broaden my perspective and help me when I went to Middle Temple. "There's more than one way to play the game, or 'to skin a cat,'" as the local saying went. Dinner went well. The journalists were interesting and entertaining. That evening further infused my desire to go to England to study law.

I was diligent. I worked hard, determined to excel at my job. I treated everyone fairly, in particular those who came asking for an interview with the General Manager (G.M.). I never pulled rank. I always obliged if asked to type a letter, or listen to a complaint. I helped people. Later on in life, my attitude came back to help me. The Transport & Harbours accountant whom I'd once helped was promoted to the position of Commissioner of Income Tax. I had been erroneously assessed for income tax earned in one of my later ventures, for one of the years while I was still working at the Transport & Harbours Department. A simple telephone call to him cleared up the error. Without this, I would have had to pay heavy legal costs because of a "belief" by the official making the assessment, that I was cheating.

But I digress. A year passed quickly. Mohan and I settled into an uneasy truce. I spent one weekend a month with my parents. They often questioned me about what I did and how I spent my time. I told them, "Life is simple. I go to the movies on Mondays, I'm busy at work, read a lot, entertain Mohan's foreign guests from time to time, and life simply seems to speed by."

"What about children?" my father asked.

"Dad," I replied. "There's no time for that in my life. I still want to go to England to study law. I'm saving my money and in a couple of years, I'll be off."

"I don't understand you," my father replied. "I offered to send you away before you went to Barbados to get married, and you said no. What brought about this change? Aren't things working out for you?" The concern in his voice reached my breaking point.

My defence crumbled, I broke down, and started to weep. My mother and father looked at each other quizzically wondering 'why the tears, what's happening?' He got up from his chair and put his arms around me.

"Dry your tears and let's talk about what's troubling you. I've always suspected that something was wrong. Are you and Mohan not getting along?" he questioned.

I sobbed harder, hysterically. My floodgates had opened and there was no way to close them. Both parents tried to hold me and comfort me; I was encircled in their arms. Then my father went to the sideboard and poured some brandy into a glass. "Here," he said, "drink this. It'll soothe you. Cry if you will, but you must let us know what's wrong."

Eventually, I dried my tears. I tried to look at them both. "Mother and Dad, I couldn't tell you this before because I was so ashamed and overwhelmed. Mohan and I are married but in name only. He couldn't consummate the marriage in Barbados; we sleep in separate rooms. So, you see, there can be no grandchild for you."

They were both astounded. "Why didn't you tell us about this when you returned home? We wouldn't have allowed you to live with him. Tab, don't you trust us to do the right thing for you? Where have we failed you?"

I replied, "You both know there's always been gossip about me. Looking directly at my Mother, I said "you've always chided me for 'laughing and talking' with everyone. I didn't want to bring further disgrace on your shoulders. I thought I could handle the matter and gradually ease out of my current situation when I eventually went to England to study. Mohan couldn't follow me there."

Dad interrupted. "How little you know of life! Mohan got married to you because you were the solution to resolving his money problems and advancing his future. He visited me after his return from Barbados and asked to borrow twenty-five thousand dollars, against the money you'll inherit when I die."

"What?!" I exclaimed, "Why didn't you tell me this? The nerve of that man! This explains why he avoids family functions? Work has always been his excuse, but I've long suspected there was another reason."

"He asked me not to worry you about this. He planned to establish a printing and publishing house. I was quite impressed by the extensive work he planned to do, but doubted his ability to turn his dream into reality. I asked him how much of his own money he was going to invest. He tried to beat around he bushes, but he had none."

"How shocking," I replied. I've always understood he was independent; he's a lavish spender, and boasts about how he provides for his mother and aunt."

"Do you give him any of the money you earn?" my mother asked.

"No," I replied. "I assumed responsibility for providing food. I buy whatever I need."

My father said, "Let's put an end to this discussion. Telephone him. Tell him you're spending the night here; he'll see you tomorrow after work." I looked at him through eyes that bespoke my worry, but this didn't stop his directions to me.

"Telephone your boss in the morning. Explain that you have a family emergency and need the day off. We'll travel to the city tomorrow, you'll gather your belongings, and my boys (Dad's clerks) will take care of the rest."

I tried to interrupt again, but he dissuaded me. "You're my daughter, under my protection. There's no alternative. You're returning home. I'll make sure this marriage is dissolved."

"Dad, let's leave it for a while. I feel better now that you and Mother know the situation. I can continue for a while longer," I tried to say.

He was angry. Looking directly at me, his eyes conveyed that he was issuing an order and nothing I could say would change it. "You aren't going back to his home ever again, except to retrieve your belongings. There's no argument that'll induce me to change my mind. It'll be unsafe for you once he knows I'm aware of what he's done to you. Say no more."

I telephoned Mohan and told him not to expect me until the following evening after work. He was upset, but I managed to avoid a quarrel. I felt I could make magnanimous promises I knew wouldn't be kept.

CHAPTER TWENTY-NINE

MITIGATION. As I lay in my old bed that night, thoughts of the future kept me awake. I feared that Mohan would expose the rape and abuse that had happened in my childhood. I would be regarded as the 'Scarlet Woman,' a person to be stoned and dishonored. Passers-by would cross the street to avoid me. No one would touch me. It was easier to avoid this by just enduring what had happened. How could I make this go away? I remembered my trying to roll off the roof in my effort to commit suicide. Why did I stop to look around? I should have rolled down when I had the chance. Another mistake.

I argued that truth and redemption could also have made me whole again but I had muffed my opportunity when I was stilled by Henry's threats. Childhood respect for authority had kept me prisoner. I had retreated into the silence of despair. Perhaps this was the role in life I had been born to fulfil. I always remembered my mother holding me tight and warning that what Cyril had done to me was secret and never to be revealed. Instead of being comforted, an additional burden was added to my already tortured mind. Would I be admonished if I revealed what he'd done to me? Childhood fear of telling what was supposed to be secret and being punished, had perhaps been part of my reason to believe that happenings like these were ordained for me and I would have to deal with whatever fate I met in silence.

I'd confided this sordid story to a stranger who used it to blackmail me into a loveless marriage because of my supposed inheritance. I was totally to blame and nothing could absolve me.

Parents were beacons in the lives of their children. I didn't want to fall from grace. I craved their praise and approval and I'd accepted the mantle of guilt to gain this approval. There was no way out.

During the night, strange apparitions reappeared in my dreams; half man, half beast, - they walked beside me claiming that I belonged to them. My childhood nemeses returned to my world. Snakes slithered after me, vampires tried to rape me and suck my precious blood, the headless horseman tried to run me down as I tried to escape the ghosts who had come out of their graves to frighten me and kill me so I could join them. Creatures I couldn't see howled and cackled as I tried to escape.

When morning came, and it was time to rouse myself, I felt weak and disheartened.

My father suggested it was better to take the later ferry across the river and so avoid the questioning looks and the usual crush of passengers on their way to work. This would also be better as I would avoid a meeting with Mohan.

Going back to the home I would no longer be part of, gave me an eerie feeling. I didn't want to linger in the house, but It took an hour to get everything I owned into suitcases and boxes. As we were about to leave I thought 'a note for Mohan is easier than conversation with him. I won't have to listen to his threats, reprimands, and recriminations. This is the coward's way out, but at times it was better to be cowardly and avoid further complications.'

Dad waited while I wrote the note. He asked to see what I had written. He was being careful. My note said *I wasn't happy and it was time to make a fresh start. My parents were now aware that he'd blackmailed me into marriage and advised that it was best to end it. I'd taken my clothes and personal belongings and I wished him well.*

As I settled back in my childhood room that night I contemplated my future. *Would Mohan make trouble, or would he bow out gracefully?* I hoped that life would make me a concession and everything would end peacefully.

I should have known better. In the weeks that followed, he tried to call me at work, but calls from him were not connected. He wrote me long letters, which my parents intercepted and returned. He asked Mike to plead his case.

My replies were all the same. "Please leave me alone. Speaking to me won't solve the problem. My leaving is final; after the appropriate time, I'll seek a divorce."

A month passed and I began to breathe a little easier. I knew that an uncontested divorce would move faster through the courts and hoped for the best. I trusted that Mohan would understand that a marriage born out of blackmail could not survive. It was time to put an end to an impossible situation.

My relief was short-lived. One afternoon, on my way to catch the ferry, I was cycling along, intent on not being late for the ferry home. I stopped at the Traffic Sign at the intersection of Water and Hincks Streets. Traffic was always heavy at this junction because of gridlock created by buses, cars, donkey carts, cyclists, and people on foot. Out of nowhere, it seemed, Mohan appeared. He grabbed the handlebars of the bike, so I couldn't move on. Two men suddenly appeared. I was frightened beyond belief. He said to them, "Take her to the car. I'll get rid of the bike." As they approached, my fear led me to scream. Then I shouted, "They're trying to kidnap me, help, help me, please."

Mohan tried to make me stop. He said, "I only want to talk to you, Tab. You're my wife and you have to come with me. You must obey me. This is the law."

I screamed all the louder. Suddenly a crowd had formed a circle around us. "Thank God," I said to myself. "At least he can't drag me out of here."

Mohan pleaded with them. "She's my wife. Her parents don't like me, and they won't let her speak to me. I only want to talk to her. Let us pass. I'm not going to harm her. I have rights and privileges."

A woman from the crowd shouted, "You're lying. Look at her and look at you. You're too old for her. Let her go. "By this time, the throng had grown and traffic was at a standstill. This attracted the attention of a passing policeman. He stopped and asked, "What's the cause of all this commotion?" The crowd replied, "He's trying to kidnap her. He says she's his wife and he wants to talk to her."

The policeman asked Mohan, "Why are you trying to take her away against her will? If she's your wife and she doesn't want to talk to you, the law says she's free to do this."

"Buddy," Mohan cajoled. "I don't want to hurt her, but she won't speak to me. I love her and want her to come back home to live with me. She has to come with me, that's the law."

The crowd got in on the act, making jeering remarks at Mohan, while offering advice to the Policeman. I said, "I'm on my way home. I need to catch the ferry. I have no desire to reconcile with this man. He has obstructed me and he still has my bicycle."

The policeman said to Mohan, "Return the bicycle to her. You can't force anyone to go with you against their will, regardless of your feelings. You've no rights on her person. If you try this again, you'll be charged with obstruction and kidnapping.

I'll accompany her to the ferry." He turned to the two men who were waiting to drag me into the taxi and said, "You'll be charged as accomplices if you ever try anything like this again. The sentence for kidnapping is imprisonment. I'm sure you won't like to spend time in jail."

The crowd cleared and made a pathway as the policeman directed my passage through. Then he jumped on his cycle and accompanied me to the ferry. He gave me his name and number, and told me to call him if there was any recurrence.

I barely made it to the ferry. It was a few minutes after the time for the scheduled departure. I hoped someone would see me and not 'cast off' (loosen the moorings) before I got there. Luck was with me. Vincent Cummings, a schoolmate from my primary school days, now ticket collector, saw me and signaled the captain. The captain delayed the ferry so I could get aboard. The ramp had already been removed. Vincent took my hand so I could jump aboard then threw my bicycle to someone in the crowd. The Captain had waited a few minutes for me but he would make up lost time on the journey across the river. This was special treatment because of my position as Secretary to the General Manager.

Vincent saluted and touched his cap in deference as the vessel moved from the dock. He and I had been friends, sitting side by side at school, whispering help with spelling and reading. Now he was employed as an 'unclassified' worker, while I held the important position as Secretary to the General Manager. The worlds which made us once close, now separated us. We were in different classes of society, in addition to the fact that he was black and I was brown, and such a friendship between male and female even though it was platonic, was impossible. We moved in different circles.

I was shaken to the core as I parked my bicycle and headed to the top deck. If Mohan could hire some thugs to kidnap me, what else would he be up to? I must escape, leave the country, change my name and disappear. The near miss of his attempt frightened me. What if I hadn't screamed? What if the crowd hadn't gathered around and challenged him? What if the policeman hadn't appeared? What if I had fainted and Mohan and his thugs had just picked me up and lumped me into the car?

I felt I was going to have a seizure. I couldn't let this happen. I didn't want to become a spectacle. I couldn't handle the gossip. I took deep breaths. Every so often my mind would stray back to the attack, and I would become fearful and start to tremble.

The ferry docked and I rode swiftly home. Mother and Dad were sitting in the gallery having a cup of tea before dinner. One look at my face told them something was wrong. "What's wrong?" they cried in unison.

I burst into tears. I was home, safe in the bosom of my family. "I was almost kidnapped," I said. A passing policeman saved me. Mohan isn't going to let me go. He'll hound this family until we're all destroyed."

"We'll see that doesn't happen," my father replied. "I'll give him a run for his money. I'll talk to our lawyers tomorrow and also have a chat with Sergeant Blackmore. In the meantime, I'll ask Mike to keep an eye out for you and accompany you to work and back again. Last time he was here, he blamed himself for introducing you to Mohan. He said he never thought Mohan would make a play for you, or that you'd even get involved with him."

Mike was happy to take on the role; he cycled with me to work, and then went to his own office. He became my constant companion. This was the start of a blossoming friendship.

Trouble loomed again. Mohan didn't give up easily. He was on the warpath. Three months after the kidnap attempt, I received a call from Detective Sergeant Bayne at the Brickdam Police Station. Brickdam was the suburb in Georgetown where

I'd lived with Mohan. Sergeant Bayne explained, "We're investigating a serious complaint made against you by your husband, Mohan Bahadur. He's in hospital with internal bleeding caused by ground glass. I'm in charge of the investigations and I require you to come down to the station for questioning."

I asked for some more detail. He said, "I can't tell you anything else. Your husband said that he drank his cough mixture to help ward off a cold and he became ill. You must appear at the station for questioning. If you fail to do this, you can be arrested and charged."

I was aghast. Mohan was doing everything he could to coerce, frighten, and terrify me. His aim was to destroy me and my family. I thought, *Will I never be free of this man? What have I done to deserve this?* Trouble had fallen on me from out of the blue. In my ignorance, I had decided that if no one knew the secrets of my childhood, I would be safe. *I little knew that something within me would cause me to betray myself, and someone I trusted would use these secrets to blackmail me.*

There was no time to contact my parents. I called our family lawyer. He advised that it would be best if a member of his firm was present during the interview at the police station. He would telephone the officer, then collect me on the way to the station. He stressed, "On no account are you to go alone or with anyone else."

What a debacle of trouble was popping up and exploding all around me! Would it never cease? I promised myself that never again as long as I lived would I trust someone with any knowledge I felt was sacrosanct.

Mohan had made the accusation. The police were summoned to investigate the incident the previous day. Mohan was found bleeding from his mouth and was taken to hospital. Happily, he hadn't swallowed much of the mixture, but he was still in hospital being monitored for further complications.

His complaint was that when I collected my belongings from the matrimonial home I added the powdered glass in an attempt to murder him. I was aware that he relied on the mixture for health reasons and followed the chemist's instructions exactly. He usually shook the bottle then swallowed the dose directly from the bottle, without swirling it around in his mouth. I'd tried to kill him in this way because I hoped the cause of his death would go undetected and I would get away with murder.

"I've never returned to that house since I collected my belongings," I replied. "If the only evidence you have against me is Mohan's word, you have no case against me. Mohan is attempting to harass me and you're helping him."

My lawyer advised Sergeant Bayne, "You should examine the medicine bottle and check the date the medication was dispensed. Check your evidence before you threaten arrest." He then indicated that we should leave, and I got up to comply.

The Sergeant turned to me and said, "I have some more questions for you."

I was angry. Mohan's word that I tried to kill him wasn't sufficient evidence to drag me down to the police station for questioning. Sergeant Bayne should have verified the facts before he summoned me to the Station. He seemed more complicit with Mohan's desire for vengeance than in investigating the complaint.

Before I could reply, my lawyer said, "We're leaving. I suggest that unless you have something more substantial than Mr. Bahadur's complaint, you should not harass Mrs. Bahadur. I have it on good knowledge that the medication was dispensed after Mrs. Bahadur left the house. You're trying to turn this incident into a media circus. Rest assured, I'll be registering a complaint with the Commissioner of Police about police harassment."

My father was indignant when he heard what had transpired. "It's time to expose this creature for who he is. We'll file a petition for dissolution of marriage on grounds of non-consummation.

He'll suffer loss of face. He's a spiteful loser preying upon a young girl he blackmailed into marriage for money. He couldn't consummate the marriage because of his own inadequacies. The man's evil and it's time to call his bluff and put him down."

Has there ever been a creature more miserable than I am? I asked myself. *There were two yokes around my neck. First, I would need to prove that my hymen was still intact in order to start proceedings for divorce on the grounds of no-consummation, and second, Mohan knew all about the rape and sexual abuse and he'd use this as his defence.*

I felt condemned. *"Prisoner at the bar, do you have anything to say before sentence is passed?"* Deepest misery invaded my consciousness. It was time to own up to the miserable happenings that had fettered me and burdened my life. My parents and family would be devastated. We would fall from grace into the mire of hellish gossip. How would my parents deal with the betrayal of the life they had so carefully charted and lived? They had built a home and barricaded it from jackals, but the jackal lay within the fortress. I'd wronged them by my silence and perpetrated another crime when I confided in Mohan. Sir Walter Scott once wrote, *"Oh what a tangled web we weave when first we practice to deceive!" How apt, in my case,* I thought. I had deceived myself into thinking that I could break my bond of silence and trust another person with my secret.

"You must talk to your parents before this charade goes any further," I chided myself but I couldn't disentangle the chains which bound me to silence all those years. I couldn't bear to hurt them. *The truth of my silence lay in the fact that I'd sinned in the eyes of God and the Church when one man raped me, and another violated me sexually for several years. I was brutally torn asunder, yet in the eyes of the Church I would be viewed as a fallen woman. Men, to whom I wasn't married, had sexual relations with me. "Adultery" – sex without marriage – was the greatest sin of all. I asked myself, why did women have to bare the heaviest burden in situations like this? Blame always rested with them*

for deeds completely out of their control perpetrated on them against their will.

One day morphed into another until it was too late for disclosure. My lawyer made an appointment with Dr. Rodney Charles, a leading gynecologist, for the following week. Dr. Charles was in his sixties, renowned for his work with feminine illnesses, and well-respected in the community. In those days, people seldom visited doctors unless they were ill with something they couldn't cure with household remedies which hadn't been effective. I had visited a doctor only once before when a compulsory medical examination was necessary for all civil service positions.

I felt shamed at the thought that I would have to expose my genitals to a male. An internal examination with his finger would determine whether my hymen was intact, but I'd no choice. I hoped some "miracle" would happen and my deceit wouldn't be exposed.

Well, well! Miracles do happen. What a relief! I didn't question it. After his examination Doctor Charles confirmed that my hymen was intact. I couldn't believe this. Medical examinations weren't as sophisticated as they are today, and British Guiana wasn't as advanced in the practice of medicine as in the USA and England. I tried "guessing" at various reasons, but in the end accepted the result as a miracle from God, and a well-deserved break from the various misfortunes that had beset me throughout my life.

I breathed easily, glad that I'd postponed the "evil" day when all would be revealed.

The petition for dissolution of the marriage on grounds of non-consummation was filed along with a certificate from Dr. Charles stating that my hymen was intact. I wondered what Mohan thought of it all. *Did he believe that some childish quirk had caused me to confess to happenings that had occurred only in my mind? Had I deliberately misled him into believing this because I wanted to be a heroine awaiting rescue from her captors?* I couldn't find an answer but hoped he was suffering from the laughter of his friends and co-workers at the turn of events.

In due course Mohan filed a defense which stated that the fault lay with me. I was frigid and had an aversion to sex because I'd been raped as a child.

We settled down to await a trial date.

My lawyers made it clear to Mohan and his defence team that all communications to me should be addressed to them. Mohan retained a prominent lawyer to represent him. I wondered where he would get the money to pay the lawyer. This was a little reprieve in my life. I was fighting for vindication.

I hoped this would put an end to his machinations against me. My fight for freedom from my ill-conceived marriage awaited court hearing. Mohan was busy with news about the political upheaval in British Guiana, and I hoped this would distract him and cause him to leave me in peace. There were other issues to be dealt with.

CHAPTER THIRTY

RA OF CHANGE (40'S 50'S 60'S). As I was going through these major changes in my life, so was British Guiana. Indians and Negroes banded together to form one political party. Election results under new regulations swept them into power. This caused major concern in the British Parliament. The leader of the party, an Indian, was considered to be pro-Communist.

Britain and the U.S. did not want a "Cuban" crisis in their backyard. An unconfirmed report that the Archbishop of Guiana was attacked on his way to Berbice (another county) and that there was a general breakdown of law and order, provided the solution for action. The Constitution was suspended and a state of emergency declared. The British army was rushed to the country to maintain law and order.

Much like the Hindus and Muslims of India, Britain proceeded to drive further wedges between Negroes and Indians to lure them into a fight between themselves. The CIA became involved in the dissemination of false information intended to increase disharmony.

We were all astounded at the state of affairs. Our faith in British justice was torn asunder. We'd grown up singing songs about being part of the British Empire. We considered ourselves loyal British subjects, and believed that justice would unveil the truth. What was truth indeed? Where was the 'democracy' we had always accredited to Britain? Were we just pawns in Britain's quest for wealth and power? We did not like the answers to our questions. Much like all the other commonwealth countries, our British masters had sold us out.

British Guiana slowly lost its sense of well-being and became a country divided against itself. The two major races who had previously lived and worked harmoniously together, became bitter enemies.

Incitement to violence to disrupt and invoke disorder heralded the end of justice for Indians in Guiana. Arson and murder became everyday occurrences.

The violence perpetrated on Indians in Wismar, a small village situated across the Demerara river, opposite the local bauxite company was of significant importance to me. Women and children were raped, Indian men beaten and murdered, homes set on fire. Indian children who sought refuge in the homes of their Negro neighbours who'd dwelled peacefully with them and who they trusted and always addressed as Auntie, Uncle and Cousin, were handed over to gangs to be beaten and raped. When their penises couldn't function, the gangs had inserted foreign objects into the bodies of victims.

It was rumoured that the CIA, government officials, and management of the bauxite company knew that the attack was planned. They simply folded their hands and awaited the result. The Indians of British Guiana were 'led to the slaughter' on the altar of fear of communism and the power of greed.

The Indian population lost its faith in justice, and so did I. The land of our birth held no future for us and for our children. Promises of justice from Britain were just idle words designed to entrap and lure us into a false sense of security. Britain and the USA had sold us out and set in place a government we could not trust. Evolving from what was indeed slavery under a different name – bound Coolie – we were now abandoned and forgotten because of avarice and the fear that communism would disrupt the accumulation of wealth.

The campaign of violence was successful. Death, destruction, and fear were the ultimate results.

Britain granted a new constitution to British Guiana, elections would be held, and independence would follow. Changes were made to the electoral system. Proportional representation replaced 'first past the post.'

Elections were rigged. Names of the Dead and Guyanese in other countries filled the voters' lists. This was the final blow.

Forbes Burnham became Prime Minister, Cheddi Jagan became Leader of the Opposition. The country was renamed "The People's Republic of Guyana."

The Western world courted Burnham in the hope of alliance against communism. He ignored them after independence and started nationalization of industry and commerce.

Our Negro and Bound Coolie (Indian) forefathers, had endured their periods of servitude. Together we had broken the yokes placed around our necks. Now one race had replaced the masters and become rulers of the other.

Violence, murder, rape, theft, and destruction became the new order. This was a salutary lesson. Indians realized that British Guiana had become a country in which they could never be free. Their White masters were replaced by Negroes. They were citizens with no rights. Justice had disappeared.

Fear drove Indians to move their homes to areas where there was a concentration of fellow Indians. They preferred to live as "squatters" rather than face robbery and destruction of their property as well as violence and rape of their families. Rape of children, young and old, was an abhorrence and could never be forgotten or condoned.

Indians *en masse* began their exodus to Canada, England, and South American countries, taking with them whatever form of their wealth they could gather. The population began its decline, and the economy spiraled downwards. The Government tried to halt this by imposing currency restrictions. This was no deterrence. The saying grew, "stricter the Government, wiser the population". Money and people departed for greener pastures.

Guyana remained within the Commonwealth of Nations and was allowed access to markets in Britain and also to retain some of the defence arrangements Britain offered its former colonies.

The violence which erupted during the conflict continued against the Indians. They lived in fear of robbery and violence, without redress for the crimes committed against them.

Today, Guyana is ranked one of the poorest countries in the world.

CHAPTER THIRTY-ONE

LIFE NEVER STANDS STILL (THE 50'S). My own life was also evolving during this period. Political upheaval heralded many changes. There was a gradual shift in relationships as 'race' became an element for promotion or appointments in Government positions. Friendships between Indians and Negroes slowly disappeared. The sterling relationships with my father's Negro musician friends ended. Listening to their music had been a part of our childhood. The landscape of the country had begun its change. Resentment festered.

My job with the Transport & Harbours Department became more important. It was essential to keep transportation by land, rail, and water moving. Communications within the country couldn't be disrupted. We all felt and hoped that the effect of politics on racial relationships would wear off and life would return to its normal pattern. We were prepared to await the outcome. This was naïve.

I hoped that the case for my divorce would be listed for hearing in a short time, but as soon as a date was set, Mohan and his lawyer managed to get a postponement. They had the help of the Registrar who still felt the sting of being slighted when I'd rejected his proposal to be his "kept" woman and concubine.

In the ensuing years, Mike and I became an item. Our friendship was growing. He was my close confidant, but I had learned my lesson well. I kept my own counsel with regard to secrets. I never did tell him of my early trauma, and even though he always pressed me to tell him about my job, I resisted the temptation.

Finally, good news. A trial date was set. My lawyer called me at work to let me know that the case would be heard in six weeks. This would provide ample time to prepare.

Mohan and his lawyer asked for an independent medical examination to establish my 'virginity' and my lawyer in turn asked for an independent examination regarding his impotence and virility.

"What a shemozzle," I sighed. My chickens had come home to roost. An application was made to the Court and two Doctors selected. Costs would be equally divided between Mohan and me.

I summoned my courage. The inevitable had been delayed for two years. I had to face the music. There was no time to think of the effects of the examination on my reputation. I would be judged and condemned. "Well" I consoled myself, "if that happens, it won't be the end of the world. I would escape to a foreign country, hopefully to England or a remote possibility, The United States."

I still held a British passport and I felt I could easily obtain a job in London, beg lodgings and help in getting settled from my maternal Uncle who had settled there after the war and his discharge from the R.A.F. Consoled by my thoughts, I braved the outcome.

The medical examination was held at the Public Hospital. I was an object of curiosity as I walked the halls to get to the examination room. My mother hadn't accompanied me at my request. I didn't want her to face the nightmare.

It was torment indeed. I lay naked on the table, covered by a thin sheet. Two doctors prodded and poked me. One felt my breasts and made a rude comment. I had never felt so humiliated in my life. Then I heard them discussing the outcome. "She isn't a virgin; she's had sex with someone or others before. Nice, sexy figure, great breasts." A nurse, an older mulatto woman intervened, "Have you completed your examination?" They looked ashamed as one of them nodded a reply. "Well, it's time for you to examine the other patient. He's in the room next door."

She walked over to me, smiled in sympathy, and said, "Get dressed, honey. A nice cup of tea will settle your nerves. It's over for the time being."

I got up, dressed, thanked her, and went away. I collected my bicycle and decided I wanted to be alone for a while. I cycled to the Promenade Gardens where I thought I might have some privacy to ponder my thoughts. Nature would rescue and restore my equilibrium. The silence, broken only by the rustling of trees, and tweets from the birds, would calm my nerves and help my thoughts.

The gardens were beautiful in the sunlight. Manicured lawns and flowerbeds added symmetry and grace. My mind, body, and soul had been put through the wringer. Everything within me ached. I felt more alone and helpless than ever before. "Would my childhood defilement and humiliation never leave me? Violation was perpetrated on my persona, and memories of this always dragged me down into hellish territory. No matter how hard I tried, "IT" always walked by my side, just like my shadow. "IT" controlled me, placed an anchor around me, and dragged me into the deepest parts of the ocean from which there was no escape.

Wrung dry by my tears, weakened by the onslaught on my soul, I prayed to God for deliverance. *Let me die*, I pleaded. *My burdens are too heavy. I cannot live a lie any longer. I have turned into a person I do not like. If I despise myself, then surely others must also do so.* How ashamed I was to have had my body exposed, and comments made that assumed I'd fornicated with a man or men and that I would make a 'good lay.'

I felt entrapped, bound by chains wound tightly around my body, squeezing the life blood from my veins. "*Let me die*," my mind screamed. Even then I couldn't do the deed myself. Coward that I was, I lacked the courage to bring about my own demise. I hoped and wished for Divine intervention. Time stood still. I was caught in the vortex of something I could no longer control. The only way out was the truth and that was too difficult for me to handle.

A couple, hand in hand, passed by me. They looked at me quizzically, but kept going. My sanity asserted itself. *I have become an object of pity, it's time to get home, get a hot shower and wash away the lewdness of the doctors which they have transferred to me by their touch.* I felt drained, my usual self-control had deserted me, and left me tottering on the brink.

There's more to come, I told myself. *If you let your thoughts strand you on the isle of despair, you'll be lost forever. This is just the prelude to the battle ahead. Stand firm. People only destroy you with their remarks if you let them. Close the door on the morning's events. Do not ingest their thoughts, remarks or behaviour. You will survive. Survival should be the foremost thought in your mind.*

I rolled my bicycle slowly out of the gardens, caught the next ferry, and prepared myself for the discussion I would have with my parents. They were anxiously waiting, I knew. In their minds the examination today was a formality, the outcome assured. What was I going to tell them? I couldn't avoid disclosing the childhood rape and abuse. They would feel I'd shamed them, but there was no satisfactory explanation that could shroud the truth. My mind whispered, *"It's not what you did, it was what was done to you. The guilt belongs to others, not to you."*

But another thought surged out of the cloud. *They'll ask, why didn't you tell us?*

CHAPTER THIRTY-TWO

TRUTH AND CONSEQUENCE. As expected, my parents were awaiting me in the gallery. One look at my face told them that something was wrong. In unison, it seemed, they chorused, "What's wrong? What's the matter?"

I dropped despondently onto a chair and said, "My world has collapsed. Truth has come back to bite me."

"What truth? What are you talking about?" my mother probed, her eyes mirroring a million questions coursing through her mind.

My father looked at me, aghast at the thoughts soaring through his own mind "Take your time, and tell me what that wretched man has done now."

"Mother, Dad," I responded, my body drooping with dejection "it's not him, it's me."

"What have you done, child?" my father responded anxiously, his face registering his belief that mischief was still afoot.

"It's a long story," I began, words spilling out of my mouth without my conscious consent. "I know I should've told you, but at the time I was afraid you'd blame me and I was so ashamed. I couldn't face you and I feared your wrath, so I kept silent."

"What are you talking about?" my mother interrupted. "This isn't a time for riddles. What happened?"

"Do you remember that Sunday, a long time ago, maybe when I was four or five years old?" I asked, "When you found me in a pool of blood in the 'Last Room?'"

"That was a long time ago" … she began, with a puzzled look, then stopped short. "I thought if we said nothing to you about it, you'd forget what happened."

"You do know that Cyril raped me and my hymen was broken at the time?"

"Yes," she responded, her hands open wide with questions she needed answers for, "but you were so young, I thought it would have grown back, and that you wouldn't remember what happened."

"Hymens never grow back," I shook my head. "And that's not all. The same thing happened again and again. I was sexually abused from the time I was seven years old until I got my period when I was ten."

"Who could've done this dastardly thing to you, and why didn't you tell us?" my father thundered in anguish and anger, unwilling to believe that something like this could happen in his household.

"Henry did this to me. When I cried and said I'd tell you, he told me it was a normal thing for brothers to do to sisters. I told him I didn't believe him. I'd never heard of this before; he wasn't telling me the truth. He slapped me and shook me and told me he would do it all over again and this time he'd hurt me more." Tears settled in my eyes. It was difficult to control the emotions flooding through my mind.

"He said that you'd never believe me and would punish me for telling lies about him. You've always taught us to obey our older brothers and sister. I knew nothing of the world, nothing about sex. I only felt the pain, humiliation, and degradation of what was happening to me. The agony and shame of it shattered my physical and mental well being. I thought if I kept silent, I could hide my shame. No one would know and I would keep that part of my life secret. I longed for your solace and comfort, your arms around me, but you were both always too busy at the times when I gathered the courage to tell you about it. I was afraid to talk about it; I was even afraid to let on about my unhappiness. I was scared that I'd lose your love. I lost interest in everything, even in my schoolwork, and that's why I failed that scholarship examination". The words continued to tumble out without stopping.

My mother started to sob. My father got up from his chair, holding his head with both his hands as if to keep it in place, and started to pace the floor. "What have they done to you, to me and this family?" he cried in anguish.

"I should never have told Mohan. I know that now, but once I began I couldn't stop." I'd kept my secret shame to myself for such a long time, talking about it was a relief. "What am I to do now? I've made things worse all around and my stupidity is costing us all."

My father shushed me. "Let's talk about this now. Get it off your chest and out into the open. Your mother and I will listen. Always remember this: you were a child, under my protection, and the protection of your mother, sisters, and brothers. We all failed you. First your cousin and then your own brother violated your trust and did these horrible things to you. We will listen; we'll do everything we can to help you; you were never to blame, child. Your brother played upon your trust, and he'll pay for this. Mark my words. He'll pay for this many, many times. He's not my son anymore. He'll never set foot in this house again."

My father got up and poured us each a shot of brandy. My mother was still in shock. Her world had disappeared and everything she had worked and hoped for had been ravaged and destroyed. I felt a buzzing in my ears which grew louder. My brain seemed to be shutting down. My body started to shake uncontrollably. I had lost all power and control over it. It seemed to have a mind of its own. I had no resistance to battle what was happening to me. I felt I was going to faint. I closed my eyes, tried to breathe deeply, and slowly regained my jurisdiction. I gulped down the brandy. It warmed my body and slowly, I returned to reality.

My parents looked at me. "Are you okay? You look as if you're going to faint," my mother said, as she moved a footstool closer to me, concerns on both their faces reflecting the sadness my words had brought them. "Rest your feet." She tucked me in a blanket, and then she and my father started to argue about what the next step should be.

"Hush," I whispered. "Don't blame yourselves. You were both busy trying to make life better for us. You knew about Cyril, but you didn't know about Henry. I can't talk about it now. It's a place I try to avoid. Whenever I tried to hide or run away he always found me. He even lied to you once when he summoned me and I didn't want to go to him. He told you that he was taking me to his room because I was failing so badly in school, and he wanted to help me. You looked at me sternly and told me you would brook no disobedience to my elders.

"I can't relive those years of torture. He played with my mind. In my waking moments and even in my nightmarish dreams, I was chased my zombies, ghosts, vampires, snakes, and alligators, all bent on destroying me. Somehow a dominant part of me established a foothold in my mind and gave me comfort. It reminded me that I was important and had to stand up for myself. I learned to vanquish the mind invaders and I gained strength.

"When my period came I gathered enough courage to say to Henry, '*Enough, no more. I'll report everything he'd done to me over the years to you, Mother and Dad, and abide with the consequences.* He tried to beg and cajole me, but I remember stomping my foot and in my mind grinding him into the dust. He knew that somehow things had changed and I was now in the driver's seat. He didn't leave it there, but attempted to regain control when he told me, '*You were born bad. You seduced and incited me to do the things we did together,*' I silenced him by telling him that he'd lost power and control over me, and he was free to go ahead and do what he wanted. I didn't think that he would be believed.

"And that's basically it. My mind was tampered with. I'm always insecure. I don't think much of myself and I always put 'me' last. I don't know where we go from here, how we're going to deal with this new information, but the trial must go on. I want to be free."

I felt a sense of relief. The truth was out. I had shared it and it wasn't reaching out to bite me. My parents looked at me with such anguish on their faces, I felt vindicated. They loved me and showed such sorrow, I was the victor in the end. *I didn't want to hurt my mother further by reminding her that she'd told me that what Cyril had done to me was a secret and could never be revealed.*

My father shook his head. "We had no idea of the turmoil you've lived through. We always thought we were protecting you because it's so important not to have sex outside of marriage. You have to be blessed by the Church before you can lie in bed with another man. All cultures believe that, and I also believe that a man can send you back to your parents and sue for divorce if he finds his bride isn't a 'virgin'. You know that your mother and I weren't accepted by the Anglican Church until she was able to obtain a divorce from her first husband. However, our sins were only forgiven by the Church because they relied on my financial support."

"Well, Dad," I sighed, my shoulders sagging with the weight of everything, "I've one day, tomorrow, to compose myself. The trial starts next day. The Doctors' report will be available to the Court, but perhaps it's best if we allow the legalities to play their course. I'll offer no explanation to our lawyers; let them jump to their own conclusion. The doctors who examined me will attest that I wasn't a virgin; Dr. Charles will verify that my hymen was intact when he examined me. Our case is that Mohan was unable to complete the sexual act. He can't now change his response when he sees the report."

I stretched out my hands and took theirs in mine. "You know I love you both dearly and would do anything in my power to spare you the shame you're going through now. I've always been proud to be your daughter. Sometimes I wished that I could run to you with my arms outstretched, and you would open your arms wide to catch me, but you were always so busy, I'd just lower my head and move on."

"It's not for you to protect us. The shoe is on the other foot. We failed you, and I don't know if we can ever forgive ourselves for not recognizing what was happening in your life. We should've known when you started doing so badly in school that something was amiss. We just thought you were going through a phase and it would pass as you got older. Will you ever be able to forgive us?" Dad entreated, his eyes sad and weary, grief-stricken for all that had happened and wishing he could rewrite history.

The innermost part of my soul cried out, hoping that my tears could erase the past "Mother, Dad, you've always done what you considered to be best for me. Sometimes I wish I'd taken you up on the offer you made to send me to study in London instead of marrying Mohan, and lived with the fall-outs from whatever he did. But we can't erase past events. We have to live with the consequences and make the best of everything."

As I lay in bed that night, I heard a tap on my door. My mother came in and lay beside me. She put her arms around me as we lay their side by side. She whispered, "I thought you were being deliberately difficult when you were always in trouble for little things, being rude, answering back when you should have been silent, and I never thought beyond that. I should've loved you more, not shown disapproval. I'll never let that happen again". She squeezed me tightly as if she could rid my body of the pain and humiliation of the past.

I fell asleep with the thought, *"How much more would this have meant to me during my troubled childhood years, but it's better late than not at all. The slate has been wiped clean. My parents had erased any doubt left behind that somehow I was to blame.* Blame belonged to the perpetrators. *There was nothing I could have done that could have prevented what happened. I was the victim. I needed to come to terms with that or I could never move on. For some reason we always remember our failures but take our successes for granted. Evil always seem to play havoc with our thoughts, but it was possible to minimize this by remembering the positive things it engendered. I must be strong. I must be courageous. Walk with my head held high. Acknowledge who I am, and despite it all, what I've accomplished. That was all that mattered.*

I didn't go to work the following day. In many ways I felt at peace with myself. It was time to think of myself, not be worried about my parents and certainly not about my reputation. They were right, I should have thought of myself rather than of trying to prevent what was being done to me hurting them. A convoluted way of thinking, but that was it. The time had come to leave that part of my life behind. I had moved on with my education, held important positions, and earned a reputation for being an excellent secretary.

I told myself *'you've come out ahead of the game. It's time to appreciate the person you are'.*

CHAPTER THIRTY-THREE

L IFE'S UNPREDICTABILITIES. Dawn next day was spectacular. From the window in my bedroom, I watched the sun rise
on the horizon bringing light to vanquish the darkness of night
and energy to sustain life. I hoped this would be an omen for
my own life. Hidden secrets were out in the open so there was
nothing to fear. I was in control. No matter what happened, I
would be free. Dwelling on the yesterdays of my life had shrunk
my world and limited my thinking. The future would be mine
to shape; my dreams could become reality. Thinking outside the
box provided a pathway for a new life bright with sunshine. The
past had done its damage. No matter the outcome, it was time to
leave it behind and move on.

I chose my attire carefully, paying particular attention to my
make-up. I wanted to be the archetype of a successful woman,
accomplished, and in control. My father would stand by my side
and accompany me to Court. There was nothing to fear, no hidden secrets to rush out of Pandora's Box.

As boarded the ferry, I heard whistles from the crowd on the
lower deck. I smiled in their direction. I was bolstered by the
energy generated from their admiration. I reminded myself that

I was one of the privileged. My father owned the "Big House," several profitable businesses, and especially the cinemas. Their vocal admiration was a pleasant moment of nonsense in their morning; this was a good omen. My father frowned at them, but I squeezed his hand and told him they meant no disrespect.

We arrived at the Victoria Law Courts in good time. This place held many happy memories for me. Now I was a supplicant seeking justice, not just an onlooker.

The trial was set to start at 9 a.m. The courtroom was full. I saw several newspaper reporters in the crowd, but recognized no one. *Well*, I thought, *here it goes. I'm going to be the next major news item in the newspapers for the next week or ten days. So what? It'll soon be forgotten. If this meant that no likely suitor would want to court me because I was flawed, that was just too bad.*

Court started with the usual pomp and ceremony. The Clerk of the Court announced the case for trial before the Court.

My lawyers were Cameron Singh and Gerald Fitzroy. Mohan was represented by Fred Ebenezer and Samuel Adams.

Gerald Fitzroy rose and addressed the Court. "May it please your lordship we are asking that this case be held 'in camera' because of the nature of the allegations and the sensationalism which would follow."

Mohan's lawyer, Samuel Adams, objected. "Your Honour, this is a case which strikes at the innermost soul of a man's ego. To be impotent calls into question the entire fabric of manhood. The respondent has been maligned. He's a noted news reporter and well-respected. He holds an important position in society. These allegations of impotence are false, and we expect him to be vindicated. The public's need to know should not be violated."

The judge looked at me and then at Mohan. "I don't think justice will be served by allowing this case to become a sensational news item. I'll have no melodrama in my Court. The plaintiff's application is granted. Bailiff, please clear the courtroom."

The request for my father to remain was disallowed.

Before he left, my father told me he would be waiting outside the courtroom and would be present in spirit. He gave my hand a little squeeze, looked at me, smiled, and left.

The trial began.

Gerald Fitzroy addressed the Court. "My Lord, my client, Tabitha Bahadur, is the plaintiff in this case. She was married to Mohan Bahadur, the respondent, in Barbados. The respondent hasn't been able to fulfill the legal requirements of his marriage contract. The plaintiff and respondent lived together for eighteen months. When her parents became cognizant of the fact that the union had not been consummated, they rescued her. She's been living with them under their care and control ever since. It's no secret that Mr. and Mrs. Rajnarain have always disapproved of the union."

The judge nodded his permission to proceed.

"I call Dr. Rodney Charles to the stand."

Under examination, Dr. Charles affirmed, "The plaintiff's hymen was intact when I examined her and I gave her a letter certifying this." The letter was produced and marked 'Exhibit 1.'

Mr. Fitzroy continued. "Did you notice anything in her behaviour that would affirm or deny that she's frigid and consequently this could have accounted for the non consummation of the marriage?"

Dr. Charles replied, "Frigidity in women doesn't and shouldn't prevent sexual intercourse. Many women have sexual intercourse with men, but they aren't part of the act for many reasons."

"And what might these reasons be?"

"They may be afraid of becoming pregnant, take no pleasure from the act and find it uncomfortable, and many other reasons. I can only verify in this case that the plaintiff's hymen was intact when I performed the examination."

"Thank you, Dr. Charles."

Under cross-examination, Samuel Adams asked, "Dr. Charles, you've attested to the fact that the plaintiff was a virgin when you examined her?"

"That's correct."

"I'll now produce this letter from the Court-appointed doctors, and ask that it be marked Exhibit 1."

Turning back to Dr. Charles, he handed him the letter and asked, "How do you account for the fact that the plaintiff isn't a virgin?"

"That's easy, Sir. She must have engaged in sexual activity since I examined her."

"You're under oath, Sir, and I'm asking whether you engaged in a fraudulent scheme when you issued the first letter, entered in this case as Exhibit 1. Perhaps you made a mistake in your examination. Are you sure her hymen was intact when you examined her?" he thundered.

Dr. Charles replied, "I'm a noted gynecologist and I have practiced medicine for over thirty years. What I stated in my letter is the condition I found when I examined Mrs. Bahadur."

After a brief pause he added "I've seen the certificate by the Doctors who performed an examination under orders from the Court and I don't contest their findings. If her hymen isn't now intact, this could only be the result of sexual intercourse indulged in after my examination."

At this point the Judge interjected. "You've asked your question and it has been answered. Please move on."

I was the next witness called.

I stated my name for the records, and was sworn in.

Under examination I affirmed, "Mohan and I were married in Barbados. There was no consummation of the marriage because he couldn't get an erection. I lived with him for eighteen months. We had separate rooms. On questioning by my parents as to why there was no child in the marriage, I broke down and told them that ours was a sexless marriage. They asked for an explanation. I repeated that although we lived together, we occupied different rooms. Mohan and I had tried to copulate after the wedding but he couldn't get an erection, so there'd been no sexual intercourse between us; nothing of the sort had taken place between us. My parents advised me this was an unnatural state of affairs and no good could come of it. They recommended it was best that I returned home. The following day, my father accompanied me to the house Mohan and I were occupying and we removed my belongings."

"Why are you seeking an annulment, rather than a divorce?" my lawyer continued.

"There are no other grounds for divorce or legal separation. I asked Mohan to consent to a dissolution of our marriage. He didn't agree. He said our marriage vows bound us together until death and he could never accept a law which said otherwise."

"Did Mr. Bahadur try to contact you after you left the matrimonial home?" my lawyer questioned.

"Yes," I replied. "He attempted to kidnap me outside the Stabroek Market when I was on my way home, but a passing policeman intervened."

My lawyer then addressed the Court. "Your Honour, this is a copy of the incident report."

The judge accepted the copy, and told him to continue.

"Was there any other incident you would like to add?"

"Yes," I replied. "Mohan accused me of trying to murder him. The evidence he produced was a bottle of cough mixture, which contained ground glass. I was summoned to the police station, but after questioning, the sergeant agreed there was no evidence to support the accusation.

"This is our case, Your Honour."

At this stage, I felt nervous. I looked over to where my lawyers were sitting. They both looked confident and somehow transmitted this confidence to me. There was nothing to fear. I felt quite sure that Mohan had told Samuel Adams about my early trauma of rape and abuse. How would I respond to that? I believed it couldn't be used as part of the cross examination because Dr. Charles' evidence was that my hymen was intact when he examined me.

Samuel Adams thundered, "You're frigid and afraid to have sexual relations and that's the reason your marriage couldn't be consummated."

I said, "I'm not frigid. I'm a normal woman. I'm quite aware of sex and sexuality; Mohan couldn't get an erection and therefore couldn't perform the sexual act."

When the same question was asked and answered several times, my lawyer objected and the judge agreed they should move on.

Mr. Adams continued. "You're frigid because of childhood abuse. Do you deny this?"

My lawyer objected vehemently, "Your Honour, there's no foundation for such cross-examination. The defendant is trying to besmirch the reputation of my client. Dr. Charles stated under oath that the petitioner's hymen was intact at the time of his examination. No evidence to support the defendant's theory of 'frigidity' has been introduced. The defence is introducing a new component which is unsupported. This is insinuation not evidence."

The judge said, "Unless you intend to produce further evidence in support of your questioning, please move on."

Mr. Adams said, "Thank you, Your Honour. I have no further questions of this witness."

Mr. Fitzroy addressed the Court. "This concludes my case for the Petitioner."

The Judge then called on Mohan's lawyers to present their defence.

Dr. Sinclair Jacobs was their first witness.

His written report of the examination of both Mohan and myself was presented earlier to the Court. The document was given to the lawyers at the start of the trial. His evidence was in the main affirmation of the details in the report filed. I was not a virgin. The doctors couldn't say whether or not I was frigid, and that my frigidity had resulted in Mohan's inability to have intercourse with me.

With regard to Mohan's virility, Dr. Jacobs explained, "Mr. Mohan Bahadur was unable to get an erection and therefore couldn't provide a semen sample. I can't attest to the cause of the loss of virility, or impotence, only to the fact that the examination could not be completed because he couldn't ejaculate and produce any semen. In short, he couldn't get an erection."

"Shouldn't you have given him a second examination?" Mr. Adams asked.

Dr. Jacobs replied, "He was given sufficient time and materials which would cause men to get an erection. As far as my examination is concerned, I can only report that he didn't get an erection and so couldn't climax. That he should be given a second chance is not in my discretion. "

There was no cross-examination by my lawyers.

Mohan was next called to the stand and sworn in.

In answer to his counsel's questioning, he stated, "The plaintiff and I were married in Barbados. Our marriage couldn't be consummated because every time I tried to make love to her she would gasp and cry out. I became discouraged. I wanted her love and I couldn't bear it when she showed that making love with me was causing her distress. I only want to make her happy. I know that we can have a happy life together and I'm still very much in love with her."

His counsel asked, "You've lived together for eighteen months; how did she react when you indicated that you wanted to make love to her?"

"She would just go into her room and lock the door. When I tried to open it, she said she had a broom inside and if I did get in she would fend me off with it. I kept hoping for a change, and bought her gifts of perfume, jewelry, and flowers. When there was no change in her attitude, despite everything I could do, I became discouraged and accepted that this would be our life together. It's better to live with her, than without her."

"Despite her petition, you're still willing to take her back to the matrimonial home and resume your marriage?" Mr. Adams continued.

"I'd willingly welcome her back. As a matter of fact, I'm hoping this would be the outcome of this matter."

Under cross examination by my lawyer, Mr. Fitzroy, he seemed to lose control. He stated, "We've taken vows that we would be together 'till death parted us' and the Court should not disrespect this."

"Why did you fail to get an erection on your wedding night? This was a time of joy and happiness and a celebration of your love. This is the main purpose of marriage."

"I did have an erection but Tabitha didn't want to engage in sexual activities. She said it was unnatural behaviour. I tried to get her to respond to me, but when she wouldn't, I didn't want to hurt her feelings or do anything that would make her think of me as 'evil'. I thought time would settle the matter and that she would ultimately come to terms with her squeamishness."

"Why didn't you pursue the question of intercourse when you returned home?"

"I respect Tabitha. On her return home, she said she wanted her own room and would have nothing to do with me sexually. I didn't want to displease her so I agreed."

"You've lived with this woman for eighteen months, yet there's been no sexual activity between you. How do you account for that?"

"I didn't want to lose her. I told myself that half a loaf was better than no loaf. I was patient. I hoped she'd come to terms with me as her husband one day, and I was content to wait."

"You state that you are virile, so why didn't you get an erection during the court appointed examination?"

Mohan replied, "The Doctors' offices were too busy, there was no privacy, and I felt I was being judged and laughed at."

Mr. Fitzroy continued, "You've heard that the petitioner has had sexual intercourse with someone because her hymen isn't intact? How do you feel about this?"

He replied, "I love her and I forgive her."

"This concludes our evidence for the defence," Mr. Fitzroy told the Court.

Our respective lawyers summed up the cases they had presented to the Court. My lawyer asked for dissolution of the marriage on grounds of non-consummation. Mohan's lawyer said that the case was "inconclusive" because we hadn't proved that his client was impotent. Consequently, the case should be dismissed.

The judge said he would deliver his judgement in two weeks and the case was adjourned.

Mohan attempted to get over to me, but my lawyers quickly escorted me from the courtroom.

CHAPTER THIRTY-FOUR

THE CLOCK TICKS SLOWLY. I left the courthouse with my father. He had hugged me, then held me at arm's length, looking at me carefully in the face, trying to assess how I was coping. I recounted the proceedings and confided that the court case had gone much better than I anticipated. "Thank God that's over, Dad. I looked confident throughout; I did my best to hide my fears and uncertainty and I succeeded."

My father asked about Mohan. "He seems bitter and vengeful Dad, but Dr. Charles saved the day for me. Whatever he'd planned to bring about my downfall was stymied by the fact I'd lost my hymen. We talked about that and agreed that perhaps Dr. Charles had erred, but this had been beneficial to the outcome we'd hoped for.

"My lawyers are confident of success. Under both examination and cross Mohan never conducted himself in a believable manner. The defence failed to come up with anything that sounded truthful. His attempt to say that I'd been abused as a child seemed just a spiteful red herring and they were sure this would be discounted by the judge. His manner throughout his testimony added to the belief that he wasn't telling the truth."

"I'm glad that scoundrel got his just due in court. He'll never prosper, you'll see. He took advantage of you, and he must pay for it. There is justice, after all. Your mother will be pleased". His smiled as he looked at me said it all.

I wished I could take a few days off work, but I knew my boss had asked the Office Manager when I would be returning to work. British Guiana was going through a crisis and it was necessary to ensure that all systems of communication within the country were working. The government wanted "business as usual" so that politics wouldn't come into play and make the situation much worse than it was. We always wish for the impossible, but I wished that the judge had given his decision that day. I did mention this during discussions with my lawyers, but they countered that the judge had to make sure there would be no grounds for appeal, especially as the case was so unusual, probably the first of its kind in British Guiana.

The following day, while I was busy at work, my telephone rang. The caller was a friend of Mohan's inviting me to meet her after work for a chat. I asked, "Will Mohan be there?" She hemmed and hawed and then said, "He pleaded with me to help him. He's quite upset. He feels that if he can talk with you, you'll find it in your heart to forgive him. He loves you very much. I didn't want to interfere but he seemed so sincere, I felt sorry for him.

"You should know this is impossible," I replied. The matter of our divorce is still under judicial consideration. Mohan is bound by the letters my lawyers sent him. Any communication with me must be made through them. You're a good friend to both of us, but help and interference at this time does more harm than good."

Her reply stunned me. "The radio station is starting a new program called 'Lives loved, lived and lost,' Mohan is the host. The first episode will air on Sunday at 6 p.m. and the topic will be his own lost love. He wants to discuss this with you," she replied. "You're the heroine in his story."

This was a bombshell. I was angry and dismayed at the same time. "I don't care what Mohan wants, However, he should know that if he does anything which falls short of the law, we'll take action. He can tell the world how much he loves me, but it won't benefit him. I've severed all connections with him, and am now awaiting the final decision of the court. I'm looking forward to new beginnings and a new phase of my life. Forget his wants and needs; wish me well."

I hung up the telephone and thought, "This man will not rest until he has crucified me. I'll probably have to leave this country if I'm ever to be at peace."

That Sunday he did indeed start his radio show. He talked about his love for me and the tragedy that had been created in our lives because of parental interference and the betrayal by his friend, Mike, who was now courting his lost love. He was a good orator. The public loved it. The ratings went through the roof. It was reported that the audience were looking forward to the next episode with eager anticipation.

My lawyers quickly put an end to that. They served the radio station with a 'cease and desist' letter. If they continued to air the show, legal action would result.

Reaction was swift. Mohan's show was cancelled. However, for a long time I was subject to the jabs and puns about his love for me. I had become a 'person of interest'. I consoled myself by thinking this notoriety would fade in time or as soon as something else reared its head.

Two weeks later, on the date appointed by the court, the judge delivered judgement. My marriage was annulled on the grounds of non-consummation. I was free to get married in church. I could finally hold my head high. Gossip about my "carryings on" had proved to be an embellishment to gain sensationalism. My life was my own again.

I breathed a sigh of relief. There were secrets in my life I vowed never to share, but this didn't prevent those secrets from continuing to haunt me and mock my well being. "Will they ever disappear?" I questioned myself.

Freedom meant many things, but there were still cords that bound me. Life had limitless possibilities but limitations were placed on a female. Females didn't possess the same rights as men did. I could come up with bright ideas, but the rewards fell far from me. I desperately wanted to travel to London where I could begin a new life, study law and become a practicing lawyer. There was only one female lawyer in Guyana and she was from a family of lawyers. I dreamed the dream but it was like a bubble, floating away and disappearing before I could catch it.

Inevitably, the question arose, "When are you and Mike going to get married?" I usually replied, "Marriage is a long way ahead. My annulment won't be final for a year. I'll think about marriage then. In the meantime, I just want to live and enjoy being single for a while."

I liked earning my own money, being dependent on no one. Of course, I lived at home with my parents so board and lodging were free. I figured that by the end of my year of waiting, I would have saved a sizeable sum and I could set out to capture my dream. Would I be able to break through the glass ceiling? Women always seemed to be judged by their sex rather than by their aptitude. This was a time when no one thought women could ever equal the abilities attributed to men or even rise to higher pinnacles.

My parents counselled me. If I wanted a family, I had to get married soon. Child bearing years would end by the early thirties. I thought, *just soon enough to make it impossible for me to become a lawyer, return home, and start a family*. Mike was also pressuring me. He had been walking alongside me for more than five years and was a regular visitor to my home. He was my partner at dances and parties, and I know he had discouraged a few young men who wanted to woo me.

The role of a woman in those years, in British Guiana, seemed to be only that of housewife and mother. I had grown attached to Mike over the years. He had become a good friend and a constant companion. We could make a go of life as man and wife. He promised that he would give me everything I desired "earth, moon, and stars". We had a great friendship, and perhaps life with him would give me peace, security, and happiness.

My parents promised to deed me a house in Georgetown where we could make our home.

I pondered, I pondered, and I pondered. I was tired of fighting. My parents were probably right. I would find happiness in marriage and let my dream slip away. I agreed to get married to Mike six months after the decree of dissolution was made final. We went to the best jewelry shop in Georgetown. I selected a ring and he paid for it.

My parents were overjoyed. I would be settled at last. They felt a home with children and a loving husband would fill me with happiness and dispel the past. I bought into that dream, but secretly feared it would never become my reality.

CHAPTER THIRTY-FIVE

WEDDING PREPARATIONS. It was time to celebrate, time to be happy. The wedding would be the biggest and best Vreed-en-Hoop had ever seen. Two celebrations were planned. The first would be a feast where the entire village would be feted and entertained, and the second a traditional Guyanese celebration. The wedding ceremony would take place in St. Swithun's Anglican Church, the day following the village feast. Guests would be entertained to a banquet, with dancing to follow.

After the ceremony on their return to the venue, the happy couple would be showered with rice and flower petals. The rice would ensure that their union would be fruitful, the flower petals bespoke the richness and happiness to follow. Before entering as Mr. and Mrs., the couple would be greeted by the mother of the bride, who would offer them ceremonial glasses of wine, a token of their new status and the joy their marriage would bring not only to themselves but also to their families. There would be speeches and the cutting of the cake, the first dance for the bride and groom, and then the start of the festivities, dining, and dancing.

My wedding dress was specially ordered. The wedding cake was to be made by my mother, and decorations done by Art Coggins, a celebrated cake decorator. An orchestra was engaged and decorators hired to turn the cinema hall into a place of splendour.

Our home and the front of the cinema would be illuminated by 'fairy' lights for a week before and a week after the wedding. It would truly be a grand celebration. As there was no electricity in the village, these illuminations alone would express the happiness of the family and the importance of the occasion.

I began to feel a little queasy after a while. I kept busy at work. This time around I wouldn't be forced to give up my job. It was the expectation of the General Manager that I would return from my honeymoon three weeks after the wedding, but I would be away from work for four weeks.

I was again projected into the limelight. The wedding was fodder for the Gossip Gang who seemed always to be able to corner me to find out how far along things were and any special details of related happenings.

I felt tired and I wanted to run away and escape from it all. Alas, I felt I owed my parents the joy this wedding was bringing to them after the turmoil of the previous years. I shopped for furniture and furnishings for my new home. Deep down I hoped everything would be all right this time around.

Invitations were sent two months before the wedding.

Wedding invitations to the villagers were sent in the Indian tradition. Rice was dyed yellow with turmeric, and a village woman who specialized in the tradition was hired to deliver the *'nauta'* (an invitation) to the feast taking place the day before the wedding.

The master chefs of the village were hired to prepare meals for both occasions. Everything was slowly coming together. I had fittings for the wedding dress and changes made when my parents were not satisfied.

Relatives came to visit. Joy and feasting were part of my pre-wedding celebrations and I couldn't change that. Everyone was happy for me and nothing could stop them. I thought it would obliterate the unhappiness of the past, but it only erased it for a time.

Our home was changed into a hive of activity. Laughter, joy, and happiness filled the air and surrounded me with love. It was a gift to me that spoke of forgiveness, love, and understanding.

The week before, huge cooking pots appeared. Cooking would take place in the yard. Tents appeared as if by magic. All efforts were centred on the tasks in hand. Food preparation was all important; decorations to the cinema hall had turned it into an important venue.

The cooks held various conferences with my parents. Pre-dinner appetizers were ordered from the city and would arrive the day of the wedding. Rum and coca cola, whisky and sodas would come from my father's rum shop. Everything was settled. This event was meant to erase the past, wipe the slate clean, and give me a fresh start in my life.

The local butcher slaughtered sheep and prepared the meat for curries. The cooks took over after that. There was singing and dancing by Indian dancers throughout the night. The next morning, six women appeared; they were responsible for preparing the roti and puris for the feast.

I was expected to make an appearance at the feast, but this was limited to half an hour. I had to get my rest so I could 'shine' on my wedding day.

Truth to tell, I was transported into the land of the fairy tales of my youth. Someone waved a magic wand, the past was forgotten, and the future promised to be happy. The tale would end "they lived happily ever after". I wondered "Dare I wish for a happy ending?"

CHAPTER THIRTY-SIX

M Y WEDDING DAY dawned bright and clear. I made a promise to myself, *"This day is going to change my life. I'll put aside my past and any fear that still lingers. My wedding day will be the start of a successful life, a new beginning filled with dreams and hopes. I'm not the shrinking child where fear walked beside me, nor the wife chained by a husband who'd used blackmail to coerce me into a union. I am free. Mike is a good man. We're going to be happy."*

Nora, one of the maids, interrupted my thoughts. She was very excited as she delivered a parcel. I told her to leave it with the others, but she was intrigued because it arrived by special delivery, giving rise to her curiosity. Her face was bright with anticipation and excitement as she pleaded, "Please Miss Tabby, it's your wedding day. It's so beautifully wrapped; it must contain something beautiful."

I looked at her face, so full of anticipation and joy. *Perhaps I could be gracious and succumb to her pleadings.* I opened the parcel slowly. There was a small box inside. I thought, '*This looks like a jewelry box; who could've sent me jewelry? This is most unusual.*'

I lifted the cover. Inside lay a gold bracelet, which gleamed and glittered as the diamonds inlaid within it caught the light. I opened the card and almost lost my composure. I read, "You're my wife. I'll not stand in the way of your getting hitched to Mike. You swore before God, 'Till death do us part.' I'll be waiting for you and I'll love you always."

Nora noticed the shocked look on my face and started to apologize. "It's not your fault, Nora." Please let my dad know I'd like to see him when he has a moment."

Nora returned. "He's on his way."

"I should've expected something like this from Mohan," I whispered as I went into his outstretched arms when he saw the horrified look on my face. He held me close and stroked my back. "Whatever's wrong, we can make it right."

"Please send this package to our lawyers and ask them to return it to Mohan with a 'cease and desist' order. I can't let him spoil this day. There'll never be another one like this in my life, and I want to remember it always. You've done so much to make it happy for me. No princess could have asked for more."

I shushed my father when he said, "Let me ask Nen Nellie, your godmother, to come and keep you company. All the relatives wanted to be together with you, but I thought you might want to be alone."

"I'm all right, just irritated and annoyed. It's simply Mohan's way of trying to provoke me and spoil my day, but I won't let him. I'll go and linger with them instead."

My wedding celebrations were perfect. It was the first day of my new life, filled with humorous banter, much laughter, and joy. Crowds gathered outside the village church and then followed the bridal party to the reception. It reminded me of wedding scenes from movies, and it was happening to me in my own backyard. The happiness of the crowd and the wedding guests embraced me. I was their fairy tale princess.

As we were about to leave the reception that night, my father hugged as both. His face was inscrutable as he turned to Mike,

"Tabitha is not property. She's a vibrant woman and I love her dearly. She's endured a lot, but that's the past. If you ever lay a hand on her, or ill-treat her, back home she comes. She's now your wife, but she'll always be my daughter, under my care, and don't you ever forget that."

What brought about this admonishment? I wondered, but hid it at the back of my mind. *What was my father trying to say?*

In the happiness and joy of the moment I decided the past was the past. *I'll close the door on it and concentrate on the future. Dwelling on the past is simply a waste of time. It brings nothing but pain. Welcoming the future provides new avenues for happy thoughts, new ideas to ponder, new worlds to conquer.* Doubts and uncertainties seemed to slip away. The future was up to me. The fairy tale ending, *"And they lived happily after"* would bless my union with Mike and it was the legacy I would create.

As I walked down the stairs to get to the car, I looked up at the sky. The moonlight added enchantment. If it's to be, it was up to me. There was nothing and no one to stop me. I was starting life with a clean slate. There were no secrets to unburden.

The leaves of the flamboyant trees rustled as the wind disturbed their peace, provoking a feeling that disturbed me. *Is this an omen?* I wondered.

CHAPTER THIRTY-SEVEN

WOMAN IS NOT EQUAL TO MAN. Sometimes, no matter how hard you try, nothing ever seems to work out. This was still the time when husbands made all the decisions and wives had very little or no input. Women were simply expected to fall in line and obey. Quite soon, it appeared the honeymoon period was over. Our first quarrel arose when Mike asked, right hand held out as if to receive something and face set in forbidding lines, eyes daring me to refuse "Where's your pay check?"

My face mirrored the shock and surprise I felt as I replied, "I banked it, as usual. What's the matter? Do we need money for something? Are you short?" I smiled reassuringly. "Whatever it is, we can fix it."

"We're married now, and I control the finances," he scolded, the look on his face daring me to refute this, chastising me because I had erred. "During a conversation I had with Nelson, my brother, he advised that control of the finances rests with me. What you earn should be given to me. Men control the finances of the Union."

"Why are you bringing this up now?" I questioned. "Surely, if you had a problem you should've discussed this with me, rather than with Nelson? We could have arrived at a solution agreeable to us both. Raising this question now makes me believe that you stuck by me all those years because of money, not because you loved me". My face registered the anger and surprise I felt.

"I don't see why you're making this such a big issue. Husbands look after finances and wives have no problem with this. Wives agree because this is normal. Why are you being difficult?" His hands were now folded across this body, as if he needed to keep control and not give in to his temper.

"I'm being difficult because it seems your brother wants to influence the goings-on in our marriage, and I'll have none of that. Decisions are made by us, not by you alone. We combine our earnings and determine a workable budget. Planning for the future is our responsibility, not yours, not mine, but ours; our future and what we achieve depends on both of us." I glared at him. There was determination in my voice; we were enjoined in battle.

"Well, that isn't what I want. You'll hand over your pay cheque and I'll determine where the money goes," he retorted in a commanding tone.

"Too bad," I laughed. "You told me during our courtship that your earnings were greater than mine. What exactly is the amount of your monthly pay cheque?" I raised my eyebrows and stared at him, through stony eyes, daring him to refuse to disclose that information.

I was adamant about learning what he earned, and eventually, when he confirmed the amount, I realized I was the better wage earner. I felt sorry for creating such a big issue about money. What we earned together was the important factor. He obviously didn't want me to know that I brought in more than he did. This didn't sit easily with him. It could mean loss of his control in our marriage. That we worked together to build our future was more important than who brought in what. I didn't like his brother being a part of our planning, and was daunted by the knowledge that no matter how much I disapproved, Nelson would always have a say in our financial affairs.

I knew Mike was aware that his brother had tried to establish a love relationship with me years ago, but I hadn't reciprocated. I wondered how much this rejection was behind his determination to interfere.

I reminded Mike of this but he ignored me and broached another complaint. "When is your father going to transfer ownership of the property he promised to you?" *Why is he bringing this up again? Is this meant as a put down? Is he accusing my family of offering him a bribe to get married to me?*

I shook my head in disgust, *would I never learn?* "I thought you loved me, Mike. I didn't know that Dad's financial assets played a part in your love. I feel foolish. This isn't you. It's your brother's interference in our affairs. If something bothers you, let's talk about it. We must make decisions which affect us both together, not because of someone else's advice. Your brother is probably jealous. But understand this, I'll make a success of our lives together. You'll help, not hinder because you're a part of this venture. Let's make our own decisions. Don't let other people interfere. Nelson is the main wage earner in his family and whatever affects him is of no concern to us; what we do in our household is our own business. We don't need help or advice. Did you ask him for guidance?" I probed.

My conciliatory tone must have fooled him into thinking I was falling in line. "You don't know what you're talking about," was his response. "I don't much care about these new-fangled notions about women's rights. I want you to give me your cheque each month, and I'll make the budget." His face was set in a forbidding stare. I suspected that if there was a table nearby he would be pounding his fists on it.

"Shall I give up my job, and just keep house for you?" I countered with a smiling face knowing we couldn't live on his salary.

"If I go out to work and earn money, I expect to have a say in how it's spent. It's that or nothing. The choice is yours. I won't allow your brother or your family to interfere. It's no concern of theirs. I've grown up, Mike; I'm not the person I was when Mohan felt he had control over me. No man, husband or otherwise, can exert control of me. I'm not an animal to be horse whipped and trained to obey. I've learned my lesson well. I value the person I am and I fight for my beliefs."

Mike didn't give up easily, "I want an answer about the property. If I'm not careful, your brothers will get it all."

What's wrong with these men, I asked myself, but I smiled "You seem to have forgotten that the property was promised to me, not to you. Don't disregard that piece of good news. If and when it's transferred is my problem, not yours."

I shook my head wearily, my body slumped in dismay and disgust. "If this is so important to you, why don't you speak to my father about it? I'm not going to pursue it. Remember his parting words to us when we were leaving on our honeymoon after the reception. If you have a problem, discuss it with him. Don't take it out on me."

I felt torn between two cultures; the Indian culture, which placed male values as the determining factor, and the culture I had gleaned from my education. In that split-second I determined that I needed to assert myself. I couldn't live under male domination. I wasn't chattel to be bought and sold. Women had equal rights under the law.

I continued, "This quarrel can end here and now. I'll repeat this again. We, not your brother nor your family, decide on our welfare and our plans. I won't tolerate any discussion with them about my affairs nor any gossip about me when I'm not present. I've faced marital problems before and I'm not afraid to face them again. I'm married to you and will be mindful of what you care about, but their opinion means nothing to me." The tone of my voice, the shrug of my shoulders, and the strength of my words took him aback.

I was quite surprised at my own response. But it spun from all the little changes that tarnished my concept of romance and wedded bliss. I was expected to cook, clean, and do the laundry; in fact, every chore that made a household run. It seemed I had given up all the benefits I enjoyed in my parents' household for a mythical happiness that existed only in fairly tales.

I was bemused by my thoughts. It seemed that in my struggles to catch a rainbow, I missed out; somehow its enchantment and promise had eluded me but left me with the hope, *Next time will be better.*

Mike interrupted my thoughts. "I'm going to visit Boysie Ramcharan. What time will dinner be ready?"

"I'm glad you brought that up," I replied. "This is a good time to talk about our future. I'm not going to do all the household chores, cook your dinner, earn money, and take orders from you. I, too, wish to spend time with friends, but this isn't possible. Two full-time jobs are more than I'm prepared to manage. We need to divide the chores, prepare a budget where we have equal input, and manage our spare time to ensure equality. We have only one car. I expect use of it when I want to get out."

"This is highly irregular. I'm tired repeating this. I don't support women's rights. I'm the boss in this household."

"You're playing mind games, and I'm not going to be a part of it. Marriage means sharing and from here on, we will share. I'll prepare a list of duties I think you can and should manage and we'll take it from there." I glared at him through stormy eyes, daring him to refuse.

A housekeeper to do cooking, laundry, and household chores would ease the pressure of household responsibilities. If Mike still thought he could push me into handing over my cheque to him, he had another thought coming. I was going to prepare a budget where he would pay for the items assigned to him and I would pay for those that fell into my portion. I wouldn't let him control what I earned.

I'm no longer going to be party to men who get married to find someone to ease their burdens through life. I'll be a slave to no one. I'm going to be happy and not allow myself to become downtrodden. The time has come to assert myself and take my future into my own hands, I whispered to myself *but I didn't want to return to my parents' home because this would reflect on me. Everyone would whisper "Another failed marriage!"*

My father had always reminded us that we were each responsible for our future and our happiness. He always asked, 'If you want a coconut from the tree, will you lie under the tree and wait for a capricious wind to gust and blow it down to you, or are you going to climb the tree and get it for yourself? Remember, Jason wanted the Golden Fleece. He didn't pray to the Gods to give it to him; he prayed for courage and strength to find it and claim it for his own.'

Dad was an avid reader and a wise man. His tales always had lessons to be learned, much like Aesop and his fables. He always told us that the first step towards a goal was the hardest. If you can forget your fears and take that first step, the rest came easily. He reminded us all, boys and girls, that this was the way forward for everyone.

The time had come for me to loosen the shackles that held me prisoner. No one could help me. "If it is to be, it's up to me". These words would continue to be my credo, the doctrine that would motivate and inspire me to speak up for myself. I could support myself financially. My skills were marketable. I didn't need someone to provide for me. Women were just as capable as men. The very fact that I was the major wage earner and my boss valued my work, signified this.

There was no doubt in my mind that I could make my marriage work and secure a good future while I was about it.

I said, "Mike, we've arrived at the turning point in our lives. We're partners, not 'boss and slave.' I will not turn my salary over to you. I'll prepare a spreadsheet. This will show our assets and our liabilities, and detail our monthly costs, which will include our hiring someone to do the chores I now do on my own. I will divide the cost between us. That'll settle matters pertaining to the household. On the question of when or whether the promised property will be turned over to us, it's best that you speak to my father about this."

"I don't agree," he retorted, and turned to leave.

"I won't be put off by your tantrums," I cautioned. "If this doesn't satisfy you, we can go our separate ways. I'm accustomed to gossip. I want our marriage to work, but you must understand that the world is changing. I want your love and your respect. Happiness can only be ours if you understand that man and woman are equal, and neither is the dominating factor. Marriage means we're equally joined and we have equal rights."

He walked out of the house, got into our car, and drove out of the yard.

My heart was heavy, and my mind churned with unhappy thoughts. At work I was treated with respect, the quality of my contribution was recognized. I was human, not beast. At home where I should have been happiest I was regarded as chattel, owned by someone else. Life wasn't fair, and then I remembered, *"if it is to be, it's up to me."* If I felt I was beating my head against a stone wall, I had the power to change it.

CHAPTER THIRTY-EIGHT

DOWRY OR GIFT. I understood Mike had to maintain "face" with his brother and his friends. It would take a while before change happened. I went ahead and employed a housekeeper. Mike had thrown my list aside and grunted when I told him of my arrangements. Our quarrels were shelved, but we were an uneasy household.

Things changed when he decided we needed a new car. He didn't have the capital himself and needed my help. "Hurrah," I laughed quietly. "My time has come."

I showed him how much better we would have been if we had pooled our resources, and he agreed. We bought the car, registered it in both our names, and divided the monthly payment equally.

Mike was gracious. He thanked me for reorganizing our finances and life settled down once again. We danced the last Saturday of each month at the Caribe, the social spot for the Georgetown crowd, picnicked on Sundays, and life was full and happy again. I had time for reading, dreaming, and dressmaking. I improved my culinary skills, cake baking, and cake decorating. I decorated wedding cakes for my friends and family, and became an overall expert in the kitchen. I was happy at work.

Life settled down and I was relaxed and content. Then our quarrels started again. Transfer of the property reared its head. Mike raised the question one evening after dinner. I said, "Mike, my father will transfer the property eventually, whenever he gets around to it."

"We've been married for over a year, and he's done nothing about it. Perhaps he's changed his mind. This is so unjust. Promises should be kept," he countered staring me in the face, his eyes full of blame and condemnation.

This argument had come at a bad time. It was the start of my period, my workday had been heavy, and all I wanted to do was to get to bed with some pain killers.

"Did you get married to me because of the status of my parents and my inheritance?" I queried, weariness in my voice. "This property is something promised by my father to me. He didn't offer it to you as a dowry, it was a gift to me. The property is mine. I'm happy with the situation as it is. Why can't you be happy also? Won't you be as proud as a peacock if we're able to buy a home for ourselves without any help?"

"You always twist everything I say. I'm looking out for your interests. If you don't want to remind your father of his promise, he may give the property to one of your brothers. How would that make you feel?" he responded with a self-satisfied look, daring me to contradict him.

"It's his property to do with as he wishes. If he desires to give it to my brother, that's okay with me. I don't need to have the status of property owner to be happy. He gave me an education and a skill which I can use. It would demean me to remind him of his promise," I countered wearily.

"I can't understand you. He promised you the property. You should remind him of this and ask him to transfer it to your name. Even if we don't live there, we can rent it; it will supplement our income and help us to get ahead faster." His look, his tone, and his body language indicated his feelings, "*Why are you so stupid. Don't you know that you're missing out?*"

"Mike, please don't bother me. I'm exhausted. I have a migraine and I'm going to lie down. I refuse to have any discussion with you about property. You made me a lot of promises before we got married and I've never reminded you of them. If the property is a problem in our marriage, then it might be better for us to split up. We can live apart for a year and then apply to the court for a divorce."

I turned, went into the bedroom, and slammed the door. The sound of its reverberation through the house eased my feelings somewhat.

He waited for a few minutes, and then I heard him opening the door. "It might be better for you to sleep in the other room for a while. I want peace and privacy," I said in a tone which brooked no response.

He countered disparagingly, "You can't even have a child. Who are you? You're right. We're not happy. It's time to say goodbye and start again. Nothing can come of this marriage." He quietly left the room.

It was a sobering reflection. More things to ponder, more solutions to find for what seemed to be turning into an insoluble problem. I didn't want to remind my father about his promise. Living in a big and rambling old house wasn't part of my reality. The adjacent land was also promised to my sister and one brother. The entire property would have to be surveyed before it could be transferred.

I felt a sense of humiliation when I thought of reminding my father that I was awaiting transfer of the land. My parents provided me with tools, an education, and a good upbringing, and it was up to me to build a life without further help from them. It was true that owning the land would elevate us financially, and the rent it could bring would be pure savings, but asking my father about his intentions was like attaching a weight to my ankles and forcing me to run a five-mile race.

I drifted off to sleep but my night was tortured with dreams where everyone and everything seemed to be after me. It was a return to my childhood with snakes and vampires. *Will I never be free?* I wondered.

I got out of bed to go to the washroom. I fell to the floor and passed out. When I regained my senses I opened my eyes and saw Mike looking at me. "What's the matter?" he said. "You fainted and fell to the floor. You were out for about two minutes. What's happening?"

"I don't know. I was just going to the bathroom. I mustn't have been totally awake and perhaps I slid on the mat or something," I replied. "It's a good thing it's Saturday and I don't have to go to work. I'll just remain in bed. You'll have to help yourself today." I hated to ask, but I would have liked to have a cup of tea. To my surprise, a few minutes after, he brought in a tray with toast and coffee.

"I'm sorry about last night. I noticed how tired you looked. It wasn't the time for a discussion. I just don't want to see you lose out on something promised to you. Your father does favour his sons even though he loves his daughters more, and I suspect that if he isn't pressed he'll forget you." He was at his conciliatory best.

"The property belongs to him. He promised to give it to me, but I won't feel good if I pressured him. Our quarrels always start with that property. Can't you forget that promise?" I pleaded.

"It really burns me up to think that they'll deprive you, but if that's what you want, we'll forget it." I didn't believe his conciliatory manner of dismissing the subject represented his true feeling and I knew this wasn't the end of the matter.

"You promise?" I persisted, with a doubting look on my face.

"Yes," was his reply. I won't mention it again.

We settled down, but I felt uneasy. Perhaps there was jealousy because my brothers had gone abroad, attended universities, and returned home qualified in their professions. They were well respected and to all accounts, their future was secure. However, I must admit, they were somewhat condescending to us because Mike didn't have the same education or earning power and we lagged behind them.

Status was never important to me. Now I understood that because of my past, Mike thought I was second-best and property ownership would raise my status. I was the scarlet woman. Being a businessman and owning property would equalize our situations and make him feel better. "Should I speak to my father?" was the burning question. I was content in my marriage. However, I'd never felt the ecstasy of being in love, sexual intercourse was a hit or miss affair, and I could well do without all the bother, except for the fact that children were a necessary part of my life.

I decided to write to my parents and ask if they had changed their minds about giving me the property. I explained that I wanted to make plans for the future and property ownership was important. I was careful to stress that if they had changed their minds, I would understand.

My father replied that he was already in process of getting legalities concluded. He was glad I had raised the matter because a new business venture had kept him busy and that had delayed fulfilment. He added that when we visited at Vreed-en-Hoop again, he would discuss the transfer. Formalities were in hand and he expected the whole process to be complete within the next three to six months.

I shared the letter with Mike. I could see the joy in his eyes. Status was very important to him. The stigma of being married to a divorced woman would disappear. I stilled the doubts in my mind, but they kept recurring.

CHAPTER THIRTY-NINE

MIKE'S FAMILY HISTORY. To be fair to Mike, he'd bought their family home from his parents when they had fallen on bad times. His mother still lived there and it was an unwritten condition of his ownership that she would end her life there. He couldn't dispose of the property until she died. Perhaps his own insecurity was causing him to make sure that my father's estate didn't all go to my brothers.

His parents' marriage had been rocky throughout. His father, Ramharry was well-educated. He fell in love with Erlinda, one of the daughters of a wealthy landowner and the Union was blessed with five children. Ramharry earned his living as a Coconut Estate Manager in Essequibo, one of the counties of British Guiana. In the early days, the family lived with him in Essequibo, but when the children reached age school age, he bought property in Vreed-en-Hoop. The family took up residence there and he returned to his job in Essequibo.

Life was lonely and he soon found comfort with the daughter of one of the Coconut Estate workers. This caused conflict with Erlinda. Conflict brought out the worst in him. The family dreaded his return to Vreed-en-Hoop every three months and sighed with relief when he left. Unfortunately, the expense of maintaining two households was difficult.

Money was tight. The family in Vreed-en-Hoop could barely eke out an existence from the money Ramharry provided. Erlinda was determined that her children shouldn't go hungry. She decided to go into business. The backlands of her home were turned into a "kitchen" garden where she grew tomatoes and other vegetables. She bought a cow which fed on the grass in the back yard. The cow calved, milk was provided, and the calf was sold. She earned some money from these 'home' businesses, but not enough to satisfy the needs of her growing family.

Her fortunes changed the day a peddler stopped by at her house and displayed the merchandise he was selling. He explained that a city merchant imported discarded and unused remnants of cloth from clothing manufacturers in the USA. They were bundled willy-nilly in pound lots and shipped to the colonies. Peddlers like him sold the bundles to people like her who couldn't often travel to purchase what they needed from stores in the city. There was always a variety of material so everyone was satisfied.

Ready-made clothing wasn't available in British Guiana. People either made clothes for themselves or employed seamstresses and tailors.

He showed her a catalogue with a variety of ready-to-wear clothing for men, women, and children. She went through the catalogue with him and an idea blossomed. She would buy remnants from him and employ a seamstress who lived nearby to make clothes and hats for children. She would sell these garments as well as needles and thread and other sewing accessories, which were difficult to obtain locally. She had no money, but owned the land she'd inherited from her father.

Despite land ownership she couldn't obtain a loan from the bank. Banks wouldn't deal with her because she was a woman.

This didn't deter her. She went to the local money-lender, signed a note, and embarked upon her project.

Houses in Vreed-en-Hoop were built on stilts to avoid damage from flooding. She hired a carpenter to enclose the bottom and build her some shelves. She bought a sewing machine and set up her business. Her venture took off and was profitable for a few years. She built a reputation as a fair trader but was unable to keep up with the local competition which followed her success. Several enterprising villagers followed her example, and two similar shops sprang up. They undersold her and forced her out of business. Eventually, as larger businesses opened up, they couldn't compete and were themselves forced out of their businesses.

Meanwhile, Mike's father lost his job and returned to Vreed-en-Hoop. Jobs in his field were few and far between. He undertook accounting and bookkeeping duties for businesses, on an 'as needed basis,' but the household depended on the money Erlinda earned. The loss of his job and the difficulty obtaining a similar position meant loss of face, and he took out his frustrations on Erlinda and the children.

Ramharry died during a Yellow Fever outbreak several years later.

Mike's working career began early. He became the major wage earner. The family plan was that his earnings would help pay for Nelson to attend secondary school. In turn, Nelson would help pay for his education after his graduation.

In the years that followed Mike renovated the family home.

After Nelson graduated, Mike felt it was too late for him to return to school. Time for education had passed him by, and he felt he would be better off if he continued in the workforce, especially as an opportunity for promotion to company secretary had opened at the same time.

Times in British Guiana were changing. Wages and working conditions were key elements in the dissatisfaction of the working class. Women wanted equality. Political pressure was the only way out.

India had a hard-fought battle for independence. The British Raj no longer held sway. British Guiana could follow the lead of colonies fighting for freedom from Colonial rule.

Erlinda still ran her shop on a much smaller scale. She had earned the respect of the village through her entrepreneurship, her kindness, and fair trade dealings. A devoted Hindu and leader in the Temple, she taught Hindi to anyone who cared to learn. She was a recognized leader in the East Indian community.

Janet Jagan, American born wife of Cheddi Jagan, leader of the People's Progressive Party, started a women's arm of the Party around this time. Erlinda was inspired. She became one of the early recruits. *(As an aside, many years after Guyana's turmoil, Janet was elected President of Guyana, the only American woman ever to hold the title of 'President' of a country).*

Erlinda worked with her and joined the fight for better government. Her older sons, Mike and Nelson, didn't like her involvement in politics, principally because she was a woman, whose place was in the home, but she was determined to join the crusade for fair wages, and equality for women.

I had the greatest respect for Erlinda. She was the mainstay of her family, providing for her children and encouraging them on.

She was kind to me, and the best mother-in-law. She always sang my praises and offered encouragement. When she noticed the 'goings on' between Mike and me, she frequently reminded me that she'd told me Mike was 'difficult' – always looking for something he could turn into an issue.

CHAPTER FORTY

PROMISE FULFILLED. Legalities settled the division of property promised by my father, and ownership was transferred to me three months later. My father insisted that the deed should be in my name only. If I wanted Mike to be joint owner it was up to me. However, he made me promise to wait a while before making any changes.

Mike wasn't happy about this. He felt ownership gave me too much control and also shut him out of the process. We leased the house, and the rent was a big boost to our income.

Life settled down, but no matter how hard we tried, it seemed I couldn't get pregnant. The fault, of course, always rested with the woman. When I could no longer bear the aspersions of failed womanhood because pregnancy was not happening, I decided to take matters in my own hands.

"Mike," I said, "I've doing some research. I've found a doctor who has succeeded in treatment of women having difficulty getting pregnant. It's expensive, but I think it'd be worthwhile."

He jumped at the idea. "You're always dieting and exercising and I'm sure that's the cause of our not getting a child. Your pregnancy would make me very happy because I've heard whisperings that I'm at fault and that you've made a second bad choice of a husband. You've always seemed more interested in a career than in being a mother. Consulting this doctor is a good step."

Sometimes I wondered where the Mike who courted me had disappeared. On the outside, it seemed we had a happy life, but whatever love I felt originally had fallen to second place. He always berated me in company, drawing attention to my failures and what he considered my shortcomings. We quarreled over this, but nothing ever seemed to resolve the situation. It seemed he was determined to put me down in company in order to underline his dominance and control.

Rather than feel the discomfort of quarrelling in public I started declining invitations to the usual run of dances and picnics. Instead, we went to the movies on weekends. The euphoria of a good movie always gave me something to think about. Movies continued to be an education for me and unconsciously changed my focus on "happiness." I returned to the time when I was two people: one who dwelled inside my consciousness, and the other who smiled and made the correct responses. It was like a Jekyll and Hyde-like existence.

I created a world inside my head where I was the best person I could be. I longed to have a child to nurture and to cherish. The ache inside me was sometimes unbearable. When this ache happened, I put more effort into my job and the response of my boss to my suggestions and ideas became a panacea.

The doctor who was recommended questioned me closely. He outlined several medical procedures he said would help, but after six months he suggested that the fault might not lie with me.

I asked, "Doctor Bissessar, what would you suggest?"

"Tell your husband to come and see me, and we'll take it from there," was his reply.

I was afraid to approach Mike with this. His comments always tore me to shreds. I didn't show any reaction to his remarks, but this didn't deter him.

I broached the subject. "I've been going to the doctor for over six months with no good results. He'd like you to make an appointment to see him."

"Why would he want to see me?" he countered. "I have no trouble in that direction. Not like Mohan," he laughed.

I replied, "There's more to it than just ejaculation. I read in a magazine that sometimes the sperm count is low, and this could be a problem. The Doctor will explain everything to you." I couldn't resist adding, "Don't talk to me about Mohan. You introduced us and praised him to high heaven. You just stepped out of the way when he turned his attention to me. If, as you say, you loved me, why didn't you put up a fight? All the suspicions you mentioned after the marriage, why didn't you air them? I want a child, and if we can't have one together, adoption will be our only course."

He was very unhappy about this. Men did not like their virility questioned. They waved their penises like wands and women were expected to sway in longing, content for them to be the master. They seemed only anxious to please themselves, giving little thought to the expectations of their partners. 'Good' women were not expected to take pleasure from sex.

Why am I having to be bothered by this? Hadn't I had enough in my childhood and my first marriage? Why am I having to forever do battle with sex and sexuality? All I want now is a child. Surely the fates will be kind to me. I've been brutally used to satisfy lust. Now I only want someone to love and care for, someone who will love me, my soul cried out in anguish.

It was my turn to storm out of the room. I took the car keys and strode towards the door. Mike tried to stop me, but one look at my face told him not to bother.

I drove to the Sea Wall in Georgetown. It was the gathering place for all on Saturdays and Sundays. On Saturdays the Police Band entertained with musical performances. They gave renditions of popular music in the pergola, erected to add beauty to the area. On Sundays this was a common meeting place. It was always possible to meet someone you knew here and exchange a word or two in pleasant conversation.

Like Vreed-en-Hoop, Georgetown was situated on the coast and thus was also below sea level. Walls had been built by the Dutch to keep out the ocean and prevent flooding in the city. Fishermen frequented this spot at high tide as fish was prolific. Small fish we called "four-eye" fish could be seen swimming in shoals. Shrimp was also plentiful and fishermen would take specially made nets and walk to where they were swimming to make a catch. When the tide went out, we could see little crabs and other small creatures running around in search of food. At night, it was the haunt of lovers, an idyllic spot which gave zest to their love.

The porch was deserted. I wearily climbed the two steps which led to the platform. I told myself, "My life has no purpose. Living has again become burdensome. I've lost the will to exist. In addition, life with Mike is also becoming oppressive. We hardly ever walk side by side. He always walks six steps ahead of me whenever we go out. We don't hold hands. When I reach out to him, he always grunts and asks, 'what do you think you're doing?'"

A voice in my mind replied, "You try too hard on yourself and do too much. Go on a holiday by yourself. Try to relax and maybe the future might not be so bad after all."

As it grew dark, I decided it was time to return home and face the music. Mike was sure to raise a quarrel, and I was too tired. He was out on my return. He had had his supper without me, so that was that.

On his return home, he told me he would go to see the Doctor.

"I'm simply overjoyed," I said. "I want a child to cement our lives together."

Six months into his weekly visits to get needles of vitamin and other supplements, I arose with one of my migraines and the need to vomit. On his visit to the Doctor, he told him about this. "Well, Mike my boy, I think we're on our way. Take care of her and you both come to see me next week."

Doctor Bissessar confirmed that I was pregnant, and I gave a whoop of delight. He said, "Mike, I told you something was cooking in there. You must take care of her now. She's fragile and will need extra care. We don't want to lose this one."

Mike was overjoyed. I thought he would have hugged me and was disappointed when he didn't. I guess he didn't want to show emotion to the Doctor.

Of course I'll take care of myself. This child growing within my body will provide the happiness I couldn't find with a partner. Finally, my life will bring me emotional warmth and well-being. I needed no counselling in that respect.

I bought and read all the books I could find on prenatal care. My mother told me that this was all a lot of rubbish, but I replied, "These are modern times, Mother. Positive thoughts, talking to the baby, caressing it by rubbing my tummy are significant breakthroughs in pre-natal care." My parents were both overjoyed, as was my mother-in-law, Erlinda.

I registered with the most accredited family specialist doctor, a noted maternity specialist in Georgetown, and decided to follow his advice precisely. Headaches still bothered me. They were a misery, but I imbibed a local painkiller, which seemed to help me through these periods.

Coincidentally, at this time, a Commission of Enquiry was sent down by the British Parliament to investigate incidents of violence which happened during a strike of sugar estate workers. The Commission was scheduled to be in session for three weeks.

Their job was to enquire into the death of workers during an attempt to break a strike on one of the sugar estates, and the rioting and nationwide strikes which resulted. Political leaders stood firm in their demand for justice,

The Commission of Enquiry needed verbatim reports of all proceedings. Court reporters were few and far between. There were few stenographers equipped with the necessary requirement of 150 words per minute in shorthand or who were experienced in this field. I was one of a few and top of the list because I also held a certificate for 160 words per minute in addition to my experience as a court reporter.

My services were requisitioned by the government. Despite protests by my boss, I was seconded to work with the Enquiry. The length of time required would mean my pregnancy would be nearing the end. "If birth occurs early what would happen?" I enquired. "We'll solve that problem when we come to it," was the reply.

I spoke to my doctor about this. He was dubious but said he wouldn't intervene if I wanted to serve as a reporter at the Enquiry. He was willing to prescribe Thalidomide, a new drug on the market, recommended to ease headaches and make pregnancy easier. I told him I would consider it if my headaches and general feeling required medication, but I didn't want to ingest anything unnatural. He reminded me that I was taking locally made painkillers for my headaches, but I replied, "I've been taking these painkillers since my periods first started, so they're old friends."

Pregnancy was a delightful state. Growing a baby inside your body is a privilege. I'd believed this miracle would never happen to me but then it did. This baby was mine and mine alone to love and cherish.

For the first time in my life I was doing something which made me happy. I was engaged to perform a task for which few people were qualified, and at the same time my body was performing its own miracle.

The country was locked in political hurdles, but I felt the British would make everything right.

As I mentioned before, we were brought up on songs which rang with praises for being part of the British Empire. We believed justice would prevail. Were we not British too, as part of the Commonwealth? There was nothing to worry about.

Little did I know that my world would fall apart and I would be forced to leave the country for fear that my children would never be safe.

CHAPTER FORTY-ONE

CHILDBIRTH. The Commission was scheduled to end its enquiry ten days before my 'due' date. I thought this would give me time to decorate the nursery and make sure that everything I needed after the birth was available. I felt so tired after work, my time at home was spent in bed.

Labour pains came two days before the due date and lasted for more than 24-hours. When it seemed the baby was about to be born, I was rushed to hospital and into the birthing room. He popped out quickly. The nurse told me it was a boy and rushed away. I heard the nurses calling to each other to get the doctor there immediately. I asked what was wrong, but received no answer except that I should concentrate on expelling the afterbirth. This came quickly after and I asked, "What, now? Where's my child, I want to see him?" They told me that he was in an incubator as he weighed under five pounds. As soon as the doctor examined him, I would be allowed to see him.

Worry filled my heart. I heard the Doctor saying, "The baby must be premature. She delivered before her time. Have you examined him? Are there any deformities?"

"No, Doctor" was the reply. "He has both feet and both arms, fingers and toes. He's just so small."

"Well, take good care of him. Feed him slowly every two hours. I'll return in the morning to check on him."

He then came over to me and said. "He's perfect, missing no limbs, just a little small. He doesn't seem to have grown since last I saw you."

"Why are you asking about limbs?" I asked.

He replied, "He's a perfect baby boy, just a little underweight."

"But why are you asking about limbs?" I queried again. "Is something wrong, something I should know?"

"We've had a couple of births recently where the baby's limbs were deformed. You've nothing to worry about, your child is perfect," he replied.

"Do you know what caused the deformities in those babies?" I asked.

He replied, "No one knows yet, but a drug which might be responsible has been taken off the shelf. In fact, there was an article in the papers about this drug; it's called thalidomide."

"Thank God," I breathed a sigh of relief. "It's indeed a good thing that I didn't fill that prescription you gave me."

He smiled. "It was wise of you to decline it. It had good reviews in the medical journals and it was prescribed by me in good faith."

He patted me on the hand and left.

Where there should have been joy there was only a heavy weight on my mind and in my heart. *My child was so small and would he survive?* The answer came from within.

There's a solution for everything. It takes time and patience and the result may not always be what is desired. I promised myself that I would find that solution. Man could fashion anything he wanted except life. If life was given to you, then that life would be cherished and nurtured. A fierce desire grew in my breast. My son will live. I wanted happiness for this child more than anything else on Earth.

I got out of the hospital bed and went to the nursery. Everything was quiet. The nurse in charge had probably stepped away for a moment. I slipped in and found him. *My son will live.* He was a tiny slip of a baby boy. I touched his head, his eyes, his ears, his nose, his mouth, and then his hands. I put my index finger in his left hand and his fingers curled around it. Emotion filled my body. Tears filled my eyes. I could hardly breathe. My heart pumped rapidly.

I felt a hand around my shoulder. The nurse had returned. She said, "Honey, it's going to be all right. He'll need special care, but children grow quickly. They have the desire to live, and their whole being is attuned to this. Let me take you back to your room. Birthing is a terrible ordeal, but women are special, and they can do what man cannot. Both you and your child will be okay."

It was hard to leave him, but I docilely accompanied her back to my room. My body was becoming limp with a tired feeling. But there was hope. *"If it was to be, it was up to me."* That mantra reaffirmed itself firmly in my mind. My efforts would make everything right.

We were in hospital for eight days. I refused to leave him behind. I was told that I could return home and visit him during the day. There were still arguments about his birth being premature. However, women seldom make mistakes about their due dates. When I'd found out about my pregnancy, I'd carefully noted it on the calendar. Perhaps the doctor had made a mistake, but it was certainly not about the end of my pregnancy with the birth of my child. It would take extra care to protect his growing years, but I was with him every step of the way, and difficult though the road would be, I would not falter.

CHAPTER FORTY-TWO

MONEY DOESN'T GROW ON TREES. I believe we're all born with coping mechanisms, but our attitudes to problems which offer no obvious solutions determine how well we adapt to change which puzzles us.

My infant was a precious bundle, the miracle of life. I pushed the thought that he might not survive to the back of my mind. Raising a child in the tropics where sanitation is never given a second thought would be a challenge.

The names we agreed on for the child were Christopher Mohandas, powerful names in my estimation. Even though the Anglican Church didn't like the East Indian name 'Mohandas,' I insisted on giving him a name that would identify his racial origin. I have always been a Gandhi admirer. The qualities of his character, his determination and his devotion and dedication to freeing India from colonialism always inspired me. Christopher Columbus discovered the New World. I hoped that the affiliation of names would hold my son strong.

He was baptized, but taking no chance, I also asked my mother-in-law to go through the Hindu ritual of birth and blessing.

Christo was a colicky baby. I was at my wit's end. He hardly slept for any length of time and was only comfortable when I held him. We consulted various doctors who gave different advice. I took him to the Creche in Georgetown where mothers went to have their newborns checked and weighed by midwives. I listened carefully to all advice and followed their instructions.

He slowly gained weight, but at three months old he was still grossly underweight. I was always jealous when I saw other children, plump and happy. I comforted myself that my nurture and care would make things right in the end.

Of course, everyone blamed me for producing an underweight child. I always remarked, "Isn't it wonderful that's his only drawback?!"

It had been my intention to return to work, leaving Christo in the care of a nursemaid. This was usual practice in those days. When various emissaries from work continued to visit me to ascertain when I would be returning to my job, I finally told them that I couldn't leave my child until he was at least a year old.

I felt sad, but was buoyed by the answer, "We can't hold your job open, but we can create a position for you whenever you choose to return." It was good to hear that. I had earned the reputation of being one of the top secretaries in Georgetown and an asset wherever I worked, but at this time in my life another charge was given to me and I recognized there were other facets of life.

There were repercussions awaiting me. *How were we going to manage without my salary?*

Christmas was always a big event in our lives. I couldn't go over to Vreed-en-Hoop for Christmas Day celebrations without getting Christmas gifts for everyone in the family. I would lose face. My siblings would know that something wasn't right and gossip over the fact that money was a problem. I didn't want their sniggers or their pity. Something had to be done. I could withdraw some of my savings to tide me over, but this rankled. I had to think of the future.

Various solutions to our loss of my salary and how to make up for it were constantly in my mind. I asked Mike to brainstorm with me, but he pooh poohed everything I suggested. He insisted that it would be a come down for us if I used my sewing skills and supplied ready-made children's wear to the stores in the Stabroek market. He also added that he didn't want sewing girls in his house. He reminded me that his mother tried this and eventually had to cease that line of business because it hadn't paid off.

Eventually, I said, "Look, I'm one of the top secretaries in Georgetown. Why don't I have classes for budding secretaries? I could teach shorthand, typewriting, and English grammar?"

Our principal language was English, but the general population spoke Creolese, the local dialect started during the period of slavery and continued thereafter by the indentured Coolies from India.

Mike said, "Let's wait and see. Something may turn up." He seemed anxious to avoid the subject.

I replied, "If we have to wait, why don't you make a start in the property market? You know people are always buying and selling houses. The few real estate brokers seem to make a thundering lot of money."

"I'm always busy at work. I don't think I'd have the time but let's wait and see," he replied.

"Do you think I can try my hand at that? I don't know anything about it, but I can learn the ropes. I won't lose anything. Dad speculated in the property market, and it can be very rewarding. He bought and sold houses, kept and rented some, and this became a major source of income," I replied. "We can't go on like this. Your mother has promised to oversee the care of Christo, but she has her own life, too."

He replied nonchantly, "You're always anxious about every-thing. It won't hurt if you used your savings to tide us over until you can get back to work. I don't know what your concern is all about."

"I've seen too many people come up the front stairs of our house in Vreed-en-Hoop to borrow money from my father be-cause they thoughtlessly took the future for granted. I don't want to end up like that. I have too much pride and you know I won't go to my parents for help. Once Christmas is over I'll get into some sort of home-based income earning business." He didn't like where our conversation was taking us.

I was infuriated. I knew that whatever increase in salary normally given at the end of the year, and the usual year-end Christmas bonus, would make only a tiny dent in what we needed for our household expenses.

I didn't realize at the time that "saving face" was more im-portant to the male psyche than female efforts to earn money. Women were "kept," men earned money and retained control, but what could women do when the household budget couldn't provide for all its requirements?

It didn't help my mood when he said to me later, "Men rule the Earth, women just follow." I thought but did not air my thoughts, *That's why your poor mother had to struggle so hard to put food on the table, while your father was content to 'lord' it over everyone, never once suspecting that if they could combine their efforts, prosperity would follow.*

CHAPTER FORTY-THREE

NEW ADVENTURES. Christmas was fast approaching. I hadn't resolved the Christmas gift problem. Getting a gift for everyone and for old relatives who lived nearby would take some doing. I agonized over this. I couldn't go empty handed because everyone would begin to wonder and question. I decided to fashion and sew dresses for the nieces and suits for nephews. I got into a flurry of baking for older relatives.

The children loved their clothing and the adults appreciated the wide assortment of goodies nicely arranged in Christmas baskets. I still managed to tuck a small bill in baskets for the 'not so fortunate.' Everyone was overwhelmed. I felt good. It had taken many hours, but with a small outlay, Christmas was saved.

The upshot of this was new found confidence. One door had closed, but I only had to push others and they, too, could open and welcome me.

A small 'commercial' school for young ladies was something I could manage at home. *All secretaries and steno typists were female, so why not?* I asked myself. Men got jobs as clerks without any training, except sometimes in book-keeping and accounting, most skills required for clerical jobs were part of 'on the job' training.

Girls rarely held clerical positions in offices. This, again, was a put down for girls. Boys and girls all graduated with "A" levels, but boys were able to obtain jobs immediately after leaving primary school, while girls had to be proficient in secretarial skills.

Twelve students represented an ideal number. This meant my living room had to be cleared to accommodate the necessary desks and tables. There was just enough money to fund furniture and typewriters. Students would be required to purchase their own textbooks. I wrote to Pitman and Gregg Shorthand examination centers in England and registered the school as "The Modern Business School for Young Ladies."

It was time to approach Mike and ask for his help. He put forth every reason he could find to dismiss my idea; it wouldn't work and I was only wasting money, which could be used in other ways was his constant reminder. I needed his help to get furniture made and the room set up and I pressed him to assist with this. I planned to start advertising my school almost immediately.

Mike recognized I was adamant. He told me I would become laughing stock when my efforts failed. Women did not start businesses. "I have to try, Mike. I can't do this without your help. We'll both benefit. I have everything going for me. I've been a successful secretary and court reporter, my family is prominent, and friends will support me. You know there's a dearth of good secretaries in Georgetown. I will train young ladies to become good secretaries, and businesses will come here to recruit them."

"We'll see," he replied. "And who will look after Christo while you're busy with your students? You only think of yourself. The child needs you."

"I've spoken to Catherine, our housekeeper, and she's agreeable to extending her working hours until four in the afternoon. After I see what takes place, I'll get someone to come in from four o'clock when she leaves, until seven when classes end. He won't suffer in the least and I'll be within call, if need be. The morning session will finish at eleven thirty, and the afternoon will start at four thirty. I can handle any emergency which may arise. Let's be practical about this, and don't split hairs. You can take over the care of Christo when you return home from work and when the school becomes successful, I'll hire someone to take care of him. I know you won't mind helping me. You can dictate the passages to the shorthand students so we'll both put our shoulders to the wheel and the outcome will be successful. Let's do this together. We will make this venture a reality."

Telephones were not readily available at the time in British Guiana. I needed help to get one. I approached the Office Manager of the Transport & Harbours Department. He wished me luck on my venture, reminding me I always had a job there if I changed my mind about the school, and within two weeks I had a telephone. *First hurdle over,* I thought. *Good to have friends in the right places.*

Advertisements appeared in the Sunday newspaper the following week. My telephone kept ringing. I was concerned that the ringing would awaken Christo and start a round of wailing, but he cooperated and slept almost right through. I had six enrolments for the day class and an equal number for the 'after work' class.

When I received the first fees for education in my school, I felt an elation within me that I had never experienced before. Fees for the first two months were almost twice as much as I had earned at work. In addition, I felt that a trust had been established between me and my students for the betterment of their future. I treasured this and was determined that no one would ever regret placing their future in my hands.

One morning, quite to my amazement, an Indian woman dressed in traditional headwear, head kerchief and orhni, greeted me at my door. She was accompanied by a young man who seemed to be about fifteen years old. "Missus," she said in broken English, "I bring this boy for you to train and *eddicate*. (educate)

"I cannot take him," I replied, "this is a school for girls."

"Take him," she begged, pushing him closer to me. "He's a good boy. He'll study hard and make no trouble." This was the first time some one was begging me to perform a task for which they were paying me. I looked at her closely and was favourably impressed by her manner and her confidence in my ability. She trusted me even though we'd never met.

"What can I teach him?" I asked.

"Teach him to type and work with numbers so he can find work in the Estate office. I don't want him to be a cane cutter, and that's what will happen if I can't leave him with you. His mother was my daughter. The father marry again and the step-mother don't like him. Help me make a man out of him and give him a future". Her eyes betrayed her feeling of anxiety. She feared that if her grandson wasn't accepted in the school, his future was in jeopardy. She'd hit upon that spot in my heart which told me I had to help him.

I turned to the young man and asked, "What's your name, son?"

"Narain," he replied, with his head hung low.

"Don't you mind attending a girls' school? The girls may tease you." I smiled.

"Ma says I have to come here and the girls won't bother me." He replied in low tones.

"My fees are high; can you pay them?" I asked the grandmother.

"Yes, I understand," she replied, "but I know that if you take him in your hand, he'll succeed."

I was intrigued. "How did you hear of me?" I asked.

"When I was going home on the bus I heard people talking about you. They said you'd worked in high places and you'd pass on this learning and training to your students. They told me where you were living, and the boy helped me find your house. We come from Lenora on the West Coast. I'll make sure he gets up early to catch the bus and make the 7.30 ferry to be here for 8.30 every day. Please take him into your school. Everyone says you will make your students successful."

Here was an uneducated woman living on the sugar estate trying to educate her grandson in a manner that would elevate his position in life. It made me think.

I was flattered and humbled at the same time. Should I or shouldn't I take the boy? He had finished primary school, could read and write, but had not attended secondary school. He could be a prime student for bookkeeping and accounting, but I knew nothing of those subjects. However, the thought struck me. Mike could spend half an hour every morning with him, and this could be the start of his teaching career. I could also start learning alongside him, and if I kept ahead with two or three chapters in the text book, that would take care of everything. It was an opportunity and it beckoned.

I enrolled Narain in the upcoming session. He would be the sole student in book-keeping but would join the girls for English language and typewriting. I would provoke his sense of learning and get him to expand his knowledge through reading and discussion.

Enrolment was good. There was a steady stream of students for each of the two sessions. I needed help so I hired three new teachers. I couldn't clone myself, but I had to build a consensus of teaching methods. We brainstormed and held sessions to discuss curriculum and the manner we would disseminate knowledge and bolster our own knowledge and our skills. Students needed inspiration to forge ahead. Teachers were obligated to use my teaching methods so we were all on the same page. They were also required to update their own skills.

Within three months, enrolment for each session had risen. When I'd first conceived the idea of opening a secretarial school, a long-term plan wasn't important and held no significant place in my future. The school was simply a means of providing much-needed income. Now it seemed what I was offering had hit a niche market. It was the first vocational school of its kind in British Guiana and this initial success was important. The groundswell in enrolment was exciting. Suddenly a door had opened for me. I'd filled a need and best of all provided a career opportunity for girls, and a new enterprise for myself.

This was a major milestone in my life. This career opportunity was both challenging and exciting. There were few boundaries or obstacles. Teaching had started something unique in my life. I was making a difference in the lives of young girls. The knowledge that I imparted would help emancipate them. Getting good jobs with good salaries boded well for their future. My perspectives of life changed.

My thoughts ran away with me. I could relocate to a new property where I could build a school and foster a career to span the remainder of my life. The political landscape was changing, but I had put my faith in British justice and hoped whatever the outcome of the political changes, it couldn't alter the plans I was making for the future. Further, Mike was on board. He would help me. Success would be ours.

Mike and I talked about this, and we decided to engage the services of a property agent who would find us a suitable property. We would either alter the building to accommodate the school or demolish the structure and erect an edifice we felt would make an ideal home and premises second to none for the school.

I looked for opportunities to enhance my knowledge of teaching, either through correspondence courses, or enrolling at the local university. I felt motivation and innovation would play a major role in the future of my girls. I needed to examine trends in teaching and motivational techniques in England and the USA.

My personal aspiration was to guarantee that each student had optimum skills and after that it would be up to them. There was much to consider, but the future loomed bright and happy.

I'd found something rewarding to fill the rest of my life. My school would rank second to none. My future lay in the achievement of my students. Success wouldn't happen without delving into areas of study that were new to me, but it was a plan.

Meanwhile, I started an after lunch session and this was working well. It was a busy time but I was happy.

Amidst it all I discovered that I was pregnant. Happy, happy thoughts. This time I hoped I would give birth to a daughter.

I took pregnancy in my stride. A lesson learned from the last pregnancy was that I should take no prescription drugs to counteract anything that impinged on the health of my child.

My pregnancy wasn't easy. My ankles swelled, my head ached, my stomach seemed to want to empty itself after anything I ate. But there were happy thoughts of the child growing within me and the future I was building. True to my vows about taking prescription medicines, to ease any pain and discomfort, massage therapy at the end of each week and rest during weekends eased the discomfort I experienced.

Birthing was easy. The baby was late. The due date had gone by unnoticed as I continued working in the school. One day I felt somewhat uncomfortable, but didn't recognize the signs I was looking out for. After I closed sessions for that day, I noticed a slight change in feelings and went to the toilet. My water broke; I picked up my bag and told Mike, "It's time to take me to the hospital".

The journey took twenty minutes. The nurses took one look at me and ordered a stretcher. The baby was born on the way to the delivery room. I thought, *how lucky can you be?* People complain of hours of pain. She was small at only 5 lbs 2 oz. Her voice was powerful, though, and I felt all was at peace within my world.

I remained in hospital for six days; I was becoming a bit antsy because the due date for end of term examinations was fast approaching. Mike promised to take some time off from work, but I felt it was my responsibility to make sure all went well. I felt examination jitters as acutely, as did my students. Their success was important.

As I was leaving, the hospital staff reminded me that it was necessary for me to rest and take things slowly. Once I was at home, I couldn't keep away. When I saw the expression of relief on my student's faces, I felt my actions were justified. They always put their best foot forward when I was present and it seemed to produce good results.

Results were, as usual, excellent with an almost 100 per cent success rate.

It boded well for my plans when we found an ideal location for the school. The building wasn't quite what I wanted and we decided it would be easier to demolish it and rebuild to our specifications.

The contract for erection was concluded, architectural drawings approved, and there was no problem getting a mortgage from the bank.

I breathed a sigh of relief. I had two children and a career which wouldn't take me away from them. I could never become the lawyer I had hoped to be, but quite by chance, would have a career in education. I could challenge the young minds of girls and they could aspire to build a future for themselves, using their little "grey cells" to propel them forward. Life was good.

Unknowingly, the drums of disruption were rolling. British Guiana was on the brink of turmoil, which would destroy racial relationships for decades. Law and order would be replaced by injustice; the economy would sink to one of the lowest in the world. Peace and prosperity were doomed and I would have to determine whether I would be a second class citizen in the country of my birth or flee as thousands were doing. The brain drain had begun.

Citizens of British Guiana would migrate to almost all corners of the world in their desire to flee and be free. We had all welcomed the birth of a new generation of politics and government. Many had endured death in their search for a better life. But the descendants of all the thousands who were brought to serve as slaves and those who'd been indentured as Coolies to work on the sugar plantations like their predecessors, were conflicted. Superiority of race had become paramount and had taken precedence over the initial motto of peace, progress, and prosperity.

Yet again, I get ahead in my tale.

CHAPTER FORTY-FOUR

D REAMS HAVE A LIFESPAN. *To dream, to reach for the top and create a better world for themselves would be the goal of my students. Their talents would be recognized, regardless of their sex. Their skills would impact not only their own lives and the lives of their children, but also their country.*

My parents concentrated on furthering the education of their sons. It was time to make sure that girls had skills they could use to take them to the top.

Mike protested when I wanted to visit the site of the new school. He told me he was protecting me from gossip. I ignored his arguments. I suspected that he wanted to be seen as the "big cheese" and any visit by me would undermine this. He warned me, "Tab, the men will disrespect you if you visit the site. Women don't get involved in construction. I'm protecting you."

"The world is changing, Mike," I cajoled. "Take our own circumstances. Look at the progress we've made. My maternal instincts told me I couldn't leave Christo's care to someone else. The school was born because I used my education to give us an income. I was able to provide maternal care and add to our earnings." I spoke with a plea in my voice, but my face had a stony look. I was taking a stand.

"Remember this, Mike, she who pays the piper calls the tune. Without me there would've been no school; it's time for men to get accustomed to the fact that women are not brainless creatures, and that also includes construction workers."

He walked out of the house, got into the car and disappeared, but I was adamant. He returned to find an empty house as I'd taken my two children for an evening stroll.

Next day, I visited the site on my own. The contractor hastened to show me around. I asked questions, suggested minor changes, and advised I would be back at the end of the week. I gained the impression that "I had made his day" with my visit. I was respected for the work I was doing, and the success of my students. I'd become an important figure.

After dinner, I discussed the changes with Mike. He grunted, but decided not to demur. I was quite surprised when he told me later, "We'll go the site on Friday after work, and I'll let the Contractor know that we're paying an inspection visit.

Expansion was a heavy load. I realized that I'd set a huge curriculum for myself but I felt inspired. Failure was not an option. There was no thought that I couldn't accomplish what I had set out to do. My goal was to change lives. I would provide motivation by giving my students a visual picture of what their future could be.

Date of completion was set to begin the new term. Enrolment peaked. Our financial future was assured. This was propelled by changes in the political landscape. Parents were mindful that without employable sills, children would find it difficult to obtain jobs in their new countries of residence. The focus of life had shifted. No one wanted to remain in Guyana. We had become a country where the future was bleak for Indians and non-blacks.

Our first thoughts were that we should seek immigration to Britain, and the United States. Like Australia, Canada had a 'closed door' policy towards people of colour. People of Portuguese descent had left for Canada in droves and had spoken of the excellent opportunities available, but this was useless speculation. We were brown, not white.

Miraculously, it seemed, Canada opened its doors to people of colour. Our horizon widened. There was new hope for the future. Change doesn't happen overnight. Wishes take time for fulfilment. In the meantime, it was necessary to live with the new situation.

The political landscape continued in a vortex. As the solidarity that had joined Indians and Negroes together disintegrated, enmity between the races crescendoed.

Businesses were coerced into paying for protection. Indian merchants and professionals were asked to donate funds to the 'cause'. If they refused, gangs attacked their businesses and homes. If payments were not large enough, cheques were torn up in their presence, and cash strewn at their feet, with the admonition of the words "you can do better". Those who demurred, knew what the future held for them. They would be targeted by gangs, their homes destroyed, and their womenfolk raped.

It became the norm for gangs of Negro youths to roam the streets, attacking and robbing the unfortunates. Fear ruled the city of Georgetown. The countryside was not immune. Rape and robbery also happened here. 'Choke and rob' became the order of the day.

Negro leaders spoke openly of the need to attack and take possession as a means of subduing the Indians. Arson and murder became commonplace.

The landscape changed. Fear became part of the human psyche. There were iron bars against windows and doors. People existed within the confines of violence because there was no recourse. Fear ruled the roost and this boded only ill will for Indians.

Our Slavery (African) and Bound Coolie (Indian) forefathers, had endured their periods of servitude. Together they had broken the yokes placed around their necks. Now one race had replaced the masters and become the rulers of the other. *Justice disappeared.*

Not everyone would be fortunate enough to leave the country and seek their future elsewhere.

These changes heralded a death note for my hopes and dreams. My children's future was at stake. Safety was just as important for my own family as it was for my students. Uncertainty had only one choice. *Change it to certainty.*

CHAPTER FORTY-FIVE

GOALS CHANGE. It wasn't easy for me to sit back and ignore the happenings around me. Rape was anathema to me. Fear ruled the day. I wondered why women always seemed to suffer the brunt of violence. Extra security was needed to protect the school even though someone took pains to let me know that I wasn't targeted.

My students, black, brown and white, had done well overall. The reputation of the school was second to none. Wives of foreign embassy staff who wanted to hone their secretarial skills were inspired to enroll.

I was content with the progress, but very unhappy at the changes wrought within the country.

I mulled over what I considered the "Big Betrayal." Britain divided India into India and Pakistan when Nehru and Jinnah couldn't settle the problem of leadership between them. Jagan and Burnham faced the same problem. Britain had again shed its responsibilities and divided my country, this time symbolically, through proportional representation.

Picking up roots and settling elsewhere was a tough decision. I would have to give up my beloved school. I had worked hard and created a bastion of learning. Technological advances would herald change, but there would be no local Technical Institutions to advance that knowledge. My soul was filled with disquiet. What would become of my own children? What would happen to the legacy of education for women already on its way?

My children's future took precedence. There was no way out. No matter the cost, rape was violence second to none in my soul. I felt death would be preferable to having my children molested in this way.

I tried to talk about my fears with Mike but his reply brought me no comfort. "Tab, we have a good thing going here. We're independent and well-respected. We've just built a new home and a new school. We live in a prestigious neighbourhood next door to a beautiful church. We cross the street and the Promenade Gardens greet us. We are well respected. Why would we leave all of this? Survival is important. We'll cooperate with the new regime. Let's try it and see if it works. I'm not closing the door, but I feel we shouldn't make sudden decisions."

I shook my head, tears in my eyes. "I'm afraid of the future. These people seem to strike at the heart of what disturbs me most. I can't bear the thought of men molesting and raping women at will and fancy. I'll go mad if this happens to one of my children or one of my students."

"That's nonsense," he admonished, looking at me through eyes filled with stern resolution. "You're letting your paranoia get the better of you. People have started guarding their homes with wrought iron frames against their windows. We'll do the same. We're well-respected. No one will harm us. I know someone who could design a pattern for our windows, and this will be a first start to keeping us safe."

My heart said, *if we're so safe, why do we have to put up iron bars?* My head said, *go with the flow, but make plans to leave.* "I don't know,

Mike; let's start sending money out of the country. Many people are already doing this. I must have some safety net and a plan for the future. I can't stand by and see people being hounded and robbed, chased from their homes, and their children scarred for life. If I could make a difference, I'd fight for them. But I'm only a woman with no physical strength. I'm so afraid. Life's crashing down around me. I thought I had a plan for the future. I dreamt of our children attending university abroad, and returning home to a future bright with promise. That's all gone now. Everyone is leaving, and I too must prepare for this."

He hugged me. "Tab, you should leave the planning to me. It's a man's job. I'll take care of the situation. You should trust me more. I've already been making enquiries. I know someone in the Canadian Embassy and he'll start work on our applications."

I didn't trust him. His words were just a palliative excuse thrown in my direction. I knew that I would have to start proceedings myself. Mike and I looked at the future through different eyes. I couldn't remain in a country where my children wouldn't be safe. If I didn't leave this country I loved, my psyche would die. I would be living a lie, fearful of the fact that harm would be done to my children and to me. How could I close my eyes to what's happening to people of Indian descent. There were two standards for justice. Racial prejudice said it all.

Mike and I had been at odds with each other for some time. My teachers had enrolled in a swimming class and they were encouraging me to join them. Mike didn't like this. He warned me, "You can't be friends with people who work for you. There is a great divide. The minute you start to swim with them, they will cease to respect you."

"What's wrong with friendship?" I asked impatiently. "We're all equals. I'm their boss, but I'm at a loss to understand how they could take advantage of my friendship. They respect me and the they value their reputation as teachers at the school. What disrespect can come from going to swim with them? We're all equals." He gave me a withering look, and stormed out without an answer.

My housekeeper was waiting outside the room to see me about dinner preparations. When she came into the room, she found me in tears. She put her arms around me, and held me close. She wiped my tear-stained face with her apron. "Madam, it'll all pass. We work for you, and we love you. You value what we do for you and we've earned your respect. You treat us all as equals. Dry your tears, and do as you wish. We all value your opinion, and we look to you for guidance."

A few days after, Mike told me he needed to speak to me on a business matter. "You don't need to make an appointment to speak to me, Mike. What's bothering you this time?" I questioned. Classes started on time and I was in a rush.

He was taken aback by my tone, so he responded in kind. "This isn't a convenient time. Let's speak after school this evening."

I was exasperated, but my tasks in the school awaited me. "Okay. We'll do that," I retorted impatiently.

Swirling thoughts took control of my mind. Was someone in trouble? Was he in trouble? The day couldn't go fast enough for me. I breathed a sigh of relief when school was over and we went in to the office. "Well, Mike what is this all about?"

"There are two things I wanted to raise with you. I don't like you swimming because men will gape at your body and they'll disrespect me for permitting you to swim in public."

"And the other?" I queried, my face expressing the exasperation I felt, my eyes wild with anger.

"I've been speaking with my family, and they want to know when I'll be transferring ownership of the school to myself."

I was thunderstruck. "You and your family should be thoroughly ashamed. Without me, there would be no school. The school was my dream, and my reality. I share ownership with you because you've helped me along the way. In my mind, the school has always belonged to 'us'. What is this all about?

"You still don't get it Tab. Men make the rules. They are the authority figures. You constantly ignore what I try to tell you about running the school. Students appeal to you, not to me. When something isn't quite right, I should be the one to settle their problems. I am the manager."

"Do you think the title of owner will make them turn to you, Mike?" I disdainfully replied, my face ablaze with anger and frustration. "This is just a red herring you're throwing at me; I'm surprised you think so little of me. Women have made progress; Indian women in this country are not subject to the whims and fancies of their husbands and I hate to remind you of this, 'my father did not give you a dowry when he transferred the property to me. That property was gifted to me solely, not to you as a bribe to marry me.

"Transference of ownership of the school is a moot point any way. You can have it all but I won't be here. I will seek immigration to Canada and I'll take the children with me. If you don't want to come with us, that's up to you. You can have total control of the school at that time but ownership will always remain with me.

It pains me to abandon this school. Your help was invaluable. We're partners, not boss and slave. We cooperate and we get along. I pursue my friendships, just as you do, your own friendships. My teachers love and respect me. I'm their advisor and their friend. I'll go swimming whenever and wherever I please. If men find my body beautiful and gape at me, that's just too bad. Looks can't hurt".

My heart was in turmoil. 'Flaunting' my body in public was an accusation that irked me. Being the object of male attentions because they desired my body was simply his excuse to control me. It was demeaning. Sex with Mike was an act I performed as part of my wifely duties. I took little pleasure in it and it never seemed to make any difference to him.

What was happening to Mike? Did he feel that my success in the school was threatening his male persona? Was he trying to control me?' Why doesn't he acknowledge that without me there would have been no school? I've never implied that the school was mine. I'd never even thought of ownership in that way.

I always managed to avoid confrontation even when he tried to put me down in public. Indeed, it was a battle to keep my temper. If we went for a walk, he always walked ahead of me as if he was the bwana in the jungle, the supreme leader on a jungle trek. Our friends secretly smiled. Perhaps the time was ready for me to think of myself and the children. Mike was uncertain of his future in a foreign country. It was going to be hard for him to leave. The success of the school hadn't only upshot us to prominence and wealth, it had also raised our status. We had earned respect because our students achieved and progressed. People looked up to us. We played a prominent role in education and they respected this.

There was confusion and darkness. Where had I gone wrong? Suddenly the words, "if it is to be, it's up to me" floated into my horizon, like a ray of sunlight. "Yes," I told myself. "I will make plans. I'll try to send as much money as I can out of the country even if I have to borrow some. I can start afresh. What I've accomplished here will be the building block for the future."

There were rumours that the money drain on the country was so high, the government wouldn't be able to pay its bills. To survive, the new regime would soon be putting embargoes on money leaving the country. I would get some advice from the bank and prepare for this.

"Something on the back burner" eased my concern. A plan was in place and this would suffice. If Mike didn't want to leave the country, he could stay and run the school. This would be a break for me. Although I ignored his comments and criticisms, they rankled. I hid my feelings by living through the fiction I read. It would be nice to be free of it all. My children would be safe in another country and I'd forge ahead with a new future.

CHAPTER FORTY-SIX

NEW BEGINNINGS. Canada beckoned. Leaving Guyana for a new country was a simple decision but very sad. My first choice for a new home was Canada. Pierre Trudeau, world renowned leader, had flung the doors open for me, when he acknowledged that Canada would benefit if restrictions with regard to applicants of 'colour' were lifted, and the Canadian immigration system was open to all. The Canadian Parliament enacted appropriate legislation. This provided an avenue of optimism for me. It was my hope that in this country of my choice, I could find peace, happiness, and contentment. Politics had changed Guyanese culture. Fear had overtaken the happy-go-lucky freedom and friendship which previously existed. There was an uneasy peace between the races. Simple conversation was filled with innuendo. It was difficult to talk about what was happening in the country because we looked at occurring and recurring events through different eyes.

A friend and former student, broached the need for a secretarial school in Barbados. She had returned from Canada where she attended Ryerson Polytechnic to further her skills in shorthand and had been offered a job in Barbados. I confided that I didn't want to move to the West Indies because I feared a situation similar to Guyana might exist. Indians might be regarded as interlopers. She laughed derisively. "That would never happen in Barbados. Barbadians have a different mindset."

I shook my head and smiled as I remembered an incident that happened while I was in Barbados. Our village Priest had given me a referral letter to the Priest of the Church in Bridgetown. The letter stated my family and I were upstanding Christians and asked that I be allowed to take the Sacrament of Holy Communion at his Church. I visited the Vicarage on the Saturday following my arrival and presented the letter. The Vicar had smiled during a pleasant chit chat and welcomed me. He confirmed that morning service would be held at 10 o'clock the following day.

On arrival at the Church next day, I decided to sit in the second row from the front. This was normally where my family sat when we went to Church in Vreed-en-Hoop. No one sat beside me. To my surprise, the theme of his sermon was "He who humbleth himself shall be exalted." He'd looked at me frequently during the sermon and I felt it was directed at me.

I looked around and saw that white parishioners sat in the front seats, coloureds sat at the back. I recalled seeing this on the bus trip to the Church. After the service he'd held out his hand to greet me. I'd smiled, and pretended that I didn't see his outstretched hand as I said goodbye. It was a salutary experience at the time. 'Coloured people were generally considered to be of no account, second class citizens.

It's my belief that the human mind dictates how we treat our fellow humans and how we accept those we think are below us on the human totem pole for many fathomless reasons. In Canada, justice, fair dealings, and ethical values, so essential to human existence, represented the breath of life, and were the norm. We could find a haven here. My children would be safe.

Immigration application forms were available at the Canadian Embassy. I made an appointment and collected a form. I hoped to avoid rumours of my impending emigration. Some of my former students held important positions in the city. I bumped into a few at the Embassy, but managed to avoid their questions about the future of the school.

Mike was angry that I'd gone "behind his back" to secure the document. However, he didn't object when I asked him to add his signature and deliver the forms to the Embassy. Time elapsed and in the interim I wondered whether the application was still lying on his desk at work.

I was on tenterhooks. I continued to give my full attention to the school. Enrolment was always higher than expected. People of Indian descent were intent on sending their children abroad to find their future in another country and they wished to provide them with employable skill-sets. It was quite natural for me to identify with their hopes and aspirations. Politics had changed Guyanese culture. Fear had replaced the happy-go-lucky freedom and friendship which previously existed. There was an uneasy peace between us. Simple conversation was filled with innuendo. It was difficult to talk about what was happening in the country because we looked at occurring and recurring events through different eyes.

The racial divide created barriers. Truth and justice lived on different plains. Interaction between Blacks and Browns simply disappeared. We had different objectives, different beliefs, differing skin colours. Indians who cooperated with the new regime were labelled traitors. Government positions very seldom went to Indians, regardless of qualifications and suitability. Protection from civil authorities was non-existent. Indians were indeed 'second class' citizens in the country of their birth. The freedom for which we had all so valiantly fought, had been replaced by anarchy and hatred. We were 'no account' descendants of Coolies.

Events pushed the urgency of our immigration to the forefront.

One night we were awakened by noises coming from the churchyard next door. Mike and I rushed to the window to find out what was happening. It turned out that two police vehicles and policemen with dogs were trying to apprehend someone who had stolen a mango from a vendor at the Bourda market, a short distance away. They were followed by a group of angry black youths, men and women.

We heard someone say that the person was hiding beneath the church. Police dogs were sent in to get him. It turned out that the culprit they were pursuing was a young Indian lad, about twelve years old. He begged for mercy, but two policemen took turns striking him with their truncheons. He fell to the ground. They kicked him, then threw him into their van. He was taken away by the policemen.

I was demoralized. My body was shaking; I could barely stand. It seemed a dagger had been plunged through my heart. A child had been tracked like a vicious criminal and subdued by violence I'd never witnessed before. I asked myself "Is this the new justice? Can my children become victims of this hatred?" Endless thoughts aggravated my mind. I was afraid. I needed to flee.

Mike tried to calm me. We discussed the disappearance of friendships we'd once thought inviable and the prejudice and hatred prevailing throughout the country, all brought to life by the ambition of one man who wished to become 'monarch'.

"You're right, Tab. This is no place for us. What satisfaction did those policemen get from the cruelty of their actions against a defenseless child? I never imagined that life in Guyana could fall this low."

"Hatred has no boundaries," I lamented, "It has taken precedence over normal behaviour. Authorities turn a blind eye to what's happening; in fact, our Prime Minister encourages it".

People of Indian heritage have become prey to satisfy a desire to appease the cruelty wreaked on African slaves who were transported across the oceans, violated, abused, and forced to carry out the orders of their masters."

"Negros look around with resentment as they notice that Indians have become more successful and better off financially. They begrudge this. They take matters into their own hands. Egged on by the new government, and the blessing of their leader, the new Prime Minister, they vent the hatred they feel for anyone of a different colour. I can't live in this country any longer. We may never achieve anything close to what we're leaving here, but our children will, and that will make our sacrifice worthwhile. It breaks my heart, but the Universe is sending me a message."

Mike looked at me thoughtfully, his face reflecting the concern he felt. "We had a great childhood. Friendships included all races. We were in and out of one another's homes. We played, laughed, and poked fun at each other. We used racial epithets and slurs, but they didn't have the same barb as they do now. We were individuals each vying to finish our education and get good jobs. This has all changed. Even our friends look at us differently. The infusion of "race" into relationships has generated too much ill will and bad feeling. I understand your fears, Tab."

"Life has played a cruel joke on us, Mike. Just when we thought things were looking up for us, we have to leave it all behind and start afresh. Even if I have to scrub floors and work as a maid, it'll be better than having to live in fear and persecution. I'm proud that we built this school. I'll always look back and wish that things could've been different, but regret can't be a part of my life. Wherever we go and whatever we do will make us successful. I know that this school changed my outlook on life. A new future now beckons. I can't change the past, but I can make sure that the future is better. It's up to us once we leave here. Let's focus on the future now. Today we start again."

Playing the waiting game was no longer an option. I made enquiries at the Canadian Embassy about our immigration status. I was pleased to learn that an immigration officer would be conducting interviews within the next four months, and we would learn before then whether we would advance to the next level. This was good news, but I was still on tenterhooks. I argued with myself that we were ideal candidates. We had scurried away a tidy sum of money into Canadian banks. We owned an established business. We were good candidates.

Two weeks to the day of the poor Indian waif was beaten and kicked, I happened to look over to the churchyard beside us. Entering the gate was a Negro man riding a lady's bike with a young Chinese girl on the seat behind. He leaned the bicycle against the steps leading into the church and pulled the young girl under the building. The space between the Church and the ground was barely three feet.

I called out, "Mike, there's something wrong happening under the church building. I just saw a Negro man pulling a young Chinese girl under the church. Run over and see what's happening. I'll phone the Vicar and ask him to join you. But you must hurry."

He grabbed a stick and rushed out. When the Vicar heard my story, he quickly disconnected the telephone and he and his housekeeper were down the stairs rushing to the scene. It was dark under the church and they could hear sobbing. The Vicar hailed out, "What are you doing under the church? I've called the Police and they're on their way."

The man rushed out. In his haste to escape he pushed the Vicar out of the way. The Vicar stumbled. The man tried to grab the bicycle, but Mike was too quick for him. He fled on foot and escaped.

The young girl wept, as she told her story. She was 14 years old. "I was returning home after a private tutoring session. Mom asked me to go to the Bourda market to buy some oranges. I parked my bicycle against a lamppost just outside the doors and locked it. As it's Sunday, there wasn't the usual hustle and bustle. Before entering the market 1 looked back and saw a black man fiddling with the lock. I ran back and challenged him, 'That's my bike. Leave it alone.'

"He told me, 'if you want your bike, you'll have to come with me. If you don't, I'll tell your parents that you were meeting a boy in the market. You know they won't like this.'

"I was afraid of losing my bike. My parents are poor and I'm their only child. They work hard. They saved their money to get me this bike so I could attend secondary school. I didn't want to lose it. They'd sacrificed so much for me. I did as he said and jumped on to the back seat. I didn't know where he was taking me, but I thought I'd meet someone on the road and cry out for help. He pulled me under the church and started to fondle me, threatening that no one would hear me if I cried out. He said he would slap me, choke me, and beat me. Even if I cried out no one would hear me and he would choke me to death after he'd had his way with me; the only way I could escape this was by consenting to his actions. My parents would never know what had become of me. Thank God you rescued me and saved my bike."

We were all horrified. I brought her over to my home while we awaited the arrival of the police. When they did arrive, they said they could do nothing about the situation. If we had apprehended the perpetrator, they could have charged him.

I asked, "Aren't you going to file a report?" I looked from one to the other. "You're supposed to report the crime, not ignore what happened."

"No purpose to that," was the reply. They were nonchalant about the whole situation, and I heard their lewd comments as they walked out of my driveway. Sexual proclivity brought them joy.

All the victim wanted after that was to get home to safety. Mike and I took her home. Her parents were overjoyed to see her. When she was late getting home, they had become alarmed.

I advised them, "This has been a traumatic experience for her. If you need help or if she needs to talk to someone, you know where I live. Come and see me. She must be careful. No one is safe from these hooligans."

On the way home I whispered, even though no one could hear me, "Mike, this can only get worse. These people have become so brazen there's no stopping them. They feel they have a right to anything they desire. They don't fear punishment because the officials who should be preserving law and order, are all in cahoots. The British don't care about us. They preached "law and order" when they were in control, then put us in an untenable situation because they feared that Jagan would turn the country into a communist state. What do we have now? The Burnham government fosters rape, robbery, violence, and blackmail. Can this country ever make progress?"

We were both sad. It was difficult enough reading about the happenings in the local newspaper, but experiencing them firsthand, and being unable to do anything to help was very troubling indeed. The inability to right the wrongs done to people of Indian descent, especially to women, rankled in my heart, but I was weak and afraid of repercussions.

I thought of my students to whom I tried to impart knowledge and ambition. I hoped that the lessons learned under my guidance would help them fulfill their dreams and their lives would be happy. I felt like a traitor because I was deserting them. I decided to keep the school running from abroad, if this was a possibility, and return twice a year to make sure everything was working. I knew this would only be a half measure, but it would assuage my guilt at deserting them.

Life is never simple. To complicate matters further, my father was diagnosed with cancer of the bowels. This took center place. Everything was put on the back burner. We consulted major specialists in Georgetown, but no one could help. The tumor was incurable. We did not give up. My brother James the doctor, arranged admission to a hospital in London where he was working.

Dad decided he needed a few days to put his affairs in order, and we made travel arrangements for the following week. I visited him daily. One day, as we were sitting together on the sofa in the living room, he took my left hand and held it with both hands. He turned one palm up so he could trace the lines on it with his finger, and said, "Your future doesn't lie here. It's time to seek your fortune in another country, Canada, Britain or the United States. Our neighbours have forgotten that violence imprisoned them in slavery. Perhaps they feel that if they follow the path of terror, they'll gain whatever they think was lost because of slavery and perhaps that same violence could make them rulers." He guided my hand to his heart and held it there. We smiled at each other, and then I hugged him and kissed him. I felt honored and cherished. I was once again that little girl who ran around the yard chortling with glee as she tried to catch the butterflies.

Two days after, I received a telephone call from him asking me to travel over to Vreed-en-Hoop on the next ferry. I laughingly replied "You know I have exams this morning, Dad. They'll be over at noon and I will travel on the 1 o'clock ferry as usual".

He said "I need to see you now."

I replied "Don't fret; you'll see me; I'll be there before two o'clock."

Sadly, this was not to be. I received a call from my mother just as I was heading out to catch the one o'clock ferry. She told me "your father died just after lunch today."

I foolishly asked "Are you sure he's dead. He spoke to me only a few hours ago and he didn't sound as if he was dying."

"Come over. Let's not argue. The pharmacist, Doctor Small came over to see if he could be resuscitated. He's just left. I need you beside me."

Grief overwhelmed me. I blamed myself because I did not heed his call. I will never know what he wanted to say to me. Perhaps he'd just needed the security of love, and I had put my other duties ahead of his need.

The sorrow at his passing was unbearable. When tears overwhelmed me and I couldn't control them, I was comforted by my Uncle George, my father's youngest brother. "Tab, he loved you and was always proud of you and your accomplishments. When your Aunt and I we visited him during his illness and we were talking about family, he'd confided, "I have such a swollen head when it comes to that girl, sometimes I thought my head had become too big for my hat." I sobbed all the more. I'd not heeded his last wish.

Dad's funeral was the largest ever in Vreed-en-Hoop. Hundreds lined up overnight and took part in the procession to the church. We all walked behind the hearse on his way to his funeral service. My mentor, the love of my life, had left for greener pastures. I needed to heed his advice and get away as soon as possible.

Plans for our departure speeded up after the funeral. Everything fell into place. Our immigration application was approved. Preparations for our departure began. We decided it would be prudent not to sell the school. Mike agreed that he would return from Canada and manage it with the help of the teachers who had been with us from the start and two additional assistants he would hire.

Departure was sad, but inevitable. The fulfillment of my dreams would never happen. I scolded myself for my cowardice in not enjoining the battle. The people who had wronged us had chosen a weapon I couldn't defend myself against. Rape and violence left me inert and quaking with fear.

I consoled myself. "*You may be down, but not out. You're following in the footsteps of many who've given up kingdoms and fled for safety. There is opportunity in the new country of your choice. You'll find feast, not famine. You'll succeed if you muster your will power and work hard. Fine thoughts, indeed, but where do I start?* I asked myself. My inner second voice replied, *you'll find a way. Fortune favours the brave. If it's to be, what's the answer?* It was up to me.

Everyone was sad to see us go, but there was a tacit understanding that the future of Guyana lay in chaos. People would survive but there would be a shift in values. Everyone knew that growth in the economy would be stifled. Guyana's sons and daughters would build the economy of other countries they'd call 'home.'

CHAPTER FORTY-SEVEN

NTHUSIASM AND HIGH HOPES. We arrived in Canada one cold December night but we took winter in our stride. We rented an apartment and enrolled the children in school. Mike returned to Guyana at the end of February. Leaving us was a difficult decision for him, but he felt that if we continued to run the school, the political situation could change, and I could be persuaded to return.

Although there were some racial overtones initially, by and large, our new life in Canada wasn't difficult. There were too many nice people around who welcomed us and helped us learn the ropes. Friendships followed. While money wasn't tight, I needed to assess my potential in the workforce. I was encouraged by family and friends to start a secretarial school in Toronto, but I felt I needed a University degree. As a start to a new career, I decided to enroll in evening classes in Business Management at Centennial College.

As the months went by, I felt a craving for ethnic foods and spices. There was only one West Indian shop in Scarborough which catered to the needs of new immigrants from the East and West Indies. An idea crossed my mind. New immigration rules created new needs and opened new opportunities. Indian food had become popular in England with the influx of Indians from India and Pakistan. Would a Guyanese Indian restaurant work? Canadians were very laid back in their acceptance of new food ideas and reluctant to change. Curry spices are pungent. There were often complaints from tenants in apartment buildings about cooking smells of fellow residents from Indian countries. I thought, *"A take-out curry business might be just what we're looking for. It would be a tough start from a physical viewpoint, but if it worked it could be used as the foundation stone for an import trade of vegetables and fruit from Guyana and the West Indies."*

I mulled over this during my early months. I missed my home in Guyana. The small apartment we occupied seemed somewhat stifling and confining when compared with the beautiful home we had left behind. While I took the children for walks and everything was still new and exciting, the basic idea of a home was missing. I decided to go house hunting. When Mike returned, we would select a home together but I would have done the groundwork.

Things were moving ahead, but time dragged. News from Guyana continued to be bad. It seemed everyone wanted to leave. The economy was failing, the government had decided to nationalize industries, and plum jobs only went to one sector.

There was also dissension in the school. The teachers weren't getting along and Mike was having difficulty. Enrolment was still high, but students and parents continued to ask when I was returning.

When he returned to Canada at Easter, he confided, "Tab, I never thought I'd miss you and the children so much. I don't think I can return without you."

I asked, "What will we do with our investments there? We have the home and the school. We just can't give it all away. What about our responsibilities to the people who've put their trust in us and relied on us for help in giving their children an education?"

"I've spread some news around that we might be selling, but I was told no one would pay the price our school is worth. Perhaps you could return instead of me and settle down the teaching staff. I'm having difficulty with them. They don't accept the changes I think are necessary. I'll take care of the children and scout around for some business we could invest in here."

It was very disappointing to learn that Mike was encountering problems with running the school, but there was no way out. I also doubted that he would make progress finding employment. It would be very difficult for him to enter the labor force in any capacity that would equate what he'd left. Even university graduates from countries outside Canada were finding difficulty in the job market, and his accounting skills were too basic in comparison with a Canadian graduate.

I sighed heavily. I completed the courses in which I had enrolled and aced them. I left college with the understanding that I could renew my registration to complete my Certificate on my return.

I trudged back to Georgetown with a heavy heart. Just when I thought I had put my finger on something that would pan out for us, I had to return to pick up the pieces.

My presence at school was like a panacea. Everything settled down. Life returned to some state of normalcy. Everyone wanted to know what it was like in Canada. The burning question was, "Had I come back to stay, or would I be returning to Canada?"

Things had changed rapidly in the months I had been in Canada. It seemed the fire had gone out of life and the embers remaining would soon die. There were a few offers to purchase the property, but running the school was a different proposition.

All members of my teaching staff had their eye on immigration to Canada and all expected that they would be leaving within the next three years, if not sooner. They said, "You've shown us the way to the future. We have no desire to remain."

That put an end to my hopes of quietly easing myself out of the school and at least getting back part of what it was worth. I consoled myself that during the Second World War, victims had left their mother countries with only the clothes they wore. Those who had remained lost their opportunity, and forfeited their lives. I decided I would remain until the end of the year, but with the understanding of the students that after year-end they would have to complete their education elsewhere.

While shopping one day, I met a friend from my high school days. We talked about the unrest which had settled over the country and the sadness of it all. He said, "I'm not going anywhere and I have no children. My wife will stop plaguing me if she has something to occupy her. She's of mixed race, as you know, so she fits in perfectly. Would you be willing to sell the operation to me?"

I pondered the situation. "Provided we can negotiate a fair price."

We made an appointment for the weekend; they could inspect the books at that time and understand the operation.

I telephoned Mike that night. "Things are looking up. I might have a sale for the school, after all. Someone up there is looking out for us. Have you been able to find anything for yourself or for investments?"

His letters had been full of complaints. "I require a license to sell real estate. I have to look after the children, so can't enroll in classes. Nothing seems to work without you, Tab. I need you here."

"You need to get a grip on things, Mike. We have to make sacrifices. We just can't expect that we can move from the Guyana situation into the Canadian scene effortlessly."

"I came here for you, Tab. You told me that things would work out and I'm depending on that. You have to sell the school. When you return to Canada, we'll talk about what we can do."

My heart was heavy. It was true that I had forced the issue of immigration because of my fears but I expected that the future would be the responsibility of us both. When we sold the school, our income would disappear. Delving into our capital for living expenses would rob us of our safety cushion. In exasperation, I closed my eyes and consigned the future into the hands of the Universe.

The meeting with my friend and his wife went well. I think they were more impressed with the house than with the school. We made a good deal. They were also sending money to Canada and so could pay us part of the agreed price in Canadian dollars and get a mortgage from the bank for the remainder. The price was well below what the home and the school were worth. With the income from the school, they would be able to repay a mortgage within a couple of years.

I could now spend time packing my personal belongings for transport to Canada. Everything else had been sold with the school.

As is usual, after the deal was signed, there was a clamour at the door. Everyone, it seemed, was interested in purchasing the school.

The deed was done. When I eventually left for Canada at the end of the school term, just before Christmas, my heart was filled with grief. It was difficult to say goodbye to all my employees and well-wishers lined up to say their farewells. I hoped I could live up to their expectations of my success in Canada. I wondered if I had done the correct thing by turning my back, for good reasons I admit, from material success, and now, when there was no going back, I wondered whether I had thrown away something irreplaceable.

CHAPTER FORTY-EIGHT

CHANGE IN OUTLOOK. Canada was extremely different from Guyana. There was simply no comparison. Life in a Third World Country in the tropics was vastly different. Everything in Canada was new and every aspect of life was distinct. Change was everywhere. From Summer to Winter, nothing could be taken for granted. We were minorities in a land of 'White' people who were unaccustomed to dealing with immigrants of differing colours and customs. It was the place of New Beginnings for everyone.

Back together in Canada, Mike and I seemed to be always at odds with each other, more so than when we were in Guyana. Nothing I did seemed to be what he wanted or pleased him. I decided we were both spending too much time together, so it would be better and more cost effective if I got a job.

Jobs seemed to be few and far between. I was always met with the words, "We require Canadian experience." Someone suggested the public service, but this didn't fit exactly with my expectations. There was too much red tape. I needed a job where I could expand my knowledge and use my aptitude. While this was only a temporary situation, I needed insight into the workplace and the Canadian way of looking at things.

I registered with an employment agency, had several interviews, but was always met with the excuse "overqualified for our position." It seemed to me that I could make little headway in my quest, so I decided to accept "temporary" assignments. This would enable me to say, "Yes, I do have Canadian experience. After one of these "temping" jobs at a legal firm, I was surprised when I was summoned by the Personnel Manager. She said, "You must have made a great impression on Mr. Smith after only one week. We're offering you the position as his Secretary."

I was pleased. However, I was taken aback when I was told that one of my duties would be to collect his laundry at the end of each week.

"Is this one of the normal duties for secretaries?" I asked.

"As you know, Mr. Smith is a perfectionist. He works long hours and is very successful. We try to make him happy. He can't always get to the laundry on time, so his secretary has been collecting his dry cleaning for him. That responsibility would fall to you."

"Thanks for offering me the job but I can't undertake the "laundry" responsibility. It's not part of a secretary's job, and that makes the job not in my league."

"I'm sorry. He's quite impressed with your competence." She smiled.

We left it at that. I wondered how uncomfortable it would be to finish off the afternoon at work, but I wasn't prepared to do a job which I felt was a 'put down' because I was 'brown'. Once I gave in, there would be no end to the errands I'd be requested to run. I couldn't see myself burdened with laundry, walking down Yonge Street and being greeted by someone I knew from my former life. (I could just hear the thoughts ... how the mighty have fallen. I was scared of the rumours that would follow.)

So be it, I thought as I put on my coat and prepared to leave at the end of the day. However, I knocked on Mr. Smith's door before I left, as a courtesy. He seemed surprised when I stretched out my hand to say goodbye. He wished me luck. We smiled at each other, and I departed.

Perhaps I was out of my depth, I pondered, as I walked to the subway. I felt I had to take a stance and keep my dignity. I pondered over the values in Oliver Goldsmith's 'she stoops to conquer' and wondered if I had indeed overplayed my hand. Before I could become too depressed I remembered 'fortune favours the brave,' straightened my shoulders, and moved on.

Mike grumbled when I told him what had happened. "You should be looking at our business plans, not wasting your time. What do you think you'd like to do?"

"You're right, Mike. Thoughts have been racing through my head. Let's sit down on Sunday and look at possibilities."

That Sunday before we could get down to business, we talked about racism and being marginalized. The children were having trouble at school. They were taunted and called "Pakis". We fell into the category of immigrants from India and Pakistan, the newest type of brown coloured immigrants to Canada. My children were heartbroken. Their world had changed. They had enjoyed a privileged childhood with servants at their beck and call. Now they were taunted and jeered at for something they could not change.

Fears and bigotry had been passed on to Canadian children by some parents' fear of many things. Their children had become bullies. They had rights, whereas the newcomers had none. 'White' people were supposedly more intelligent and therefore superior.

"Just ignore the taunts," I said to them. "Let's talk about our future here. This is our home now. You know that being born a different colour doesn't make you less of a human being. Ignore the taunts, and if they get worse speak to your teachers. You're both bright children. You can overcome this. We've come here seeking asylum. We ran from those same fears. There's no way out. Things will change as evolution takes place."

I hoped that things would settle down at school, and they did. One day a spider appeared in Gloria's classroom and pandemonium struck. The children were shrieking with fear. Gloria went up to the spider, caught it, and released it outside. She was the heroine of the day and simply accepted as a regular girl thereafter. My son was good at math and football. Popularity followed and the turmoil soon died down.

The children's happiness was an essential part of my own adjustment and contentment. I couldn't be happy if they weren't. I had plucked them out of an environment to which they were accustomed and moved headlong into the turmoil of the same element from which we had fled. It was my hope that living in an upper middle class neighbourhood would isolate them from this form of bullying. *Surely educated people were better informed and knew that racial prejudice was a black mark against every axiom of liberty, truth, honour and justice that Canadian society bespoke,* I thought.

There was another hurdle which presented itself at this time. I received a phone call offering me the complete collection of Encyclopedias, a 'must' I was told for every student. I replied, "I'll think about it." The caller tried to impress upon me a sense of urgency.

"We're selling them off at $20.00 below the book store price. This is a one-time offer, and you must commit today to the purchase."

"I can't do that at this time. I have to do some research," I replied

"Encyclopedias contain knowledge. You must have children. You don't want them to lose out," he said.

I was patient and polite; a trait I'd brought with me from Guyana. "I agree with everything you've said, but I still need to do some research. Leave me your number and I'll call you if I decide to make the purchase."

"All this haggling is not worthy of you. You know that you want to buy the volumes. Why not say 'yes' now?"

"I will say 'no' now, perhaps another day." I thanked him and hung up the phone.

I felt certain he understood I wasn't making a purchase.

The next day I answered the doorbell. There was a delivery van in my driveway and a delivery man at my door with a huge cardboard box. He grinned and said, "I've brought you the encyclopedias you ordered. You've taken a very important step in your children's education. I need a cheque for $50.00."

"I didn't place an order" I smiled and shook my head from side to side. "I won't accept delivery of something I don't want and can't afford. You'll have to return the books to the dealer." I attempted to close the door, but couldn't because he had placed his foot to block any attempt at this.

"I must borrow your phone to report the matter to my boss," he commanded, glaring at me with a fixed stare.

"I'm sorry, but you'll have to go to the corner store and use the public phone. If you don't remove your foot now, I'll get my son to call 911." He muttered an epithet about Pakis and how they smelled, but removed his foot. I watched his departure, thankful for small mercies. This was my first exposure to high pressure selling, bordering on force, and intimidation. Never in my imagination should something like this have been possible. I was shaking.

My peace was short lived. The phone rang. It was the original salesman. He began with a string of epithets about uneducated Pakis coming to live in Canada, ordering books, not accepting delivery, and not forthcoming with payment. I quietly disconnected the call and left the phone off the hook.

I was disillusioned. I trembled at the thought of what might have happened if I'd let the delivery man into my home. I was also ashamed. I shouldn't have listened to the salesman in the first place. He had obviously typed me as an uneducated immigrant who could be bullied into paying for something she didn't order.

This was a salutary lesson. Being polite didn't necessarily earn kudos. We were now living in the great, big, wide world of Canada, a first world country, and everything good and bad, had a place in it.

Another lesson I learned was that people tended to take advantage of persons of colour, especially new immigrants. I speculated on the many reasons for this. Perhaps it was due to a lack of understanding of a different culture, a presumption of superiority which they'd inherited because of their birthright, the feeling of the day that they needed to protect themselves from lowering their standards, their belief that all men were not created equal. The reasoning was endless, but I could find no justification for any of this. This pondering was the start of my trying to understand and accept the situation my family had to live within, how I dealt with it, and what knowledge I could impart to my children to ensure they wouldn't grow up with a feeling of inferiority.

I couldn't change the colour of my skin. I couldn't return to Guyana, or migrate to India where my colour would allow me to blend in, because the language would not. English was my first and only language and I had been brought up with English customs. I had to live with this. Even though I had been warned that I would always be a second class citizen in Canada, I believed that at least justice was not colour blind. I could live with that. I would start my own business together with Mike. I would cater to the growing West Indian and Guyanese community and I would prosper.

What and where could I start? I returned to my thought about food gratification and the fact that immigrants from Guyana, Trinidad, and the other West Indian islands missed the foods they had grown up with. Curry and roti were popular Guyanese dishes and delicacies West Indian people craved. I told myself that McDonalds, Colonel Saunders, among several others had created an empire from food. I would follow their example, start one shop, and let the future roll on. I knew that cooking meant physical labour, and a step down from my previous jobs, but I knew I would succeed.

I had excelled at cooking and baking in Guyana. I had learned my cooking lessons from the kitchen help in my parents' household. I'd never expected that the skills they had so lovingly taught me would be so important to my future. Recipes for my curries and puris were always in demand. I breathed a sigh and repeated this mantra to myself: "one small step and good marketing could ultimately lead to creation of a niche market in the food empire, if it is to be, it's up to me."

As a sign of the times, "*Would my being a cook and selling my products demean my image in the eyes of my customers or would they flock to get what I was producing because of its superior taste and quality?*"

CHAPTER FORTY-NINE

A BREAK AT LAST. In the midst of these thoughts, the telephone rang and my attention was diverted to other matters. The employment agency I had registered with was trying to schedule an appointment for an interview. The position was Senior Secretary to the Senior Vice President of Lionsgate Financial Services, a much respected financial company with headquarters in the Netherlands. Lionsgate Financial was a worldwide organization.

I demurred at first, but the consultant cajoled me and pandered to my vanity. She told me this was a company in which I could grow. She had given a glowing report of my qualifications and experience, and the personnel officer was looking forward to meeting me. The company needed an immediate replacement for the previous incumbent. I asked, "Did you tell them I'm not white?"

"I did, but they told me that didn't matter because competence not race was what they were looking for," she laughingly replied.

Her words seduced me. I agreed to attend the interview and do my best. However, I decided to play down my qualifications and say nothing about my high earnings and teaching career.

I wanted the experience of being interviewed by a company of this high caliber. Even if I didn't get the job, it would be nice to see if their offices were as resplendent as those I had seen in the movies.

Mrs. Maguire, the personnel manager was an "officer" of the company. To become an officer was a high achievement in management status. Officers were part of the hierarchy.

The interview went well. I was shown around the office and introduced to some executives. I thought the interview was over and I would learn the outcome later, so I was surprised when she redirected me back to her office. She closed the door and waved me to a chair.

She smiled, seemingly to put me at ease. "Mr. Fenwick isn't an easy person to work for. He has high standards and his expectations of work performance are difficult to meet. Miss Easterbrook, his last secretary, left abruptly for personal reasons. I've got a good feeling about you. Mr. Fenwick is away for the balance of the week, and I don't want to lose this opportunity as you may find something else in the meantime. I'm offering you the position as his Secretary. This is a senior position and we're looking for someone with the right personality and qualifications."

I was flabbergasted to be offered a position on the spot. The salary was good and she even threw in an extra week annual holidays when I told her this was one of my conditions of employment. I accepted and promised to do my best.

On the way home I argued with myself that this job would keep the wolf from the door until my Curry and Roti shop was established. The workload would be heavy. In addition to a 40-hour week I would also have responsibility for looking after my family, running the home, trying to finish my studies at Centennial College, and establishing the business. Roties had to be made and baked individually. They couldn't be mass produced. "Too heavy a load?" I questioned myself. I remembered

my father's words again. "If it is to be, it's up to me." I told myself, "*Make room in your consciousness to accept the load, and you can
make it happen.*"

Life has a way of pushing you in the right direction. *Was it destiny? Would it deter me from establishing my own business in Canada?
Was it life's way of teaching me to manage my opportunities on the road
to fulfillment of what was indeed in store for me?*

I felt elation at gaining the job. The storm clouds were lifting.
Here I was, forty years old, an immigrant, non-white, being given
a first insight into what I thought would be closed to me despite
my accomplishments because of my colour. Nothing was impossible, it seemed. I had made the right choice to leave Guyana.
News from there was always depressing. There seemed to be no
end to the problems being encountered by the Indo-Guyanese,
as Indians who were still in Guyana, were now called.

The job signified new beginnings and an end to my old life in
Guyana. "Yes," I said to myself, "fresh starts, new approaches to
problems, anything can happen, the world's my oyster."

Of course, Mike wasn't happy. He berated me for making the
commitment and asked, "Who'll look after me and the children?"

I replied, "This is exactly what I'm doing. If we don't husband
our resources, our capital will disappear, and what can we hope
for then? Despair over missed opportunities? I don't think so. It's
time for you to assume some responsibility. You're at home, so it's
up to you to research the availability of properties to open our
shop. You can make sure that the children are off to school and
be here when they return."

He glared at me. "Is this what you've brought me here to do?"

"You have our roles confused, Mike. You're supposed to be
the bread winner, and I'm supposed to be the mother who looks
after the children and home. You turned over your role to me
after our son was born and we couldn't make ends meet because
I couldn't return to work. You can't always wait on me to start

things; you have to do your part now. We've been accustomed to a steady income from the school, but this ended when we sold that business. Things will work out but we must each put our shoulders to the wheel."

He looked at me in disgust. "I'll do as you wish, but don't blame me when things go wrong."

"The secret to success is to visualize that success is indeed happening. Nothing will come to fruition if you think it'll go wrong. Positive thinking brings positive results. Let's pull together on this. We'll be successful, I'm sure of that," I counselled.

He seemed somewhat mollified by my conciliatory tone, but my heart was in turmoil. The children had heard our bickering and after he left the room they asked what was happening.

"We're in a new country now and a new situation. The home and life you knew when we lived in Guyana is past history. In Canada we have to take care of everything ourselves. The simple tasks and the difficult ones also have to be done by all of us. You both have to help me with the household chores and help your Dad with the yard."

"What about the swimming pool, Mom? Who'll look after that?"

"You're both too young to go near the pool if no adult is around, and you must never invite your friends to come over for a swim unless you ask either your Dad or me for permission. An adult must supervise you and your friends when you're in the pool. That's the law."

"We know, Mom. It's cool to have a swimming pool. It makes us special."

I smiled at them. "Everything will be fine."

We had bought a house in an upper middle class neighbourhood before I returned to Guyana. The deal had closed shortly before I returned to Canada. With the help of some friends, Mike moved us in. Moving was not a big deal. There were no large items, and the apartment we'd lived in had been sparsely furnished.

The children were happier here. The home was more in line with what we left, though smaller in size. Now they had their own swimming pool and this was a big deal. School was just five minutes away. Children came to call when they moved in. The neighbours were friendly enough, but I kept my distance.

Waiting at the bus stop made me a friend, Jackie James. Our friendship endured for years. She set out to make sure that I was welcome. Our family were constant guests in her home. She had a pool also. Nancy, her daughter, gifted to my daughter the complete series of *Nancy Drew*. These books were passed on to my three nieces, and then to my granddaughter. Our friendship endured even though she eventually emigrated to the United States, and then we lost contact.

In contrast to Jackie, there was another neighbour who lived next door to Jackie. He also worked in the Sun Life building, home of my new employer. We would travel up to our different floors on the same elevator, but he never acknowledged my existence. I would enter the elevator, say hello, everyone would reply or smile, but his facial expression never changed.

Later on, I heard that he was blaming my children for using "swear words" while they were playing with his son, Charlie. He had also made derogatory comments about the neighbourhood 'going down.' Mike didn't go out to business, we entertained lavishly every weekend with our relatives and new friends, so we had to be part of an underground illegal organization, possibly the "mafia."

Christo and Gloria had complained about Charlie's language before. They didn't like playing with him because he tried to bully them and he felt using "swear" words made him a 'big shot'.

One afternoon I came home from work and found eight children playing outside. I was happy. I didn't mind the neighbourhood children playing in our front yard. I felt it was better for me to know they were just outside rather than wondering where they were.

Gloria tried to introduce me to them all, but Charlie uttered some expletives about their delaying the game. I must admit that I was taken aback. He hadn't acknowledged my presence. The other children had chorused a greeting with a smile but he'd remained sullen and silent, off to one side.

I walked up to him, "Charlie, those words you're using aren't polite. Do you know the meaning of them?" He hung his head and pursed his lips.

"Obviously, you know they aren't words you should repeat. Why do you use them?" He didn't answer. I smiled as I gazed at his face. He looked totally confused. He'd never received questions like this before from any adult. "Do any of the other children use them?"

"No," he finally said in a low voice staring into the ground.

I smiled, and in a gentle tone said, "I'll make a bargain with you. Before you use any words you don't know the meaning of, look them up in the dictionary or ask your parents what they are. When you come over here to play with Christo and Gloria, I expect you to be civil and polite. Swearing and use of words I consider are offensive will only cause me to set you apart. Then you won't be permitted to join in their play. Do you understand?"

He looked around at the children who had gathered around and lowered his head. He'd lost face and couldn't deal with it.

He looked at me and I smiled. "Come on, lad. Say you're sorry, and get on with your play."

The children chanted, "Hurry up, Charlie. You're in or you're out."

He said, "Sorry" as he looked at me for the first time. I held out my hand, and he placed his in mine. We shook hands, and the children whooped as they returned to their play.

I moved my head from side to side thinking 'what's next?' as I went through the door. *We will be blamed for everything that goes wrong around here,* I said. Obviously the children are popular. The swimming pool was the drawing card. If it took a swim in the pool with a hot dog and lemonade after, I felt that was a small price to pay for their happiness.

Thoughts entered my mind. "*Would I ever be accepted? Would my colour, rather than who I am define me?*" My future awaited my actions. I smiled '*If it is to be, it's up to me*'.

CHAPTER FIFTY

L UCKY STRIKE. My job was turning into the very interesting opportunity I'd always dreamed of experiencing. I thought I would find efficiency. Instead, it seemed I was projected back to my first job, which I considered operated on archaic inefficiency. No one respected the twenty-minute break for coffee, the telephones were always busy with private calls, secretaries worked only for their own bosses, even though they could have helped out in other areas, when time hung heavily on their hands.

I eased into things gradually. I didn't want to rock the boat. There was a hierarchy, of course. The secretary was as important as her boss. As secretary to Harrison Fenwick, Senior Vice President, I was a Senior Secretary and ranked high in the pecking order of office staff.

Mr. Fenwick was away when I started. My first day on the job, the day on which my future was to be built, was important. I had my own office. It was small and private, a store room really without a window, but it was my own. I was given office manuals, shown my boss's office, and left to my own devices. It was necessary to acquire an understanding of the business I was in; procedures and functions mattered when efficiency was called for. I asked about Mr. Fenwick, his status, likes, and dislikes. If I wanted to function efficiently, I needed to know the personalities and expectations of fellow workers.

Collection of laundry and personal errands were at the back of my mind. I smiled to myself. I'd mentioned the laundry incident at my last temping job to Mrs. Maguire during my interview. She told me that personal errands were up to me; however, the mailman usually did these chores for Senior Staff.

My first day at work stretched out interminably. The hands of the clock moved slowly. There was simply nothing to keep me occupied. I wandered over to Mr. Fenwick's office. There were two baskets full of mail on his credenza. Mrs. Maguire had warned me that I was not to touch anything until his return.

"If I'm to be a good secretary, efficiency counts. Secretarial jobs aren't just shorthand and typing. In my book, secretary also meant being an assistant. If this was a faux pas, too bad. Nothing ventured, nothing gained," I told myself.

I started opening the letters. I didn't know what the fuss was all about. These were only replies to a survey. I filed them according to action required and then set about clearing the pile of other mail accumulating in the second basket. These were also sorted. I then looked for the relevant files and determined the type of action required.

Sorting the mail gave me some insight into the workings of the company. By the end of the week my research had paid off. I had basic knowledge of the industry and the company's position within that industry, together with the role my boss. My first week had been put to good use.

Things were working out well at home as well. My thoughts centred on planning for the future as soon as I settled into my job; I would prod Mike into action and we would go looking for a suitable venue for the shop. Life took on a pleasant hue. I wasn't sitting down and waiting for the world to come to me. I was going out to greet it.

Mr. Fenwick arrived soon enough on Monday morning. I gave him time to read the newspaper. His name seemed to suit him. Harrison Fenwick had attended a private boys' school in England and his demeanor bespoke this.

Immigrants from England were highly prized employees in Canada, I understood. They signified the customs in Canada which, of course, had been founded by English and French settlers. I also had an English education, albeit in the Colonial empire, but we were on the same wavelength.

He commended what I had done with his correspondence. "I've never had someone like you working for me before. If you can do as well with your shorthand, I'll be very pleased indeed".

I raised my eyebrows. "What now? What have I said?" he asked.

"Nothing at all," I replied with a knowing smile. "However, I'd like some guidance on preparation and typing of the treaties, "financial contractual agreements", the company has negotiated, and now awaiting formal execution. I understand these have been piling up and are overdue."

"What about them? They're late already and should have been sent for signature six weeks ago, but there was no one to get them ready."

"I'd like to suggest that we make one original, and then photocopy the six copies we require. Typing would go much faster and the copies would have a better appearance if they were put in folders and bound. I've looked at the carbon copies and for the amounts these treaties represent, the presentation of our final contract should convey their importance."

"Come now, what are you suggesting? I don't think you understand our procedure. Carbon copies signify that there have been no changes from the original, and that's how we operate."

"Perhaps I haven't presented my case properly. Photocopies become originals when they're signed. Signatures on these documents make them legal. They don't have to be carbon copies," I countered.

He said, "I've never thought of our contracts in that way. It's a good idea. I'll ask our company secretary to seek a legal opinion on this before we make any changes. Thanks for the suggestion. I can see that we're in for interesting times. What did you say you did before coming to Canada?"

His telephone rang and I took my leave.

Later on in the day, he came into my office. "You were right. We'll start photocopying the documents. How long before we can clear this pile up?" he said pointing to the stacks of files.

"It'll take a couple of weeks. I'll need to get clarification on some of the wordings and this may take some time."

"At last, someone intelligent. Where did you learn about originals?"

"I have a legal background also," I replied. "I was Secretary to Sir Thomas Bingham, Chief Justice of Guyana."

"We'll work well together. You can start preparing the contracts we make to bind our commitments, before we send them over to the lawyers for vetting," were his parting words.

Later that day Rose, the receptionist, enquired with raised eyebrows, "What have you done to that man?" He came out of your office and said, "I think I've died and gone to Heaven."

I laughed. "He recognizes my value."

I mulled over my day. I could see myself working here in the niche I had created, but was this what I really wanted? This was just something to tide me over. I wanted to be my own boss, to determine my own future. Would this job become my stumbling block?

CHAPTER FIFTY-ONE

WISHES BECOME REALITY. We fell into a pattern at home. Mike seemed content with the way things were. Whenever I asked about venues for our restaurant, he always made excuses. I debated with myself, "Should I let it go and concentrate only on my own job?" I was part of a worldwide organization, even though in a minor capacity. The job kept me busy during the day and at college two nights a week, plus time to study. With the household chores and meal preparation, there was little time left for social outlets.

I recognized that something within me wanted more. Despite my value to the company, we were still in a period of history when women seldom, if ever, got promoted to senior positions. I couldn't see myself being content with a secretarial position in five years. I wanted to be my own boss, responsible for my own destiny. I needed to emulate the success I enjoyed with the school and most of all I wanted to take control of my destiny.

I remembered having to haggle over vacation time. I didn't trust that salary increases wouldn't encounter the same problem. No matter how good I was at work there were two strikes I could never overcome. I was a woman, and I was brown, neither the correct sex nor the correct colour. The job would serve for two years at the most and then it would be time to move on.

We started researching commercial retail rentals in local classifieds and viewing properties on weekends. This dragged on for a while. As we couldn't find something suitable on our own, it was time to get help. Colin Porter, the realtor who had assisted in the purchase of our own home, found a colleague who dealt in commercial rentals. It took another three months, but we eventually found ideal premises in Scarborough, about half an hour from our home.

Renovations, equipment, and supplies completed, our bold venture was ready for action. Dependent on how business developed, further plans would follow.

Our grand opening was in October. I hadn't anticipated as many people as the crowd which stormed our door. We ran short of everything. I cooked rotis until I was red in the face. We needed help and fast.

Assistance came from a former student. She was awaiting a visa to the U.S. so I knew this could only be a temporary measure. However, the main shift of cooking fell to her and she was great, just what we needed.

Business was good. There was never a dull moment. Money literally poured in and we began to plan for the future.

There was never much time for my personal life. My world consisted of several pigeon holes. I worked at my regular job, part-time at the restaurant, attended night school to finish by Certificate in Management, looked after the home, and nurtured the children. Proper planning enabled me to do all these things. I didn't neglect my health. I rose early in the morning to put in a 45-minute workout, interspersing this with swimming in the summer.

Two years of this drained me but I didn't give up. After completion of my Certificate at Centennial College, York University was my next target. A degree would be a string to my bow. This would satisfy the yearning within me that had begun when my brothers went abroad to further their education in the field of their choice, a path not available to me, because I was a woman. I'd always envied my brothers. They were given opportunities I yearned for. This was my chance.

During this period, I became a proud Canadian citizen. Tears of joy streamed down my face as I swore the oath and sang our national anthem. I was Canadian, I belonged. I couldn't stop smiling. The winds of change pushed me forward. I could become whatever and whoever I wanted to be. Canada was the land of opportunity. I'd left the past behind; the future was up to me.

I understood that the concept of women at work and equal opportunity were difficult philosophies but there was always hope. Attending university and pursuing further education was a dream. As I stood at the threshold of fulfillment, I couldn't be denied.

It was a hard grind. Five years at night school paid off. At the graduation ceremony nobody was as happy and contented as I was. The music of Elgar's 'Land of Hope and Glory' brought tears to my eyes.

This day counted as the completion of one of the major milestones in my life. I remembered the yearnings of a young girl, twelve years old, sitting on the back steps of the family home, hoping to see a falling star, and wishing that if somehow she could go to university abroad, her life would change, the past would disappear, and who knows, maybe, she would be made whole again and the violations to her body and her soul would fade.

Time never distances you from good or bad. You embrace the good and it becomes part of you, but you wear the bad like a leaden mantle because it seldom, if ever, disappears. It remains part and parcel of your soul.

I determined to seek psychological counselling and reach some understanding that would give me comfort. If I came to terms with the past, perhaps the mantle I carried with me could become less burdensome.

CHAPTER FIFTY-TWO

PROMOTION. My status at work improved. Ellen Maguire had found a new love and there were other interests she wished to pursue. Working in her old job was not part of her future. That opened up a position I could fill.

I was promoted to the post of Officer Manager and Head of Human Resources. Ellen and I'd had our differences when I introduced new concepts and ideas for more effective management which were counter to her own management principles.

This promotion was an opportunity. My education was opening doors to the future. Data processing and modern trends were revolutionizing the storage of data and information. Technology hovered on the brink of world revolution. Innovators saw the future expanding with technology; the naysayers thought the world would continue to exist as they knew it and technological improvements would totter and fall off into oblivion. They were wrong. Technology was in its infancy; it would grow and expand with no boundaries.

Furthering my education was paying off. I'd studied subjects which led to a certification in Business Management at Centennial College. At university I was given the opportunity to turn my knowledge into reality. Personnel management was a refresher in understanding people potential. My intuition that different approaches were needed with different individuals because we're all different, was established. To help my former students achieve what was best for them, I had changed my approaches to suit their personalities. Getting along with people came naturally after that.

I looked at the company as a cohesive whole and pondered the concept that if everyone worked together as one organism, rather than fighting to hold on to the pigeon hole they considered their sole 'domain,' this could create ultimate efficiency. This was an avant-garde of new ideas, of different ways of approaching the same problem, against a background of a determination that markets were changing. It was my belief that conglomerates would take over and smaller players would be swallowed up in their wake.

Ideas are like avalanches sweeping down the mountainside, either consuming the imagination of forward thinkers or burying the naysayers in their wake. Ideas are not exclusive. We all have ideas. Some may be similar; others could be different. If we combined them, the impact could be formidable. My first objective was to get departments talking with each other, committing to the same objective, with everyone working together to achieve one goal, a well-oiled corporate machine. Motivation is a key element in life. If we're not motivated to join the revolution of change, we remain stagnant. If we deny ourselves the opportunity to move forward, we seldom achieve the optimum, and never reap the benefit the future offers.

A committee of members from all departments was appointed. We set goals together and created a new personnel manual. It defined the workforce and the responsibility of each individual. Our credo became our mantra. Each department held training sessions where everyone could ideate and concepts could blossom. Company sponsored education was offered to all employees who wanted to update their skills. We felt this would lead to a

cohesive, well-oiled entity with everyone participating in its success and new ideas could become the avalanche sweeping down
the mountainside. They could consume the imagination, burying the pessimists in their wake. Employee commitment to these
new ideas grew into a huge wave, a pride of 'belonging.'

When employees become empowered, they take pride in
their jobs, regardless of status because they realize that they are
all integral parts of a whole. Salaries better than the average,
benefits second to none, promotions that could be earned with
further education, gave every employee pride in their jobs and
self-respect; they realized their importance in the whole scheme
of operations and everyone pushed in the same direction.

As this wave grew, I earned a second promotion. This was a
huge improvement in my standing. It attested to my competence
and value. I always thought that race would play a role in my ever
getting further ahead, but somehow it seemed that the value of
my work to the company made everyone colour blind. What an
achievement in itself! I would receive major benefits, including
the use of a company car. I would also spend two weeks in the
Netherlands at the company head office. Travel and accommodation were business class.

This moment in my life held considerable importance to my
future. Suddenly, it seemed, I didn't think of myself as a brown
woman; I was Canadian. I paid taxes, worked hard, and best of
all, I was proud of my country and its reputation in the world.
Being Canadian meant holding on to the values my country represented and being part of them. Finally, the feeling of homesick-
ness for the country of my birth began to slip away. I belonged.

It was the eighties. How I felt didn't portray how well I was received outside the office by people who didn't know me. I looked
on in amusement when I attended conferences. People looked
in my direction and quickly looked elsewhere to avoid eye contact. The looks always changed when they found out who I was.

I didn't hold this against them. This was part of life. I told my-self that they felt awkward because of the difference in colour and background. Talking to someone they didn't know meant taking a big leap in the first place, and they were confused be-cause, suddenly, their world had changed and this was all new to them. People of colour and women were becoming part of the landscape.

I felt secure in my new environment. Once again, I was el-evated to a position of authority and consequence. I went to the best restaurants and to concerts and plays. I was part of the crowd who cheered our baseball and hockey teams to victory. This job had given me a place in the hierarchy of a multinational company and expanded my mind and being, with an explosion of cultural activities.

I still continued to work laboriously at the shop. My Saturdays were always spent cooking and helping to fill the orders which were always heavier. The shop had gained recognition. West Indians loved our cuisine, sometimes coming as far as New York City, or buying supplies while on holiday. We were still looking into expansion in another location but Mike felt it would be dif-ficult to manage a second shop. I mentioned hiring more people, or expanding in different ways but Mike's excuse always was that this was impossible. His outlook on life in Canada was different to mine. He was content. The shop was prospering. Why make changes? He remained isolated in the context of managing a business catering to Guyanese and West Indians. This limited his vision and confined it to his past experience. The expanded horizons available in Canada held little appeal.

CHAPTER FIFTY-THREE

S TORM CLOUDS REND THE TREE OF LIFE. Differing outlooks on life began to tear us apart. Instead of being proud of my accomplishments at work, Mike looked on these as a threat. He felt he needed to discredit me in order to uphold his own importance. He aired our disagreement by denigrating my accomplishments. He escalated his put-downs of me in public. I ignored his jibes by trying to turn them into a laughing situation, but my tolerance of this continuous ridicule was almost reaching boiling point. Sometimes I longed to retaliate, but I held back because open warfare would interfere with my children's lives and I felt would achieve nothing.

While the restaurant was growing and solidifying itself, and I was trending upwards in the echelons of business, my children had also blossomed. They had done well at school. My son was attending university and my daughter in her last year at high school. They had friends of all races and were very comfortable in their new environment.

I held high hopes for their future. The disappointment of my siblings when they were forced to pursue disciplines chosen for them by my parents was always at the forefront of my thoughts.

My parents had limited their choices to what they thought would best guarantee financial security for their children – Doctor, Dentist, Barrister, Solicitor. One sibling, in particular desired to further his studies in engineering. He had worn his regret like a mantle, always contemplating "if I'd studied in my chosen field" rather than observing, "I've made a success of this career."

I promised when my son was born that his happiness was all I desired. I felt that if he pursued the career of his choice, he would justify his place in the world simply by being happy and content. I hoped my daughter would follow in my footsteps.

At the time of their birth, I was a staunch Christian and believed that children were gifts from God. Now, with the advance of scientific knowledge, I wondered what motivated the sperm, let loose by the cataclysmic upheaval of sexual gratification, to swim madly towards their goal of fertilization. Was it God, Chance or Destiny?

As a child, I always questioned the reason for my birth. Was the trauma of my childhood atonement for my sins purely circumstantial, or because of some remote reason I could never fathom? Happiness eluded me in my youth. I was determined that the same fate would not befall my children.

My daughter was blossoming. She was charming, articulate, a good listener, and beautiful. She had done well in school and with her educational attainment and could attend any university of her choice. Whatever discipline she wanted to pursue was her choice. I knew she would be successful and happy.

I sheltered them, or tried to, from the bickering that had become daily conversation in our household. They comforted me, when they saw how hurt I was after a particularly brutal encounter with their father. They tried to bridge the widening gap between us, but neither Mike nor I would give in.

We had it all, Mike and me. The restaurant was doing well, which meant Mike was doing well, I was climbing the ladder and excelling at my job, the children were persistent and persevering. They were making inroads in their search for further education. We had achieved what we set out to do when we left Guyana. No longer did I regret leaving the school. I was proud and happy that we had all settled down to life in Canada without any severe fallout. There were many opportunities still to be pursued, and there would be no end to our success.

Mike and I were not marching to the same beat of the drum. He was content with the shop remaining as it was. I wanted to expand. He dealt with the difficulty of supervising. I countered with the opportunities that awaited us. I took matters in my own hands and contacted a real estate agent to help us find a new location for our business. Our bickering increased to the point where we began to air our differences in public.

We were attending a party hosted by one of his cousins. It was a happy affair. Friends and relatives and fellow Guyanese were there. We laughed and danced to the beat of Caribbean music. After a particularly long session on the dance floor, I looked around for Mike. Someone said he was in the dining room. I halted just outside when I heard his cousin say, "Mike, you're a lucky man. You struck gold when you married Tabitha. She's beautiful, charming, and brilliant. We all thought you were foolish to leave the school and come to Canada, but look at you today, you're all set, you're in the money again."

I heard Mike's laughter and then his words, "It's easy for you to say that, but Tabitha's hands are always in the till. She drains the cash."

I didn't let him proceed further. I entered the room and said quietly but with the determination to stand up for myself against a downright lie, "Mike, you're a liar. I never take money from the till. In fact, you may call me an unpaid worker called upon at all hours to help you out of a jam. I give you and the shop my all, but seldom get anything in return. Give me the keys to my company car now." He started to object, but one look at my face which reflected the storm he'd set loose made him think twice. I took the keys and drove home.

I was so angry at his latest put down, I felt like telling him to find other accommodation. He had shamed me. I never asked for an accounting of proceeds from the shop, assuming that most of it was going into family savings. I used my salary to defray household and other expenses.

"What am I doing wrong?" I asked myself. "Is he jealous of my success at work?" Then a thought wormed its way into my mind. "You've given him permission to treat you like this."

"How did you reach this point in life?" I asked myself. "You've never called him on his put downs before. You've bitten your tongue and lamented in secret. This is something he's been accustomed to doing for so long, he doesn't even realize that the day would come when you would find his taunting so unbearable, you'd lose it and be forced to take action."

Memories of all I'd endured danced before me. I remembered the remarks when people laughed at us in Georgetown, Guyana, because he never walked beside me. He had to show, as he walked ahead of me, that he was the leader and in control, much like his father had done. I remembered the looks on the faces of my teaching staff when he made remarks to diminish me, or when he would, in the midst of important instructions to the girls at school, interrupt me with trivialities he felt should be included in my talks. All designed to put me down. I was overwhelmed by the memory of it all. How and why did I endure this? What had I done to myself?

I remembered how ashamed, and diminished I had felt during our holiday in the south of France when he behaved so intolerably to me because I'd refused his sexual advances that night. He had shouted and called me all sorts of names. It didn't stop until someone came and knocked on our door and told us to cease our disturbance. I was embarrassed and afraid we would be asked to vacate our room next day. Nasty words and quarrels during the day then sex at night to make it right. This was his pattern.

Here I was, a woman, respected by my colleagues, a force in business, allowing myself to be verbally abused by my husband, the man who was supposed to protect me. I had allowed this to happen over the years of our marriage. It was easier to absorb everything in order to keep the peace. I hadn't counted on his disrespect of me because of my silence.

I vowed it would happen no more. This was the end. New beginnings needed to happen. I decided that the time had indeed come for me to take issue with him.

When he returned home, he came up into our bedroom. I didn't wait for him to speak. "I didn't appreciate what you did and said about me today," I barked at him with a forbidding look and daggers in my eyes.

His reply added fuel to the fire, "I said it as a joke. Can't you take a joke?" He seemed to want to quell my anger by placing blame on me.

I interrupted, fury in my face, eyes and heart, "Was demeaning of me a joke? I've never stolen money from your till. I've never even asked you for an accounting of income from the shop. I pay all the bills associated with our home. Why do you have to lie? In fact, why did you want to make such a derogatory remark about my stealing money from you? I'm not a paid employee, and I labour there harder than you've ever done. The shop doesn't belong to you solely. I have a stake in it."

"I told you it was a joke. Can't you take a joke?" he muttered angrily shaking his head in disbelief that he was being blamed for an innocent remark.

"I don't know why I've allowed you to behave this way towards me. Is it too much for you to acknowledge my worth and importance to our success?"

I was astounded by his reply. "When you have a jackass you have to ride it."

"If that's what I am to you, then I'm a jackass no longer. You just managed to end to our marriage. Our life together was always a farce. I've never been happy. Despite everything I've done, you obviously think of me as chattel to be used and abused. Don't ever come into this bedroom again. This house belongs to me. Find other lodgings. I will seek legal advice, and we'll proceed on our own paths from here on." My body was shaking with anger and disgust. What had I done to myself all these years?

I turned to get back into the bedroom and noticed my two children standing in the corridor, staring at us with shocked faces.

I said to them, "You don't have to choose sides. You've lived with us and you both know that we never seem to be in agreement about anything. I've tolerated your father's behaviour of me far too long. I can't go on like this any longer. Your Dad will find some place to live. I will remain here and this will be your home until you decide otherwise."

They were both stunned, but in their hearts I believed they knew that it was time for us to sever relations.

Each had stepped up to defend me over the years but they were torn. This was a major decision. Like an earthquake, the tremors would be far reaching and ultimately affect their own lives.

The tide of abuse and put downs over the years had reached their boiling points and broken through the chains of bondage. Enough! No more my soul cried out. Your marriage is over.

CHAPTER FIFTY-FOUR

ON THE BRINK. My first action next day was to make an appointment to consult a lawyer. My feelings must have been reflected in my demeanour. There was a rumour around the office that something was out of kilter. No one would hazard a guess about whether it was personal or business, but George, the office mailman brought me a chocolate. "Boss lady, you're not smiling today; this will restore your spirits, you're all business, no chit chat, no smiles."

A simple act, but it caused reassessment of my thoughts and my future. *Change is happening. Whatever it is, it'll bring happiness and smiles. This is a celebration, not a wake. I'm severing the yoke I helped place around my own neck. My prison sentence is over.*

I got up, straightened my jacket and went into the mailroom. "George, you're a genius."

"Glad you recognize that, Boss lady, my pleasure, as always," he replied. He'd provided a much needed jolt to my consciousness. This was not the end, but in fact a new beginning. For the first time in my life I would be free to laugh, to be happy, to be insulated against the barbs that had become an everyday part of my life. I reminded myself, *'Today is the first day of the remainder of my life.'*

I knocked on the President's door. "Mr. Woodruff, please indulge me, are you free for lunch? I've some personal business to discuss with you and it would be better said away from the office."

"You're not going to quit on me, are you?" he jokingly replied, eyebrows raised, hand waving me to a seat.

I smiled. "We'll talk about it over lunch and perhaps a glass of wine."

This was an important day in my life. I had made a split decision, which would cause change. I wanted to set the record straight. Women never seem to have the same rights as men but the future was clear to me. Because of my ability, I was promoted to the rank of Senior Vice President, the only woman in the officer hierarchy of the entire corporation worldwide. I was at the brink. Life could turn either way. I mattered. I had value and I will survive.

I engaged in positive thinking. I told myself I wouldn't be expected to resign my position. The hierarchy would be supportive of me. Because of my efforts, the company now worked like a well-tuned car.

The restaurant was almost full. We knew a few of the diners and acknowledged them. We were shown to a table in a quiet corner.

"Now what is this all about? What's bothering you?" Taylor Woodruff asked after we settled down.

"I'm filing for divorce. Mike and I are separating. I've called it quits."

"This is certainly a sudden decision. I've always thought you guys were hitting it off well together. Just goes to show, you never know. You've always told everyone their future is theirs to make or break."

"Mike and I have had our differences throughout the years, but I've always backed down for the sake of the children. They're both adult now, and its time for me to look out for myself."

"Is there someone else waiting in the wings?" he asked, looking at me with a twinkle in his eye.

"No. I just want to legalize my situation and my finances, and then I'll revel in my freedom. We've been married for nearly thirty years, but we've grown apart. We work and live in different worlds and we see life through different eyes. We never seem to understand what motivates the other. There's just too much bickering and quarrelling, too much jealousy of success and ability. It's time for us to go our separate ways. I want to be free as a bird, to flap my wings whenever I please. Simply put, I just want to be happy." I looked at him with questions in my eyes, not knowing what his reply would be.

"That certainly wasn't what I was expecting to hear. But it changes nothing here. We'll have to find some additional jobs to keep you busy". He patted my hand and smiled. I took a sip of wine.

"If you need my assistance at any time, just ask." We laughed. I had said the same to him many times, when he'd approached me about some triviality.

I was relieved at the tone of the conversation. I questioned myself, "Why are you always so insecure? You know your value to the company. You always say to others 'an end heralds a new beginning.'"

My mood lightened as the day progressed. I was looking forward to getting home and starting the job of straightening out various changes our separation heralded.

My heart sank as I turned the corner and realized that Mike's car was in the driveway. That meant he was waiting for me. I didn't think I had any reserved energy to deal with him. But the meeting could not be postponed. As I put my key in the lock I realized I was dealing with the situation from a vantage point. He had always been the instigator in our disagreements. Our roles were now reversed.

As I opened the door I called out, "Mike, are you upstairs packing? I'm so glad we can settle this situation amicably. It'll be good for both of us and better for the children."

"I'm in the kitchen waiting to talk to you about this nonsense of separation and divorce," came the reply in a put-down tone, just as if I was being chastised for a wrong I'd committed.

"It's no nonsense. I'm serious. I met with my lawyer, John Engel today. He advised that we can get a dissolution within a year, provided the divorce isn't contested. I told him this is an amicable situation, we've had issues over the years, and we'd grown further apart in Canada. He advised me to prepare a list of our assets and how we wanted these divided. His legal team would take care of the rest."

"Tab, I don't know what has gotten into you. I've never stopped you from doing whatever you wanted even when I didn't agree with that. You travel on business all over the world and you never discuss this with me, you get a car from the company and you never even ask my opinion on the make or model. You don't even come to help me in the shop anymore."

"As to the last, you practically accused me of stealing from you. You told your cousin that I was dishonest. Why? What brought that on? Why do you persist in pulling me down and shaming me? Does that make you feel good? Can't you even admit that I had everything to do with our success, first in the school and now with the shop? You landed a gold mine when we got married, but it has run dry. I'm looking forward to going my separate way and then I'll have to please no one but myself. The children are grown and they wouldn't be a burden to you. The earnings from the shop will all be yours, and the building will increase in value when you decide to retire. You've nothing to fear, just keep the shop running," I replied.

"You don't know what you're doing. Who's advising you to leave me and disrupt our little family? There must be someone else and you've been carrying on with him behind my back."

I laughed. "Think whatever you want. I'm tired of it all. I can take everything we own from you if I wanted. That's not the way I think. When you walk through those doors, I'll watch you go with peace in my heart."

"But what about the children? They ..."

I didn't allow him to finish. "I've thought of leaving you many times over the years but I felt it wasn't the best choice for the children. I didn't want them to grow up in a broken home. Now I'm not so sure. Their childhood was full of our bickering, your 'put-downs' of me, and seemingly impossible arguments. I did them a disservice. I should have protected them better."

"And is that your last word? My family would like to speak to you. They all feel you're doing the wrong thing"

"Mike, I don't want or need advice. Let's leave it at that. The sooner you move out of the house and get settled, the better it will be for us all. This is the end of our lives together, but think of it as a new beginning where we can both be happy. Let's not make this an issue. We don't even think on the same wavelength. Our goals in life have always been different."

"Tab, I can't live without you. I'd rather die. You're my world. I can't stand the loneliness of life without you. We've been married for such a long time; why would you think that either one of us could exist without the other?"

"I'm not going to argue with you, Mike. I've made up my mind and there's no turning back."

"Is there someone else? Am I being replaced? Is that what all of this is about?"

"Think whatever you want to. You've had your way all these years. You exploited my feelings. You showed no respect for me despite everything I've done. I can add much more but I won't."

Someone had probably put the thought in his head that I was leaving him because I was head over heels in love with another man. It never seemed to have occurred to him that it was his behaviour that had led to this. It was just easier to put the blame on someone else, rather than accept that it was his fault. He slammed the door as he left. I thought 'freedom at last'. I poured myself a glass of wine, took in deep breaths, and pondered.

CHAPTER FIFTY-FIVE

INTROSPECTIVE. My life was a muddle, first with rape and violation, then by Mohan. I'd had doubts about going through a marriage with Mike. Before we were married, I asked him to free me from my promise to marry him. He'd reassured me by saying hat everyone felt insecure before '*taking the plunge*' and it was just a case of 'jitters'. Rather than argue with him, or ask for postponement of the wedding, I had given in too easily. Somehow, I always felt it would be easier to make peace with myself rather than deal with the disappointment of others.

I upbraided myself for putting 'me' last. I never realized the damage I was inflicting on my psyche. Everything bottled up inside demanded reparation. The elasticity of the human mind can only stretch so far, then 'pop,' just like a rubber band, it breaks.

I asked myself, "Who are you? Why do you think so little of yourself?" The answers came pouring out.

I don't know who I am. I've always blamed myself because I couldn't and didn't defend myself from early rape and incest. I didn't fight hard enough. I was constrained by my own fears that no one would believe me, and I dreaded the outcome. My cowardly silence gave consent to the abuse.

I'd been living a lie. I wanted to be loved and liked. Despite being a victim, I believed I would be penalized by blame and rejection. My easy acceptance and friendly behaviour was a signal to my abusers that I was easy prey, and not likely to raise a fuss. I gave in to Mike's bickering because I feared that putting up resistance would cause more disagreement between us. It was easier to accept defeat and live with the consequences. I'd become an easy victim because of fear and cowardice. If I'd fought back, perhaps our marriage may have ended earlier, or perhaps not?

It's difficult to reconcile the role of abused woman with the same woman who made a success of her career as secretary, teacher, and business school pioneer in Guyana, as well as Senior Vice President of the Canadian operation of a respected worldwide company... and in addition to it all, pioneered a thriving Guyanese take away food business along with a partner who always professed to know everything about anything, but lacked the courage to start the venture or make change.

The other you, I told myself, is that shrinking violet who cowers behind a veil where she can shut out her accomplishments and usurp the blame from those who wronged her.

There was much to learn about myself. A lifetime had been wasted. I blamed myself for my inability to stop the heinous abuse which was being perpetrated on me in my childhood, yet all I had to do was to scream and shout. Victim mentality was my scourge. I could do nothing to avert the abuse meted out to me as a child. In addition to the pain and humiliation, I felt disgraced, shamed, and dishonoured. My childhood was stolen from me by lust. I lived in a fantasy world to preserve my sanity. That world was my survival until the dams broke loose.

Salvation is at hand, at last. I'd finally summoned the courage to put that world of horror in its proper perspective. True, something irreparable was done to me but unknowingly, I kept it alive by burying it in the recesses of my mind. It didn't lay buried, but seeped into my subconscious and coloured my life. I became an unwilling dupe. I allowed other people to put me down, screaming inside while none of it was reflected on the outside. I wondered again, had I called Mike on his actions earlier in our marriage, would our lives have been different?

I pulled myself up with a jerk. Here I was again, taking the blame. Life happens. Everything takes time. Decisions are made against a background, rife with the unexpected, all encased in a huge balloon waiting to explode.

The lost child was emerging from the ashes and beginning to deal with her life as she dealt with people in business – fair and honest, no longer ingesting fears and failures and making them hers. Out with victim mentality. 'Blotting paper is absorbent, but when it becomes too full it's just a soggy mass of nothingness,' I affirmed to myself.

I had finally begun to regain my perspective of life. The world would be murky for a time, but that would soon pass. There was a sneaking feeling in me that what I was saying was all talk. If I slipped up, I could start the process all over again. I encouraged myself, "All it will take is the courage to move one step forward. There are always regrets when you make drastic changes in your life."

Questions stormed my mind, "Do you turn back the clock and return to where you were twenty-five years ago? You're dealing with an aging body, your mindset has changed, but you're not as naive as you once were."

I reminded myself, "The world doesn't stop turning. You must advance with it or you'll be left behind."

I tried to reassure myself by the reminder that 'Endings resulted in New Beginnings.' Forest fires caused devastation, but new growth followed. For the first time in my life I was in sole control, there was no one to report to, no one to admonish me and, did it really matter, no one to cherish me and love me.

True enough, my children, Christo and Gloria, were very supportive. In their growing years, they had been caught between the snide remarks and put-downs by their father, but they loved us both. They both thought our separation was the best thing and showed a maturity in their approach that made me very proud indeed. They assured me that my happiness was all that they desired. They always wondered what kept me tied to a marriage that obviously wasn't working.

I never involved them in my battles with Mike. When they found me in tears after a confrontation or quarrel, they would hug me and tell me they loved me. To all accounts, I still wondered how our constant disagreements disturbed them.

It was too late for regrets. What was done was done. I hoped their lives would be happier and trusted they would choose their partners wisely. I also hoped that the behaviour patterns they'd seen evolve from us, their parents, wouldn't affect them. That, of course, is every parent's wish. Children can leave their parents, but parental upbringing is part and parcel of them.

When news of our separation spread, it was grist for the rumour mill. I was a person of note, so anything about me was information of interest to the Guyanese community; everyone speculated about a situation no one could understand. Some of the gossip was hurtful so I stayed clear of all. Friends and acquaintances called on the pretext of commiserating with me. I knew they only wanted to obtain the latest information 'from the horse's mouth,' so they could get their moment in the limelight when they told what they had learned from me.

Six months passed quickly with nothing resolved regarding division of property. I was becoming impatient. I wanted to get my life back together again and uncertainty was vexing.

Quite unexpectedly, when hope started to ebb, my lawyer telephoned me. He'd received a call from Mike. Mike had fired the lawyer who was advising him to contest the settlement. He agreed to the division of property we had outlined, provided he obtained more cash. My lawyer advised that Mike was taking advantage of me, and I should not agree to his latest demand.

I told him all I wanted was my freedom. I would mortgage the house and give Mike the money. He tried to reason with me, but I affirmed that all I wanted was to cut the legal ties which bound me.

The settlement was agreed to and we both signed off on it. Legally the process would take a year before the divorce could be granted. However, I knew everything else had been settled and I would just have to wait on time to ebb. I considered all ties were cut and my life was my own. "Freedom, at last," I told myself. The world's my oyster. There is no one to question my actions or chastise me.

My doctor suggested that I seek counsel from a psychologist as part of my resettlement. He knew my life hadn't been easy. Years before, while he was treating me for migraine headaches, he referred me to a psychologist. I didn't continue my treatment after the first visit. Twenty minutes into our session, the psychologist had observed, "the problem is your husband, isn't it?" I was struck by the accuracy of his diagnosis, but didn't want to delve into the problem for fear of the outcome.

If I saw a psychologist again, I would have no reason to hide my problems or the mental burdens that were part of me. The mind is complex. Clinical depression places a question mark on your ability and on you, as a person. Talking about my problems could create understanding and acceptance within me. The past was the past. Hiding it, even from myself because I couldn't live with the shame, kept it alive. It was time for closure. No matter how "put together" I appeared on the outside, my past experiences had walked beside me and shaped the person I'd become.

I had always recognized that I was two people: the 'thinker' and the 'pacifier', two very different people living in one body but having separate compartments in my brain. Not a case of Dr. Jekyll and Mr. Hyde, of course, just different.

Mental illness was not generally understood at the time. It carried a stigma. Seeking treatment was considered a weakness and could bring shame. Talking about it with the shrink, as I referred to my psychologist, would open that period of my life again. The years had built scars around my wounds until they were tightly encased like the kernel in a coconut. I felt if it remained a closed item I could deal with it, and perhaps it might even disappear.

My doctor did refer me to a psychologist he thought could address my problems. The trauma of returning to my childhood was so debilitating, I couldn't talk about it. I concentrated mainly on the problems relating to Mike and me.

Canada was not like Guyana. Women had freedoms. It was true that women didn't receive the same pay as men, for the same job. I was lucky. The changes I instituted gave the company a makeover. Because I was in charge of human resources and administration I was privy to the salaries everyone was making. When I felt I was being short-changed, I questioned this. The anomaly was fixed and I was content.

Giving the shop to Mike meant that my dream of taking it to the next level would never see reality. It would happen, but when it did, it would be the materialization of someone else's dream.

I gave a heavy sigh. I built the school and had to leave it. I built the shop and had to give it away. What was I going to do when I retired?

As the months passed there was a gradual shift in my vision. I was happier than I had ever been. I mourned the loss of friendships with most of Mike's family. Thirty years of family relationships are never easy to cast aside. I had considered myself the 'Empress' in Mike's family. I helped everyone and they returned whatever I gave in full measure with their love and respect. It would take time for them to accept the new reality.

I felt overwhelmed when I received a bouquet of flowers at the office with a note which said, "Thinking of you. Let us know how we can help." The note was from my soon to be former sister-in-law. We bonded when her younger son was diagnosed with prostate cancer. He was only 14 years old. Chemotherapy wasn't working. How do you tell a young boy that he is going to die, that all treatment had failed?

We soldiered on together despite the prognosis and tried to grant his every wish, hoping it would make his last days happy ones. The end came too soon, but before he passed he tried to tell us that he was happy. A shared moment in time, but a lifetime of friendship to follow. His mother and I bonded; we became sisters. Our friendship survived. She'd reached out to help me.

I didn't contact her when Mike and I separated but I heard that she vigorously defended me against the ranting of the family.

Another sister-in-law also reached out to me. She had also felt the family anger when she decided to separate from her husband, Nelson. She'd graduated from housewife to bank clerk. Financial independence was hers.

Mike's brother, Nelson, didn't recognize this. He couldn't come to terms with the fact that women were emancipated, and their opinions mattered. Strange thinking for a man who'd attended Oxford University for post-graduate training.

Life in Canada was very different from life in Guyana. The ability to earn a living in a respectable job expanded women's horizons. Nelson continued to live in the Guyanese colonial world he'd left behind, with the expectation that his wife would continue to comply with his wishes. It was difficult for him to recognize that wives were not chattels and money they earned belonged to them.

When their bickering became heightened, Nelson's wife asked him to leave the family home. Mike's family always ran interference when one of their own was threatened. They embraced him and ostracized her.

We three, bonded by marriage, became a triumvirate against the onslaught of criticism levelled against us. We were Canadian women, equal in every aspect of life.

CHAPTER FIFTY-SIX

DAWNING OF A NEW AGE. Gradually, my fellow employees became the family I had lost. Working relationships became stronger. There was time to listen and I easily filled the place of mentor in their corporate lives, sometimes even into their personal lives. My workplace friends nicknamed me "Dear Tabi."

Coincidentally, this period heralded the beginning of the emergence of women in the business world. If women excelled at their jobs, and earned promotion, it was their right to expect to be paid at the same rate as men. Many businesses adhered to this to some extent, but they were in the minority. Promotion in many cases necessitated sexual favours. This was utterly demeaning. Women are not possessions and shouldn't be dependent on men's sexual gratification to fulfill their aspirations, especially when in some cases they were smarter and even better educated than the men who were their managers.

We build walls in our heads, walls erected by assumptions that physical strength excels and equals mental acuity. Men created laws to ensure that this fact was enshrined in the concepts and precepts of human thinking. Women were encased in a protected role to keep them cloistered because their beauty and physicality created desire in men. Their role was to give birth, nurture children, and keep the home fires burning. They couldn't fight in wars, pilot an airplane, nor could they till a field or enjoin in battle where physical strength dominated. They were born beautiful, a signal from nature that they were to be loved, cherished, and protected. Beauty was a valuable asset. In ancient chronicles, a thousand ships were launched to free Helen, daughter of Zeus, and wife of Menelaus, who was captured and borne away by Paris, Prince of Greece.

Many thousands of years have elapsed since the birth of these concepts. Each generation has chipped away at the hypotheses. History recorded the feats of women like Boadicea and Joan of Ark, but these always were classified as 'exceptions.' Women who excelled in thought and action were most times considered to be 'witches,' burnt at the stake, and hopefully cast into the hellfire of damnation. Mercifully, education became universal and gradually a new shift in thought started to prevail. The shift was so gradual that it went almost unnoticed. The dawning of the realization that women could think for themselves had begun.

With men away on the battlefield, women became the main workforce during the Second World War. They kept the home fires burning and proved their mettle. They clamoured for inclusion at the doors of learning institutions and excelled at disciplines previously thought to be male prerogatives. Doors slowly opened for them.

I considered myself lucky to have been given the opportunity to use my knowledge to create solutions to systems, fast becoming outmoded. Was it providence, I always asked myself? No one asked me for sexual favours and if they had, that would have been the end of that. I would have boxed their ears and fled. My role in business was paramount to how I thought of myself. The other part of life was a myth; my psyche had regained its rightful place.

Ideas generated outside the box earned me the position I held. My company colleagues told me that I could pull a rabbit out of the hat and this gave me an aura. I was always 'all business' and not open to dalliance with the opposite sex, but I was a good friend to have. Even the wives of my colleagues called for advice when they needed help.

Way back my father said to me, "Think one step ahead, don't follow traditions too closely, and you'll always be invaluable. Ideas come from the brain. Feed it. Research and knowledge are invaluable tools."

My quest for knowledge never ceased. Seminars, lectures, emerging trends gave rise to new opportunities. Technology was continuing to change the world and this was awesome. If we always followed traditional procedures, we would soon be gobbled up and become defunct. Everything was moving forward, methodology had to keep pace. Businesses which ignored the future would do so at their peril.

Morale boosters in the form of small modifications challenge the mind. Motivation increases the zest which creates new ideas. That zest was a machine that needed to be oiled and cared for as we moved into the new age technology was carving for us.

Creating a new mentality for women wasn't an easy task. We'd been conditioned for such a long time, it was difficult to break the yoke. Women slowly began to take their place beside men in the boardrooms of business, in the chambers of justice, and in the halls of parliament. Evolution was a process that couldn't be forced nor could it be ignored.

Throughout the ages, women had fought the battle for equality and the clamour had grown louder. I had unwittingly enjoined myself in that battle. Purely by chance, I'd obtained a foothold in the hallowed halls of men's prerogative rights and forged one step ahead to become one of the 'first' in the series of women in the company hierarchy.

Looking back at my own life, I questioned my own fight towards financial independence and understood that for some reason, it was not solely a fight for financial freedom, but a fight to win equality for me as a woman. My role was to prove that I was equal to and even better than the men who held sway. I couldn't win the entire battle; I could raise the expectations of women so that they became emboldened by my success, and fought the war themselves.

Unfortunately, the realization dawned that we would have to fight the war on two fronts, at home and in business. I'd failed at home.

CHAPTER FIFTY-SEVEN

REFLECTIONS. While reflecting on the past, as we all do from time to time, it was impossible not to observe the great divide which existed between Mike and me. It seemed we were never 'in sync'. We slept in the same room, but there was always controversy in dealings and communication. If I dissected my own role, the children were my first priority, my jobs the second, my mother the third, and I can't really tell where Mike fell on the totem pole. We lived together, slept together, but our union ended there.

Mike always told everyone how much he respected me, but he'd never said that to me. It was all criticism about the way I dressed, changed the colour of my hair, and talked to people. He objected when I asked people's opinion about anything. He felt that he was the one I should turn to for advice regardless of the fact that he wasn't knowledgeable about what I was asking. How could I ask for thoughts from someone who condemned every idea with the words, "That can never happen, people don't think like that, that's a stupid idea."

I liked to travel, but he preferred to stay at home. I pushed and we made several trips to the U.S. and to England and Europe. If anything went wrong, it was always my fault and I needed to put it right. He always expounded on everything, and secretly I think he was happy to have made the journey, but he never admitted this. He grew dependent on me to set his world straight, but I never did hear the words I longed to hear: "Thanks, Tab. It was a great holiday."

In retrospect, this was perhaps how he saw his parents behaving and thought that it was the proper way to approach marital bliss. He never seemed to realize that any woman would get weary and jaded if she performed a task to the best of her ability, but never heard the words, "Thank you; that was very good."

I only belabor this because it seems such a waste of life. I always questioned the purpose of my birth during the period of my "troubles." I was told that God loved me and He would reward me when I died and went to Heaven. Whenever I tried to ask about sex, I was told it was a sin and I shouldn't go there. To put it mildly, even thinking about "it" was sinful unless God blessed the union when you were married in Church. Outside the boundaries of marriage, that sin was sometimes rewarded with a child born out of wedlock; mother and child suffered a fall from grace. Men got off with a handshake and a wink.

Church and religion held full sway during my early life. I understood that a fall from grace would send a woman hurtling down into the bowels of Hell, a frightful existence, as was told to me several times. Perhaps that was why I was afraid to let my parents know what was happening to me. If I didn't reveal it, no one would know. I could enter the pearly gates of Heaven without anyone realizing that I had sinned. Who knows?

Getting back to reality was never simple. Quite unexpectedly, the years of my childhood, damaged, ravaged, savaged would invade my mind. I still ask, "Why?" A man's sexual urges rule, it seems. Once it happens he must seek gratification time and time again. Some twisted thought caused the perpetrators of rape and molestation to focus on me, a child, a helpless victim. Rape is one crime against a woman from which she never recovers. It's a life sentence.

Having two personalities helped me ease the pain. Over the years dominance shifted from the inner child to the outgoing woman. The outgoing woman was in charge most of the time, but many actions reflected the voice of the inner child. Sometimes I felt I had come to terms with what happened in my childhood, then a sudden jolt would return me to the past and misery would invade my being. It wasn't only the acts of rape and molestation themselves that were troubling, but also the feeling of unworthiness, shame, and rejection, that swamped my being, and seemed to always hang on to my psyche, so that nothing appeared to grant the forgetfulness I craved.

Outwardly, I was the executive who could always be counted on, yet inwardly I feared rejection and humiliation. I was told many times that my bosses relied on the cool, calm, and collected 'me' that greeted the world. I wondered what it would be like to be a fly on the wall if they ever knew the true me. Would they reject me and cast me out?

Keeping what transpired a secret was very important at this stage of my life. A person who'd been raped and molested was always looked upon as tainted, and branded for life. The stigma was a life sentence. Humanity seldom embraces the fact that the act of rape is a horrible crime, which disfigures a person and brands her for life through no fault of hers. Rapists always seem to get off with a light reprimand.

Putting all that aside, I felt I was finally on my own and on the road to finding freedom from the person who was raped. I would merge my two personalities. This was the only way upward to peace and happiness. I needed to rid myself of all the hurts, peel back the layers placed around my psyche, and confront the issue. I asked myself whether there was enough courage and strength in my heart to start that journey which could lead to acceptance and peace. I needed help, but I could trust no one to keep my secret.

I began my search for freedom from the perils of my youth with astrologers, psychics and seers, then finally psychologists. I thought they could show me the way to inner peace. I'd grown up a devout Christian, but Christianity failed me when I heard sermons condoning the actions of rapists and murderers in Guyana. If indeed there was a merciful God, why didn't He punish the wicked and the transgressors? Why did we have to await death to finally get redress for the wrongs done to us? Why were women and children, girls and boys, most often the brunt of crazy, horrible sexual deeds? To survive we were required to follow a code of conduct that starts with secrecy. That code protected the transgressors, but did nothing for the violated. There had to be a more just system where men who were sexual predators paid for the heinous crime of sexual violence towards females of all ages and boys.

CHAPTER FIFTY-EIGHT

HELP FROM THE STARS IN THE SKY. I needed help. After considering my options, I decided to try astrology. If astrologers could predict behaviour based on Zodiac signs and movement of the heavenly bodies, they might help me understand my personal history. Astrologers in India used this science to forecast behaviour patterns and perhaps I could gain an understanding of myself and my life patterns through the use of this science.

The first guru I consulted in my quest was Canadian. He had studied the Ramanya and the Mahabharata, Hindu religious scriptures, rich in philosophy and morality. He showed me around his office and pointed with pride to the framed letters from well-known people thanking him for his help. The letters were full of praise for the assistance and guidance they'd received. I would never have thought a few of them needed help of any sort. They always gave the impression of never having encountered a problem they couldn't solve on their way to prominence. Some of the people whose pictures decorated his walls were known for the brilliance of their rhetoric, which held their audience captive.

It was difficult at first to accept that there was a relationship between the heavenly bodies and the human world. I knew that the moon, responsible for oceanic tides, was also rumoured to have an effect on human behaviour, hence the term lunatic. There was also the question of the horoscope and the Zodiac signs.

My astrologer explained, "Indians, Chinese, and Mayans worked on the premise of this relationship with much success. The positioning of the planets affected people born under particular signs, in different ways. Supposedly therefore astrological phenomena played a part in world happenings. Astrological forecasts were his specialty."

Researching the field of horoscopes and predictions for the future is fascinating. That your birth time categorized you into astrological groups presented a fathomless font of study and conjecture. Matchmakers used horoscopes to match temperaments and behaviour patterns. Arranged marriages usually turned into successful unions, and their efficacy made them worthwhile.

I remembered that a matchmaker was the intermediary in the match between my father's youngest brother and my future aunt. They were the happiest couple I've ever known.

Study of the moon and stars took me back in time when I saw myself, a young seven-year-old, sitting on the back steps of our home, gazing into the sky. The nights were cool, and the rustle of the leaves as the wind blew in from the seashore made the landscape serene. The glow of the moon and stars almost seemed to bathe the landscape in a magical aura, darkness with enough light to distinguish shadows. I'd believed that if I caught sight of "a falling star" and wished on it, I would be taken to a magical, mystical place where I could learn to play without fear, the past would disappear, and I could run about, happy to be alive and above all, loved.

Buoyed up by this reminiscence, I concluded that astrology could indeed help me reach self-understanding. I arranged for three sessions. During the first session he read the palms of my hands. He told me the lines revealed I was twice married, had borne two children; there was trauma and sadness in my life, success in business, a good aura and a future with many challenges.

I saw him twice after that. He slipped into the role of psychologist and we had some very interesting discussions. I never mentioned the horrors of my childhood. He always told me that my sessions with him were enlightening for him. We discussed the science of astrology and the many ways in which the planets, including the moon, sun, and stars interacted with the world. That timing of birth was significant because while we shared the same astrological group, there were many differences.

According to him, our future is mapped out for us at birth and we couldn't escape it. In olden times, in India and China, it was customary for seers to prepare astrological charts as soon as a child was born; parents eagerly looked forward to this forecast representing what the future had in store for their children. In all likelihood, I believed, parents used the charts as a guideline for training and education.

I was anxious to see my astrological chart. He prepared a full version for my next visit. The chart showed my progression through life. It was not direct in every respect, but even with generalities, I could place myself within its framework. His forecast included finding a partner who would bring happiness into my life. One sadness was that I would outlive this person and his death would create emptiness in my life.

I ridiculed the idea of marrying again and told him that that would never happen.

"It will happen, and sooner than you expect. You'll write me one of these letters." He pointed to the wall, "and I will frame it and hang it there."

I didn't know this was the last time I would see him. Two days after our meeting, he was shot and killed in his home. As far as I'm aware, his killer was never caught and brought to justice.

I felt sad at his passing. I knew that his chart, though not as detailed as I expected, was accurate with regard to the past. Most of it jibed with my own experience. I was skeptical of the future and very distrustful of "getting into bed" with another man. Having a man in my life was of no importance, or perhaps I had yet to meet my soul mate, if such person did exist. I chuckled at the thought.

CHAPTER FIFTY-NINE

INTROSPECTION. Divorce proceedings moved quickly after the first flurry of negotiations. When I went to visit her my mother scolded me. "Why are you being so foolish? You're putting an end to your marriage for no good reason. Quarrelling is nothing. Mike has been faithful. What do you really want from life? I know Mike is 'picky,' but your father wouldn't have condoned this behaviour."

"Freedom from the past unhappy years is very important to me at this stage of life. I've worked hard to attain financial freedom, Mother," I answered with a smile, intended to reassure her. "Mike has helped, but something within him doesn't like the fact that I spearheaded the ventures that led us to where we are today. He uses my achievements as weapons to demean me. I've had enough; I can't continue my life under the same circumstances."

Deep within her, I knew she was aware of everything that had gone wrong, but Mike had been to see her and narrated his many complaints about my behaviour. She'd reminded him that I held a responsible position at work, which couldn't fit into a nine to five schedule. His insecurity, caused by his lack of not knowing exactly what kept me away, caused him to create a fanciful picture of what he suspected was in play.

She reassured me with her next words. "I know his complaints are petty and unfounded. No one can fault you for neglecting your household duties. I don't know how you do it all. You spend all day Sunday preparing meals for the week. You even do his laundry, washing, and ironing. He can be petty, too," she mused, "After all, you're the best judge, and if you think separation will make a difference in your life and you'll be happy at last, you must do as you wish. Remember, though, a woman without a man is defenseless." She patted my hand and gazed into my eyes. I felt her love, but somehow I knew she feared that what I was doing could only lead to my downfall.

"That era of man's domination is gradually coming to a close, Mother. Women are as brainy as men, but like everything else, acceptance takes time. Men have physical strength. Women excel because of advances in education and technology. Losing their leadership role doesn't come easily to all. What do you think Dad would have said?"

"I've never said this to you before, child, but I'm proud of your accomplishments. I've been critical of you because you're strong and I noticed the widening separation between you and Mike. I scolded you because I feared this day of separation would come. Your father was always the boss and I loved and respected him. We were happy and I hoped you would be happy also, but we lived in a different time.

"You've grown into a strong woman, outspoken and deter- mined. You're also brilliant and strong-minded like me. We don't give up. I never imagined that you could've moved so far up the ladder in a 'white man's' country. They were always the bosses when I was young and we had to obey them or there would be trouble. I smile when I imagine them listening to you and recognizing the wisdom that comes from your mouth. I sometimes thought that Mike believed you were selling your body for promotion because he couldn't believe you were as sav- vy as he is not."

"Mother, I love you. You're so shrewd," I said, gratitude for her words bringing me comfort I'd always craved. "I've always thought you didn't even notice how difficult it was for me to keep pace with everything. I knew you expected nothing less of me, but it seemed you took everything I did for granted and wanted more. It wasn't an easy passage over the years, as you know, but I used my intelligence, my knowledge, and my people skills. I put my shoulder to the wheel and carried on. You recognized how tirelessly I worked, and that my days were proverbially without end." She smiled, closed her eyes, and said a little prayer. I was happy.

I couldn't expect my family to break off a lifetime of friendships they had built with Mike, but I always felt put out when, despite our separation, they accepted his hospitality and then tried to cover it up.

Mike had always been very critical of them, and had lorded it over them because we were financially better off than they were. Relationships hadn't come easily. However, I had no desire to create waves. He was, after all, the father of my children and I wanted them to respect him. They were witness to the happenings between us over the years. I had laughingly explained that it was just his ego talking, as he was indeed a very kind and considerate person. Their looks of disbelief had said it all.

Christo's and Gloria's relationships with their father turned out to be far happier after our separation. They did their best to bridge the gap which existed in his life. I was proud of them. They respected us both and they were impartial. I didn't want to rock the boat, so even though family gatherings were very important to me, I didn't create waves. My family celebration of Christmas was scheduled for Christmas Eve and Easter celebrations took place on Easter Sunday. This left them free to spend time with their father if they so wished.

Mike bought a condominium and a nice new car. There was still acrimony that I had abandoned the marriage. Truth to tell, we should never have gotten married in the first place, but I didn't regret that we had two wonderful children who were open-minded and didn't pass judgement on either of us. They loved us both and remained unprejudiced.

Friendships took the usual course after our separation; some friends sided with him and others with me. I had integrated Guyanese culture with Canadian culture and so had the best of both worlds. My Guyanese friends were a little envious of my success, but proud of me all the same; my Canadian friends enjoyed the differences in culture.

When two people are facing the end of a relationship, most important is the understanding that they each have a parallel duty to their children. Fighting over petty things ends up becoming a degrading experience with neither party gaining the edge. Making children a party to what's happening in the relationship is criminal. Sometimes we forget that our children are part of each of us and all they want is not to take sides but love us both.

My children were adult. I hoped that in time they would understand that my own happiness was important, and love and trust me enough to know that I could no longer endure my place in the union without losing my own self-respect. It hurt me to leave them even though they were both adults, but they seemed to have accepted the change, and weren't interested in 'who was to blame.' This was great.

I know now that I'll always question whether I did the right thing by raising my children in a home which wasn't happy, but always full of wrangling and unrest. "Whatever possessed you?" had frequently crossed my mind. They may have been happier if they hadn't witnessed the quarrels and rancor we caused each other.

That was over now. I would soon be legally free and able to face the new challenges of being a single woman. "Freedom at last." I pinched myself to check that I was still in the land of the living.

It soon became common knowledge that I had separated from my husband and was in the process of getting a divorce. I had no desire to start a liaison with anyone. Friendships had blossomed with both male and female colleagues to the extent that I seemed to be always offering advice, in my role as 'Aunt Tabi.'

A few male colleagues resented my advancement and there was always some scheme afoot to trip me up. They couldn't understand why a woman held the position they felt could be better performed by them, and were envious of my success. It was a man's world, one code for men and another for women. Colleagues tried to enlist women in the company in their plots to oust me, but they fought a losing battle.

Rumour had it that the few who weren't happy with my promotion were developing schemes to trip me up. One particular case got to the President who advised that any disagreement between us would best be settled without reference to him.

Wrangling for promotion was also present. Prudent handling and an understanding of human nature resolved the matter. Men thought I could be influenced while belittling me behind my back. Eventually they realized they were just wasting their time.

One day the President asked, "How did you manage to settle the rivalry between the prospective candidates?"

"I just gave it space. One thought he could use lobbying, the other settled down and worked hard. They should have known that I would help neither, and if they couldn't fill the bill I would have recruited outside. The only thing that mattered was finding the right person for the job."

He smiled and said, "You're an old fox, Tab. Where did you learn those tricks?"

"People give themselves away. You can almost predict the outcomes based on personality and behaviour. When I ran the school, behaviour patterns were important. To get the best of the students I found out what motivated them. This showed me the way to inspire and challenge them. There were no true failures. Even the few who took longer to pass examinations ultimately became successful."

He smiled. "You're doing a fine job here, Tab. The future bodes well." I smiled at the thought of where success could lead. Little did I know how change would affect me.

CHAPTER SIXTY

CHANCE AND CIRCUMSTANCE. I was busy at work, but had to deal with changes in my own life. Christo was engaged and would soon be married. Gloria was chomping at the bit. She wanted to find an apartment and start life on her own. While I encouraged their aspirations, I felt dejected at the thought of losing their companionship. I had to help them leave the nest even though I dreaded it, hoping they would continue to live with me as long as possible. The house would be empty without them and totally unsuitable for me. It was time to shake the past and venture into new avenues.

I felt attached to the house but argued with myself against keeping it because it held years of memories. Security for old age loomed large. I needed to think of the future.

The house echoed with loneliness when they were away. I worked longer hours and was almost the last to leave the office. I laughed when Rose, the receptionist, told me I had to find a lover. I shook my head and told her I wasn't interested. However, the thought remained in my head. I had made too many mistakes with my choice of a partner. I still wondered where I had gone wrong.

There had been many eligible young men seeking my attention in my younger days. The ones I was drawn to, always seemed to be in love with other girls. Perhaps past relationships caused insecurity, but always at the forefront was the fact that I didn't really want to get involved. I had been blackmailed into marriage with Mohan, then fallen headlong into a relationship with Mike because I felt I owed him for standing by me when I'd left Mohan.

Perhaps I was afraid of the consequences. I wanted companionship, but feared the outcome of a relationship that wouldn't pan out for me. It was safer to plunge myself into my job where I could find fulfilment, rather than into nurturing friendships. I had taken two risks with marriage. The onus was years of searching for self-actualization and compromising my true self, but on the bright side I felt I had borne and nurtured two incredible children. They were different, one driven to find success, the other determined to make the world a better place for children.

What did I have to lose if I risked another liaison, I argued? My dignity, my self-respect, my sanity. The eighties and nineties were prudish in their rationale of sexual behaviour outside marriage. There were few single men around so my choice would be limited. I'd never dallied with flirtations since the time in my teenage years when I thought I was helping a school chum understand mathematics, and he believed I was 'into' him. I remembered telling him, "I'm willing to share my intellect, develop our friendship, but not to select a life partner."

Years later, when we met at a social function, we laughed over the incident, but he'd whispered, "I still regret that you didn't think of me as your 'chosen'." I'd felt a few flutters of regret in my heart at the time, but had come to the conclusion that he was viewing the situation in a different light. I was now, after all, a successful businesswoman. I had chosen a career which allowed me to share my knowledge and develop my ideas; it had taken me to heights I'd never dreamed of. *"Beautiful dreamer!" The reality is that you can never achieve your dream of happiness. Men feel challenged by you. They look at you as 'the competition,' the female outsider intruding into the world of male dominance.*

I remembered my first conversation with the Chairman of the Board of our parent company, a powerful man in the world of finance, on my first visit to Amsterdam. He had asked me, "Do you ever find it difficult in your business dealings because of your race?"

I smiled as I answered, "Race is seldom a part of the equation. My being a woman in the position I hold is challenging for most men. They're astounded when they find they've met their equal in knowledge and competence. Accepting this is difficult for them, and sometimes the situation becomes complex." I added, "It just means that I have to work a little harder to 'wow' them, and they become my champions."

I saw him looking at me with renewed respect. My answer had won his vote of confidence and this augured well for my career.

I decided that I was being foolish as I made plans for my future. Before my separation, it was my plan when I retired to take the shop to the next level, or volunteer for work in education, perhaps in Third World countries, or even return to university to obtain a degree in law. My world had changed. I was single again and new challenges awaited me.

I felt a calmness and return to sanity. Romance in real life and romance on the screen were different. "And they lived happily after," seldom happened in the real world. The twists and turns of life are difficult to fathom.

I was scheduled to attend a conference in New York City along with the President, Taylor Woodruff, Sean Baker, and another male colleague. We all travelled down together, which was unusual.

Sean Baker was a handsome man, with lovely blue eyes that twinkled with fun, sometimes at my expense, but someone I'd classified 'gentleman,' someone I could trust. Everyone loved

Sean. He was easy-going, it seemed, listened carefully, and was always prudent and correct. We'd worked together for over fifteen years and shared a platonic friendship. When he took my case to store it in the overhead compartment, I rebuked him and told him I was quite capable. He shrugged his shoulders, his blue eyes twinkling at my discomfort. I often teased him about the comb in his pocket, and his need to make sure that every lock of hair was in the place to which he'd assigned it. He was indeed a handsome English gentleman and he knew it.

We were good friends. When I was out of sorts for one reason or another, he always tried to calm me, and I did the same for him. We had our differences, and became hot-headed about them from time to time, but in the end, we always managed to sort things out. I often used him as a sounding board and he did the same with me.

The conference went well. It was a grueling three days. Our team was brilliant, and we received many compliments on our work from fellow attendees. After dinner and the closing ceremony I mentioned that I was going for a walk to ponder everything we accomplished, and to clear my head. Sean reminded me that I shouldn't go for a walk outside on my own as it wasn't safe for ladies, and he offered to accompany me.

New York is a city that never sleeps. We chuckled over some of the gaffes we all made, then returned to the hotel.

Some of the attendees were in the bar and they hailed us when we arrived.

"Join us for a night cap," they chorused. We all had early flights the next day but it seemed churlish to refuse. There was much laughter and chatter. We were all pumped up and energized.

Too soon, it was time to say farewell. Sean offered to accompany me to my door to make sure I was all right. I affirmed there was no need, as I could take care of myself and the hotel was a safe place, and not like the streets outside. However, we were on the same floor and I decided not to make an issue of it. "I'll see you to your door. That's the least a gentleman can do."

We had an early flight the next day and I was anxious to get in and pack. At the door, I held out my hand in fun, a twinkle in my eyes, to thank him for his chivalry. He took my hand, drew me to him, looked at me through eyes filled with love, then he slowly bent down and kissed me on the lips. I never knew that a kiss could be that sweet and evoke such rapture in my entire being. What ecstasy? I was lost. That kiss awakened a feeling I had never experienced before. My body came aglow with a craving for fulfillment, for more, for the beauty of a physical love I never knew was possible.

That kiss changed my life. It opened a world of sweetness, pleasure and excitement, of desires waiting for fulfillment. I was lost.

CHAPTER SIXTY-ONE

A CLOSED DOOR OPENS. I pushed the door open wondering whether I should invite him in, but knowing I couldn't. My body was alive with a desire that was new to me. I was filled with a happiness and a need I never knew existed. I wanted to feel his arms around me, to take the arousal one step further but the past kept interrupting my thoughts.

I stumbled through the door and closed it. I left him standing outside, waiting. How easy it would be to forget responsibilities and give in to the exquisite sensations cruising through my body! I hugged myself and felt the delicious feeling of love, sensuality, and yearning for sexual gratification. The crescendo of sensations rushed through my body. I forgot the inhibitions I had imposed on myself. I felt the only choice I had was to open the door and let him in.

I was saved by the bell. The telephone started ringing. It distracted me and I turned to answer it. When I was away on business, I was conscious of the fact that I needed to know my children were okay. True, they were adults, but emergencies can happen. It turned out to be the hotel receptionist confirming my wake-up call for next day.

I rushed back to the door, and opened it, but no one was there. I looked around. Sean was nowhere to be seen. Disappointment swamped my body and soul. The telephone rang again. My heart fluttered. I slammed he door shut and ran back to answer it. It was Sean. "I didn't want to hang around after I heard the telephone, but can I come around so we can talk about this?" he added.

"We can talk about it now. It's safer. Distance will prevent us from making fools of ourselves."

He laughed. "Are you afraid of your emotions? I've loved you since the day I first met you in Harrison's office over fifteen years ago. I looked forward to coming to work each morning because you were there, part of my working life. You seemed to be happily married and I stifled my feelings. Kissing you tonight just happened, but now I can start a new chapter in my life. I can't turn away now because I kissed you and this opened closed doors in my heart and gave me an insight into what could exist between us. There's no turning back for me now."

"The exquisite feeling of love enveloped me also. I've never felt desire like this before". Emotions welled up inside me that I never knew existed. "I need time to think about this," I replied. One part of me whispered, "Why not," while the other said, "Remember you don't engage in dalliance."

"Come on, Tab. We've worked together for over a decade. Our friendship was a haven for me. Just being with you made my day happier. Now that we've kissed, we can no longer return to the past. We must explore what the future holds. Let's discuss this matter now."

"I know that, but I fear this insanity of ours can only lead to unhappiness in the end. Go to bed. Dream of me as I will dream of you. Let's not be hasty. Knowing that you love me is paradise indeed. Taking it further isn't in the cards for me. You're still married so we aren't free to pursue this. We can have an affair if our hearts so desire, but we cannot rush into something that we'll both regret."

"My soul longs for you. The dam I created between us has burst its banks. I can't close it now. Why can't we meet and discuss this?" Sean pleaded.

I blurted back, "I'm too weak and can't trust myself. Let's savour our new-found feelings. I'm going to be out of the office after tomorrow for a week in Halifax. When I return, we can discuss our future. Let's give ourselves time and space. We need to explore the possibilities which lie before us. I hold a position of responsibility, and I have a duty to the company. We're both officers. Can you imagine the scandal that will take place if we're found having an illicit affair?"

"All right, Tab. You always pour oil on troubled waters. But I refuse to be a star-crossed lover. You are the love of my life and I won't let you go. Whatever the consequences, I'm prepared to deal with them."

"Good night, Sean. If our love is to be fulfilled, this will happen. We must be patient. Our heads, not our bodies must control the future."

It was difficult to get to sleep. *I was elated, but tortured and tormented at the same time. Could I have an affair with Sean? Did I have to tell him of my past? Would he think less of me for it? What about my career and future? Would my family chastise and condemn me? What about the difference in our race? What about my children?*

It seemed I'd come full circle, back to the days when my actions made headlines. Could I brave the scandal? Sexual promiscuity was questionable. It could lead to divorce proceedings. The questions poured forth, with no answer appearing.

At last I fell asleep, only to be tortured by the nightmares of my childhood. It seemed that I was again the heroine of Nathaniel Hawthorne's, *The Scarlet Letter*. The verdict was out. I was to be stoned because I had fornicated and broken one of the Ten Commandments.

Next morning, Taylor indicated that he wanted to talk to me and suggested that we share a cab to the airport. He was off to Europe that evening and needed clarification on some issues that had arisen during the conference. I was off to Halifax the following day as I was a speaker at a conference on Human Resources and Skills development.

I welcomed the breather. Sean and I would both be too busy during the day. He had left me a cryptic message, but I hadn't returned his call. It's true that love was all encompassing, but there was a time and place for everything, my fears argued with me. We were not star-crossed teenage lovers like Romeo and Juliet. We were adults who, I felt, should know better.

The question was, "How do you deal with emotions which had surfaced to the forefront and were such an important part of human existence?" I had never felt like this before. It was such a beautiful feeling; I couldn't let it escape or elude me.

As I boarded the flight for Halifax the following day, idle thoughts entered my mind. "I'm a person who is loved." I walked with winged feet. My footsteps hardly touched the ground; there was a glow within me and passion filled my soul. Whatever the future held, this was my moment. I would refuse to think of the repercussions which could follow when my new love was discovered. My heart sang. For the first time in my life, I was truly in love and was loved in return by someone I respected and had known forever.

CHAPTER SIXTY-TWO

A DIFFERENT OUTLOOK ON LIFE. The conference in Halifax was well-attended. Colleagues from Ontario greeted me. They laughingly told me that my talk would be the highlight of the meeting for them. "Flattery doesn't work," I replied. "I know you'll all be trying to poke holes in my arguments". We laughed together. It would be good fun. I had researched my topics and was well versed to defend my vision. My conclusions were that, in the coming years, conglomerates would dominate the markets and this would lead to a global marketplace. Larger players would take control, and put the squeeze on smaller players. Eventually amalgamation or elimination would happen. My forecast would be met with much skepticism, but I foresaw a future very different from the past. Globalization would become the dominant marketing trend.

After my talk, there was much discussion, most of the attendees disagreeing with me and pooh-poohing my projections. I reiterated that new players in our industry would determine the future. The Old Boy Network was reaching the end of its days. Technology was marching inexorably ahead. Small companies would be swallowed up. Billions would replace millions when we talked of market share. Industries couldn't afford to bury their heads in the sand but rather should look to the future. The world was changing. Survival meant that we would have to change our outlook as markets became world driven. Technology had added a new element into the science of business.

On an impulse, I decided to remain in Halifax for the weekend. I rented a car, got a map, and decided to wander where fancy took me. I stopped at Peggy's Cove, one of the tourist highlights of the region. The lighthouse, calm and virginal in white, dominated the vista. It was a beautiful area to contemplate nature. Mankind was just a simple dot on nature's landscape. As the waves pounded the shoreline, I felt as free as the seagulls adding beauty to the landscape. It seemed the waves were whispering, "Go with the flow. Destiny awaits you. You can't change what has been ordained". Somber thoughts, but somehow they seemed to calm my soul and improve my outlook.

There weren't too many visitors, so it seemed, and I was all alone. A woman traveling alone was an unusual sight. I fell into conversation with some fishermen who hailed out to me. They laughed when I asked for directions to Malone Bay and Lunenburg, world heritage sights. They requested maps. I looked aghast at their request and laughingly told them I had none. They chuckled and said, "Just like a woman." The truth was, I was enjoying this interlude with strangers. This was all new to me. I had never thought of doing something like this before. They were part of the landscape and their easy, carefree approach to life added a different element to the day. I envied their nonchalance, but I knew that this was just an interlude. I was someone who had somehow become driven by success.

Nova Scotia is beautiful, the countryside unfolded into picturesque landscapes which seemed to push my questioning thoughts into the background. There were few travelers on the road and I took my time. My anxieties seemed puerile when I looked at the majesty of nature and the pastoral beauty which greeted me at every turn in the road.

As night fell, I parked in a small town and asked directions to a bed and breakfast inn. I realized that my colour made me stand out, and traveling alone made me an oddity. Everyone was friendly and willing to help.

Directions took me to a large old house, which had been converted into an inn. I imagined myself the heroine in of a novel, being graciously welcomed into a charming stately old home. I thought, *Sean should be here. We aren't two star-crossed lovers, we're simply two people filled with the excitement of discovery of that love, and we're now basking in its glories."*

The receptionist greeted me with a warm smile and a friendly welcome. She told me I was lucky. There was only one room left. It was part of a suite and had recently been refurbished. The price was naturally more as it was the best suite in the inn. She insisted that I inspect the room before making my decision to stay there for the night.

The room was on the second floor. When she opened the door, I held my breath. I was projected into the Victorian era. *A room for an heiress,* I thought, *beautifully decorated and a setting for a Victorian drama where a lonely girl awaits her swain to rescue her. Sean only has to appear and we could indeed ride off into the sunset. A pleasant thought!*

I oohed and aahed with delight. The ambience was picture-perfect and it matched my feelings.

Betty, the receptionist, was as pleased as punch. She confided that she had been showing the room all afternoon. While everyone liked it, most had said they preferred a simpler room, and of course, the lesser cost. She had a cheery personality and a pleasant manner, which gave me a feeling of confidence.

She continued, "Would you like to dine with us this evening? We're noted for our local cuisine, and it's always busy on

Saturdays." I accepted. She sent a porter for my luggage and added that I only had to call if I needed anything.

I decided to rest for half an hour in the comfort of my luxurious surroundings, dress for dinner, and then explore the sights and shops. Pleasant and interesting as the town was, everything was just a backdrop to the thoughts that churned and tumbled in my mind. I headed back to the inn.

Laughter, music, and light conversation greeted me as I arrived in the dining room. As the Maitre'D was taking me to my table, a voice reached out from across the room. "I'm dining alone and you're alone, it'd be great if you would join me. Dinner conversation always makes food taste better. It'd be a pity to waste our evening sitting alone in all this splendour?" The invitation was from a white American woman. She seemed to be in her thirties, pregnant, and her smile was inviting.

Why not? I asked myself. She's right, *camaraderie during a meal can add pleasure to my experience. The only thing that can happen will be that I'm stuck with her bill.*

As I sat down, I said to the Maitre'D, I said, "Separate cheques, please. I can't have this lovely lady paying for my dinner."

We chatted for a few minutes, exchanged names, then ordered dinner.

Clarissa was interesting and seemed to be about eight months pregnant. She tossed her head during our conversation. Her hair moved from side to side, and this added to her aura. She touched her belly with her hand, and smiled. "My husband is looking after our three children," she confided. "When I return, he'll come over for his dinner. This works well for us when we go away on holiday together."

She was vibrant and animated as she confided that the family were on their way to Buffalo to visit relatives. "Only in America," I laughed. "In Canada, we won't be undertaking such an adventure at this late stage of pregnancy. What happens if you have early labour?"

"My husband, Lawrence, will take me to the nearest hospital, and the bonus is, my child will have dual citizenship." She chuckled at the possibility as she touched her swollen belly.

"Why are you traveling alone?" she questioned. During dinner, we developed a convivial relationship. We were two strangers passing in the night. The chances of our ever seeing each other again were slim. Besides, I'd had a glass of wine and decided to throw discretion to the winds.

"I needed some time on my own to ponder my future. A knotty problem has arisen. It can be life changing and I am torn. Should I, or should I not?" I closed my eyes and let out a big sigh.

"Every problem has a solution. Endings signify new beginnings. You obviously aren't married because there's no ring on your "heart" finger. Have you fallen in love with someone?" Her eyes were questioning and eager.

Our eyes met. *Shall I take a chance and reveal all? My new found love is obviously causing confusion in my life. Perhaps recalling everything will help me find a solution.*

"I've fallen in love with a man I've known for umpteen years. We were friends and confidants, but all that changed when he kissed me. It revealed a part of me I never even knew existed. Perhaps this is just a passing fancy. He's married, but he says he fell in love with me the first time he saw me, years and years ago." I shrugged my shoulders, raised my eyes in question, and awaited her answer.

Clarissa became animated." Tell me about this man. You're an attractive woman. I can see why any man could fall in love with you. You're an oriental beauty and there's an aura of tranquility surrounding you. How long have you known him really? Do you believe he's in love with you, or is he just trifling with your affections and you're just a passing fancy on his part? We have to get to the bottom of this, before we can move on."

I smiled. "You sound like a lawyer cross examining the accused. So many questions and so few answers. I don't want to believe him, but I do. He's always struck me as honourable Englishman. We've been close friends for years."

"Why don't you have an affair and see where this leads?" She pursed her lips and smiled, daring me to answer truthfully.

I sighed. "I can't. In my mind an affair means living a lie. Cheating is dishonourable. I can't sell myself short. If it doesn't work, I couldn't live with the fall out. I'd be devastated. You know that all dishonour would fall on me. Men never seem to receive any blame. As an aside, explain this to me. Why do women always have to bear the shame of star-crossed lovers, and having sex without the mantle of marriage? Happily, I wouldn't have to bear the mortification of having a child out of wedlock."

We laughed heartily at the thought of it all, but we both questioned the assumption that the woman was always at fault in the circumstances; society in general had decreed that sex had to be licensed by marriage, and vows exchanged. The marriage bed was sacrosanct.

I confided, "To be honest, I have a lot to lose. My career is at the top of my list. I've worked as hard as the village blacksmith to fulfill the responsibilities I've undertaken. My motto is 'duty first, obligations next and everything else thereafter.'"

Clarissa took my right hand in hers. "From the little snippets you've told me of your life, it wasn't a cake walk. You're one of the leaders of the female revolution for equal opportunity in business. You've accomplished very much indeed. Don't you think it's time to think about yourself? You admit to feelings of sexuality, as that's what this kiss aroused in you. Have you ever known the delights of physical love? It's quite something, I can assure you."

We laughed, "And you're carrying the effects of that."

"She'll be our last. I'll get my tubes tied after she comes. I can assure you that the pleasures of the bedroom keep love growing. Too many women today never realize the joys of the marriage bed. They look on it as just another chore to be endured. I always think how stupid that is. Sexuality is not a treasure to be hoarded. It gets better through use."

I laughed as she continued, "I know you aren't comfortable with this talk of female sexuality and needs. Few women are, and the others – Lord bless them – keep saving themselves for God knows what."

"You seem to be very knowledgeable about these situations. You're not a sex therapist, are you?" I joked.

A paroxysm of laughter, which we couldn't seem to control, greeted this statement. When it stopped, we would look at each other and it would start all over again. Eventually, our mirth concluded, she indicated that we needed to return to a solution for my situation.

"I think that our dinner here tonight answers my question. I'm at the crossroads of my life. I can just muddle along as I've done in the past or I can embrace this feeling of love and pursue my dreams of happiness."

Her answer was thought provoking. "That sounds simple enough, but both ways would take a lot of courage and consume you. You know the result of continuing along your present path of focusing on your job and success in your business endeavours. Is that what life is all about? It is for men, but they're made differently. They can have a fling on the side to satisfy their sexuality temporarily until the next opportunity comes along. Women are made differently. This is your last chance. You'll never get another. Do you have the courage to turn aside from convention and embrace this last chance of love? Will success satisfy you on cold nights? Who will comfort you when you're old and sad? Will you forever carry the flag of unrequited love?" She smiled as she blurted out the questions, giving me a look that told me exactly what she thought of that.

"This is too heavy for me to ingest, Clarissa. You're forgetting the reality of life. If I don't work who'll support me? If I turn my back on my job, I'll never find another. What am I going to do with the rest of my life? How will I be able to face my family or my children?" I questioned.

She raised her hand, as if she needed to interrupt the flow of conversation. "I have one question for you. When you're standing at the pearly gates of Heaven waiting for St. Peter to open the door, and he asks, in senatorial tones 'Tabitha, what have you accomplished in your life?' Are you going to say that your greatest joy was your success in business? What will you do when he starts closing the gates and tells you that you've been a failure? Ask him what you should've done?" I tried to interject a few words, but she continued, "He'll tell you that you're a failure. We're put here on Earth to be happy. Success and happiness are as related as they are unrelated. Success in business and happiness are two different things. St. Peter will tell you that we creatures are sent here on Earth to be happy. You can't shun happiness and believe that success in business can equate with the joy that comes from love. Love is the reason we're born. Love brings us together. Fulfillment of that love comes from the ecstasy that sexual relationships bring between two people."

All the questions I needed answers to, swirled through my mind. "So, St. Peter closes the door on me. What happens then?" I couldn't wait for her answer, so I could start the next.

She narrowed her eyes, her face revealing the thoughts swirling through her mind." Tabitha, you're being deliberately obtuse. You know what I'm telling you. Simply put, it is embrace your love, experience the joys of love, and trust the future. There are no guarantees. Success comes to those who dare. I'm daring you to take the choice of happiness even if it means the loss of your future in business. If you have yearnings for this Sean of yours and he has yearnings for you, you both have to find a way out of the maze. It isn't going to be easy, but you'll never regret it."

Clarissa provided me with food for thought, even perhaps, a solution. There were still many questions without answers, but the truth was that the answers lay with Sean and me. We both had to come to the realization that we could put our trust in love, and journey on. The alternative to that was to forget that the doors of love had been swung wide open, and awaited me. I shook my head. That was something too difficult to contemplate. I had to find the right answer.

Our dinner was stimulating. The Maitre'D offered a cognac or liqueur on the house. We both declined. He said, "I've never seen two people totally unknown to each other having such a stimulating conversation. I'm very glad you sat together. Perhaps our restaurant provided a setting where you both found what you were looking for, invigorating conversation and good food!" He smiled. We paid our bills, left a handsome tip, and parted with hugs and promises.

It had been a long day, chock full of strange happenings. I wanted to call Sean, but this was not possible. I fell asleep in my Victorian room, dreaming of love and happiness, echoing the words I had read so often 'and they lived happily ever after.'

Next morning when I woke, I wondered whether this adventure would prove to be the turning point for me. I would return to my real life after my Nova Scotia experience, but after that, what? Would I continue along the road to a successful career or forge a new future for myself?

CHAPTER SIXTY-THREE

T
O HAVE OR HAVE NOT? Safely back in my own home was really a return to my old life. It was a letdown after the excitement of the previous days. My old fears returned. I spent a restless night still unconvinced that I should leave the safety of my present position and grab the future with both hands.

Life was always hectic at work. I had been absent for a week and it seemed everyone had some question they wanted answered. The morning flew by. Sean appeared at my door. "You've been busy today. I passed several times but your door was always closed. I'm happy that you're back. I missed you. Are you busy for lunch? His tone was quite business-like."

I thought of making excuses but decided it would be better to have a discussion now. Postponing the issues between us would only make them loom larger

"I can be ready in half an hour if that's okay, Sean. I'll meet you at the elevator."

We were alone for the first time, neither of us comfortable with our new situation. Conversation was strained as we strolled to the restaurant. He asked about the conference and my talk. This gave us some time to settle down until we could move to the main issue.

"What are you going to do about us and our new-found love?" The question jumped out at me.

"I don't know, Sean. Let's not rush into anything. If we take a slow approach, we may find this is just a storm in a teacup." I hoped my voice would be friendly but not forthcoming.

He smiled. "I thought you'd say something like that. This is a major issue for me, Tab. For the first time in my life, something I desired over the past years since meeting you, seems to be within my reach. I'm afraid to let it rest. I want to settle matters now. I need to know what your commitment to me will be. I'm dedicated to loving you for the balance of my life, and I hope and wish you feel the same way."

"Sean, you seem to forget that you're still married. I'm single and can do whatever I want. You're married and have a family who depend on you". I raised my eyes and gave him a quizzical look, hoping the answer I heard would be the one I wanted to hear.

"I know we can't take my family out of the equation," he replied taking hold of my hand under the table.

His touch was electrifying. I thought, *how can I go on working together with him? Would I be strong enough to control the emotions which flood my mind and made me weak? It would be senseless to provoke a physical relationship between us. And how would it end? Such a situation would make it all the more difficult if we had to end it. Even before starting I was concerned with the ramifications of dealing with the situation when love had lost its luster.*

"We're two adults who've suddenly found we love each other. What do we do about it? Do we plunge into an affair like teenagers enjoying the first flush of love, or can we be sensible and examine the pros and cons before jumping off the cliff? Once we make a decision, it'll be difficult to reverse it. Let's hasten slowly. I think we'll find a way forward," I answered, a part of me hoping to hear the answer I craved, that I couldn't even repeat to myself.

He looked around then back at me, "I'm serious, have no doubt about that. I've been to see a marriage counsellor and have spoken to a lawyer. I'm an honourable chap and I can't seduce you into having an extra marital affair. I have too much respect for you to suggest such a thing."

His face had such an intense look, I weakened and wanted to throw discretion to the winds and say, "Let's run away, together, and deal with the consequences later."

My past experiences with love were disastrous. I remembered that I had once been forced to act hastily, almost on the spur of the moment. These decisions came back to haunt me. At that time, I felt that whatever happened I could deal with it. Experience now counselled me. *Take your time, there's no need to rush. You're dealing with the rest of your life, your future. Don't mess things up.*

Thoughts of past events flowed through my mind, each one taking shape into lost memories, as I travelled back in time. I had never felt like this before. Having found this love of my life, I didn't want to lose it. This was something I'd longed for in the past as I sang the love songs in my youth, or replaced myself as the heroine who found eternal love, in one of the movies I'd seen in my youth.

A somber thought demanded my attention at that moment. He's 'white,' you're 'brown.' You know that 'white' men fall in love with coloured women and after a cooling off of passions, they return to the comfort of the 'white' domain.

Lordy, Lordy, what a problem! I'd fallen in love so quickly and so desperately that I'd forgotten to put race into the equation. As hard as it was going to be, this had to stop here and now.

"You're deep in thought," Sean interposed. "Tell me that you've found a solution for us?"

"It's a bitter solution, Sean. I can't entertain this love between us. We stand between a racial divide. The races have affairs, but marriage between them seldom, if ever, happens. We work for the same company and an affair between us would be tantamount to robbing the company. We couldn't work well together, there would be constant wrangling and disagreement when the affair ended, and in all conscience, I cannot let this happen."

"What are you trying to tell me, Tab? I'm an honourable man. I want our love to hold on to until the day I die, and even thereafter. I've loved you since I met you and I'll love you for all eternity." There was disappointment in his eyes, and his body seemed to sag.

I questioned myself, '*am I throwing something irreplaceable away?*'

"This is how you feel today, Sean. Things happen, love is challenged, and it becomes difficult to cherish the feelings we have now. We'll end up hating each other. It's time to return to the world of sanity." These words out of my mouth gave me he the feeling that doomsday was at hand. I hated that part of me which uttered them, and wanted to recant, but I felt inertia invading my body.

We finished our lunch and left. He said he needed to get some air and we parted company outside the restaurant. I wanted to curl up and sob. I had turned away my love. It was over and done with. A taste of the pie, but no fulfillment. I braced myself. "*Tab, my girl, leave it at that. If it is to be, so it will. Let it rest.*" Two days ago, I had been in my world of fantasy. Today, reality had set in.

Sean called me at home that night. I told him my heart was breaking. There was no future in our love for either of us. We were star-crossed lovers on the brink of a happiness, which would elude us forever. We'd had our moment in the sun and we had to be content with that.

CHAPTER SIXTY-FOUR

L OVE'S SHINING LIGHT. It was difficult to avoid each other at work. Sean respected the decision I had made and while there seemed to be a change in our attitudes to each other at work, it seemed no one suspected anything was wrong. Three months passed by, then one morning the rumour mill started up. A colleague from another company had asked Rose, our receptionist, how Sean was bearing up since he had left his matrimonial home.

A lot of questions about reasons and speculation as to why this had happened flew around the office. I was appealed to for clarification and confirmation. I was told that everyone came to me for advice and since I had my finger on the pulse of the organization, I knew exactly what was happening. They didn't believe me when I said this was news to me, also. I shrugged my shoulders and said that Sean should be given space to settle his affair. I couldn't still the voices in my heart, though. I wondered what was happening and whether that would include me.

Saturdays always meant a return to work to catch up with accumulating paperwork. I liked the calm and silence of the place, the freedom to concentrate without the constant tapping on my door or the endless ring of the telephone.

There was a tap on my door, and when I looked up, there he was.

"May I come in?" he asked, with a smile on his face.

"What are you doing here?" I asked. "I usually have the entire office to myself. It's amazing what you can get through in half a day without interruption. Have a seat." I questioned myself silently. *"What's he doing here? It's Saturday."*

"I've missed you, Tab. You've heard that Bridget and I have separated and I've asked her for a divorce. I've just lived for the day when I could declare my love to you without hindrance. I've kept my distance with much difficulty, but I can hold off no longer. She's seen a lawyer and we're in the settlement process. It hasn't been easy for Bridget and the children to understand my reasons for wanting a separation from a marriage that has lasted for over thirty years." *My face must have reflected my shock, but he continued.*

"I confessed to them, 'Separation has been uppermost in my mind for years, I haven't been happy for a long time, but I kept on going because it was the 'thing' to do. I've fallen in love and want to grasp this last chance at happiness. Our children are now adults and should understand that I can't remain in a union which has become burdensome. I've given my future considerable thought and decided it's time for me to be true to my feelings. Living in a relationship which isn't working when the chance of happiness is within reach, is something I can't let happen.'"

I was stunned. "I heard through the gossip line that you were living in the city and going through a trial separation. Our co-workers kept trying to find out what was wrong with your relationship at home. I often wondered whether this was a trial separation which could lead somewhere for me? You kept your doings secret and I never intervened. I missed our friendship. We've both been busy and you've been away very often on business. I thought everything was over between us and we should give ourselves some space."

His face took on a somber look. "When I told Bridget that I'd fallen in love with someone else and asked her for a separation and divorce, I didn't mention you. Bridget was shaken and I became confused. She said we should see a therapist and not rush into things. She loved me and had done her best to make the marriage work. She had no idea that our lives had fallen apart. I had become distant over time but she felt this was normal and probably due to the pressure of business". She was heartbroken and confessed she had never expected this. She wondered whether it was too late to see a marriage counsellor.

"The children are very disappointed and inconsolable. They blame me for not seeking counsel when I thought I was at the crossroads and the marriage was falling apart.

"I told them that I'd remained silent because of the responsibility I felt towards them and to my marriage. I wanted them to have a good education and a good start in life and so I'd bided my time. I confessed I had no rational answers to give to their questions. I'd fallen in love decades ago, but bided my time. I affirmed that they would always be part of my life and, hopefully, when they got to know the person I'd fallen in love with, she would become a part of their lives also. They weren't satisfied and kept asking me to reconsider. This was very traumatic for them, and for Bridget also. They kept bombarding me with questions for which I had no answers."

I interrupted with a questioning look, not quite understanding the feelings coursing through my body. "I don't understand. Out of the blue, you told them you're leaving home?"

"Tab, you must understand that Bridget and I have been at odds for years. We've never looked at the world through the same eyes. It's true that we've never spoken about separation before, but it's been in my thoughts constantly. I've been unhappy and Bridget knows this. It's time for us both to go our separate ways."

"This is indeed a bombshell, Sean. It has generally been voiced that this was the very last thing anyone would have expected of you." My mind was full of questions, but answers would have to wait.

"You should know that I tried hard not to leave after their tears and recriminations. I told them I would reconsider. They were all happy, but it was like a death knell. My heart felt so heavy I could hardly breathe. Bridget held out her hands to embrace me; as she walked towards me, I turned away from her, tears in my eyes. I'd tried to say what they wanted to hear, but the future looked dark and dismal."

"It isn't going to work, is it?" she said regretfully. "If your heart isn't in it, life won't work out for us. My life has been happy with you. I did everything I thought you wanted. You've been strange and distant for some time, but I thought this was because of the pressure and demands of business. I never thought you'd be unfaithful, or fall in love with someone else. It just shows how life can change out of the blue." She held my hands. "You've been good to me and I've been happy. If you decide to go now, I can't stop you."

"She turned towards the children and they hugged her as they walked away from me. I felt guilty. I'd promised to love and honour until death parted us, but I couldn't help the feeling of relief that overcame me. I'd cleared that hurdle. There would be many ramifications to be dealt with, but with you at my side, I felt I could conquer the world, be good to them, and to myself and to you at the same time.

"I came in here today hoping to have a frank talk with you. I'm hopeful that I can talk you into a future with me. When the divorce is final, I'll ask you to marry me. In the meantime, I hope I can court you on the quiet."

I really couldn't believe what I'd just heard. Sean was serious, while I'd doubted him.

He held out his hand, "Come upstairs to my office. There's something I want to show you."

I hesitated. "I'm not going to take advantage of you, Tab. It's just something I want you to have. This is the beginning of my courtship."

"Okay," I said. I took his hand.

Touching him was electrifying. Ten thousand volts of happiness shot through me. It was difficult to control my body from not leaping into his arms. There was no denying it. I had become a prisoner of his love. Whatever he offered, I'd take. I couldn't help myself. His magnetism, charm, and naked love had won the day.

He stretched out both hands to help me out of the chair, and then looked into my eyes as he drew me forward into an embrace. He kissed me, and it was even sweeter than the first. My body lit up with desire. Only one thought remained in my mind. I had to satisfy this lust, if that was what it was called, or my heart would break.

"Tab, you still love me? I wasn't sure. I hoped and prayed, but you were always so cool and distant, sometimes I despaired. Oh my love, my love! Will you be my wife when I'm free? I can't let go of you now. My heart has been aching these past months. I couldn't eat or sleep. Suddenly there's hope for happiness. Let's go upstairs to my office."

I was weak with desire for him. Holding hands, we stepped into the elevator. He kissed me again. My body felt that it belonged to him, not to me. He told me 'close your eyes' when we stepped into his office. Then he left me standing. "Now, open your hands." He placed a bunch of flowers into my outstretched arms. The aroma was enchanting. I opened my eyes. I was holding an enormous bouquet of red roses, beautiful, fragrant, and awesome.

"Today I make a formal promise to ask you to marry me when I'm free." He knelt down as he said the words. "I will be yours forever, until death, and I hope that you'll accept this token of my love. I will love and honour you always."

There were tears in my eyes. "I love you, Sean. Yes, Yes, I accept your proposal and gift of love. I'll always treasure today and I will always love you." He kissed me. This time we couldn't break away. We both needed to feel the crescendo of our love. I never knew that it was possible to have a sexual encounter standing up. Stars exploded, cherubs sang, and paradise was mine.

CHAPTER SIXTY-FIVE

I NTERLUDE OF LOVE. It was difficult to maintain a business relationship at work, but we tried. We hoped no one suspected the change from colleagues to lovers.

Months later, I told my children I was seeing someone and had been spending weekends with him. They asked, "Why don't you alternate your weekends? We like your being here some-times. It's a lovely family feeling. We also need to get to know the person you're dating."

I thought I should come clean. "Why don't we all go and sit at the dining table!"

The dining table acted as our boardroom table also. It was the place where serious matters were discussed. Many a thorny prob-lem had been dissected here and settled. Discussions around the dining table lent a certain ambience to the solution of a problem. It was a ritual they both knew, so they looked at each other and back to me.

"I'm seeing someone," I said, "someone from work. You don't know him, but I think you'll like him when you get to know him. His divorce is before the courts. We don't want to flaunt our relationship. When the divorce is granted, we'll speak to our bosses in the hierarchy and take it from there."

Christo and Gloria both piped up. "You can spend the weekend just as easily here. We always wondered what was happening, but didn't want to intervene. No more excuses; we need to know this guy also, to be involved. We're both sad you and Dad had to go your separate ways, but you're both easier to deal with now. You were constantly fighting and bickering and your quarrels only got worse. Let's meet this new love of yours and see if you're any better together. Your new love doesn't know what he's getting himself into. You can be tough when you want to be."

I was flabbergasted. When I told Sean about this new happening, he seemed pleased. "I'll have to be on my best behaviour, then. Perhaps we could all go out to dinner?"

"I think we have to be prudent, Sean. We can't flaunt the change in our association. At the moment we're still colleagues. I think opinions of us will change once the news of our liaison gets out. Let's clear one obstacle before we create the next."

He told me he was excited. On Friday I left work early to get home before he arrived. I told him I would park my car on the driveway so his car could remain unrecognized, hidden in the garage. We laughed at the subterfuge, but we were just being careful. We both had senior positions within the company, and we didn't want our private affairs bruited about in a way that would affect relationships with our clients.

It was different when I went to his apartment. He was an unknown, just one of the many transient renters, a temporary habitué.

Sean arrived before Christo and Gloria. I poured him a drink of his favourite Scotch and a glass of Chardonnay for myself. We were both somewhat on edge, both having second thoughts, both fearful that the outcome would not produce the results we hoped for.

"Perhaps it might have been better if we'd met elsewhere for dinner. I don't want them to think I'm trying to usurp their home," Sean said, as he interrupted my thoughts.

"My thoughts also, but it's too late to do anything about it now," I replied.

Sean replied, "It'll be difficult for them dealing with a strange man who's courting their mother in what used to be their father's bedroom. I think this won't work. After dinner, I'll just return home."

"Sean, we're both nervous. Is that why you arrived without a bag? A wise decision! Let's say you're only here for a visit and to meet them and perhaps have dinner together."

"Subterfuges can be daring, but they seldom work. We'll see," he replied with a look of optimism.

Christo, Marigold his fiancée, and Gloria arrived together. It seemed they had planned their arrival to coincide. I had a moment of fright. What if they didn't like him? Perhaps I should have consulted them before I'd gotten involved! What can I do if they hate one another on sight?! A thousand questions jostled each other, all impatiently waiting for an answer.

I needn't have bothered. After polite greetings, they all sat down. There was one awkward moment when roles had to be assumed but Christo asked politely, "Sean, I understand that you've kidnapped my mother. What can we do about it?"

There was a moment of laughter. This was a role reversal. My children would have to become part of his life, and he would also have to play a major role in their lives, if they let him. Their acceptance of him as a suitable consort for their mother was vital. How would that affect their relationship with their father?

I had met Sean's children on their visit to the office over the years. Christo had worked one summer as an office boy, so he had met Sean briefly. Gloria greeted him, "It's nice to meet you at last, Sean. You've been usurping my mother's attentions for some time. Careful you don't make us jealous, but it's nice to meet you at last."

We all settled down to pleasant conversation. They all had so many things in common that conversation flowed easily. I left them for a while to finish preparing dinner. The evening was very enjoyable and time seemed to disappear.

Eventually it was time for Sean to depart. "Aren't you spending the night, Sean? We know what you and my mother are up to."

"The next time, perhaps Christo. I did come prepared to spend the weekend, but thought we should get to know one another better before assuming your acceptance of me. I want to do this correctly. I love your mother dearly, and have loved her silently for years. I don't want to compromise her in any way, or assume that I can spend weekends here without meeting you first, and letting you know we're planning a future together."

Gloria said, "We like you, Sean. You complement my mother. She is so relaxed and different in her conversations with you, that I'm astounded. Thank you for considering our feelings. You're right. It's natural that we should get to know you. We know Mom loves you and you love her, and we want to join the bandwagon. We want her to be happy".

Our dinner together was pleasant filled with chitchat and laughter.

Christo, Marigold, and Gloria said they were meeting friends and left. The evening had gone well. Sean and I agreed that our weekend of sexual gratification would have to wait. We were content. We kissed each other good night under the stars in the back garden. He was happy with the outcome.

Sean had consulted a lawyer and was in process of finalizing his divorce proceedings. This would take time, but we were hopeful everything would go well.

Meantime, we decided to sneak away on holiday together to India. I wanted to visit the land of my forefathers, somehow to understand our cultural differences and customs. My childhood had been spent in Guyana where, as colonials, we were brought up as Anglicans and never had the opportunity to understand Indian mythology.

Knowledge of India seemed unimportant because we considered ourselves more British than Indian, in fact superior to the people of India. We were taught that our future lay with British traditions and customs rather than with our Indian forbears because we were British citizens. This all changed when British Guiana was granted independence, and renamed Guyana.

Our immigration to Canada had coincided with the surge of brown people from India and Pakistan. We were referred to as Pakis and there was resistance to brown people buying houses in certain neighbourhoods. Somehow, I was never openly targeted, but, as you'll recall from my early days in Canada, my children received racial taunts from their schoolmates. They'd mentioned being subjected to heckling and expletives at the time and we discussed the question of racial discrimination and its consequences. As time passed it seemed whatever discomfort they felt was dealt with, or they'd decided to deal with the situation themselves.

They were different in many respects from their schoolmates. Our swimming pool and large backyard were drawing cards and we didn't object to their friends visiting, the children did well at school; they spoke and wrote better English than their classmates. The girls romanticized over Christo, and Gloria simply excelled at everything she did. They were cut up by the feeling that they were being judged by the colour of their skins, but we never turned it into a problem; it was simply a fact of life... One more hurdle to cross until people realized that skin colour didn't make for superior or inferior human beings.

When we told them that we were taking a holiday together and we were thinking of traveling to India, they asked us "why" and Sean said, "Your mother wants to find her roots. Your great grandparents came from India and she thinks this adventure into a past culture would be very meaningful."

I added, "India was always regarded as the jewel in the British Crown. Back in Guyana, even though few of us spoke the language, many Indian customs still prevailed. Religion, food, and arranged marriages were all India-based. In your grandfather's cinemas, Thursday nights were always reserved for Indian movies. These movies always intrigued me. Even though I couldn't understand the language, I was always entertained."

They laughed at us and told us to be careful.

We booked our holiday with some stealth. It was the first time we would both be absent from the office on holiday at the same time. However, Sean said he was going to visit his family in Ireland.

I was going off to Europe on a business trip, following which I would join a group tour to India. Jokingly, to many who asked 'Why?' I replied, "I'm off to find my roots."

CHAPTER SIXTY-SIX

UNDERSTANDING THE COUNTRY OF MY FOREBEARS. Sean and I met in Mumbai. His flight arrived before mine, but he was waiting for me at the airport.

Our journey to the hotel placed us in a traffic situation that existed in no other part of the world. He was excited, I was cautious. I couldn't understand how cars, buses, cycles, rickshaws, 'holy' cows could all travel at the same time on the same road in the early hours of the morning. Car horns sounded continuously, without seemingly having any effect on the flow of traffic. The cacophony of sounds in the still of the night evoked unsettling feelings in my mind. I wanted to say, "Let's turn around and go home." The confusion did have an enchanting edge to it, but it was also totally unnerving. It seemed I was visiting another planet. I asked myself "Where was traffic order?"

The hotel was much more to my liking. Opulent and gracious, I was swallowed up in luxury. This was a far different situation from what lay outside.

Despite my many adventures, India still remains a mystery to me. It was as wealthy as it was poor. 'Fagan-like' children had been turned into beggars and thieves. My heart was full of pity but I shrunk from the dirt and disease which I associated with poor hygiene. Beggars wanted to touch me or hang on to a piece of my clothing. I opened my handbag to give a child a rupee, when suddenly there was a swarm of children, all trying to tug my handbag from me. Fortunately, a constable arrived in the nick of time. He swirled his truncheon like a magic wand, and the children fled only to reappear as we ran to the car and drove away. They didn't give up easily, but tried to follow us on foot.

Tourists were easy prey. It seemed that everyone wanted a piece of our dollar: merchants, hawkers, carpet sellers, and would-be tourist guides. We solved this situation by hiring someone to accompany us when we were without a guide. The glitz and glamor of jewelry, and furnishings left us in awe. We were urged to buy, but the wares were eastern and we lived in a western world. I couldn't resist the carpets, though. I had to take a few home with me.

We visited the Taj Mahal and mourned with Shah Jehan, the loss of his love Mumtaz. What a wonderful memorial! I wondered at the mastery of the architect who'd designed the place, the artistry and craftsmanship of all the people who had brought this creation to life. The splendour that was India's past had disappeared from daily life, leaving only monuments to remind us of a time when Indian Maharajas and Moghuls were the all-powerful; and wealth and power were displayed by the glitter and glitz of gold and precious stones, which decorated the palaces of the wealthy – a stark contrast to the mud huts which lay beyond.

The India that was, became alive as we listened to our guides. I could appreciate the greed of the British when they started their trading through the East India Company. Much like the Spanish in Mexico they eventually displaced the rulers and took control of the country.

I was strangely moved by the emotions which flooded my mind and brought tears to my eyes when I set foot in the Mahatma

Gandhi memorial gardens. I remembered pictures and newspaper reports of his many sacrifices as he sought to free his country from the invaders who had taken control in the 1800's. This wizened little man had inspired a nation and brought the powerful British Empire to its knees.

The British hadn't departed without a final blow. They left an India divided against itself, adrift in a sea of distrust and anger, where men fought not for love of their country but for achievement of power, so they could emulate what they had learned from the people who'd ruled them for three hundred years, controlled and abused them, and plundered their resources.

They left a legacy of fear and distrust with little or no understanding of how their actions would shape the future of man's relationships with his fellow man in this country, which once was "The Jewel in their Crown."

One country became two countries, India and Pakistan; hatred between two peoples who once lived together was sealed. Lines were drawn on religious ethnicity. This would involve separation and movements of millions who had once lived together in harmony, from one area to the other, leaving death and destruction in its wake.

Indians and Muslims had battled between themselves throughout the centuries but they were united in the march for freedom. Imprisonment of mostly the Hindu element of the Indian Congress followed. Britain then tried to woo the Muslim community in hope of putting down the 'insurrection.' The result was that Muslims now wanted to be repaid by giving them a Muslim country. Division of the country would see India ablaze with fire, murder, and mayhem, as the fury of Hindus and Muslims wreaked havoc on each other.

Partition amplified the problem of religion. People were uprooted from lands which had been their homes for generations. Hatred magnified itself and the result was fire and brimstone.

India was an inferno, a conflagration, perhaps a funeral ceremony, not unlike the pyres lit for the departed as bodies floated down the river Ganges.

I felt proud of my heritage and consoled myself with the thought that if my forefathers hadn't left India, I wouldn't have been born. Marriages of my grandparents and parents couldn't have taken place. My lineage was Hindu, Moslem and Madrasi (Chennai).

The visit opened my eyes to the past glories of India but I couldn't see myself in this setting. I was brought up with Western traditions. The only thing we shared was the colour of our skins. We spoke different languages and were different in outlook.

Although Indira Gandhi, a woman, was elected Prime Minister of India, she'd enjoyed privilege and popularity as the daughter of former Prime Minister Nehru. Had I been born and lived in India as an ordinary citizen, I could never have achieved the position I now held in an international company. It was hard enough for women to be successful in the Western world, but forbidden in the East where women to this day still await emancipation. India continues to be unique in many ways.

Sean constantly poked fun at me reminding me that in a previous life he was an officer in the army of Robert Clive who was responsible for finally displacing the Maharajas in India when he won the battle against Suraja Dowlah. He always teased, "I fell in love with a lowly Indian girl, gathered her in my arms, as the villagers raced after me, and took her to my little grey home in the West, where we lived happily ever after."

I always replied, "If thinking that we've met before in previous lives where you were master of the world brings you joy, go ahead with your thoughts. In present time, we're equals. I have one question for you: 'what would your mother have said to you when you brought home your Indo English children to see her?'" My gaze was triumphant. I smiled, *let him talk his way through this.*

"You're mine, Tab. My love for you holds you captive, just as securely as it did centuries ago." He always managed to look me in the eyes when he said this. His look captured me in an embrace that locked us together, it seemed for an eternity. I was indeed a slave kept shackled by his love. I couldn't say 'no' to this man. Sometimes I actually believed his ramblings of our historical past encounter.

"You're a romantic, Sean. We can always pretend that we're star-crossed lovers in a starry-eyed love story that spans centuries. These stories always have happy endings... and they lived happily ever after. Do you believe in destiny?"

"I do. I fell in love with you the first time I saw you over seventeen years ago. I danced with you at your first company Christmas party. Do you remember you had us all singing "White Christmas" when we talked about Christmas in Guyana? I wished that life was different at that time, and I could capture you and ride off into the sunset. We both had commitments. I settled for friendship because you were so 'proper,' I was afraid I'd lose you if I confessed my love for you. The years passed by, then destiny decided it could wait no longer and brought us together. And now, my darling, I'll never let you go."

In that happy frame of mind, we decided to pay a visit to an astrologer. In India one custom was the belief that astrology predetermines our life here on Earth. We talked about the effect of interplanetary configuration at the time of birth and a destiny predetermined for us. Reading my horoscope each day was routine for me. We had nothing to lose. The Beatles had visited India to learn about Transcendental Meditation. We were interested in our destiny ... and we were in India.

Our guide recommended that we visit the astrologer in the hotel lobby. He was reputed to be well renowned because of the accuracy of his predictions, which were based on astrology and mathematics, intuition and meditation. His credentials included a letter of thanks from Margaret Thatcher, former British Prime Minister, for work he had done for her.

The astrologer dressed in Hindu costume, complete with turban, was intrigued. Here was a white English man and a brown Indian woman from another part of the world. "Are you married" he questioned. Sean replied that this was our plan. He looked carefully at us as if trying to gain an insight into our souls. He gave a satisfied grunt, then explained that order in the universe depended on interplanetary configurations; the effects of this order on life on Earth were similar to their effect on the seasons and weather patterns. Our lives followed a charted course depicted at the time of our birth and our destinies were predetermined. (I'd heard this before from my astrologer in Canada).

Because I was born in another hemisphere, he had to make adjustments to my time of birth. I threw him a curve when I told him I didn't know at what time my birth occurred. He frowned, as he said that time was important because the constellations were never still and predictions were an exact science. However, he would approximate my time of birth, but the readings would vary slightly.

His booth was filled with books, which he consulted from time to time. He drew graphs and plotted points. With a groan of satisfaction, after fifteen minutes, he produced a chart. This chart was supposed to have predicted my journey on Earth. Starting with childhood, he forecasted sorrow and trauma, rebellion in my teenage years, but brilliant in school. He took my palms and interpreted the lines on them. One was supposed to show the past and the other the future.

I was fascinated by the accuracy of his predictions of my past life. How could the lines on the palms of my hand reveal my past?

The lines on my right hand predicted a future full of love and happiness. I would be faced with a choice, which would determine my career path. He finalized the reading by saying, "Behti, life always offers a choice. Follow the pathway that brings happiness. Materiality is never satisfying. Step back, ask yourself what really matters; Your aura is good. Your future is in your hands."

I was somewhat subdued when he finished. There was a lot of thinking involved with the results of his forecast. Sean took my place at the table.

He knew the time of his birth, and this drew a sigh of satisfaction from the seer. Volumes flew off the shelf and back on again as they were selected and then rejected. Then there was a sigh of relief, turning of pages, and finally, plotting of graphs and the production of the chart.

Sean and I had talked about his past. It seems he had loved his mother, but found that nothing he did ever pleased her. His humiliation reached its height when she vented if his activities fell short of her expectations. To keep his equanimity, he'd done exactly what she expected him to do, and ignored what would have made him truly happy. He was always blamed, but seldom praised. Her disappointment had played havoc with his psyche. He began to believe that something was wrong with him. His life had followed the pattern which she determined. Even when he tried to explain that he wanted a career which flowed along different lines, she was adamant that he didn't know what was good for him.

It was his secret wish that as soon as he could leave home he would do so. On graduation from university he filed Immigration forms with the Australian, Canadian, and U.S. embassies. The Canadian Embassy was the first to reply. He went for an interview and came home glowing. He was going to live in Canada.

An uncle had immigrated to the United States and was doing well in the Navy. Sean was not interested in either the Military or the Navy. He was a happy camper when he landed in Montreal and boarded the train to Toronto. Finding a job wasn't difficult and as his career advanced; he settled down to life in Toronto.

The years passed and it was time to get married and start a family. They had two children. The passage of time created differences and the marriage became a sham, kept together only because of the effect of a broken home on the children and also that divorce was frowned upon. He'd confessed during the early years of our friendship that it was easier to remain in an unhappy relationship than to strike out on his own.

When we were just friends, both complaining about life, he'd shared his feelings with me. "Tab, it's hard for me to break the vows we exchanged when Bridget and I got married. 'Till death do us part' is a life sentence. I never knew how difficult it would be to keep this promise. But there we are. I can't risk losing my place in society and being pointed at. Divorce is an American tradition."

I'd told him then, "What you mean, Sean, is that if you promised to drive your car into Lake Ontario, and you knew that would result in death, you'd still do it?"

"I promised before God. That's different. I don't want to be cast into Hell when I die."

I'd smiled when I told him, "You're damned if you do, and damned if you don't. Sometimes, when we're at the crossroads, we have to make tough decisions. If present conditions in your life affect your health adversely, you have to find some way of coming to terms with it and making peace. When emotions are bottled and suppressed, your actions can become irrational and uncontrollable."

He smiled. "You should've been a shrink."

"No, just a good friend, Sean."

It never occurred to me at that time that our friendship could turn into love. I had imposed strict rules on myself. I would never fall in love with a 'white' man. That vow would be sacrosanct. No doubt I was prejudiced, but also sure that all 'white' men would ever want from someone like me, of Indian descent, and a different culture, would be an adventure in bed. I wouldn't be true to myself if I allowed this to happen. Breaking the 'code' imposed on 'good' women was not the person I wanted to be.

I was brought back from my reverie when the astrologer signaled that Sean's chart was ready.

I listened carefully. His reading of Sean's chart was strangely accurate. He said Sean was a dutiful son and also a dutiful husband and father. He had lived his life based firstly on the wants and needs of his parents, and after he travelled across the ocean, hadn't broken away from rules imposed on him since childhood. He had followed them rigorously because a certain code of conduct was expected of an English gentleman. His own wants and desires had taken a backseat to the expectations of others.

The astrologer predicted that our future would be different. Our birth signs were in harmony. We would at last find the happiness we both craved. We would travel the world together and discover the laughter and love that had eluded us; best of all, we would both find contentment. One of us had to die before the other, but the soul of the one who had died would await with patience the passing of the other, so we both could journey into another universe together. We had been searching for each other throughout several lifetimes, but this would be our last journey.

Death seemed a far off happening in the future, and we laughed about it. Most important was that happiness would be ours. Love would enable us to find places we'd never dreamed of and would provide us with the contentment we had always craved. We were giddy with excitement. No matter what the future brought, we would find solutions. Our future was bright and promising.

Our visit to India had been one of highs and lows. It provided a good background for us to discover things about the other which were new and different. We had only been together for at the most three days at a time when we were both away on company business. We were spending three weeks discovering India and ourselves. Every night I fell asleep in his arms. Every morning when I awakened he was beside me. The bliss and joy of rolling over and being enveloped in his arms gave me a feeling of love and belonging that was blissful.

Our future was going to be an exciting adventure. We were content.

CHAPTER SIXTY-SEVEN

OUR NEW FOUND RELATIONSHIP. Returning home and to work required strict adherence to the code of conduct we had agreed upon. Strictly business. It was difficult not to look across the room and exchange smiles, to touch when we were alone in the elevator or to throw cold water on points Sean raised for discussion, and which we disagreed about. Love didn't blind me to the realities of business and I couldn't put aside my vision, my knowledge, and my ability. We saw the business world through different eyes.

Sean told me he couldn't fight me in the boardroom. He saw the world differently. Telling me that what I was proposing was not workable was not chivalrous. He couldn't speak adversely about anything I said. This was a new slant in our relationship. He felt hurt when I didn't agree with him or when I argued against his proposals. There was tension in the boardroom between us and this didn't augur well.

He couldn't see that I wasn't pitting myself against him. I felt that the industry, and indeed our company, were at the beginning of a renaissance, which heralded the explosion of new ideas and new ways of doing business. The ideas I presented were futuristic but there was evidence that they would become reality. Technology was offering us new concepts and new ways of determining the 'How's, Where's and Why's' of everything. The past predicted how the future would change. Nothing stood still. He argued that what worked well in the past was tried and true; it functioned well and we should stick to what we knew. I argued that if, like ostriches, we stuck our heads in the sand, we would fall into obsolescence.

Arguments at work filtered over to our private lives. He started avoiding me after work. Then our weekend together at my home was cancelled because he needed to see his children. I didn't buy this. Reality was setting in. Our love had crescendoed with our holiday. We needed to spend some time apart. I asked myself, 'Is this the beginning of the end?'

Heartbreak filled my being. To Christo's and Gloria's question, "Where's Sean this weekend?" I replied, "He's spending time with his children." I saw the surprised looks on their faces as they chorused, "Are you guys quarrelling?"

"Perhaps? Just a little time apart so we understand where we're heading."

"Cheer up, Mom," Christo replied, a smile on his face. "It's nice to have you to ourselves this weekend. Let's invite some of the cousins over tomorrow. They miss you and keep asking about you."

"No," I quickly replied shaking my head from side to side. "I'm going shopping today, and tomorrow I plan to spend time with a new novel I've been longing to get into."

"Well, we'll leave you to it, but don't mope too much. These things have a way of working out and whatever it is, you'll be better off. Try to be happy". They both hugged me and whispered, "Perhaps he's the first of many loves which will follow."

I chuckled. "Perhaps you suspect there's another side to your prim and proper mother." A light moment to end a disturbing question.

Shopping for clothes I didn't need was a good idea. I was no exception to the sentiment that clothes enhanced appearance. Looking my best altered my feelings. I gazed at myself in the mirror in the dressing room and murmured, "You may have a broken heart but you don't have to advertise it. Appearance is everything." When I again looked at myself in the mirror after the many fittings through the day, my eyes mirrored my thoughts. *Although I loved Sean with all my heart and being, I couldn't compromise the values that were dear to me, and which had earned me a place in the corporate world. I'd be living a lie, and this would cause me to disrespect myself. I'd made a vow to myself, 'to be the best and do the best within my capabilities.'*

Reality had set in. I had no doubt he loved me, but his feelings were not as strong as mine. Our view of the future differed vastly. I saw the future with conglomerates dominating the industry and acquisition of small players becoming the norm. Technology would simplify methodology. The world would become one local marketplace.

Sean couldn't envision such a world. He believed in the 'tried and true.' In his perception, technological revolution could never happen within the immediacy of our lifetime. He couldn't believe that present concepts would become archaic within the span of a decade and new methodology would blossom in its place.

He was not singular in this regard. It was the feeling of the time. Most of our colleagues shared this feeling. It was comfortable and they had all achieved high positions in government and business organizations. It was difficult to picture changes to the future when the present worked so well.

I laughed at myself. Why did I ever believe that I could find true love in this lifetime? I tried to console myself that at least I had experienced the joys of a lifetime packed into a miniscule period of my life. I reminded myself that I shouldn't be greedy, and that perhaps most couples had never enjoyed the physical and mental happiness I had packed into a few months.

I returned home to find my message light blinking. Someone had left me a message. Perhaps it was Sean. Delight flooded my mind. I pressed the message button. It was Sean indeed but from his tone of voice I knew something was up. "I'd like to see you tomorrow, if you're free. There are some things I need to discuss with you. It's business, of course, or I wouldn't have bothered you."

"Shall I meet you at the office, Sean? If it's business that is the best place."

We agreed to meet at 10 o'clock. I wondered what the business was all about, and would later spend half the night trying to find an inkling about what was so urgent and important that it required our attention. Speculation caused me a night of twisting and turning. At last I fell asleep on the thought that 'tomorrow' would come soon enough, and whatever the cost, I must grin and bear it.

Sunday morning was glorious. Sunshine heralded a day to remember, a day made simply for enjoyment with love and laughter all around. I was setting out to a meeting that would see my future love life in ruins. The dream I had locked in my heart because I felt it could never happen would die a natural death. "Perhaps this isn't in your destiny," I comforted myself, "life has given you everything else you desired and more. Be content that whatever happens today, it isn't the end of your world but the beginning of something new." The ache in my heart was not mollified. Desolation filled my spirit and my soul.

Sean's car was in the garage when I turned in to my allotted space. "Well, so be it. It was nice while it lasted. Like everything else, you know how to deal with the rotten things that happen in your life," I whispered to bolster my courage.

He had heard the elevator and was waiting at his door. There was awkwardness in our greeting. We both fumbled. A chaste kiss, a handshake, or just a smile. I didn't want him to touch me so I started the ball rolling.

"What's this all about, Sean? I'm sorry you had to interrupt your day with your children. They see little enough of you as it is. I'm sure they were disappointed."

"It's important to me, to us, that we have this discussion. Sadie was emptying one of the desks in the President's office and she found this file. She thought I should see it and brought it to me."

I recognized a copy of the personnel succession planning report we were required to submit to Head Office every three years. His face was full of doubt and disbelief. In a hurt tone, he asked, "Why didn't you tell me that I was not listed as successor to the President when this was prepared? If you loved me, you should've let me know."

I thought '*what's wrong with this man I love. Why raise something like this with accusation, not clarification? Why did I succumb to his attentions?*'" I carefully concealed my feelings. This was indeed business and I had deal with in in a businesslike manner.

"First and foremost Sean, Sadie violated the trust required of her position as Secretary to the President. She shouldn't have divulged the contents of this report to you. Secondly, did you notice the date on this report. This was prepared over ten years ago. Sadie could be fired for her actions. I wonder what are her reasons?" My shoulders were drawn back elbows at my waist, hands turned inside out, my face reflecting my difficulty at understanding.

"She's loyal to me."

"She should be loyal to Taylor, the President. And you're questioning my loyalty to you?" I smiled, shaking my head in disbelief. "You're sulking over this document. It's the elephant in the room. If you felt I'd done something disturbing to you, why couldn't we discuss it? This document was prepared over ten years ago and has been revised many times since. Why is it bothersome to you now?"

"I want to be your knight in shining armour. I'm sure you'd some input into the recommendations and I was devastated that you'd made no mention of it to me.

He looked a bit ashamed, but still tried to blame me.

I was flabbergasted. "This report was prepared ten years ago, and there have been many changes over the years. Are you trying to end our relationship, Sean? We don't have to find reasons or justify them. I'm true to my own responsibilities and have nothing to apologize for. It seems we've arrived at the crossroads. We hold different positions in this company. When lines intercross, our first responsibility should be to the job and not to our relationship. It would be dishonest of us both if we used our affiliation to better our positions. It breaks my heart to tell you this, but we have to end this relationship now. My love for you and my position within the company cause conflict of interest."

I turned away, filled with anger and betrayal. I was disheartened and sad. Tears settled in my eyes. *This accusation has thrown a wet blanket on my love and squashed the fire. It was time to relegate my feelings to the past. Why is he so insecure? This is something so foolish, it's just ludicrous. I'm better off without it.*

I shrugged my shoulders, straightened my back, and started towards the door.

He rushed after me and tried to hold me in his arms. His voice pleaded, "I won't let you go. I can't let you go. I wasn't thinking clearly. Will you forgive me?" He sounded contrite and ashamed

With my heart breaking and a voice I didn't recognize, I countered, "We're treading in dangerous waters. It's time we reported our situation to the President. I'm at the crossroads here. I know it's an unwritten rule that any association between two executives is unacceptable. Let's see what happens. Perhaps they'll transfer one of us to New York or terminate us both. Who knows? This company has been very good to me. I've never felt discrimination based on race or gender. There's no other female Senior Vice President or Vice President (for that matter) in the worldwide operations and I can never be disloyal. I'm sad that you felt you had to raise this matter as an accusation against me. We think differently, Sean, and I'm not so sure this is right for us."

"Tab, I'm certain that I can't and don't want to let you go. You're the love I've been seeking all these years. I got married because it was the thing to do. At that time, I was in love with love. I tried to make things work and stayed together with Bridget because there was no one until you entered my life. Even then, I hid my love and settled for friendship because you didn't seem interested in me. I treasured those moments when we danced together at Christmas parties or even when we shook hands. I've been lonely without you. I'd listen for your laughter, and I was jealous when I thought you were flirting with someone else. I want to be your knight in shining armour. I hated to think that you thought less of me in that report on succession planning."

With eyes raised and face creased in a fake smile I reminded him, "I don't report to you, Sean, the President is my boss. This planning document was compiled by a former Senior Vice President and your boss at the time. I'm astounded by your accusation of me. I don't forgive and forget easily. My advice is that it's nothing to be worried about at this stage. It's of no account now. You're the logical successor to the President. Everyone knows this. This worrying isn't worthy of you. You've allowed someone who's of no consequence in the outcome to cause you worry. If I were you, I'd ask myself where her loyalty lies and what she's hoping to achieve by disseminating confidential information. She obviously wants promotion, and instead of working for it, decided to use her seeming loyalty to you to accomplish this. Beware of what she brings to your attention. She's a secretary, not your confidant and adviser. If you had questions, you should've consulted, not chastised me."

"I'm so sorry, Tab. I gave her responsibility for some event planning, which she did well enough, but she far exceeded our budget. She has grandiose ideas, and some of her suggestions are not in keeping with business events. Still, I hadn't thought to question her intentions. I only felt 'let down' by you when I saw the report. "

I shook my head and narrowed my eyes. "I've nothing more to say on the subject. We both need time to understand where we're heading. We love each other, but where is this taking us? We're in the midst of an idyllic situation, but we're heading in different directions. Perhaps we plunged headlong into a liaison without giving much thought to the consequences. We need to take a 'time out' and look straight on to where our love is taking us, and whether we want to think of a life together."

"I can't live with this. What you're asking cuts me to the quick. Life without you is no life altogether," he countered, clearly expecting some other answer from me.

"It's important for us to assess our own situations from a "futuristic" viewpoint. It was good while we thought only of the present, and plunged headlong into a fulfillment of passion. The future looms large. Where's this taking us and can we survive the obstacles we're sure to face? Let's take a rest or a 'time out.' We've cleared the air over the succession planning, let's examine the future," I replied with sadness in my voice and doubt in my heart.

We agreed that this would be best.

"Can I take you to lunch, Tab? Let's kiss and make up." He smiled with pleading eyes.

"There's too much to think about. I'd like to have a little breathing room to digest it all, and come to some conclusion. I'd prefer to let things rest for a while. We both need pleasant relaxation. Time away from each other is what the doctor would order." I smiled and moved to the door.

We kissed chastely, and parted. Myriads of questions went in and out of my mind. I felt my world falling apart. Why was I throwing away something that had evaded me all my life? Shouldn't I throw caution to the winds and put an end to it all? I felt as weak as if sudden death had taken hold of my future and all I ever wanted, and put an end to its life even before it had begun. I went to my office, fiddled with a few papers on my desk, and left. I couldn't trust myself to drive home. I hailed a cab instead.

CHAPTER SIXTY-EIGHT

PREPONDERANCE OF THOUGHT. The balance of my weekend had a nightmarish quality to it. Without my car, it was difficult to get around. My children suspected that all was not right, but prudently decided not to ask. I decided it was best to retrieve my car to avoid questions on Monday. Sean's car was in the garage when I got there, but I got into my car and drove out without going into the office.

When I arrived at work on Monday morning, I was surprised to find our President, Taylor Woodruff at work. I pushed my head in as I was walking to my office. He looked up and said, "Just the person I wanted to see. Come in."

I thought, *the fat is about to hit the fire. He knows about Sean and me.*

"Well, Tabitha, some interesting news. I've been promoted to the New York office. Sean is going to be President here, and you'll take over the Services Company. Our bosses felt they couldn't give the presidency of the company to a woman despite my recommendation."

I was shocked and my expression must have revealed this. "It was a sudden decision. Both you and Sean will be reporting to

Johannes Schmidt. He'll be taking over from Erick Johansson who's seeking early retirement because of medical reasons. These are big changes made with my recommendations and they are effective immediately. I will make the announcement at the Executive meeting this morning, and afterwards inform the staff."

"This is indeed good news," I said. "I'm bowled over and speechless. Thanks for your continued support."

"You've been very good for this company, Tabitha. I leaned hard on them when they were proposing to go outside for a male replacement. Don't let me down."

We discussed the changes and what they entailed, and soon it was time for our Executive meeting.

We went into the boardroom together. Sean gave me a quizzical look. I smiled and looked away. Questions rumbled through my mind. What would all of this entail? How was I going to handle the fall out? What would it mean for Sean and me? I was sure that these promotions meant the end of any relationship Sean and I could have. It had taken the decision making right out of our hands.

There were congratulations and good wishes all around. The staff all cheered when Taylor Woodruff announced the changes. I went into my office and closed the door behind me. I had never got on with Johannes Schmidt. Over the years, he had always questioned my ability. He was a stickler for procedure, reminding us all that the past worked well at the present time and would continue on the same path into the future. He had always stated that embracing the future with the changes technology might bring was just a chancy path. Technology was still in its infancy. Changes needed to be verified before they could be adopted. He didn't understand that we were on the brink of a technological revolution, which would sweep across the Universe bringing changes we had not yet foreseen. We had many run-ins over this in the past and now I realized that it would have to be "his way" or the highway. It was also a well-known fact that he didn't think women had a future outside the secretarial pool.

Well, I told myself, *this isn't a time to prognosticate. Let's see how things fall into place before we make rash conclusions.* Surprisingly, I received a phone call from him congratulating me. He concluded, "We must work together. I need your help and your understanding if I'm to make a success of my job." I breathed a sigh of relief, but wondered whether these were just meaningless generalities, uttered at the start to gain cooperation and avoid problems until he could find a way to discredit me, later down the road.

As you know, my personal code through life had always been "if it is to be, it's up to me." I would weigh the options life offered, and make the best choices.

Sean and I had dinner together that night. He was most apologetic and pleaded with me to forget our quarrel, which he said, in retrospect, was simply a foolish misunderstanding. In view of what had transpired both with the company and his not trusting me, I told him I wanted to divulge the happenings in our personal lives to Taylor and ask his advice. "Sean, this man has been good to me. He opened doors and stuck up for me when our Dutch bosses regarded women in the workforce as being incapable for advancement into the hierarchy. I can't let this information about us explode like a bombshell. I trust him, and he has always trusted me," I stated firmly. My tone and the look on my face showed that this was what I had chosen to do, and my mind was firmly against any other suggestion.

He again entreated, "Tab, can't we forget what happened over the weekend? I'm so ashamed. I can't lose you. What can I do to earn your trust again? This promotion means nothing to me if it means I'm going to lose you." His pleading eyes and the look on his face and in his eyes were difficult to resist.

I decided to keep my cool and ease things along. I'll see what the future brings before I make the big commitment.

"Let's call a truce, Sean. First, we must let Taylor know what's happening with us. I value his advice. This could rock the boat, but it's better to deal with that now rather than wait for it to happen when we least expect it."

"If that's the way you see it, Tab; then there's no deterring you. Let's see him together tomorrow and deal with the repercussions."

A secret love in the business world is difficult. Chance meetings could happen and then the fat would be in the fire. A business friend happened upon us at the restaurant that night. We were in deep discussion when he passed our table on his way out. "Hello, you two have been having an interesting discussion. What's up? Am I interrupting a lover's tryst?"

Sean was good at masking his feelings. "She said 'no' to me again, so I got nowhere. However, congratulations are in order. You're now looking at the new President of our operating company, and Tabitha is the President of the services company."

"Great news, you guys. Congratulations to you both. No wonder you were so absorbed. Just goes to show that appearances can be deceiving," he replied.

As we watched him leave Sean agreed, "You were right, Tab. Rumours are bound to spread, and it'd be better for our news to be out in the open, rather than have people second-guessing as to whether we're in a relationship."

As we were leaving our executive meeting the following day, Taylor said, "I think it's time I got you two together to talk about future plans. This is an opportune time before we all get bogged down."

We followed him to his office and then he closed the doors. *He has heard something* reverberated through my mind. When he started to talk about the change-over, my heart sighed with relief.

We had a good discussion about future plans. Changes would be minimal. We had dealt with promotions following our appointments, but decided to hold off appointing new personnel.

At the end of it all, before he could conclude, Sean confided, "Taylor, Tabitha and I have found ourselves in the predicament of love. We both feel that our future lives are tied together. The news of our promotions have come as a bombshell. What advice do you have for us?" Having said the words and not knowing the repercussion, he was hoping to find a conciliatory voice.

"What you're saying is a bombshell. I had no idea you were romantically involved. What happened between you?" He was bowled over by what he was hearing. He had intervened before when we had our quarrels. There was an incredulous look on his face. He couldn't understand, or make sense of what he was hearing.

"We're just two people who worked together, became friends, and suddenly found out that our friendship had blossomed into something else." Sean explained trying to mask the discomfort he was feeling.

"This may just be a fling, or a passing fancy. Give it some time. I'm glad that you've confided in me, but I think we should wait awhile before we start rushing out to find solutions. You both have good careers and new beginnings. The final decision will rest with our bosses, the Dutch." He had been literally bowled over at what he heard, perhaps in his heart thankful that he wouldn't be asked to make new arrangements in the leadership team.

He wished us well, then said he wanted to speak to me alone. Sean gave me a look that said he wasn't comfortable leaving me in the hot seat but could do nothing about it.

"Don't throw away everything you've worked for, Tabitha. You and Sean have always had problems. He thinks the old ways will endure, and your vision for the future is that technology will change the ways we do business. That will always be a problem.

You may toss everything away because of your new-found feelings for each other, only to find out that you can't get along. What are you going to do then? You've too much at stake. Think carefully. You have a brilliant future ahead of you." Taylor's voice showed his concern. He couldn't understand how our present situation had evolved.

I looked at him, my own concern mirroring his words. "My thoughts have been trending this way for some time. We'll be careful. We're both career-minded and I think our careers will take precedence over our love. We'll weigh all possibilities before we make a final decision. As you rightly say, the future is ours to make or break. We aren't 'young lovers.'" I had mixed thoughts as I left his office. We had worked together for years. He had given me my first break and I hadn't let him down. He had every right to voice the concern he felt over how our relationship would work within the corporate establishment.

We both laughed. I left his office feeling a confidence that eluded me. Whatever decisions we made should be in our best interests. The question was "Love versus career". What's the answer?

Little did I know what fate had in store for me.

CHAPTER SIXTY-NINE

OCCURRENCES INFLUENCE DECISIONS. Life settled down. Sean and I were both busy at work, but we had resumed spending our weekends together. We parked our differences and settled into a relationship which on the surface was happy, but for the first time in many years I was worried about my job.

My relationship with Johannes Schmidt was difficult to manage. It seemed nothing I could do pleased him. In the middle of a storm one winter's day, transportation in and out of Toronto was difficult to say the least. I usually left home at 7.00 a.m. each day and arrived at the office half an hour later, so I was always at work before 8 o'clock. He called me at 9.30 on my cell phone and was disdainful of the fact that we were in the midst of a raging snowstorm with gridlock on all the major routes and highways.

"I've been calling you since early morning and I can't get through to you. Are we not operational in Toronto at 8.30 a.m.?" were his words of greeting.

"You did manage to reach me on my car phone," I countered. "Today's a difficult day. I've been stuck on the Don Valley Parkway since 7.30 a.m. Accidents had to be cleared before traffic could get a move on. I've no idea when I'll be at work, and this goes for most of the staff who commute. But enough of that. Your call is urgent, so what can I do for you?"

"Jaques Moreau called me urgently this morning. He's in need of a capital infusion of $2 million. He says you refused to even consider it. You know that I believe this company has a solid base and if they're in need of help, we should give it to them."

Jacques Moreau was President of a consulting company, operating in Quebec. We had purchased shares in this company and this was one of the ventures under my control.

I replied, "I faxed my report to you yesterday. We're heavily invested in this company already. They need to cut back and make changes within the company itself. Economies of scale are way out in their operations. They vote themselves large increases in salary when their income doesn't justify this. Consultant to companies in trouble is one of their major lines of business. If they can't help themselves and run a ship-shape company, how can they inspire others to hire them to resolve similar problems? They're just using our capital to keep them afloat. How often are we going to allow this? They also need a fresh approach. Companies in need of advice need new ideas because the tried and true aren't working.

"Jacques Moreau is a man of integrity, and I trust his judgement. He says that your picture of the company is biased," he reiterated.

"Have a look at the balance sheets I sent you. There's also a report from our Chief Accountant. These reveal that his company needs help sorting itself out. Why do they really need capital funding? They haven't given us specific reasons or shown how the money is to be used. I also asked our investment company for advice in this situation. Their recommendation is also to decline the advance. I've given this matter due diligence. They need to put their house in order. If we lend them money now, it's just another hand-out that will disappear in unjustified bonuses to themselves."

"I'll speak to Jacques Moreau again. You've done your research and I'll read your reports. I think Jacques should see your reports. Do you have any objection?"

"None at all. He knows all about them, because I copied him on my report to you."

"Have a good day, Tabitha. I'm sorry about the snowstorm. Take care. I'll assess your report carefully and get back to you."

I had a major clash with my boss. I knew he distrusted me simply because I was a woman who he felt had no place in the hierarchy. His opinion generally was that women were not as capable as men. Women functioned best as support workers; they didn't have the insight or brainpower to deal with the higher echelons of business and management, which he felt should be left to men. This feeling was universal at the time, but I considered that I had made a breakthrough because of my success within the company and I was every bit as good as any man in the position I held, and he should respect this. I felt resentful at the attack on my ability and credibility, and wondered what would be next.

It was soon to come. At the annual meeting when remuneration of executives was decided, I found that I was only granted a cost of living increase, and there was no bonus or increase in salary for me.

I confronted him about this. I was the only person within the companies to have received no increase in salary and no bonus. He pointed out that I'd been given a cost of living increase of 2.5 percent and that my company hadn't posted any income.

"You're aware that I took this position with the understanding that it'd take three to five years before we could post a profit. I was assured that my compensation didn't rely on profits during the grace period. I also sit on the board of the operating company and am still involved in day to day work. We're in the second year of operation. Even my staff have been better rewarded. What's behind all of this, Johannes?" I asked quietly, with determination.

"You speak just like a woman. You don't understand the facts. When your company makes profit, you'll receive bonuses and salary increases. Just like Jacques Moreau, his company isn't making a profit, so you can't lend them money. It's your own measure stick I'm using with you. Your company isn't making money; you can't expect any increase in salary."

"It's my understanding that the parent company was giving me three to five years to establish. As I told you, we're only in the second year of operation. You're breaking the terms of my contract and forgetful of the dependence still placed on me by the operating company."

"Do you have documents to support this? I haven't seen any and I've done some research. Minutes of Board meetings I've looked at, are silent on the point of your remuneration." He stared at me with such dislike, I was amazed. *What caused this?* I silently questioned.

I smiled. "I've poured my heart and soul into this venture. You remain unimpressed by what I've already accomplished, and I'm most unhappy."

I looked at him with a knowing smile as I left. "You don't like me, do you Johannes, and you resent having to work with a woman? We'll see how this all ends." I realized that my tone should have been different, but I knew that dealing with him would only lead me towards the end of my relationship within this company.

I was seething with fury. Worst of all, I didn't know how to deal with the situation. Was he trying to make things so uncomfortable for me that I'd leave rather than remain and work within the atmosphere he had created? It was true that he was in the Netherlands and I was in Toronto and I didn't have to deal with him on a daily basis. But he had questioned my ability and I felt he was determined to ensure that I didn't succeed. Did this mean I would be fired? I couldn't contemplate this, particularly as I knew it was unjustified. I didn't think that the Board in the Netherlands would want to be embroiled. There was no one whom I could appeal to. I was on the periphery of a losing battle.

I used Sean as a sounding board. He was shocked and disappointed that Johannes had treated me in such a disdainful manner. "This is totally reprehensible of Johannes. I'll talk to him about it."

"I'd prefer that you didn't. Take our own situation. When they learn about it, they'll be happy to get rid of me. The woman is always to blame. This will clean up what in their minds they would consider a messy situation. Perhaps it's time for me to call the shots and leave."

"It's your career, Tabitha. You can't let it go without a fight."

"There will be other wars to fight. If I do decide to leave, it'll be on my terms. He'll get his comeuppance one day."

I was leaving on a business trip for a week the following Monday, and would be back in Toronto on Friday. Away from it all and a different environment would help me come to terms with the situation.

Destiny has a way of helping solutions. On Wednesday I received a call from my Executive Assistant. She told me that Johannes had phoned her and requested that she requisition a check for $2 million payable to Moreau & Partners. She couldn't understand what was happening and required authorization from me before proceeding. She had asked him to wait until my return but he was adamant that the cheque should be issued immediately.

"To protect yourself, ask him to send you a fax authorizing the operating company to issue the check. It's a huge amount and proper authorization is required. As a matter of fact, ask our Chief Accountant to determine what he considers would be proper procedure and continue accordingly."

"I can't understand why this money is being advanced when we clearly showed that the figures didn't justify it. We should call a meeting of the board. I'm very disappointed," she replied.

"Just proceed as I requested. I think this battle is against me, and the money being advanced while I'm away and, against my recommendations, is a message to me. Johannes pulls the strings and if I want to survive, I have to dance to his tune. We'll see what happens, but keep yourself ahead of the game and comply with his request."

It was time to think clearly and without emotion. Could I sacrifice my happiness by reporting to this man who clearly wanted me out of the way? I would be dodging his bullets instead of putting my energies into building the company. Life had changed and I had to make a big decision.

I thought about my life, my unhappy childhood, my fight for survival, and my struggle to do the best job possible in all the positions in which I had been employed. The highs and lows of my marriages, the vague unhappiness that had tarnished everything good that I had accomplished, and the feeling that life always had to be a challenge because I was unworthy. Unworthy, because I had allowed myself to be raped and sexually abused. I was to blame and so I had to create situations which would always ensure an unhappy outcome.

I needed some advice. Sean was the logical person who could help me iron out the problems at work but asking for his help was out of the question. Johannes Schmidt was his boss also. Thoughts swarmed through my mind. I hated to give up, but I knew that battles lost before they had begun would be a futile exercise.

I decided to consult a lawyer. Johannes Schmidt had created a situation where I could claim that he had virtually fired me. I could ask for early retirement based on this. I would play my best cards and hope that I could finesse them into securing the best outcome for me.

Sean wasn't happy with this. He wanted me to go to the Netherlands and speak to the General Managers. He didn't agree that I should ask for early retirement. "What would you do with your life? You've so much talent and ability, it'd all go to waste."

"I could find another job, or just go back to university, study law, and start my own practice, or I could simply twiddle my thumbs. My pension would be more than enough to take care of my needs. Many options were open to me. The time is right. My work here is doomed to failure because of Johannes Schmidt. I have no heart for it. I just want out. The future will take care of itself."

My lawyer suggested that my best recourse would be to write a letter to Johannes Schmidt asking to be considered for early retirement based on the fact that he had made it impossible for me to perform the functions of my job through his actions, no increase in salary, no bonus, then overriding the recommendations and advancing the loan of $2 million to Moreau & Partners. He offered to draft the letter for me, but I told him it would be better for me to do this myself.

I spent quite some time drafting and redrafting the letter that would determine my future. When it was finished, I was satisfied. The deed was done; I had given six month's notice to allow for a replacement. I was committed.

I looked eagerly for a reply, anxious to get on with the future. After a month elapsed with no reply, I sent a reminder asking for a decision. The gist of the reply, which came after three months, was that my resignation would be accepted, but the parent company was not prepared to give me "early retirement" considerations.

I expected nothing less, but I was still shocked. It was time for me to approach the "big guns" at Head Office. This letter to Johannes Schmidt's boss produced the reply I desired. Johannes telephoned me. He was upset that I had approached the big bosses who had chastised him; he had always been prepared to settle with me.

"Let's not do battle over this. I have your reply to my letter in front of me. I'm looking for the conditions written in my own letter of resignation to you. I've worked these out with Miranda, our personnel manager, and I will accept nothing less. I've obtained legal advice and I know my rights."

"There you go, not giving me a chance to say what's on my mind."

"I'm only interested in hearing that my conditions have been accepted and I'm free to let the staff know that I'm leaving. The future of this company is in your hands. Deal with it wisely."

I received his letter of acceptance of my terms and conditions the following week. Everything I asked for had been clearly laid out and accepted. I was free to go.

The day of my leaving came soon enough. The staff of the operating company and my own staff were all sad. They gave me a send-off I still remember. It was all I could do not to burst into tears. They were my family; they had looked up to me. I had looked after them, nurtured their growth, and been proud of them. I felt hollow and empty inside. I grieved, but this time I wouldn't second-guess myself. It was time to let go. I had worked hard from the time when I landed my first job when I was not yet seventeen years old. I had faced many challenges and come out ahead. My journey through life had been filled with roadblocks, but exciting after all. I could let all of that go, just take life as it came, and explore other avenues.

I was financially independent, had a good pension, and benefits for life. I would spend the next six months savoring the pleasures of 'freedom from responsibility'. I could look forward with anticipation to the joys of travel and anything I had a mind to engage in. What more could I ask? The future was mine to discover.

CHAPTER SEVENTY

THE PROPOSAL. The day after my resignation, I was sitting in my home office, feet on my desk, pondering my newly found leisure, when the doorbell rang. I was surprised to see Sean standing outside holding a bunch of red roses.

"May I come in Tabitha, please?"

I wondered what all this formality meant. "Of course you may. But why didn't you use your key? If you'd told me you were going to be here, I could've prepared a little meal for us."

He gave me the bouquet of red roses. "These are for you." They were indeed beautiful and their perfume was as heavenly as only the scent of roses can be. *Flowers to cheer me up*, I thought.

I looked at him and said, "Thank you, Sean. These are very special indeed. My second bouquet of red roses from you. I'm completely bowled over. You're trying to cheer me up, I believe?'

He smiled and pointed to the sitting room. I cradled the bouquet in my arms as I sat down. It was a beautiful moment, two lovers joined together with a bouquet of red roses. He knelt down, took my hands in his and said, "Tabitha, you're so much a part of me, it's hard to imagine what my life would be like today if we

422

hadn't met. I couldn't love anyone in this whole world more than I love you. Will you marry me? My heart, mind, body, and soul cries out for you. You brighten my world. There are no barriers in our way and nothing to prevent the fulfillment of our love, our marriage, and our days of wine and roses."

My heart blossomed with joy. I was filled with a happiness I had never known. Sean loved and cared for me. I was free of company obligations, free to contemplate my own future. We would get married and live "happily ever after" just like the heroes of Grimm's fairy tales. Here was my knight in shining armour asking me to jump on his white horse so that we could both ride off into the sunset.

"Yes, I will," I smiled, happiness filling my heart and mind. He dug deep into his pocket and brought out a circle of gold. "This is a *Cladah* ring. Wear it until you select a ring that pleases you. He hugged me then whispered in my ear, "I love you Tab, I'll love you forever. This ring is symbolic of Irish traditions. It shows that your heart is taken. You must wear it with the heart turned inward towards your own heart."

He then went back to the front porch and brought in champagne chilling in an ice bucket. It turned into an afternoon filled with delicious happiness. We talked of future plans, of travel, and of our love. He kept saying, "Let's fix a date for our marriage. I want the world to know that I love you, and that you love me."

Could I ask for more? I wondered. *Love is a splendid affair. It fills life with a happiness that is overwhelming, all-encompassing and colourful. Future plans for my business life could take a backseat.*

I was encompassed by a world of emotions that were new to me. I felt powerless. All I could think about was that I was loved by someone who loved me as much as I loved him. My Prince Charming had found me and we would ride off to the land of love together.

Love is an all-encompassing emotion. Falling in love at my age could be likened to standing on a precipice. Thoughts, feelings, and emotions can be illogical at any age, but especially so with someone who carries a lifetime of unpleasant memories accumulated over decades. Questions come to the forefront. What happens if your lover falls short of your expectations? Will you be plunged into the depths of despair? Will disagreements lead to quarrels? What will the future hold for us?

Doubt and insecurity had walked hand in hand with me throughout my life. Violation had wrenched me away from self-worth. Despite all my accomplishments, I still hadn't been able to assuage those negative feelings. I could never understand why. I reached for something worthwhile, perhaps some things even beyond my scope. I accomplished these things easily it seems, but this hurt inside was like an impenetrable rock, nothing quite reached it.

I told myself time and again, "it's over, it happened, but you won out, you're ahead of the game," but this always left me with the feeling that I had fallen in value as a human being. When the psyche has been damaged, purity is forever lost and your entire being is tarnished.

As the afternoon wore on, I began to feel a strange reluctance about accepting Sean's proposal. I was not the person he thought I was. I was damaged goods. I had heard the description of "damaged goods" so often, I questioned 'humanity' and its rules regarding sexuality. A victim of sexual violence was victimized over and over again; first by the perpetrators, then by herself, and then by a society which encompasses its own rules about 'guilt' if women indulged in the pleasures of sex outside the marriage bed, or were even forced into it.

I thought, *Heavens to Betsy, I must discuss this matter with Sean. This is a secret that has worn me down for almost all my life. Would I spoil this day? He had to know that there was this kink in my mentality and being. We'd known each other for almost two decades. I was sure that he had secrets also, but equally as sure that none were as devastating as mine.*

Sometimes I wonder why it is that the brain reaches back to that innermost corner of your mind, where you would prefer to leave what's stored inside undisturbed, and plunges it right into the time when it should best be forgotten.

"Better to be sure than sorry," I told myself. The two men I'd married had always let me down. I couldn't take another chance.

We were pleasurably relaxed and excited, thinking about a future, planning ahead and fantasizing that we would find the Shangri-La of our dreams. Perhaps that "kink in my armour" was still there, but I couldn't hold on to the hope that it wouldn't interfere with my future life; if I didn't come to grips with what had held me prisoner of my thoughts and feelings, there would always be my own uncertainty to disturb my equanimity.

Courage rose out of the ashes of my tarnished self-respect. I said, "Sean, before we proceed on this idyllic fantasy of what our lives would be, I need to tell you something about myself."

He smiled indulgently, like a Cheshire cat who'd caught the muse. "You promised to marry me, and I will hold you to that promise. You're all I've ever wanted. I craved your love from the very first time I saw you. Working side by side with you all these years has been bitter sweet. Now the bitter has departed, and the sweet remains. Nothing you can say will alter that."

"I understand Sean, but I want to share with you something that happened to me when I was young."

He interrupted. "Whatever can that be? You suddenly seem very somber. It must be troublesome. Let's talk about it and put it to rest". His smile was an invitation to inspire my confidence. Nothing I could say would faze him.

"You'll think the worse of me when I tell you," I said uncertainly.

He interrupted me. "Nothing you tell me will make me think badly of you, my love."

"When I was very young, a cousin raped me. I didn't know what sex was, only that he overpowered me and caused me pain and agony. This was torture my body couldn't endure. I fainted. My mother discovered me laid out on the bed in a pool of blood. She gave me no explanation of what happened, but told me that I should tell no one about it. I know that my father threw the cousin out of our house and he was never back. But that's not the end of it. My older brother then began a period of rape and molestation, which lasted until I was ten. I was too afraid to tell my parents. I was so haunted by my fears and the trauma they brought to me; these things took precedence over everything in my life. I can't go into it all in detail. I only wanted to let you know that I'm not 'pure and virginal'."

"You, poor, dear girl! Why would you think that would make me feel differently about my love for you? I fell in love with the Tabitha you are. I wish those maniacs were here, so I could strangle them for what they did to you. If I could make them pay in some way, I would."

He looked at me with such tenderness in his eyes, dried the tears in my eyes with his handkerchief, and then held me as if I were a child, hugged me, and rocked me back and forth. I remembered how I had longed for my mother's arms around me when I was a child, how I wanted to be comforted and loved. He bent down and kissed me, not the kiss of love, but the kiss of comfort and belonging.

"Tab, dear love of my life, people who condemn the victims of rape and abuse are mentally bankrupt and you should never be stymied or stigmatized by this. You turned your anger and betrayal into making yourself a force to be reckoned with. Look at who you are today, who you've become, and what you've accomplished! Singlehandedly almost, your vision turned our company into a place where all employees feel a part of the whole organization, and the company became a flagstone. You showed that women were just as capable and in some cases better than men, and advanced the cause of equality.

"It's true a horrible thing happened in your early childhood, but you should glory in the fact that it didn't destroy you. You didn't knuckle down under the pressures of the trauma on a young and impressionable child, your mind soared to the possibilities of what life could offer, and you turned all opportunities into success. Performance in your jobs, your school, the food business, all bespeak of the person you are."

He kissed my cheek. "You're your worst critic. I love you, the person you are. You never accept the impossible, you turn it into the possible. You fight for what you believe in. Controversy fuels your imagination. Cut yourself a little slack. You could no more have prevented what happened to you than prevent the sun from shining. It was never your fault. We'll work together to ease the strictures of pain around your heart. I love you more than ever if such a thing is possible. You light up my life and give me a reason to live. That's who you are, my love, my everything." He held me tighter and rocked me back and forth.

I felt the strictures around my heart loosening a bit and becoming less tight. My inner child looked back at me with the beginnings of a smile on her face. A thought came into my mind *Things will be all right. Don't worry, this man will help ease your burdens and sorrows and be a cleansing force. Trust him; he loves you. He has his faults, but he recognizes these.*

I stirred in his arms, opened my eyes, and looked at him. "You're wonderful, you know. You've caused an eruption of the earthquake in my heart. It burst its bounds and began to scatter the self-doubt and self-incrimination that have been part of me for such a long, long time. Thank you, my darling. I was blackmailed into my first marriage because I spoke of my childhood trauma, and I've trusted no man since then. Why has it taken me so long to meet a man like you, someone who would restore my faith in myself?"

"I was always there, my love, waiting in the wings. We've lived and loved in ages gone by. Our souls danced together on a forgotten beach somewhere in the world, and we became one. We meet in different lifetimes to continue our dalliance of love and laughter. Marry me soon, and let's be one whole again."

"You're a poet, Sean, my dear... my darling ... the love of my heart ... my everything. We're joined together now and forever. I accept your proposal. We'll get married and make everything legal as soon as we can," I promised.

CHAPTER SEVENTY-ONE

ENJOINING LIVES. We decided we would start our lives together without waiting. He would give up the flat he was currently renting as soon as the lease was up.

Divorce always makes spouses angry with each other. The partner who's been left behind almost always tries to make the departing partner suffer for abandoning the marriage bed. Sean had been generous with his divorce settlement because both of us wanted to be fair. His lawyer advised Sean that he was being far too generous, and we discussed this.

"I don't want Bridget to feel we've cheated her. She has to retain her independence. If we're to live happily together, you must be generous and kind. Remember, the children will turn to her for help and she has to be in a position to help them. They're both adults and shouldn't need to ask for monetary support, but the future is always uncertain. Thank him for his advice and let him proceed with what you agreed. Half of everything is the only decent way." I counseled.

This was decided with the lawyer. We thought that was everything and we could proceed without too much acrimony, and were surprised when he received new divorce proceedings, which named me as co-respondent. It stated that we were living together in an adulterous relationship, and asked for damages.

"This isn't her doing," I said to Sean. "The legal advice she's receiving is certainly not in her interests. You should speak to her. Perhaps her lawyers want to 'sweeten' the pot, perhaps they feel that your generous offer was made because you're hiding your true worth. Generosity has been mistaken for trickery. Naming me as co-respondent is her prerogative, but I don't think this has any place in today's jurisprudence. She's also trying to embarrass me but I love you too much to let that bother me."

Sean was angry and I didn't blame him. His lawyer smiled when he said, "I told you that you were being too generous. This is what usually happens. I'll suggest a settlement meeting, and we'll see what we can work out. No one ever really wants to go to court."

In legal battles there are always two elements which offer commonality. Delays and high legal fees. Sean agreed to pay all legal costs when he thought settlement was only a formality. Now he was faced with his own costs and the costs of Bridget's lawyers. There was also the claim against me as the co-respondent.

My lawyer explained that my being sued was just another weapon in Bridget's arsenal to increase the settlement offer. He suggested that we do nothing about it, just let it float.

I was not immune from the feelings of anger which assailed me. I had advised Sean that settlement had to be fair. This was not a time for women to be cast aside, robbed, and disregarded because their husbands wanted out of the marriage. His marriage had ended before our affair had started, but in a court of law this could be torn to shreds.

Sean and Bridget met with their lawyers. Sean was fair and honest; the situation he was in was so foreign to who he was, my heart bled for him. He never expected a battle. I said to him, "Sean, Bridget's loss is my gain. Money can never equate this. If wanting more will help to ease the pain in her heart, compromise."

He stared at me and didn't offer an answer.

Sean found it difficult to deal with Bridget on this issue. They were married for over thirty years, and had two children. His lawyer settled the matter expertly by offering to provide life insurance if Sean died before Bridget.

I discovered that no matter how it pans out, dissolution of marriages is always traumatic. It's difficult to say goodbye to someone in the middle of the voyage of life partnership. Memories linger and cause anguish. Feelings of guilt reach out to strike at any moment. There's the call to stop and reconsider the process of dissolution and to return to the life you once shared.

It was difficult for Sean to get through all the issues. He was an honourable man and he wanted to do the honourable thing. Doing the 'honourable' and remaining in the marriage had been detrimental to his health. Now there was a chance of happiness.

Peace returned to our lives after the agreement was signed and settled. We could now move forward. Bridget finally signed off on the dissolution papers; it was now only a matter of time before the divorce became final.

The months flew by. We lived our lives peacefully and happily. This was the first time I was without a working career since my teens. Time hung heavily on my hands when Sean was away at work.

As I had always wanted to be a lawyer, I decided it was time for me to apply for admission to law school. Sean didn't like this. He felt it would interfere with our plans for the future and feared that my studies wouldn't allow me enough leisure time to enjoy our plans for world travel. I gave in. Life was different for me now.

As soon as his divorce was final, we started making arrangements to tie the knot and become legally married people. We decided to elope and then set off to a honeymoon where we could celebrate our love and revel in the fact that now we were bound together for the balance of our lives.

Even though we were eloping, I was still the blushing bride. Two friends witnessed our marriage, and were sworn to secrecy.

The next day we left on a journey to Asia. It was the honeymoon of a lifetime. Bouquets of red roses, a card which proclaimed his love for me, and champagne greeted us in every new hotel we used in our travels. We loved, we dined, we danced, we gloried in each other. The world was our oyster. I reveled in Sean's love and his obvious pride at winning my love. At long last I'd become the Cinderella of my dreams, something I thought would never happen to me. The Prince had courted me and now he proclaimed our love to the world.

I never knew that the happiness I felt was possible. Loved and being loved in return was the ultimate. I marveled that I was caught in such a happenstance. It must have given a boost to my ego because my entire being felt lighter, more relaxed. I began to see the world through rose-tinted spectacles.

Contentment followed as we settled down on our return home. Could I be happy in my role as a simple house wife after such a busy and productive working life?

CHAPTER SEVENTY-TWO

A DAPTING TO CHANGE. My children had clamoured for a wedding reception and were disappointed that we eloped. Sean's children were non-committal. It was difficult for them in the first place to reconcile with their father's new wife, someone who had replaced their mother, and then again I was from a different race and culture and they were somewhat distrustful.

I think they'd hoped I was just a passing fancy their father would soon tire of. However, they put on a brave face when they were told the news of our marriage.

Life settled down, but after six months I missed the challenges of business life. Sometimes I envied Sean when he shared something he thought would be of interest to me. I tried volunteer work in the local hospital, but I was judged by my colour and thought to be competent only at the most menial level, making the rounds in the candy cart for patients who wanted a snack.

I tried other avenues, but was always sent away with a quiet rejection. I changed to helping children in school who weren't keeping up with their classes. This seemed to be working out, but then there was a complaint by a schoolgirl that I was being too strict with her, demanding more than she was capable of.

Something wasn't right. My mantra was in conflict with what I was trying to do, and this was not an area which would bring me success or happiness.

I again mentioned a law degree, and applied to law school.

I had evolved with the passage of time, and life with Sean was an idyllic relationship from almost every perspective. I valued this, and while I didn't want to disturb the pattern of life which resulted - shopping, lunches, matinees, dinners, and an endless array of activities which kept me busy - missing from my life were the challenges of the business world.

We sometimes travelled together when Sean went on business trips, and twice a year on vacation. We had a second home in Florida and whisked ourselves away whenever an opportunity presented itself, but this wasn't enough; I wanted more.

In the midst of my mental disarray, one afternoon on his return home Sean greeted me. "You'll never guess what I've just learned." He hugged me and gave me a second kiss.

"You're preening like a Cheshire cat, so it must be something good. Out with it, and no horsing around," I replied with a smile.

"Our parent company is going through change. They've engaged a consulting company to evaluate their worldwide operations. Senior personnel are being offered golden handshakes. There are early retirement bonuses with full pay until age 65. What do you think?"

"It all depends, Sean. Will you be happy without the challenges in the business world? I miss work even though I'm deliriously happy being your wife. The business environment gave me self-esteem and self-satisfaction. I miss the challenges and demands of that period, but I'm content and I count my blessings every day. Being loved by you brings me joys I've never known. I still hanker for some form of education, going to university, getting started on another career path. That is self-fulfillment. Perhaps your needs are different, and retirement will give you the opportunity to do things you've always wanted to do, and never found time for, and there is value in fulfilling those rolls."

He gave me a quizzical look. "I know that I'll miss all the people who work for me and the challenges of business but I've always longed to travel the world. You know that. This is something we can do together. You like to travel to far flung places also, and we can explore everything together. India, Asia, Africa, South America, all call me. This is an opportunity to fulfill a dream. Photography is also a passion of mine as you well know. Being able to explore the world, to get that singular photograph that captures a significant moment in time, has always excited me. To achieve that is better than winning a lottery."

I looked at him thoughtfully and smiled. "Sean, sometimes, we put things off and opportunity is lost. Business and family were all I lived for. I had few dreams beyond that. But then we fell in love and you opened so many doors and avenues for me, my horizons exploded. You know that I still hanker to go back to university, but that can wait. This is your moment, and I'll make it mine too. When do I get ready to pack?"

He laughed. "Tab, work isn't life. You have to be able to see what lies beyond the corporate world. We'll travel the world together, hand in hand, explore the beauties of nature, understand the differences in people of different cultures, laugh with them, help them understand us, and take beautiful pictures. The world is ours to discover indeed. We'll find the pearl that dwells within the oyster."

It was a good night. It would take a year to set things straight, but something new and different was beckoning us forward.

This was our time. If Sean wanted freedom from commerce and our finances were right, why not? Who knows what the future would bring, and it would also solve my problem of wanting to get into a new career.

Our days changed as we planned our new future. It took eighteen months before the plans were finalized and Sean could retire.

New beginnings, I told myself. Our retirement lives together would encompass us in a world we had both yet to discover.

CHAPTER SEVENTY-THREE

THE SCENERY OF LIFE CHANGES. There were endless farewell dinners for Sean, hosted by companies with whom we did business, and finally the big reception by our parent company. Sean basked in the glory and satisfaction of his career. He was very well-liked and respected in the industry and everyone was sad to see him go. He felt sad also.

On returning from work on his final day, he told me, "It was very sad to leave, but they promised to invite me to lunch from time to time, so I'm not truly separating from them."

"This is the end of your working life, Sean, not the end of the many friendships you've made. Retirement is a big step. Transitioning to your new life will take time. But look what I've got for us. Two business class tickets to London for four weeks. We'll have a long, lazy holiday. Your first task will be to plan our trip."

"This is a most thoughtful and special gift, Tab. Just what I needed to get started." He smiled with satisfaction, as he hugged and kissed me.

We sipped wine and talked about the many adventures awaiting us. He wanted to show me the many places in London and the English countryside we had so often talked about. We would rent a car and travel the country for three weeks, then return to London for the last week.

He was preoccupied for the next two days, doing research and consultations with travel agents, discussing the best time to go, and the best places we should visit. "Our retirement years are off to a great start. Think of the fun we'll have, and the places we'll visit. The world awaits us. The magic will start as soon as we get on our mystical carpet and float off into the sunset." He hugged me and twirled me around as if we were dancing.

Two days later, he met me as I was coming out of our garden. "Tabitha, our first trip is ready for your approval. Come with me upstairs to my office." He twirled his hands much like a magician unfolding something impossible.

He could barely conceal his excitement as he sat me down and presented me with a model airplane of the Concorde.

"Why are you giving me this model plane, Sean? Is this a joke? We can't afford travel to London with the Concorde, and besides we'll have to get to New York before."

"I waved my magic wand, and lo and behold ... the Concorde is making a trial run from London to Toronto. While talking to our travel agent he informed me of this. Tickets were selling like hot cakes. He offered me the last two tickets and I took them. Best of all, he was able to cancel the tickets you'd bought, and I'll pay for our tickets home." He smiled in satisfaction. It would be the perfect holiday.

This was a dream come true for me. I had never thought that I would be traveling on the Concorde, and out of the blue it seemed, I was leaving on the Concorde for London.

Sean continued, "Furthermore, he's taken charge of our holiday plans, and will send me confirmation of places we'll visit, tickets to plays in London's theatre district, hotel accommodations, car rental, and everything else needed for a 'holiday to beat all holidays.' You'll be thrilled because everything will be spectacular."

Excitement filled me with happy anticipation. Four weeks of new sights, explorations, adventure, and love. What more could I want?

As I lay in his arms that night, I was filled with peace and contentment. I had never known or experienced love as Sean had given me. I never believed that such joys, such cohesion of thoughts, could exist. His love had taken many surprising turns. My life had become as romantic, and even more so than the love stories on the screen. I sighed with contentment.

He was busy the next day as we discussed our travel plans.

Everything booked was first class. We would motor across the countryside, spend the evenings in old castles that had been turned into hotels, and perhaps even see a ghost or two. The last week would be in London at The 'Savoy.' Best of all we would see the English performance of "My Fair Lady."

Just thinking about it all gave me pleasure.

The outcome was no less pleasurable than the anticipation of it all.

Our main destination was Cornwall, but we meandered to whatever place took our fancy. Our love seemed to throw the radiance of romance over every place we visited.

As it turned out, we seldom followed the itinerary. It was a romantic adventure. A lifetime of love, chronicled in videos and pictures to help us get through the dark and dreary days of winter. We were two long lost souls, finding each other, uniting, and dancing across the land, vowing to live together, forever and ever.

CHAPTER SEVENTY-FOUR

TO FAR TIBET. On our return to Canada, we found ourselves the darlings of our retired friends. Dinner parties and lavish hospitality became the norm. When we were the hosts, Sean would regale our guests with a choice of jazz and popular music as his fingers moved over the keyboard of his Steinway piano. His repertoire extended from jazz to the classics. There was always music and dancing, laughter, fun and joy. It was an idyllic period of life.

We craved more than that. We wanted to experience the world, travel to countries we knew only through news and television, and gain an understanding of people and culture. Sean was a geography buff and I excelled in history of the British Empire. We both wanted to see places we had only read about during our formative years, and experience the culture, traditions, and religions from which their culture had evolved.

Six months after our return, we were off again. This time it was to Tibet, part of a group tour. Sean had done his research well and his input had enabled the group leader, Mae Wong, to include places we both wanted to visit. National Geographic provided a wealth of information and we looked forward to seeing these places and experiencing what we had previously only been able to glean from television.

Tibet was now part of China. The Dalai Lama had fled to India to avoid arrest and imprisonment. China had seized everything in its path, and perhaps it was the last chance to see the country as it was before Chinese influence. Chinese migration and monopoly of businesses, were slowly usurping the Tibet that once was "the centre of happiness."

Our fellow passengers were mainly Canadians with a few Americans. Sean quickly became popular. He was knowledgeable, a ready source of information, and very charming about it all. As we travelled along in our tour bus, he was always asked to provide a travelogue. Ultimately, he became the leader of the group.

We had many adventures. We stayed in posh hotels, sat on the floorboards of lorries as we travelled to remote places, and helped the locals cook a meal.

The plight of poor people, anxious to secure a few coins from us, was always sad. It broke our hearts. We had so much, and they had so little that they needed to resort to trickery to make a living. We bought shoes for children, only to find that they were immediately returned for cash. We gave a mother money for milk for her baby, only to find that the poor child had been pinched to make her cry.

We were angry when we found out we were being duped but Sean managed to paint a different picture. Unemployment was rife, and people needed to survive. Tourists who visited their country were a means of getting money to purchase food. We enjoyed the novelty of life as it existed and helping people to live and avoid hunger was part of our experience. I remember the laughter and backslapping, as we all trooped into the local bar at 11.00 a.m. and regaled ourselves with the best cognac they had available, the brands of which we had never expected to find in a country experiencing such poverty. It was a reminder that we had plenty; the majority of the population had little.

As we trooped out afterwards, Sean reminded us of how fortunate we were; promise of a collection at the end of the tour for donation to a local orphanage, resulted. This became a practice of ours. We visited, we enjoyed, we donated to the causes we believed in, and left footsteps of hope.

Lavatories were always a problem, but it became a matter of fun when the driver stopped the bus so people could 'relieve' themselves. Vehicles which passed us by honked. We laughed. Time stood still. We visited temples and monasteries, we were entertained in homes of the locals. Everything was different and interesting. When there was a piano in our hotel, we would spend the evening singing.

Tibet gave us an added closeness and further cemented our friendship. Having your best friend as your husband increased the dimension of our love. I never dreamed that such a relationship could colour my life with happiness and contentment. I vowed that I would never let him go.

Mae Wong knew that Sean had retired from business. His leadership made our travels memorable for everyone, and she considered that if she could get him to join her company, this would help her business. She dangled the offer of a partnership in her agency before him. It would be an investment of money which would allow us to travel free of charge, but gave little advantage when it came to profit sharing. While free travel had an advantage, it also meant our roles would probably be relegated to being travel guides with duties.

This wasn't the life either of us had envisioned, and although it was pleasurable to explore other countries and impart knowledge to fellow travelers, neither of us felt it was what we desired.

As we wrested with the problem, I gently reminded him of our wants and needs. "We like to travel alone, Sean. That has been our forte. All we'd be doing is giving up our freedom and performing travel agents' duties without much recompense. It's not a lot of money, but I'd look on it as prepaying our travel costs without the freedom to go where we wanted. It's up to you. But... here's a thought: Why don't you start your own travel club? We could restrict the numbers of people, invite them to join, and choose destinations we wanted to visit. It could be an exclusive travel club."

"You get ahead of me, dear girl. Sometimes I miss the thrill of the chase in business. I treasure our time together to wander and explore little known places, as our fancies and fantasies dictate. At this time of my life, I want to savour and enjoy our love as we tour the world, free to do as we please. We're comfortable. This is an opportunity we can't miss. I've always longed to set off on the adventure of world travel and, uppermost in my thoughts had been 'would early retirement ever come along?'

"Why don't we buy a travel agency then?"

He laughed, indicating that a commercial venture was not his cup of tea. "Let's just put all of that to rest. We'll continue to do what we like, and enjoy the balance of our lives basking in the togetherness that love brings". He chuckled as he continued, "It makes no sense to put money into a business, do all the work, and get trips in return. I get carried away sometimes".

He took my hand in his, "You're a smart woman, Tab; an entrepreneur. You make things happen. Right now, all I want is our happiness together as man and wife. I miss the challenges of the business world, but I enjoy living with you, of awaking in the morning and finding you beside me."

We smiled at each other, glorying in the fact that we were happy, carefree lovers. We could discuss anything. Even when there was divergence in our views, we always seemed to find solutions that were satisfactory.

We both felt we still had a lot to offer in our retirement years, but somehow, nothing exciting dawned on our horizon.

In hindsight, I think we were meant to spend this time together, just concentrating on ourselves and our happiness. We were part of the madding crowd, filling our days with fun and frolic. Our friends were many and varied, but they were all important compartments of our lives.

Somehow, amidst all of this busyness, we still found time for discussions. We became our own psychoanalysts. I found myself talking to him about the rape and incest of my childhood years.

"Sean, I can't understand myself. Why is it that even in my adult years I felt I had to keep this violation to myself? Why didn't I confide in my parents? Looking back, it seemed the right time to tell them was when I was being blackmailed into marriage. Why did I feel that I could never let them know my shame? I really can't understand myself.

He looked at me, his blue eyes so intense with love, hoping to help me find a solution to this puzzling question. "We can only guess at the answer, Tab. You were a child. You probably felt you and your family would be ostracized and blame would fall on you, even though you weren't responsible.

You took it upon yourself to keep it secret because you knew that somehow what had been done to you would destroy not only you, but also the entire family. You must remember our generation never talked about sex. It was taboo. My mother thought sex was a "dirty" subject. She kept a close eye on me to ensure that I didn't fall into bad ways. She and my father had separate rooms." He smiled. "Think of the fun she missed. Her life was so regimented by rules and regulations; I wonder if she was ever truly happy. I looked on her as a martinet. Truth is, I was glad to leave home and make my life elsewhere after I graduated college."

I shook my head as I added, "It's a wonder, isn't it, that we survived our childhood and growing years, and found each other. We were educated in different countries, but we shared the same educational system. We read the same books, and laughed at the humour in them. I never liked geography, history was my favourite subject. We were both brought up in the Anglican faith, and now we're both distrustful of religion."

"Meant to be" he chuckled. "I've always maintained that my love for you dated back to the days of Robert Clive and his subjugation of those Indian rebels."

I decided to get into the spirit of things and assert myself. "Yes, we must have met in those bygone days, but you have the story turned the wrong way. I was a noble Rani (princess to you) and you were but a humble soldier in the army. Before the battle, I spied you during one of your parades. You looked in my direction and our eyes locked. You earned barrack duties after that. You were supposed to march and keep your eyes on the road without ogling the Indian princesses."

He laughed. "Have it whichever way you wish. We met. I loved you. I wanted to make you my wife after the war with Suraja Dowlah was won, and take you back to England. Your father, the Rajah wouldn't permit it. We parted with promises to find each other. I was posted to America by the British Army. When I returned to Calcutta, you'd disappeared. No one could tell me where you were. I went home to England a heartbroken man and remained a bachelor mourning his lost love to the end of my days."

"A likely story," I scoffed. "Why do you always insist I was just a humble slave girl?"

"Only to tease you, Tab, love of my heart. I was smitten the first time I ever laid eyes on you. You were like a 'shining jewel' from the east, 'lovely to look at and delightful to hold'. I tried to seduce you during your early days with the company, but you never seemed to understand my intentions, or perhaps never felt the same passion as I did. We worked together for decades. You were always all 'business,' always so 'hoity toity'. (I raised my eyebrows at this juncture, and let my face register my feelings, waiting to offer rebuttal but not wanting to interrupt). I never could understand your futuristic thinking. I felt the future of the company relied on its past successes, the 'tried and true' was the way forward.

I countered: "I know we can't plunge headlong into something new and untried. Time and patience are necessary when evaluating new approaches. Nothing stands still. Evolution is part of life. New generations of thinkers investigate possibilities outside the tried and true, and we move forward. Skepticism of this new wave is tantamount to fighting the battle when the war's already won. Look at life throughout the centuries. Nothing stood still. We're always on the cusp of change. Technology will redefine itself and lead the world in science and new developments, in ways not yet dreamed of. Who knows, as in Star Trek, we'll be able to say "Beam me to Australia," and in the blink of an eye we'll be there."

He smiled, indulging my rhetoric, but I ignored him and continued, "New beginnings, drastic change. The world turns. It doesn't stand still. Look at Bill Gates and what he's done and continues to do. Everyone will get into the act. It's going to be insidious. Before we know it, we'll also change. Some other genius out there will exploit his mathematical brain and find solutions never before imagined. When I read *Ten Thousand Leagues Under the Sea*, I was eleven going on twelve. I never thought that submarines were possible, but they helped to win World War Two. Look at the atomic bomb and the devastation it caused."

He patted my hand, and smiled. "You always put up such a good argument, Tab. It's never easy to find something to still your active brain. Now we know that the moon isn't made of green cheese and ham, you're going to tell me that's the next place man will colonize."

I laughed. "Not necessarily so, but will you go with me if that happens in our lifetime?"

"Tab, my sweet genius, you're always thinking the impossible is possible. Let's just accept the present. We'll enjoy our being together; the life we have now is everything I've ever desired. Contentment is what happiness is all about. Being with you, getting up each day and finding you beside me is Heaven on Earth for me". He took my hands and held them against his heart, then kissed them. "My world is the 'here and now' with you. I never believed life could be so sweet. Our souls meandered in the proverbial 'Garden of Eden' as we dallied like butterflies eagerly flitting from flower to flower. We were often called upon by some higher being to fulfill an unknown purpose and happily found each other again after lifetimes of searching. Will you fly off and leave me again?" His gaze penetrated my soul; we were conjoined forever.

Destiny has strange ways of fulfilling its purpose.

CHAPTER SEVENTY-FIVE

MUSIC AND LOVE. One of Sean's passions was music. Had he pursued a career in music, I believe he would have been popular. When we'd started living together, we bought a Steinway Grand piano. The sound of music which reverberated in our home was twice as nice. Jazz was the genre he was best at playing. My parents hadn't allowed us to listen to jazz. They felt it was the music of the Blacks, and it would lead us "astray". The classics and popular music of the fifties, sixties, seventies, and eighties were the music of 'normal' people.

Sean told me that he would make me a convert of jazz, and so I accompanied him to jazz music festivals where some of the 'greats' performed. I enjoyed these occasions and tapped my feet to the beat of the music. I found myself looking forward to the next. I wondered why my parents were so rigorous in their determination to exclude jazz from our music choices. Sean always laughed when I talked about this. He said, "Jazz was the music of choice in the brothels and perhaps they feared you'd be tainted by this."

"Music leads no one astray. I know that movements of the dance can be suggestive, but that doesn't mean sexual arousal," I countered.

"You're still an innocent, Tab, or are you putting me on?"

With gamboling eyes, and a smile on his face, he continued. "Dancing together is suggestive in the first place. There's touch with hands. Two bodies intertwine, keeping pace with the music... emotions are aroused... bodies move to the rhythm... emotions are pleasurable... feelings can lead men and women astray. We were both brought up in environments which kept a lid on the joys of sex. Men enjoyed the physical interaction of sexual connection. They were in control. Women were just silent partners in the sexual act, pandering to their male counterparts. How and what they felt weren't important." He took my hands in his and gazed into my eyes trying to penetrate the innermost corners of my soul, as he continued.

"Sexual intimacy should be a joyful union. Climaxing is the ultimate feeling of ecstasy, which should happen for both parties. Procreation depends on the release of semen from men's bodies. Men didn't care, and in some cases never realized that women could derive the same pleasure from sex as they did; they lost out; enjoyment by both parties makes the act twice as exciting. Women who enjoyed sex were supposed to be 'loose' women. What women thought didn't matter as long as they remained faithful to their husbands. Husbands were afraid of being cuckolded if women learned to experience the joys of sex," he smiled gallantly, his eyes full of love and encouragement, trying to create understanding that would ease the pressure on my body and soul.

"Come on, Sean, I know all that. What I'm really asking is why my father encouraged us to have dance parties twice a year? He hired an orchestra for the events, which were always elaborate affairs. Friends vied for invitations and felt insulted if they weren't asked. He came from an Indian/Muslim background but was baptized and followed Christianity. In many ways, we adopted what was considered the style of life which would earn us good jobs and make us worthy citizens. If you followed Christianity, more jobs were open to you. Those who still embraced the religions of their cultures were usually left behind. A recommendation from the local Parish priest was worth its weight in gold when it came to employment," I responded, still trying to grapple with the whys and wherefores and seeking to get answers to problems I had lived with all my life.

He took my hands in his, turned them over, and kissed them. "Don't be too hard on yourself, Tab. You've always said that your father was well-read. He was certainly an entrepreneur who wanted his children to have a better way of life than he had. Perhaps he just wanted you all to enjoy the benefits of a culture he hoped you would aspire to be part of, while at the same time anticipating you wouldn't get carried away by what was considered 'lower class' behaviour. From all you've told me about him, I have a lot of respect for him."

"He would have loved you, Sean. However, I don't think he would have trusted his daughter to you. Too much water under the bridge, as the saying goes."

"But your sister-in-law is English! And you said he was very caring of her?" he protested with raised eyebrows and wide open eyes.

I laughed, "That's different, Sean. She's a woman. He suffered under the whip of the overseer who was a white man who used cruelty on a young lad to make him work faster and harder through fear. Even while I was growing up, although the local commissioner borrowed money from him, my father was forced by custom to doff his hat to him and still call him 'sir.' Life was a dichotomy of various customs, based on race. I still feel angst for the slaves who, until they became free men and women were treated worse than animals, women were raped and sexually abused, men hanged and beaten to death, with little redress from the law, not to mention, of course, what was also done to my forefathers, the Indentured Coolies."

"That was a long time ago, Tab. Things are better now. I understand how racial superiority can create animosity and hatred, but look at it this way, love brought us together. There could be no truer love than ours. It took a long time to come to fruition, but here it is, and it'll remain like this until the end of our lives," he consoled. He gave me the feeling that he very much regretted the happenings of the past. They were memories of a bygone era, of things past that couldn't be erased and should best be forgotten.

"Sean, I must confess that even though we've joked about India and my being a rustic young woman, I had serious thoughts about getting into a relationship with you. I didn't trust that you'd be true to me and that after your lust and passion were satisfied, you'd simply walk away. I asked myself, 'how would you deal with that?' The answer was 'end it now before you commit yourself.' Every time I felt that I'd worked up enough courage to call quits to our relationship, you'd surprise me with a little gift, a book of poems, a CD of love songs, or a simple card telling me how much you loved me. You affirmed your love for me in so many ways, it became impossible to move on without giving love a chance," I confessed. "I grew up in a world where colour was all important. My education and capabilities weren't good enough. I had to claw my way up the ladder. White bosses were simply amazed at my erudition. One even confessed that he could be swayed by my eloquence."

"Tab, I realized you were having second thoughts, but I knew our love and life together would bring us both happiness, and I wanted to make sure you never had second thoughts. I'm an honourable Englishman. You can't judge me because other Englishmen defiled their obligations, abused their power and authority, and became less than human. I am your Sean. My life without you would have been one of vain regret. My dreams could never have been fulfilled, and I would always be grasping for the rainbow, which would quickly disappear when it was within reach and I almost had my hands on it. I've always loved you in my dreams, and then, there you were, sitting in Harrison's office. I couldn't believe my eyes. I'll never let you go. You're my life. We were bound together even before I met you."

He hugged me, left, and came back with two glasses of wine. He handed one to me and we clinked our glasses together, our hands intertwined as our glasses touched our lips. We kissed, he hugged me, and he whispered in my ear, "Till death do us part, my darling. We may have our little disagreements and become angry with each other. That's life, but I'll always find my way back to you. I'll never let you go."

CHAPTER SEVENTY-SIX

S TORM CLOUDS. In life, always when you least expect them, storm clouds were gathering on the horizon. Sean and I both loved our children and we wished to have a blended family. My children loved Sean. They loved the fact that I was happy. While his children accepted me, they still hoped that we would separate, and Sean would reunite with their mother.

We had a few disagreements when Lucinda, his daughter, changed jobs. I laughingly told him, "It's a question of attitude. New employees are expected to carry out orders, not give them, even when their ideas might be better. Attitude is more important than aptitude. Change in systems have to be marketed and accepted before implementation. These are cardinal rules for all, new employees, in particular."

His reply bowled me over. "Will you help her? Discuss the ramifications of office behaviour and office politics. Let her know that hard work and not ideas will help her prove that she can 'better' the systems in place. She can't become the boss even when her qualifications are better. She wasn't hired to be the boss. She's switched careers a few times each one in a different field from the other, and she's getting on in age. She needs to hear this truth, then it's up to her."

I raised my eyebrows questioningly. He was putting me in a situation where I didn't want to be. I pleaded, "I don't think she'll take kindly to hearing that from me. It'll only come across as criticism from the woman who replaced her in her father's life. She was the 'apple' of your eye in her growing years. She knew you were unhappy and your love for her was the bright spot, the shining star, in your own life. All that changed when we got married. Now I'm the usurper."

"That's nonsense, Tab. She loves and respects you. She has always said how much happier and approachable I am because of you." He acknowledged this wasn't going to be easy for me, but felt it could lead to Lucinda's better understanding of job requirements.

Foolishly, I agreed to try to help, but was intimidated by the challenge. Lucinda didn't like being second best in her father's life. She also felt that the aura of her father's position as a former and respected President of the branch of a worldwide company, reflected her own ability.

We met for lunch the following week. She brought me some flowers and everything was cheery and bright. She related her experiences on the job she had just quit and said she hadn't realized it was the wrong choice of a career for her. We laughed over some of the gaffes she had made.

"What are you really looking for in a job?" I asked. "Your choices have been many. What are you passionate about and what do you think can continue to hold your interest? Your choice should be something you can build upon if you want advancement."

"First of all, Tab, I'm like my father and I expect to be successful, because people see him in me. The apple doesn't fall far from the tree. I inherited his potential, and that guarantees that I have the ability to be successful," she explained.

"That's all well and good," I responded. "Education and training in the field of your choice are necessary attributes. This isn't a case of applying for a job which you think will meet your present needs, but something which offers personal fulfilment, 'what calls you?'"

"I like dress design, and I think I'll be good at it. I've researched the schools which offer a curriculum I think will help me achieve my aspirations. I'll have to attend school in the U.S. for three years, and then I can apply for a job in one of the big establishments. In four years, I can design clothes for the movies. There will be no stopping me. That's my dream and fashion will be my area of specialization."

"You do know that the big stars in the fashion industry all have a special flair, something that sets their work apart? This is an interesting career choice. Have you done research on what skills are needed? Have you ever doodled or drawn, given life to your fantasies?" I gently questioned.

"Not really. I'm taking lessons in design art, and my instructor informed me clothing design was a good choice of a career for me. Learning the basics of design will allow me to express my flair; coincidentally there's a design school in Chicago which helps foster creativeness while you learn the basics; she thought this would provide an excellent training ground for me."

"Think carefully about your career choice at this time. You want a career where you can find fulfillment, satisfaction, and a good salary. Have you researched community colleges here in Toronto? I've heard that Ryerson graduates are always in demand. One of Christo's friends graduated in fashion design, and now works out of London, England."

"Dad will support me and help me until I find my feet. I'll get work and go to night school if necessary. A job in fashion offers everything I've always wanted," she replied. "You don't have confidence in my ability, do you, Tabitha? I thought you were sure to recognize my potential."

"Consider this," I replied. "You don't have to go to the U.S. to study. Canadian colleges offer similar advantages. It'll be difficult for you to get a job in the States after graduation. Competition for jobs in the clothing industry is fierce. There's also the question of the green card. Why not try to see what Ryerson offers? Their graduates are always in demand. If you went to a Canadian college, your chances of getting a job here, after graduation, with one of our foremost designers, will be better."

"I know I can be a successful designer. Other people have made successes from nothing in particular. Why can't I?" Lucinda questioned.

I countered, "I understand that you need to follow your dreams. But be careful. People can spin you a yarn, and you buy into it because it's flattering. Reality must also play a part. Look carefully at your past choices and your feelings of rejection when they didn't pan out for you. Learn from your past mistakes. Ambition leads to dreams, and talent builds skill. You must be realistic. Demarcate where you are today, where you want to be in the future, and how you'll get there. Don't jump ship to something else when your first choice becomes tough. Acknowledge why things aren't working out for you, and what you need to correct. Success isn't a lottery, or a ticket pulled out of a hat. It comes from an innate desire to be the best you can be in the field of your choice and working hard to fulfill the demands the job entails."

"I've been told that I'm talented. You're not helping me, Tabitha... only putting me and my ideas down. I thought better of you. I valued the help I thought you'd give me," she countered.

"My advice to you, and you don't have to follow it, is this. The first lesson in the choice of a career is to find something you like doing. I'm sure that you'll do well in whatever field you choose, but you must make the right choice now. Factor in all the negatives we've discussed. This is important. Be realistic. Going off to study fashion design in the States is a glamorous choice, but does it offer a future? When schooling is over and you graduate, look at the choices open to you. Design is a closed field. Only the very best will be chosen. Will you be one of the best? Your opportunities in Canada are better. Your Dad and I will support your choice, whatever it is. Like everything else, there's a time limit. Age is that limiting factor because competition from younger graduates will always be intense, and your independence, your ability to earn a living comes into full force after graduation. The bird will have grown up and must fly the coop. Don't give up on a Canadian education."

We finished our lunch, she thanked me for my advice, and we went our separate ways.

I felt I had given the best advice I could in the circumstances. I was late getting home and I bumped into an old friend by chance. There was so much catching up to do, time flew by.

Sean looked upset when I got in and I asked, "What's the matter, Sean?"

"I trusted you to help Lucinda, not to dash her dreams. She was in tears when she called me. She said you weren't at all helpful, as you seemed only to want to disagree with her and cast her dreams into the waste paper basket."

"I'm sorry about that. I tried to point out the obstacles that lie ahead. This is the third career choice she'll be embarking on. She's twenty-five years old and it's time for a reality choice. I may be wrong, but I didn't mean to cause distress, only to get her thinking so that she'd have a clearer picture of her options. She needs to engage in something that will make her job worthy."

"You hurt her feelings, Tab. That's not the way to encourage someone who's floundering and wants reassurance."

My wide open eyes mirrored my feelings. I shook my head to show I couldn't believe what I was hearing. I was being judged and condemned. "A good dose of reality is necessary sometimes.

Lucinda has to realize that she'll be judged on who she is, not on who you are. Even if your status grants her a toe hold, she'll still have to prove her worth. You've always been very good to her, not wanting to hurt her feelings, and always pandering to her wants. She believes you only need to wave a wand and 'bingo' the world's her oyster. We're talking about her future and the reality of financial independence. One of the satisfactions of a parent's life, is that the child of the union is successful and happy. Perhaps I wasn't the right person to give her advice; you asked me to, and I tried. I'm sorry that I failed. I'll call her and apologize."

He looked askance of me, got up, and went to his office. Dinner was a silent affair. When it was bedtime I called out, "Sean, it's time to turn in."

He was terse, "I'm, not ready. I'm working on something. You go up and I'll join you later."

I spent a fitful night in bed. I didn't feel him beside me so I got out of bed to see where he was. I was hurt and dismayed when I found him sleeping in the spare room. I asked myself, "What did I do to create such a rift? What caused such a change in our relationship?"

Breakfast was a silent affair. While I was putting the dishes away, I heard, "I'm going to spend the day with Lucinda. I don't know when I'll be back."

I looked at him without a smile "Take your time. I hope you can soothe her. I gave it my best. It's difficult to hear something different from what you expected. I couldn't advise her to do something I thought wouldn't pan out for her. What's wrong with pursuing education in Canada?" I shrugged my shoulders. "I'll go into the city today and do some shopping. Some time on my own will also be good for me."

This was the first major rift we had experienced and I didn't like it. I should never have agreed to counsel and advise. Children are always prickly with relationships involving step-parents; I should have listened only and told her to do as she wished. I honestly felt she was barking up the wrong tree. The possibility of a glamorous job in the movies, and the advice that the school in Chicago would find a placement for her after graduation had been uppermost in Lucinda's mind. Nothing else mattered.

I knew from experience that guaranteeing a job in fashion after graduation was certainly not an option on which to plan the future. Referrals were always made by the school or university; hiring for the position was up to the personnel manager. Obtaining a green card to work in the States wasn't a simple matter. The future she was charting wouldn't lead to her expectations.

I spent an uneasy day at home working in the gardens and making lists of new plants for some of the flower beds. When Sean returned, he was still upset. I asked, "How did it go with Lucinda?"

"What do you care?" His usual smile was missing. There was something in his manner and voice that gave me such a feeling of disquiet, I felt dismay. *How should I deal with this, I questioned? Should I have lied and told her 'good choice' and sent her off in a blaze of happiness, rather than explaining the difficulties she would encounter? We learn from our mistakes. I shrugged my shoulders. I'll deal with this in my own way, not as I've done in the past, ingesting it all, and burying it in my own subconscious.*

"I cared enough to make time and set her on the right track. I didn't want to get involved in the first place. What's really the matter, Sean? This is so unlike you. We agreed we'd always discuss any difference that arose between us, but you've surrounded yourself with barriers of silence and won't let me in," I gently chided him.

"Lucinda told me that you humiliated her. You told her she'd never be successful in fashion, the line of work she wanted to pursue. I trusted you to help her understand the world, not dim her expectations of success. She didn't need to be reminded of past failures. You simply added to her feelings of insecurity." He sounded as if he meant to chastise me

"I tried, Sean. I couldn't tell her that a glamorous job awaited her in fashion and design because that would be a lie. She needed to understand that her success lay within herself, with a well thought out path of future education and training. She couldn't piggy-back on your success. Hiring the daughter of a friend is a thing of the past and the fashion industry is outside your ambit any way. If you want to sulk and make us both unhappy, that's up to you. I'm not perfect and giving advice isn't my forte." I thought, *damned if you do and damned if you don't. I couldn't win anyway, so why bother.*

"I've told her I'll pay for her education, no matter how long it takes," he replied.

"That has nothing to do with me, Sean. We both agreed on our finances before we got married. You're as free as I am to help our children financially."

"You owe Lucinda an apology. I hope she'll forgive you," wasn't an answer I expected.

"What are you talking about? I did my best to set her straight, to point out obstacles, so she could determine the best way forward. Let's agree to disagree on this matter. If Lucinda's disenchantment with me is so important to you that it creates a wrench in our relationship, we'll leave it there. We're two adults who thought we'd found happiness. This is a huge stumbling block in our relationship."

"Lucinda said you'd say that."

"What else can I say? Do you really believe that I'd try to put Lucinda down or should've encouraged her to plan her future on choice of a career without pointing out the negatives? I was as frank to her as I would've been to Christo and Gloria; if you do in fact believe that I was trying to belittle her, then our life together will just be one big farce, and I'm not willing to return to that state once again. I'll leave you alone to ponder your thoughts. I love you dearly, but I don't love the person you are now. I don't know exactly what was said to tarnish our relationship but I don't really think it matters. If we don't trust each other, we may best live separate lives. Do whatever you want; I'm tired and humiliated by this situation ...one I never wanted in the first place. It's time to put it to rest. Perhaps some time apart will help us realize where we should be going with our lives. A week or two away would help to cool tempers."

"Don't go away, Tabitha. I won't let you. I know that if you turn away now, you'll never come back to me."

"Perhaps that would be for the best, Sean. I need some space from you and from Lucinda's problems. 'Que sera, sera' as the saying goes. A little holiday away will be good for us all and then we can sort out our own future together."

I went to my own office and closed the door. I was shaken to the core. My body started to tremble. My mind was in turmoil. I sat on the floor and found myself in the fetal position rocking back and forth. I ignored the telephone. What was I to do? The life I had thought would be mine was disappearing and I hadn't the strength or determination to deal with the mess my advice had created.

I asked myself why hadn't I gone along with what Lucinda really wanted. Perhaps I should have agreed with her. The cost of her education in the U.S. would be phenomenal. Why didn't I realize that she really wanted an opportunity in something with a bit of flair, something glamorous to compensate for the loss of her father to me and her own inabilities. She had been floundering. She didn't need a dose of reality, only comfort that new surroundings would bring her. What I had told her was the truth as I saw it. Perhaps I needed to be more of a friend than a counsellor or advisor.

That didn't absolve her of responsibility for misleading Sean. But that was her concern, not mine. It was hers to repair and his to realize that even if I'd made a mistake, explanation – not blame – was required.

My telephone rang again, but I decided to ignore it. Whoever was calling would have to wait. There was pain in my heart as I considered a future without Sean.

The telephone stopped ringing, and then there was a knock at my door. I quickly dried my tears and got up from the floor.

The door slowly opened and Sean appeared.

"I came down to ask you to forgive me for the way I handled this situation. I know I've hurt you and I can't apologize enough. Don't leave me, please. I couldn't bear it. When I think of the words spoken between us, I'm ashamed. I know Lucinda and should've realized that whatever she reported to me was her own embellishment of the facts. Let's go away together this weekend, forget what happened, and make peace."

"Words hurt, Sean, and so do attitudes. I thought I'd moved away from living with someone and being falsely accused and hurt in the progress of life. You were upset on Lucinda's behalf because of what she told you. To assuage your own hurt, you turned on me, doubted me, and then rejected me. Adults shouldn't behave like this. I don't know what your children expect of me, but it seems I can't meet their expectations. I realize that I'm too easily hurt, but this time I wanted to deal with the situation in a different way. Perhaps I made some mistakes, but you didn't give me a chance to explain. I can't live this way. True, this is our first major disagreement, but whatever may happen in the future will only cause disruption in our lives because we can't have an open discussion. Let's give it a rest and we'll talk about it when I get back in a week."

I shrugged my shoulders and turned to leave the room when he pleaded, the tenderness in his voice showing his feelings "Let's both get away for a week. Distance ourselves from all of this. I assure you and I promise this will never happen again between us. I'll deal with the problems my children pose and not burden you with them. I'll let Lucinda know that she didn't understand what you were trying to portray to her, and became irritated and annoyed when you pointed out the difficulties rather than the advantages. You offered her help but what she was asking for was indeed encouragement, rather than assessment of the path she wanted to pursue. Let me take you away, my love, for one week. Life will be beautiful, and you have my word that this will never happen again."

"Let me think about it. This is serious. You owe a duty to your children, as I do to mine. Our marriage shouldn't come between our relationships with them. Our children must understand that they will never be rejected or set apart. Our love for them will never be the cause of friction between us," I replied with tears in my heart, rejection and upset in my mind, and a tiredness that made me feel numb.

"Let's go out for dinner and share a bottle of wine. Let's be friends again and start to put this behind us now," he smiled, as he extended his hands to hold me.

The telephone rang. The travel agent was returning a call I'd put through earlier that day. He looked at the number, recognized the caller and answered, "Tabitha's busy at the moment. I'll tell her you called and she'll get back to you."

He turned to me. "This is an important time in our lives. If you go your separate way for a week, we'll never know what fate has in store for us. If we go away together, we can resolve this matter."

I gave him a searching look, trying to delve into his mind and his heart, my own heart whispering, 'Don't fall into another trap, free yourself, men are the same regardless of upbringing or race. I was so tired of it all, but the way he looked at me melted a little of the ice around my heart. I nodded "Okay, Sean. I'll give in this time. I'll pack my bags and get ready. You decide where we're going and make the necessary arrangements. We'll have a quiet dinner tonight at home."

That night, he hugged me but the magic of our love was missing. Making up was hard to do indeed. My body was tired and unhappy, my mind unwilling to forget the trauma of the past two days. I tossed and turned as did he. We were both up early.

CHAPTER SEVENTY-SEVEN

UNDERSTANDING LEADS TO FORGIVING. Next morning, I thought my behaviour was churlish. Sean had bent over backwards to put the situation right, but I still felt hurt that he'd doubted me, especially as he had once told me Lucinda was used to turning situations around to suit her. She was jealous, of course, that she'd lost her role as the key person of his love. She wanted to impress me, to be recognized as a young woman of high caliber, knowledgeable and determined in pursuit of her dream. Unfortunately, there was nothing I could do to reverse our misunderstanding. We all needed to accept the situation for what it was and assuage the hurt that followed as best we could.

I understood how difficult it was for children to accept that their lives changed and with it the necessity of having to deal with the person they considered responsible. Although all our children were adults, the break-up of marital relationships was still challenging. I was tempted many times to leave Mike, but had remained with him solely because of the children. Later, I wondered whether I had done the right thing.

Sean reminded me to take my passport; I didn't question this, as I guessed we were going over to the States. After we crossed the border, he told me our destination was the Inn at Geneva on the Lakes, in the Finger Lakes District.

This was indeed a nice surprise. When we arrived, the reception desk personnel gave me a 'five-star' welcome. I wondered why, but concluded that as we were returning guests, we were entitled to special treatment.

When we opened the door to our room, the scent of roses welcomed me. Sean had booked us a mini-suite. There were roses in the sitting room and in the bedroom. I had never seen so many red roses in one place at one time. Rose petals were spread on the bed and champagne on ice awaited us.

I looked at Sean with questioning eyes. "Tab, sweetheart, I honour you and I love you with all my heart. There is something I'd like to read to you which expresses my feelings for you. You are the Yin to my Yang. My life would be a sea of emptiness without you. There's only you; no other can take your place." He led me to the sofa, and knelt on the floor beside me. He took from his pocket a book of Victorian love poems, and looked at me with so much love in his eyes that it melted the ice around my heart. He then read to me this loving tribute - a definition of the measurement of love from "Sonnets to the Portuguese" by Elizabeth Barrett Browning,

> *"How do I love thee? Let me count the ways. I love thee to the depth and breath and height my soul can reach, when feeling out of sight, For the ends of Being and ideal Grace.*
> *I love thee to the level of everyday's*
> *Most quiet need, by sun and candle light.*
> *I love thee freely, as men strive for Right; I love thee purely, as they turn from Praise. I love thee with the passion put to use in my old griefs, and with my childhood's faith.*

466

I love thee with a love I seemed to lose
With my lost saints, -- I love thee with the breath,
Smiles, tears of all my life! -- and if God choose,
I shall love thee better after death."

I choked up. Never in all my life had I ever received such an expression of love. I had dreamed of love while I sang the love songs in my youth, but never had I imagined that love could encompass me through the voice of a poem in which the declaration of love was so strong and all encompassing. This moment in time would last forever.

I conceded then that I was encircled by chains of a love so strong that Sean's love would encompass me forever. True love is an emotion that I had never been fortunate enough to encounter before. This was my last chance to embrace it. Luck had smiled on me. I had won the multi-million-dollar lottery. I couldn't throw it away.

We were two people from different worlds. He was Irish with English customs and upbringing. I was Indo Guyanese with an English education but born and bred in a Colonial culture, always conscious of the fact that I could never draw 'trumps' with the race card. I was tied to my Indian heritage. It was true that my background in business was varied. From being a Secretary at seventeen, I had progressed to Executive Assistant, then to Business School Owner/Principal.

I emigrated to Canada with high hopes, and ignored all the negatives I was told would greet me. From Secretary to a Senior Vice President, to President of a subsidiary company, was a roadmap few people would be fortunate to travel, more especially for a woman of colour, and especially in those years where male domination in business was the norm. My career had advanced with upward mobility in an international company. I had outstripped my siblings on whom further education had been lavished, and now I had at last found the love I had dreamed of in my youth.

I knelt down beside him and we fell to the floor facing each other. My hand rose to caress his face. I touched his eyes, his nose, and lingered on his mouth. He took my hand in his and kissed me. In that moment, it seemed there was fusion. We were truly joined together; he was mine as much as I was truly his.

"We won't talk of why we're here, only that we're together so we could have this moment in time to allow two units to fuse and become one. Our lives from here to the end of our days will be filled only with the joy of our love. Thank you, my love, for holding on to me, for not letting me go off on a tangent of self-pity and recrimination. This is the honeymoon of two wandering souls from whom the veils have been removed. Our destinies can stop flirting on the horizon of life. We've tied the Gordian knot that binds everything and everyone it touches, together forever," Sean whispered with so much love, it dispelled any doubts I still had.

Our afternoon was filled with champagne and loving sex. We delighted in the physicality of our love. We dozed through the afternoon exhausted by the passion of love. When I awoke and opened my eyes, I saw that he was awake and looking at me. His blue eyes so full of love and passion spoke to me of wonderment and joy, of fulfilling a dream he'd always had, but never believed he could find someone with whom he could give and receive that love.

He kissed me and we gloried in the delight of two bodies perfectly in tune. That his touch could excite the physical part of love in me was as astounding to me as was his love for me. I had heard the song of love, I had moved to the dance of love, and felt my body reverberate to the fulfillment of love and the joy of sexuality. My heart was full.

The scars left by the molestation and sexual violence in my childhood would always remain with me, but they had lost their power to hurt, shame, and humiliate. Despite my achievements, I had never regained my self-respect until this day. I was standing on the brink of life that existed only in the fairy tales I had loved in my youth... 'and they lived happily after.'

Days of wine and roses, glowing from happiness which comes with true love, spoke of the idyllic bonds between us that drew us and held us together. Our happiness must have radiated in our well-being. We had an aura that pulled people to us. I caught envious glances as we explored the Finger Lakes. My body felt lighter somehow. I was dancing to the melody of love and the enchantment of being loved. Life was beautiful.

We drove back to Canada in the glow of that sunshine. The car telephone rang. Sean touched the speaker phone button and said, "Hello."

"Hi, Dad... Lucinda calling. How did it go with you and Tabitha? Is she leaving you?"

I replied, "Hello Lucinda, we're on speaker phone. Thanks for calling and for the welcome home. Our time away was simply magical. I love your Dad so much, and he loves me too. I feel very special. When are we going to see you? We have to be sure that you don't miss the enrolment dates for your classes, so come over soon to discuss this with your Dad. You know that you'll always have his support and you'll always be the apple of his eye. He's a fantastic man and I love him to death."

Sean chimed in, "Thanks for calling, Lucinda. Let us know when you're available. We always love to see you as you well know. Our week away was just what the doctor ordered. Tab and I are very happy that we spent this week together in Finger Lakes. You must be happy for me too. You're my dear and loving daughter, and I feel blessed to have you both in my life. I'll always support you and do my best to advise and help you in any career of your choice. You have to do your part also. My love for Tabitha doesn't mean I love you less. Always remember that."

She sounded a little deflated, but we both hoped she would set her sights on charting the course of a career, rather than causing disruption in our lives. He took my hand in his and kissed it. We had weathered the storm and reached a place where we were so comfortable, doubt and disagreement stopped short at the doorways.

CHAPTER SEVENTY-EIGHT

TIME MARCHES ON. The years passed by, almost too quickly. We were away from home as often as we could make a trip to visit a country we were interested in exploring. In Antarctica, we visited the burial site of Robert F. Scott and drank a toast of rum to him and to his work. I had studied his voyages of exploration while at school, and always admired his tenacity and strength of purpose. Paying tribute to him after so many decades seemed a fitting appreciation of the inspiration he'd given to many, including me. During my studies of his voyages during my school years, I had toiled on with him, hoping and wishing that the outcome of his voyage could change, while knowing that nothing could reverse death, or change the past.

This was the start of our paying tribute to the heroes who changed the world because they "dared." I had always tried to hide my tears at these events, but Sean knew me too well. I could always depend on him to put his arms around me, and give me a little squeeze on my shoulders.

On that trip to Antarctica, two orcas swam alongside our vessel for almost half an hour. This was magical. We had tried to visit countries where whale watching was included as part of the scenery, but we always returned home disappointed because the whales had resurfaced elsewhere.

We were so energized on our return home that we decided to visit the Arctic. Could anything be more magical than a polar bear swimming within the arc of a rainbow in sight of our vessel, with me in a front row seat? I stood, transfixed on the Captain's Bridge, gazing at the spectacle through the captain's powerful binoculars. I always regretted not having my camera with me, but the magic of the moment was pure, unhindered by the trappings of recording the episode.

Travel with Sean was wild, wonderful, and spectacular. Our family had begun to grow also. We had three grandchildren who provided joy as they responded to the challenges of "growing up." They loved their Grandpa Sean. He was always willing to play with them and they always clamoured for his attention. They loved sleepovers with us, always begging for an extra day when it was time to return home.

We were away in South Africa when we realized that trouble was brewing in their parents' marriage. There was nothing we could do to stem the tide of separation which followed. We did our best to reverse the process, but it seemed that the disenchantment had existed for too long and a third party had stepped into the relationship.

My soon-to-be ex daughter-in-law blamed me for not commanding my son to return to his matrimonial home, and then used the children to bargain for their father's return. They became pawns in the game of chess, the end result being punishment of their father for leaving them. If they were late in getting home after a visit with him, she threatened to call the police. The words she blasted him with scared the children. They loved their father, and the trauma of the separation itself was difficult enough for them to absorb.

Sean did his best to help mitigate the effects the disruption wrought. Outwardly, the children were trying to deal with the situation and seemed to be coping, but when a stepmother came into the situation, despite the best efforts of their father, and the anger of their mother, they withdrew into their shells, and like tortoises only came out when it suited them.

The separation and wrinkles which followed caused us soul searching. I had no problem with my soon to be ex daughter-in-law. Her card to me on my last birthday we spent together, had affirmed the love and support I had given to her. She became annoyed with me because when Christo moved out of the matrimonial home, he asked me for temporary lodgings, to which Sean and I agreed.

Everything I had done to help her during the ten years of her marriage fell by the wayside. Blame became mine. One night, she came to spy on the children who were visiting their father. My car was parked outside and needed to be moved as there was 'no parking' on the street at night. Christo found her scratching my car with her keys. He had left the front door open when he went to move my car and she took the opportunity to run into the house.

I was standing in the entrance and I asked her what she was doing there. She didn't reply but held my shoulders and threw me to the ground. A post was in the way and I banged my head on it. A neighbour reported the fracas, and the police came. She was removed by the police.

I couldn't believe that something as humiliating as a public brawl could be happening to me and my family. The children rushed down from the bedrooms when they heard the noise. The floodgates burst. They were all in tears, each telling the story of abuse which followed when they didn't say the things she wanted to hear.

She had forced them into reporting stories of paternal abuse, which were fabricated by her, to the social worker assigned to the case. She'd made them write letters, which she dictated, saying they would commit suicide if they had to go to Florida with Christo, as part of their summer holidays.

All three were asked to make statements to the police that night. It was a night of confusion and horror, heartbreak and much sadness.

The happenings that night caused the court to award full custody of the children to Christo. The child psychologist who they were all seeing reported that they feared their mother and wanted to live with their father. They felt abandoned by their mother and disillusioned because of how she treated them. They feared her and dreaded their return home after their visits to their father, as all she did was question them as to the happenings within their father's household.

Once again, Sean and I discussed the ramifications of separation and divorce, especially the effects of separation on children. Children are innocent victims. They're hurt when separation happens. The home has to be divided, which causes their world to fall apart. When one parent tries to make them allies in the battle, that parent forgets that children are part of both mother and father; trying to command their allegiance only causes damage to their souls. Irreparable harm happens, and more often than not, they seldom find happiness in adulthood. Their psyche has been damaged.

I began blaming myself for the tragedy to my grandchildren's lives, their loss of innocence, and the devastation of their childhood. Did Christo's marriage fall apart because of my own failed marriage with his father? Would his children's upbringing in the atmosphere of disconcert and sadness influence their own behaviour?

Life for Sean and me continued apace. Our social life continued to be full. We always cherished the friendships we had and were never unwilling to lend a helping hand. We were content. Lucinda graduated from college and was looking for a permanent job. We were both enthusiastic about the futures of our children and this made us content.

The grandchildren were the only ones who presented a problem, but Sean assured me that they would adjust with time. "Look at our own childhoods," he would say, "they were far from perfect and take a gander at what we've done with our lives."

I hoped that the strength that had kept me from falling into an abyss, had been inherited by them. A discordant childhood builds a negative element in the soul. Dealing with this can sometimes lead to detrimental character flaws in adulthood.

Sean and I continued to try to make their childhood happy, to repair the wrongs that happened when the marriage of their parents was torn asunder. They were secretive and never really revealed what turned them into fearful little beings when they were told they had to spend some time with their mother. Was she aware of the hurt they were enduring, not only because of the separation, but also because of the way she was handling it? Tearing your children's lives apart is no way to end a matrimonial relationship.

I never knew whether they fully unburdened themselves to the child psychotherapists ordered by the court, and whether they benefitted from the help offered.

From my own experience, I knew only too well how easy it was to hide childhood pain and appear rational. They never talked to me when I tried to delve into the events during the days of separation. They never truly cleared their souls of the mantle of dread, fear, and unhappiness they were forced to bear. Like me, they tried to grow a tough shell and bury it into their subconscious, hoping they had dealt with it and lost it forever.

All I could do was to shower them with love in the hope that joy and happiness would create forgetfulness, or at least create a balance in their lives.

Sean and I loved them, as only grandparents can. They showed us a great measure of love in return and I think we became beacons of light in their days of turmoil and fear.

CHAPTER SEVENTY-NINE

THE FUTURE STARTS TO DIM. The world seemed to be shrinking for us as Sean and I continued our travelling agenda. He never liked cruises, and referred to them as "traveling on floating hotels."

I wanted so much to be part of the eclipse which would occur in the West Indies that he couldn't say 'no' to a cruising holiday, which would take us to the best spot to observe this phenomenon, and also to the volcano, Soufriere, erupting in Montserrat.

It was a wonderful experience for us both, so much so that he decided we should go on a cruise from Singapore to Australia and afterwards spend two weeks visiting friends and exploring the beauty of the country. Towards the end of our trip, I noticed that he was becoming forgetful. Our love life seemed also to have taken second place and he mentioned that he would need to take Viagra once we got home. We had a good laugh together. "It's only a passing fancy, Sean. You'll soon be my Young Lochinvar again."

His personality seemed to be changing also, and I asked, "Sean, are we getting too old for travel? You seem impatient and irritable when things don't fall into place?"

"I've been feeling a little tired, I must admit. Perhaps this stretch away from home has been a little too long. I'll see Dr. Harley when we get home. He'll fix me up and I'll be right as rain."

On the flight from Australia to Hawaii, the refueling stop on our way to Miami was a nightmare. Business class provided a modicum of comfort but Sean seemed restless and upset. When we stopped to refuel in Hawaii, American regulations had changed following 9/11, and the baggage was off-loaded. We had to reclaim our luggage, and go through customs and immigration again before we could re-board the aircraft and get to Miami.

In the past, in similar circumstances, he was always the one who remained calm. I quietly took over the role, explained we were tired, and apologized for Sean's outbursts. He wasn't amused, but when we were away again, he voiced his displeasure at the inefficiency of the new regulations which had been put into place following 9/11.

The day after we arrived safely back in Canada, I called the Doctor and he agreed to see Sean the following day. He could find nothing wrong, but ordered some blood tests and told us we should have them done immediately.

The next day, Sean went to the Medical Clinic to get blood work done. (Tests had been ordered before we left, but he had ignored them, saying they were only routine). He became angry at the inefficiency of the receptionist, vented his anger, and walked out. Behaviour like this was totally outside his character, and I wondered what was happening to him.

He brushed aside all my questions, said he would be all right, and was feeling better now after returning home.

It was our usual practice to visit areas where travel disasters happened, to pay our respects to the victims and place flowers at the sites. We hadn't gone to New York City since 9/11. He thought it would be a good idea to plan a short visit there.

As was our wont when we visited New York City, we took in a few shows, visited the disaster area, and meandered here and there. On our last day there, we had some time and decided to go for a walk around Times Square. While crossing the road, he stumbled and fell. Some passers-by helped him up and offered advice.

I was concerned. This was very unusual for him. He was always healthy and strong. On our return home, I called the Doctor's office. The receptionist told me that they hadn't received the blood work the Doctor requisitioned and Sean should get this done right away.

He grumbled when I insisted he had to return to the medical clinic for the blood test, but I went with him to make sure it was done.

Two days later, we received a call from Doctor Harley. He wanted to speak to Sean directly. My heart was heavy. This was unusual and it could only be bad news. I handed the phone to Sean with a frown on my face. Sean looked downcast as he heard the results. His white corpuscle count was too high. A visit to see the specialist the next day was mandatory.

It was very bad news indeed. We learned there was a possibility he might have leukemia. Doctor Harley told us not to panic or jump to conclusions but deep in my heart I knew there would be challenges ahead. He had been in touch with one of the senior cancer specialists at Princess Margaret Hospital and had been assured that Sean's illness would be given high priority. They would do blood tests to determine what was happening within his body, and treatment would follow. The Doctor from Princess Margaret Hospital had promised to call the next day to confirm the appointment.

We started our return home with heavy hearts. Sean looked at me and I looked at him. We had learned that there were two types of leukemia, a deadly strain, and another which could be cured or at least controlled. I said, "Let's not panic. We don't know what tomorrow promises, but we're here today, together. We'll celebrate each moment and make living worthwhile."

"Let's have fish and chips, then," he said as we passed his favourite fish and chips shop. We parked the car and walked hand in hand into the shop. We laughed and talked as if this was a normal day in our lives. My heart was heavy, but what about him? If the diagnosis was what we feared, how could we live with this dark cloud hanging over our lives, never knowing when it would burst and leave us helpless?

When we arrived home, we both rushed to the telephone to see whether the Doctor from Princess Margaret had called and left a message. No, our phone was silent. No messages, no missed calls.

Dejection filled my soul. Suddenly I felt as lifeless as a dead herring; I'd lost the use of my limbs. I slumped against the wall as if it could give me support. He rushed to my side. "None of that, Tab. I need your strength and courage to battle this thing. I'm a survivor, but I need you in my corner."

"You're right. I'm falling prey to a result we don't know will happen. Let's call the children and let them know what's happening."

He talked to Lucinda and Lloyd, and I talked to Gloria and Christo. The consensus following the conversations was that we should all keep calm. Gloria said, "I'll meet you at the hospital whenever your appointment happens to be."

Christo said, "I'll come and get you and drive you to the hospital." Lloyd was in Miami. He would visit us on the weekend. Lucinda was working but she would join us at the end of her shift. She asked Sean to put me on the line.

"We're in this together, Tabitha. I'll help to lift his spirits and be cheerful and confident. With all of us doing our best, we must think only the positive can happen." Words of comfort followed.

Although we felt somewhat consoled by the support, the dark cloud of disaster still hung over us. When bad things happen, there is nothing to quiet the feelings which seem to encompass bodies and minds, and take control, and we were no exception to the rule.

Later that evening, we received a call from Dr. Robertson the leukemia specialist at Princess Margaret Hospital. Princess Margaret is the principal hospital for cancer research in Toronto. He said he had an opening at 9.00 a.m. the following morning and asked whether Sean could make it. There was no question about timing. Of course we could make it. He asked us to bring a small overnight bag in case it was necessary for Sean to be hospitalized.

Sean moved quickly to get his hospital bag packed. I phoned our children. Gloria would meet us at the hospital at 9.00 a.m., Christo would collect us at 7.00 a.m., Lucinda would visit after work, and Lloyd wanted an update as soon as we knew what it was all about. The troops had been marshalled and we were ready for action.

Looking back, it seems strange how optimism buoyed us up. We had received a call to action and we were responding with high hopes. We expected only the best outcome. This was just a blip on the landscape, and it would soon be evicted into oblivion.

Sean underwent the usual physical examinations then blood tests were ordered. We were told that it would take some time to get the results and we should return after lunch. Everyone we saw was upbeat, kind, and helpful. If whatever he had could be cured, this was the place where it would happen.

We had some time to kill before results were available. We alerted Lucinda and Lloyd about the situation, and decided

Christo, Gloria, and I would go off on a "send-off" lunch with Sean. We jokingly told Sean that we were going to celebrate the success of his treatment in advance. The good vibes he was receiving would help to brace and sustain him. He loved beef, so we would take him to a restaurant where he would get the biggest, juiciest, tastiest steak he had ever eaten.

Off we went to Hy's. It had been one of Sean's favourite places when we worked together, and it was only a stone's throw away from the hospital. The four of us sat down to lunch, each filled with pregnant thoughts of the future, each unwilling to burden the other with his own doubts. Sean was calm, happy enough it seemed, trusting that the future boded well and we would all emerge from this moment into the sunshine of his well-being.

We hoped that the blood tests wouldn't confirm what we feared, and chattered and laughed as if enough of that behavior could dispel the doom and gloom we were feeling. We joked about this being his last supper and it was important to make the most of it. If he had to be admitted to hospital, we were certain that the food would be so bland, that in itself would drive whatever disease ailed him he into oblivion.

Soon it was time to return to the hospital. We waited with baited breath for Dr. Robertson. His diagnosis sent shockwaves through my body. Sean was diagnosed with acute lymphoblastic leukemia. Medical research hadn't yet discovered a cure for this type of leukemia. However, chemotherapy, if successful, could prolong life for two years, provided the patient survived treatment. The effects on his body would be many and varied in severity. However, Dr. Robertson stressed that this was only a temporary cure, as the disease would recur in two years.

I asked, "What would happen in two years? Can't we apply the same treatment, and prolong Sean's life?"

Dr. Robertson's tone was somber as he replied, "If the treatment is successful, Mr. Baker would need to have chemotherapy to keep it at bay. Although he would be cured, there would be ongoing tests and chemotherapy for the balance of his life, to monitor and ensure that the leukemia didn't return. At the first sign, he would be readmitted to hospital, and treatment would, of course, continue."

How was I going to deal with this problem? Sean had leukemia. This meant that whatever happened to him would be mirrored within me. He was my twin soul, my alternate persona, my life.

I was enveloped in the dark cloud that had suddenly befallen him. Internally I trembled with fear of this disease which had come to him like a bolt from the blue. Fear that this disease would take him away from me left me with a feeling of dread.

Leukemia is a cancer which affects the blood. Simply put, the white blood cells multiplied more rapidly than the red. The imbalance affected the organs in the body, and eventually resulted in death.

If Sean agreed to undergo the treatment, urgency was necessary. Dr. Robertson stressed that there were no guarantees. Treatment could begin immediately, as by chance, a room had become available and Sean was given first choice.

Pessimism took hold of me and gripped me in its talons. *A room was available only because the person who'd occupied it had died. Would that be Sean's fate also? Was this a bad omen?* I couldn't shake these thoughts, which seemed to paralyze rational reason.

Sean turned to me and held out his hands. I took them in mine and placed our hands first on my heart and then on his. "Life is precious. This is a chance, and who knows what the future may bring? A permanent cure could be found within that time." I don't know where those words had come from. Certainly they didn't echo the feeling of despair which consumed me.

He looked at me and said, "The road will be tough for you, Tab."

"It'll be tougher for you, Sean. Your body will bear the brunt of the punishing treatment required to rid itself of this pestilence. This is our battle; we'll fight this thing together. It affects us both. Who knows? Miracles happen, and if a cure is discovered by then, what a triumph that would be. We can donate your body to science."

We all laughed. "You all know I have a perfect body. It's a good body and I'll get better. I'll become famous in medical journals," he jokingly replied.

Arrangements concluded, Gloria, Christo, and I accompanied him to his room. We fussed around, making lists of everything we could think of. We waited until he had his first treatment, and left when Lucinda arrived. In the elevator, my children encircled me within their arms. "Mom, this is our fight also, not his alone or yours, for that matter. We'll weather this storm. Cancer and chemotherapy strike terror in our hearts, but we must be upbeat."

"You're ignoring what the Doctor said. There is no cure, just a stay of execution," I sadly replied through the tears running freely down my face.

Gloria said, "Mom, Christo and I've discussed this matter. We'll all take each day as it comes. Don't let the future loom large or it'll cloud everything. 'One day at a time' must be our guiding light. Let's deal with the situation as it is now. Sean will be hospitalized for six weeks, or possibly, more. You can't travel from and to Toronto every day. You'll have to stay with me at my home in the city, and you and Sean can decide how often you need to return home to look after your affairs or rather, how long you'll be able to stay away from him." She laughed.

It was the heart of winter. Driving conditions were treacherous on country roads. I felt moved by her offer. My head was splitting. Inertia had taken charge of my mind. All I could think about was "Sean has incurable leukemia" and, like a song, it kept repeating itself again and again. "What can I do?" I asked. This was something I couldn't problem solve. A malady had infected his body and there was no way to oust it. I was helpless. His care lay in someone else's hands.

I replied in a wooden tone, shooing her away with a wave of my hand. "I can't think about that now. We'll see what happens." I couldn't seem to marshal my thoughts. I thought of the pain he'd have to endure, the effects of the treatment on his body, and the mental agony he was probably silently enduring, trying not to let it disturb us. The thought that he would die was unbearable.

Gloria's voice reached out to me, "I know you can't think clearly now. He's in hospital and you're on your way home, alone, with pain in your soul and your mind in turmoil. Let's take over and ease you of all minor arrangements and responsibilities. Lucinda is with him now, and she'll stay with him until visiting hours are over. Our jobs are to keep him cheerful, comfortable, and happy. He's a proud man and it'll be difficult for him to accept help, except from you. Let's help you, and then you can help him. He needs you now, constantly by his side, and the only way you can accomplish that is by staying with me. Let's hear no more about that. Christo will help pack your bags, put them in your car, and you can drive down to the hospital tomorrow." The look on her face told me she wouldn't be denied. She had made a decision and there could be no change.

That was indeed the best solution. My head was pounding; instead of arguing, I sighed but agreed. If it didn't work, I could always change it. My life, my future, was over. There was no gainsaying that. Without him, I had no future. He had brightened my life when he kissed me, made me see the world through rose-tinted spectacles, awakened my soul, and shown me how beautiful the world could be when love blossomed between two people.

I would have to learn to live with that ache until he was well again.

I shook my head. Here was I, selfishly thinking about myself. What was he facing? The end of his life? Acute lymphoblastic leukemia was a death sentence looming large. He had been sentenced to die in two years.

Our world had turned chaotic without warning. It was downhill all the way. No matter which way we turned, the writing was on the wall. If we were lucky, we had two years together, probably a little more, or even a little less. We had to live a lifetime within those two short years.

My childhood insecurities nagged me. I began blaming myself for what was happening to Sean. This was his punishment for freeing me from the chains of my childhood horror. Doubts and insecurities rushed in. It seemed as if the floodgates had loosened because he wasn't there to halt them.

I started sobbing while on the way home. Christo stopped the car. "What's the matter, Mom? Why all the weeping? This isn't the time for that. You've got to be strong. You're not alone. We're all with you. Sean would be dismayed if he could see you now. You have to be strong for us all. You can't float away on a cloud of unhappiness. Life isn't like that, and you know it." The child was scolding the mother, letting her know she couldn't abandon her role, not then, not ever.

"I just need to come to terms with my grief and the shock of it all. The Doctor was quite clear, and he's the expert in this field. Age is against Sean. Experimental treatment is centred around the young. They can withstand the traumatic punishment the body needs to endure. Research has been active in this field, but at sixty-eight years, even though he's always been healthy, Sean's body can't survive."

"Okay, Mom. You have two years to live a lifetime. Make those two years count. You could've been given more or less, but you know it's two years. You can pack a lifetime into two years. Sometimes life creates a pattern for us. Your pattern is to make that life special. His role is to survive the treatment so you can both make those years count."

CHAPTER EIGHTY

DESPAIR. There was one incredible aspect of the relationships we had built since we moved to Queen's Concord two years before. It was a neighbourhood of friends, some closer than others, but all friends, nevertheless.

When they noticed the lights in the house, the telephone rang constantly. Everyone had heard what was happening and all were concerned and dismayed. They promised to help in whatever way they could.

The show of support was overwhelming. Sean and I had reached out to everyone when we first moved there. The community was new, and there were numerous problems with the builder. We listened, supported, and tried to find solutions. Sean became the unacknowledged leader of the group. That he had been struck down by this dreaded disease was a blow to all.

My hopelessness couldn't last in the face of all the support I was receiving. When a whole neighbourhood responded with such overwhelming kindness, despondency could find no place to hide. There was a lot of life still yet to be lived. Whatever time was left, had to be special. We couldn't waste it in vain regret. This was our future crunched short into two years. *Who knows?* I reminded myself. *A cure may be on the way and we'll benefit. We'll hold on to life and fight our misfortune every inch of the way.*

Ever confident, ever hopeful, ever optimistic, I told myself, *this is just a temporary blip in the scheme of things. When it's over, we'll all laugh about how our insecurities had led us astray.*

I spent a restless night. *What, if the inevitable happens? How can I bear to live a life alone without him?* I railed against the fates that had put this dreaded curse of cancer in his life. He had always been so healthy, seldom a day away from work, seldom with a cold. His migraine headaches had disappeared once we were married. *Why, oh why?* I asked myself. *Did this have something to do with me? Should our paths never have crossed?*

I thought, *he would not like to hear me blaming myself for what had befallen him. I knew his niece in Ireland had suffered ovarian cancer in her youth, but she'd beaten it, got married, and there was the possibility that pregnancy might even be possible.*

Thoughts wandered, tears flowed. I promised I would research this dreaded disease that had come our way, and if there was a cure for it, we would find it.

Because of Sean's age, Dr. Robertson had said he couldn't be part of an experimental research. The treatment he would be undergoing was dangerous enough, and he wanted us to be aware of this.

"One day at a time, one step at a time," I cautioned myself. *"Let's deal with this first phase and get the situation under control. For the balance of that time, we'd try holistic, non-medically recognized ways of combating the disease.*

The next morning, I travelled back to Toronto. Sean was cheerful and happy. A favourite with people, the nurses coddled him. He felt treatment would be a blast. I was buoyed up by his attitude. He told me he didn't expect me to visit him in hospital every day. His thoughts were about me and my comfort and convenience, not about himself.

I looked at him, daring him to contradict me. "If you're expecting me to leave you alone here to flirt with the nurses, you've another thought coming, Sean. You belong to me and I have to protect my property. I'll be here alongside you as you battle this pestilence that seeks to be a part of our lives. My strength will bolster yours. Together we shall overcome." I was trying to keep it upbeat.

"Come over here and let me hug you, my darling. I really expected that'd be your answer. You've filled my life with contentment and joy. I never thought for a moment during the years of my former life that the happiness we've enjoyed could ever have been mine. I can't battle this demon inside me without you. Together we'll beat it, you'll see."

He made room for me and I jumped into bed beside him. We lay together for a while, each enveloped in our own thoughts. We both wished for strength and courage. It would take the combined fortitude and strength of us both to endure and encourage, to never give up but deal with all the obstacles in our path one at a time.

We were interrupted by the nurse. She smiled. "I see you young lovers are making the most of your time together, but I must remind you that sex isn't permitted in the hospital. Lock the door next time you want to indulge."

We all laughed as Sean replied, "You can see what I have to endure, Nurse. She's so randy she can't keep her hands off my body."

"Well, I have to give you your chemo cocktail now, so that will put an end to your philandering for the time being."

Chemotherapy took its toll on Sean's body and at the end of two weeks he could hardly get out of bed. While he was cheerful about it all, his body started to develop problems all on its own. Sores in his mouth prevented proper intake of food. He developed diabetes. He had kidney failure. Then he lost the vision in his right eye. He grew weaker and weaker, lost the use of his legs, and had to be lifted into a chair. He hated the fact that he had grown dependent on help.

Sometimes I would squeeze myself into his bed and lie beside him, hoping I could transfer some of my energy to him. I left him each night with a prayer, which we recited together, asking the Universe to help him conquer the malady that had brought him to the brink. I was there the next day at 8.00 a.m. No one bothered me about visiting hours.

He became morose and began to lose faith that he would ever get well. We knew when death visited some of his fellow patients. It was an open secret. The patients all knew what was happening on the floor and dreaded the news that a fellow sufferer had failed to make it.

Concerts were held every Wednesday in the atrium on the first floor. He had been too ill to bother with such happenings. Then he heard that a fellow pianist, John Arpin, would be giving a recital. He requested a wheelchair and asked me to take him to listen to the concert. I asked the nurses whether this was permissible. They told me they'd asked for permission but the Doctor had advised that he shouldn't leave the floor as his immune system could be compromised.

He seemed quite deflated by this, so downcast as if he'd abandoned all hope. I couldn't bear to watch the disappointment on his face. I went to the desk and asked for help to get him into a wheelchair. Help arrived in the form of an aide. She whispered to me that she knew what I was about to do and she wouldn't make a fuss. She took a facemask from her pocket.

I smiled. Sean was happy. When we eventually arrived in the atrium, the concert was almost over. Sean handed me a folded note, which he asked me to give to the pianist. John Arpin acknowledged Sean's arrival with surprise. He was sad that Sean had fallen victim to leukemia. The concert had to be concluded by a certain time and he was almost at the end, but he couldn't refuse Sean's request. Permission was hurriedly extended.

John sat down at the piano and started to play "I Will Always Love You." This threw me for a loop. This was one our songs, an affirmation of our love he had so often played back home, it had become our signature tune. I recognized this was the reason he was so anxious to get to the concert. His writing, barely legible, which he had labored on because of his inability to use his fingers, was his gift to me, a reminder of his love.

Tears settled in my eyes. Could love be so strong that it provided the willpower to brave the odds so its purpose could be fulfilled? Sean's desire had been to reaffirm his love and devotion to me, to thank me for remaining by his side, and persuading him not to falter when the going was tough.

I had been the tigress protecting her young. Research and discussions with the medical staff had given me an overview of his treatment, which left me in no doubt as to the outcome. I monitored his treatment regime carefully, and always discussed it with the medical staff, and with him.

Chemo was injected into in his spine. These happenings were excruciating. I made it my duty to be present every time the Doctor came to inject the medication. My holding his hands calmed Sean's mind. He told me my energy flowed into his body and allowed him to endure the pain as the needle sought its place between the discs of the spine.

Gradually, it seemed the chemo began to work. Everyone was happy. Sean regained his strength bit by bit, and we started the slow job of getting him on his feet again. Doing something to help himself gave him a sense of purpose. At the back of both our minds was the fact that the doctors affirmed this was just a temporary fix. We needed to return to the hospital in three weeks, and thereafter once a week for blood tests, transfusions, and more chemotherapy.

We left the hospital and returned home in triumph. Returning to his home was something he had feared would never happen. Neighbours lifted him over the steps, but once in, he was able to use a walker to get around on his own.

Sean recovered his physical strength slowly, and then life returned to a kind of normalcy. We were so happy that we felt we had to share this happiness with our friends. His birthday was fast approaching so we decided a celebration was called for.

It was a happy occasion. Our friends and neighbours rallied around. It almost seemed that our lives had returned to normal. We dared to hope.

CHAPTER EIGHTY-ONE

HOPE SPRINGS ETERNAL. In his *Essay on Man*, Alexander Pope wrote, *'Hope springs eternal in the human breast.'* We hoped that the impossible would indeed become possible. As weeks grew into months, we dared to dream of a cure, discovered sooner than later. Perhaps there could be a cessation of hostilities between the leukemia and his body. Miracles happened. We prayed. Then we tried to bargain.

But the rigorous journey to the hospital once every week continued. Chemotherapy and blood transfusions became the norm.

Suddenly, we were put on a two-week visitation schedule, then three weeks, then four weeks. Sean was getting better, his body was fighting and winning. Our hopes ran high. We were in the eighteenth month of our two-year battle and it looked like clear sailing ahead.

Sean wanted to visit London once more. We asked the Doctor if we could plan a trip to England and he gave us his okay. Elated and with high hopes and happy dreams, we planned to be away for three weeks.

Excitement reigned high in our household as Sean began planning the trips. We had endless discussions about what we were going to do. Should we rent a flat or should we go to one of our favourite five-star hotels? In the end, some friends recommended a flat in Kensington.

A visit to the hospital was a must before we would be given final 'permission' to leave. Medical insurance wasn't a possibility. No insurance coverage was available in a situation like ours.

We had no concerns. We hoped for the best and expected that all would be well. Friends called to wish us well. We were going off on another honeymoon, to celebrate the beginning of the rest of our lives.

We were due to leave for London on a Thursday. Our pre-holiday appointment with the Doctor was fixed for Tuesday. We left home early on Tuesday morning to keep our appointment. Everything had been cut down to a fine schedule. We arrived at the hospital for 9.00 a.m., had a blood test, then awaited the Doctor at noon.

When the time stretched on from noon to almost 130 p.m., we wondered, '*Why the delay? What is going on?*' The nurse could give us no reason for our long wait; she just said, "You have to be patient. The Doctor knows you're waiting."

When the Doctor eventually arrived, it was nearing 2.00 p.m. He shut the door as he apologized for the delay. This caused alarm bells to go off in my head. I heard these words: "I needed to get the blood test redone; the results were not what I'd expected; it indicates that the disease has returned; I wanted to verify this."

It was difficult for him to give us such bad news. He'd felt Sean was making good progress but now leukemia was winning the battle. "The disease is acting true to form; I didn't expect this when all was going so well. You'll need chemotherapy tomorrow, and I'll expect you back in hospital in two weeks. Any delay in chemo after two weeks will result in disorientation and you'll need to be hospitalized in London. On your return to Canada, you'll be immediately admitted to hospital. A bed will be waiting for you."

I questioned, "Doctor Robertson, should we postpone our holiday? Wouldn't it be better for Sean to begin the regimen of treatment now? The holiday isn't important. His health and well-being are. We can always go later."

He smiled, the sympathy he felt at imparting such devastating news, radiating in his voice, "The disease is running true to form. The longest life expectancy after the first chemotherapy treatment borders on two years at the longest. Sean has been free for only twenty months. We never give up, we always continue the fight, but everything is still experimental. Go on your holiday. As soon as you get back, we'll continue the battle". He shook his head, his eyes full of dejection and sorrow. "The treatment you receive tomorrow will last for two weeks. Make the most of your trip together."

He shook our hands and wished us well. We had been so buoyant when he told us we could go off on our trip, we were both shocked and disappointed at the result of the tests. The carpet had been pulled from under our feet. Leukemia had taken control of Sean's body again. We both had to understand that life was telling us that we were approaching the end. Everything from now held little or no promise of success.

We returned to our flat, dejection filling every bone in our bodies. Sean got busy rearranging our trip. Two short weeks in London, then back to the awful ravages of chemotherapy in the hope that we could wrest the disease from the stranglehold it had on his body.

The next day we returned to the hospital for chemotherapy and blood transfusion. Over wine that night, we debated whether to cancel the holiday entirely. Something in the Doctor's voice had told me that only a miracle could prevent the disease from taking over. The holiday was at least something different, a last goodbye to the country he loved, where he'd lived for his first years. Familiar surroundings and a semblance of a reality which would be fleeting.

His brother James, and sister-in-law, Irene, spent a week with us in London. They told me quietly that they felt he was getting lower. They could see a daily decline in his health.

I knew this to be true. His dependence on me had grown. He told me he didn't feel safe without me by his side.

The holiday was not an easy one. In the midst of it all, he caught a cold. He spent two days in bed. When he started to feel a little better, I told him the balance of our holiday should be spent in one of our favourite hotels, the Savoy. He brightened at this. Even if he wasn't feeling up to snuff, he could still enjoy the amenities the hotel offered and relive its past majesty of home to the wealthy.

Happiness is as happiness does. He perked up and we were even able to venture outside the hotel for short walks.

I felt myself divided in two. Half of me pondered my own sadness at his leaving me, and the other half worried about how he was coping. I decided that somehow we both had to gain strength to deal with the situation, to hope that we could postpone the inevitable, perhaps even to bargain with the fates to grant us a reprieve.

I found myself longing for the days to pass quickly so that we could return to the 'safety' of the hospital, but time passed soon enough and we were on our way back to Toronto.

His health had worsened in the two weeks we were away. When we arrived at the flat, he could hardly climb the stairs. He was exhausted, but buoyed up by the thought of going to the hospital and seeing the doctors.

Blood tests were always a must before we saw the Doctor. This took time. Sean tried valiantly to sit up, to pretend that he was okay, but it was to no avail. He had to be rushed to the emergency where there was a bed available.

After the Doctor saw the tests, he requested a hospital bed immediately and treatment started again. We were glad to learn that there was some new experimental treatment they were going to try and my heart lit up with hope, but when Sean was comfortably settled, the Doctor drew me aside and told me that the end was approaching. He wouldn't last beyond the next three months. He explained that Sean's blood tests indicated that the disease had progressed to the point where hospitalization was necessary. My body began to shake and tremble. Had we been away any longer, Sean would have been coming home in a box. This news sent a chill through me. These were the last days I would spend with Sean. The end was inevitable. I needed to prepare myself for strength and courage to deal with his death and face the future without him. I had to put my best foot forward, to smile and encourage.

Instead, my heart lurched and I felt myself descending into an abyss. I lost consciousness. I awakened to a feeling of such despair, it seemed the only way out was to give up on my own life. I rallied to the realization that this fight was not about me; it was about my beloved. I owed him. He had to leave this world with the comfortable feeling that I would be able to take care of myself. I took a deep breath. I had to become the actor in a role, what was happening was not personal, I was just spouting the lines of a play. Despite the fact that I said I was feeling better, it was inevitable that tests would be ordered and I also spent that night in hospital.

Sean was, of course, alarmed when I didn't return to his bedside, but Gloria told him that I had been called away to an emergency meeting, and would return next day.

Next morning, as soon as he saw me, he wanted to know what was going on. I lied. I told him that there was a mix-up with the hospital private ward coverage; the anomaly had all been explained away, and everything was now in order. Because of his condition, he was assigned to a private ward at no extra cost. However, I had been paying for the extra facility and this amount would be refunded to us.

He said, "I'm so glad that you're looking after all of this, Tab. I haven't worried for a moment about costs. You've looked after all our finances, taken care of everything, and told me there was nothing to worry about, and I've taken all this for granted. That's my job, you know. I take care of you."

"You're in no condition to worry about anything, Sean. Just leave it to me. Your brother has offered to help with paperwork, but don't you dare forget I ran a multi-million-dollar company before we were married. Our finances are a piece of cake after that."

He smiled. "You're a wonder, Tab. Everything you put your hand to comes out smelling of roses. I don't know how you do it, but you're a marvel."

"Let's not bother about all of this now. You must put your energies into getting better. That's your job from hereon in."

It was time to come to terms with what life had given me and move on or I would become a lost soul. Somehow, somewhere, I had to find the power to give me the determination to shed my encumbrances of pain, sorry and regret, and embrace the future. We are never prisoners because 'bad things' happen, or we make mistakes. We must be precise in our determination and forge ahead. I had a duty to take care of my beloved, ease away the pressure of whatever was troubling him, while leaving him in a bower of comfort and love.

CHAPTER EIGHTY-TWO

R ECOVERY AND HOPE. Despite dire predictions, Sean surprised us all, and after another six weeks in hospital, he was allowed to return home. This was not a cure, just a reprieve. Once there's life, there is indeed hope. Hope is always a constant companion once life exists. Miracles can happen.

One evening, he asked me to leave what I was doing and sit beside him on the divan, as was our usual practice when we watched television. When we were comfortably seated, I took his feet in my lap. This time our roles were reversed. He had always been the one to hold my feet in his lap, while we watched television.

I started to rub the soles of his feet, but he asked me not to continue because the slightest touch was agony. "I guess my perfect 'bod' is letting me down," he said. "This is a serious moment in our lives together."

I laughed. "Every moment is serious, until we conquer this disease."

"Things are happening to my body over which I have no control. I'm going to ask you for a promise." He looked at me with eyes full of love and a smile on his face. "Promise me that when I die, you'll try to be happy. I'll never leave you. I'll be up there (he pointed upwards) looking down at you and loving you. I'll be gone in the flesh, but my soul will be with you, loving you as always and waiting for you."

This was indeed 'goodbye.' I wasn't ready to face reality. My heart was breaking, tears settled in my eyes. He was asking for a promise I couldn't make. How could I let him go? An inner voice said, *'you have to, you must. He needs your permission, or he'll fight death to the end. He'll not go in peace.* Sean, I'll promise that I'll try to be happy, if you promise that when life has departed your body, and the portals open for your soul to pass into eternity, you will go through. If you don't do this, we'll never meet again in another lifetime. Your soul will wander forever on this Earth, and I couldn't bear this because we'll never be able to meet again."

"But, Tab, you must promise that you'll try to be happy when I go." He protested.

"Life without you, Sean, will be existence. But I'll try to be happy. When the clouds part and leave an opening for you to pass through, don't linger here. Please go and wait for me on the other side. Our destinies now seem to be that you'll leave before me, but I know we'll meet again."

He looked at me and smiled. I knew he had no intention of keeping his promise to walk through those portals, but I hoped that some force beyond him would pull him through. Life controls us, we don't control it.

How could I keep my promise to him? He was my life, my love, everything I cherished, the yin to my yang. I loved him with every fibre of my being. How could I exist without the part that made me whole?

We had both lied as we undertook to keep the promises we had made to each other; we both knew that the other was making a promise that wouldn't be kept.

We went upstairs to bed, hand in hand. He held me tight and whispered sweet nothings in my ear. We laughed together. These moments were so precious. I wished they would go on forever, but I felt his body tiring. I turned and held him close as I whispered: "You're the best thing that ever happened to me, Sean Baker. I will always love you. You made me whole and brought out the best in me. I'm a better person for loving you and being loved by you. Thank you, my darling angel."

Next morning, he couldn't get out of bed. His strength was waning. I saw the love in his eyes as they followed me around the room. I knew how much he loved music so I filled the room with soft music, which I hoped would offer solace and calm. This was the time for him to be cosseted in a bower of love and music.

The pain worsened. On instructions from Dr. Harley, a local nurse visited twice daily to give him his morphine injections. I refused further help. He would get the greatest comfort from the personal care I'd devote to him. He was mine to protect, to cherish and love, and care for. This would be the last time we'd have together on Earth and I'd have it no other way.

Sean's soul left his body a few days later. He was surrounded by his children and my children. I held him in my arms and showered him with kisses as life drained slowly from his body. Songs of love and music, filled the air as his life slowly departed. I was glad that his pain and suffering were over as death claimed him. His battle in this life was complete. I needed to staunch the flow of tears as sadness took control of my body.

I asked the children to leave me alone with him. They looked at me with questioning eyes, but they left.

I lay beside him and placed his arm around me. Never would I know the comfort of those arms again. The love of my life had passed on. He was gone, lost to me. Being loved by him had restored my perspective of life. He had helped me come to terms with my past and shown me a world filled with love. He had brought peace and calm to my soul. How could I face life without him? But there was still work to be done. This was not the time for me to give way to my grief and mourn my loss.

I needed to make sure that his final farewell from this world would be a fitting tribute to the man he was. I looked at him, lying there, life gone from his body, taking him to a place where I couldn't reach him. I questioned the viability of a system that could wrench someone you loved, cared for, and relied upon and place him into another world beyond your reach. But this was the way of life. Somehow I had expected him to be here when it was my turn to leave, but life had played me and proved my hopes false.

There was more to the scintilla of life, I told myself. *Stop being sorry for yourself. Fear brings a finality from which there's no escape. You'll have to learn to deal with it. He was the hero who rescued you and showed you the beauty of life and love. It's your turn to accord him a final exit that depicts the glory of his life.*

My world ended that night, but there were things I had to do. I got up slowly, turned to kiss him goodbye, straightened the sheets that covered him, reluctant to leave him but thinking only of his funeral, his final exit from this world. I felt my body shaking, I wanted to scream and shout, to pound the floor with my feet, but the sitting room was full. Neighbours had quietly filled the room to show their concern and help the family through this difficult time.

Keeping my composure was difficult. I needed time to absorb the fact that death had taken my beloved away. I struggled to stay calm. Everyone wanted to talk about Sean and this helped to lighten the tension I felt. After the funeral home came to collect the body, the grief within me could not be denied. The levee I'd set up to restrain my grief broke down and I sobbed unrestrainedly, my body rocking back and forth unrestrainedly.

CHAPTER EIGHTY-THREE

FACING THE FUTURE. Sean would have liked his memorial service. It was upbeat and music filled the funeral chapel. An orchestra played the jazz he himself had so often played and enjoyed. Who knows? If circumstances had been different, as I've said before, he could have been a renowned jazz pianist! Perhaps that could happen in a future life!

His friends spoke of his eloquence and his love of the business in which he worked, his humour and his love of life, of our worldwide travels and his joy at living in a world where once 'the sun never set on the British Empire.'

His children spoke of his love, of everything he had done to show how much he loved them, and promised to be a shining example to him.

I spoke of his devotion to his children and his love for me. He had been my 'everything,' my husband, my lover, my confidant, my best friend, and my soul mate. He had brought me joys I had longed for and had never known could happen. He had taught me how to love and be loved. We had held the world in our hands and marveled that such happiness, as we knew it, existed.

My grandchildren wept, as children do, not knowing the whys and wherefores, only that Grandpa Sean had died and they couldn't understand why he was taken from them. Our children made sure that everything went according to plans.

As we left the Funeral Home to go to the crematorium, I could hear the strains of 'Danny Boy' (an Irish traditional tune) floating through the air as the bagpiper played the haunting melody in final farewell. This is the end of my life with Sean. Goodbyes, fond farewells... just widened the hole in my heart.

Life had at last given me my own, true love, but he had only been lent to me, perhaps to mould my character, to turn me into a softer, gentler, warmer person, to give me that happiness that could come only from true love. Now I had been cast adrift into a world I didn't know. How was I going to live without him by my side? What would my life be without him?

There was still one duty to perform. I had to set alight the 'pyre' that would take care of his body. Ashes to ashes, and dust to dust. I felt weak. I had promised I would turn on the switches that would start the process for cremation. That was my last duty to him.

I moved slowly forward and said a quiet prayer of hope and love. I silently promised that I would wait in this life until fate determined it was time to join him in the next world. Remembering the happiness we had experienced simply by being together would keep me warm and content. I looked forward to seeing him again when it was my turn to leave this world. There was anguish in my soul, and weakness in my body, but I slowly stretched out my hand and turned the lever to the 'on' position.

"Farewell, my one, true love. This isn't goodbye. Travel safe. We'll meet again."

CHAPTER EIGHTY-FOUR

EALING WITH GRIEF. I returned to an empty home. The silence that reached out to greet me was deafening. Despondency raced through my mind. My world was spinning out of control. I asked myself, "Where do I go from here?" No useful thought came to mind. I looked around at our home, remembering the happy days we had spent here, and wondering what the future without him held in store for me. It was so empty, so devoid of the love that once filled it. Suddenly, it seemed my body was an empty vessel; my brain was losing control. Panic stricken, I rushed to the nearest chair. I lost conscious thought.

As I opened my eyes, I tried to recall what had happened to me. My head felt heavy and my heart was sad as I remembered Sean's funeral. Tears flowed freely. Suddenly, I began to feel an uneasy sense of being watched. I looked around, then up above. I noticed a face looking down at me from above. I checked again, but there was nothing there. A few moments passed, then I again had this eerie feeling. I recalled that an Indian friend who had visited me during Sean's illness had reported that there were angels looking at us from above. I hadn't given this a second thought and now wondered whether some divine intervention had been set in force to help me deal with my grief.

I took courage from this. At this stage, I was ready to believe anything. The business of living had to go on. Even if I stumbled around in clouds of sorrow, I had to get on with the demands of life.

Almost unconsciously, I reverted back to the time when I had a split personality. I went about the business of 'settling the estate' and dealing with the fact that I was now a single person.

When I lay down to sleep at night, I hoped Sean would be a part of my dreams. I missed his presence in bed, his hugs enfolding my body in a protective embrace. In the morning, I would awaken and reality would greet me.

There was some semblance of peace brought by living in two worlds, but after a few months I came to the realization that I needed help. I needed someone to show me the way and lead me on to the new era in my life. Sean's death was the end of a happy epoch, but I was starting life afresh in difficult circumstances. I was now a grief-stricken widow. While everyone was sympathetic and offered help, I was in charge of my own healing.

Counselling was recommended by my family Doctor. He referred me to a psychologist who also happened to be my age and was also a widower; he had recently lost his wife to cancer. After some sessions, group therapy was recommended.

My friends searched the internet and found a bereavement group in Uxbridge, a nearby village. There were ten of us, nine women and one man. I was the newcomer. Their grief counselling session had started two weeks earlier. When it was my turn to tell my story, I hesitated. How could I let this group of people I hardly knew have access to my innermost thoughts and emotions? I had kept my secret feelings bottled up for such a long time, this was anathema to my being. I chided myself. We all had one commonality. Death had robbed us and we were floundering.

Unbeknownst to myself, the ambiance of the setting, and the commonality of our grief was a determining factor in healing. We all needed to gain understanding of what life held in store for us. Life and death were some things we all shared. I had to honour the spirit of life and be honest. Death had visited us all. There was nothing to be ashamed of. This was a learning and healing experience, not a case for analysis and judgement. Telling my story was the start of the process.

I looked at each of them in turn. "I feel that the burden of this grief is so overwhelming, it takes me away to the point where my own life seems to have little value. Death has left an ache in my heart, which doesn't lessen. I ask myself 'how can I look forward to a future without him?' We were together for only thirteen short years. Leukemia robbed him of his life. Our plan to grow old together disappeared. I shed copious tears, but the pain doesn't ease.

"I blame myself and look back at what I should've and could've done to help him. Feelings of guilt weigh me down for what I perceive in retrospect as my own shortcomings. I torture myself when I remember the times when I could've been kinder and gentler, at lost opportunities for enjoying his love and companionship, my thoughts engrossed only by my grief when death would take him away. Life and living are not reversible. Why didn't I understand that?"

I stretched out my hands, the other mourners next to me held my hands, and soon we were all linked together, enjoined in sorrow for ourselves and for one another.

Then everyone started talking together. That moment of relief, gained through tears and sharing, opened the doors to sunlight.

This was our moment. We bonded. Our meetings opened the doors to sunlight. Together we learned how to deal with sadness, and continue our lives without our loved ones. We became a close-knit group, strange bedfellows from all walks life, con-joined through death.

At the close of the sessions, we all promised to keep in touch and we did so until life moved us in different directions.

Eighteen months later, I sold my home and moved closer to Toronto and my children. Family gave me a sense of belonging, of having a place in the world, and a desire to see my grand-children grow into responsible citizens. I needed the comfort of their love.

The person Sean loved would recover and build a new life for herself.

CHAPTER EIGHTY-FIVE

THE AFTERMATH. The years have sped by. Living alone is never simple. There is a purpose to life and I try to find it. The past provided pitfalls and opportunities, opened and closed doors, and signified when it was time to move on. Inspiration lights the road ahead, pulls you forward, and gives solace and comfort.

One day slid into the other and years disappeared. Sean remains a part of me. *Sometimes I feel he's with me, smiling down from above.* I grab these moments, and for a split-second I feel, *Yes, he's here, and we're still connected.* But then I think, *if he hasn't gone through the open door, he'll be a lost soul roaming the earth forever and I'll be a lost soul in other lifetimes searching for him.*

I'm grateful that life gave me the courage to end two mismatched marriages, and to choose love over career when I fell in love with Sean. I experienced marital fulfillment and joy, as Sean taught me the beauty of love and being loved. I have a better understanding of Shakespeare's oft quoted sentence, *It's better to have loved and lost, than never to have loved at all.*

My grandchildren were growing up. I was the idol who gave them treats, listened to them, and could be relied upon to fill in at hockey or other activities when no one else was available. I needed to take myself away from the space of sorrow and into a new world, which was different. I remembered their greeting on our return home from a trip and wanting to be told of the worlds we had visited. They were always agog with excitement when we shared pictures and videos. To see that world through their eyes would be magical and exciting while providing something new for me. It was time to take them on foreign adventures.

I had never been to Costa Rica but I'd heard interesting things about its development and pleasurable activities for tourists. This trip with them would satisfy the needs I would have liked to have made with Christo and Gloria when they were young. I asked Gloria to research the trip. It would be designed to fit our needs and wants. Sean would have liked to have been a part of this trip, but there... that was in the past. I smiled when a past memory from our China trips came to mind. While descending the path to get to The Tiger Leaping Gorge, we were accompanied by porters anxiously trying to procure my custom because I was using a cane and they thought I would falter on the steep descent to the bottom. Sean had given them a tip for their tenacity, and they had touched my knees and blessed us both. This memory provoked a smile and a happy thought.

Our Costa Rica trip would be like that. Beautiful, filled with daring exploits, sights and sounds to inspire their young minds, and in addition, the dawning of a new age for me. Our trip turned into a beautiful adventure. They still talk about making eye contact with an alligator as we canoed down a river, getting into close contact with snakes they were allowed to handle, being entangled in trees on a cliff as our balloon cruised the jungle, rappelling down a tall tree, zip-lining from tree to tree, and horseback riding through the jungle. Our trip was evolving into a movie-like adventure with a happy ending.

Their excitement was catching. Unfortunately, one suitcase with souvenirs went missing on the return journey, and the airline never did recover it.

Their excitement was a welcome break. It opened my eyes to what could still happen. The future awaited. The past was a storehouse of memories that could be used to stimulate the future. I wasn't interested in getting a new partner. Sean was the ultimate, and his place in my heart is secure. I could continue our adventure of travelling either alone with a guide or with travel companions. While he had made everything extra special, there was still adventure in visiting foreign places.

Writing was always an interesting exercise. I found a group of would-be writers and achieved great satisfaction from our story-telling. It was a pleasant and interesting activity. Putting your thoughts on paper, making words lyrical wasn't as simple as writing a letter or a note, memo or report. I tried penning a newsletter for friends. This was well received, but after two years it became a chore rather than a relaxing exercise. It was time to put it to bed.

I tried living the life of Riley. My time was filled with the excitement of ball games in the summer, concerts that eased my mind and calmed the nerves, and theater shows in winter, which were exciting and brought me back to the reality which reflected present-day happenings.

I interspersed my days with coaching my grandchildren. This was more a way of keeping in contact with them, rather than an exercise in learning. There was one memorable moment that changed my life. During an exercise in English, I asked them to write a short story. It would be a reminder of all the stories they demanded I tell them, when they were younger and spent holiday time with us.

My youngest grandson wrote a story of a giant who lived in a forest situated in proximity to a village. Villagers feared the giant not only because of his imposing stature, but also because of his face, which was half-human and half-lion. He watched in secret from afar. When he tried to get closer, they ran away in fear. One summer evening he witnessed the festivities of the village fair from afar. The music, laughter, and joy excited him. He longed to join them, but knew from past experience they would stone him and then run away. He decided to try again, but when the same thing occurred, he became so enraged, he went on the path of destruction. When he looked at the devastation he'd created, he returned home and wept. This story had many lessons for me. Non-acceptance has far reaching implications. I'm not sure my grandson recognized the real meaning of his story, which was that exclusion can most times lead to hatred. I was overwhelmed and decided it was time to tell my own story.

Our last big adventure together was to China. Again, another historical visit for them and another eye-opener for me. On this visit, one of the highlights was a visit to an orphanage. They couldn't communicate because of the language barrier, but fun and games were open to all. One of the boys was blind and couldn't take part in the games. As was my custom, I had taken a walking stick to assist me at times when getting about was difficult. They all came to me, clamoring for my attention even though they were interrupting a meeting I had been having with local officials, and asked me to donate my walking stick to the lad. I handed it over. Whooping with joy, they rushed back to the children and presented the stick to the boy. His face lit up when he felt the cane in his hand. They held his hand and taught him how to find his way by using the stick. It was an insight into their character. Children may grow into 'meanies' but they are loving and giving. They learn their lessons from us adults and ultimately whatever is learned becomes part of their upbringing.

History is still an important part of my life. Age has not set limitations. Television offers me the best today. I can't be there physically, but I can still experience, from afar, the lives of the inhabitants in differing countries, especially those I've not been able to visit, ... and ponder the outcome of their lives had their history been different.

CHAPTER EIGHTY-SIX

LIFE MOVES ON. When the going gets tough, I never fail to remember that life never gives up on us. It offers us many compromises. We are defined by how we deal with problems which beset us. I could have remained a victim, but muddled through and became a survivor. I made the most of whatever circumstance faced me and became a better human being for it. The world turns, and I turned with it. I couldn't reverse the past, but I could work towards creating a better future. We are never prisoners because 'bad' things happen or we make mistakes. Opportunities always lie on the horizon. I've learned to shut the door sometimes gently but mostly with a bang, and move on.

I remind myself, *think of the lives of the men who abused you and what they accomplished... nothing. Compare this with your own life. Take pride in your accomplishments, and relish the spoils of victory. Think of your own personality, of who you are today. This defines you.*

The cousin who raped me disappeared from my life and I never heard of him again. My brother who sexually molested me never rose to the position of his siblings and became a wastrel and a disappointment to our parents.

I think of Mohan who blackmailed me into a loveless marriage, and the brief sojourn of our life together. He survived the break-up and lived into his nineties... Mike, my second husband and father of our children, died four years after Sean. I bear him no ill will. He was, after all, the father of my children and grandfather of my grandchildren. I believe he was a prisoner of his upbringing and his Indian heritage of male domination.

I'm a survivor of rape, sexual abuse, and marital disharmony. I realize now that my reticence to reveal what happened to me was caused by my not wanting my family to be branded and shunned. My silence throughout the horror of it all was my need to protect them as well as myself. No child should have this thrust upon her or him.

Rape is a dastardly crime and should never be pardoned. It should always remain a stigma on the perpetrator not on the person on whom the crime was committed. Rape is in fact, a criminal act worse than murder; it's a case of inflicting a living death on the victim. The sexual act, a beautiful fulfilment of love, becomes hell let loose.

My battle to come to terms with life led me into a world where dreams could be fulfilled. I travelled to the apex when I landed in Toronto, became a Canadian citizen, and not only experienced the satisfaction that success brings, but also the happiness of loving and being loved.

I have journeyed far from that little brown girl who envied the seagulls their gift of freedom. New avenues continue to open up for me and I embrace them. The joys of life eradicate the depths of despair.

Perhaps, the purpose of life is not to follow a map or continue down a rocky roadway. I have spread my wings and soared like eagles, looking down from on high, emperors of all we survey. I was born, I lived, I loved, and I persevere.

My mantra is happiness, contentment, fulfilment, and to become the best person I can be wherever and whenever that road beckons.

Ivy Graham was born in British Guiana. She immigrated to Canada in 1971 to avoid racial violence. She is now nearly 88 years old.

Her working career spans a period of 46 years spent over differing fields. She retired from business after celebrating her sixtieth birthday.

She still continues her world travels which began in her early twenties.

Intransigence is her first novel.

She plans to continue her writing career.

www.ingramcontent.com/pod-product-compliance
Lightning Source LLC
Chambersburg PA
CBHW060448090426
42735CB00011B/1942